D1610889

Command and
Morale

To Roger Lee

Command and Morale

The British Army on the Western Front 1914–1918

Gary Sheffield

Foreword by Peter Simkins

PEN & SWORD
PRAETORIAN PRESS

First published in Great Britain in 2014 by
PRAETORIAN PRESS
An imprint of
Pen & Sword Books Ltd
47 Church Street
Barnsley
South Yorkshire
S70 2AS

ISBN 978-1-78159-021-8

A CIP catalogue record for this book is available from the British Library.

Typeset by Concept, Huddersfield, West Yorkshire, HD4 5JL.
Printed and bound in England by CPI Group (UK) Ltd, Croydon CR0 4YY.

Pen & Sword Books Ltd incorporates the imprints of Pen & Sword Archaeology, Atlas, Aviation, Battleground, Discovery, Family History, History, Maritime, Military, Naval, Politics, Railways, Select, Social History, Transport, True Crime, and Claymore Press, Frontline Books, Leo Cooper, Praetorian Press, Remember When, Seaforth Publishing and Wharncliffe.

For a complete list of Pen & Sword titles please contact
PEN & SWORD BOOKS LIMITED
47 Church Street, Barnsley, South Yorkshire, S70 2AS, England
E-mail: enquiries@pen-and-sword.co.uk
Website: www.pen-and-sword.co.uk

Contents

List of Plates

An artist's impression of very early aerial combat.

60-pounder guns camouflaged from enemy aircraft.

German infantry using flamethrowers against French positions, 1915.

Field Marshal Sir John French, Commander-in-Chief of the British Expeditionary Force, 1914–1915.

A German dugout on the Aisne.

General (later Field Marshal) Sir Douglas Haig.

Headquarters staff of 1st Canadian Division in 1915.

Indian troops on the Western Front.

An artist's impression of a German officer being questioned by his French captors.

A photograph of British infantry, presumably posed, from the earliest days of trench warfare.

General Sir Henry Rawlinson, commander of Fourth Army on the Somme in 1916 and in the Hundred Days of 1918.

An imaginative reconstruction of a Royal Field Artillery wireless operator.

Artist's impression of aircraft of the Royal Naval Air Service.

A British cavalry regiment, the Royal Scots Greys, in training just before the war.

A British tank on the battlefield: the rear wheel dates this photograph to 1916.

A dramatic cut-away of a German U-boat.

Foreword

The last three decades have seen a remarkable transformation in First World War studies, our understanding of the military, political, social, economic and cultural aspects of the conflict having been greatly enhanced by a wealth of outstanding scholarship. Much work, of course, remains to be done, as perceptions of the war among the public at large appear to be still firmly, and frustratingly, wedded to the 'lions led by donkeys' and 'butchers and bunglers' interpretations of the struggle on the Western Front. For many, the images presented by *Blackadder Goes Forth* have a much more immediate impact than the writings of those who have undertaken countless hours of dedicated, archive-based research. There is no easy solution to this problem – and possibly there never will be – for, as Anthony Seldon and David Walsh remark in their stimulating recent book, *Public Schools and the Great War: The Generation Lost* (Pen & Sword, 2013), it is most commonly 'the emotion of the war and its suffering which deeply affect us, rather than the rational arguments of the historians'.

That said, the labours of scholars at home and abroad since the early 1980s have certainly not been entirely in vain. As someone who has been a professional military historian for half a century, I can personally testify to the fact that, in general, a much more objective approach to the conflict is now more widely adopted than was the case fifty years ago. Centres of excellence in First World War studies have been established at various universities, and organisations such as the Western Front Association – which was founded in 1980 and currently has over 6,000 members in some sixty branches in the United Kingdom and overseas – seem to be flourishing. Moreover, in the scholarly community and among serious students of the 1914–1918 period, the historical debate in Britain and the Commonwealth about the nature and conduct of the war has at last moved on to a point at which most would acknowledge that the forces under Field Marshal Sir Douglas Haig's command in France and Belgium experienced a distinct and positive, if uneven, learning process and achieved major tactical and technological improvements between 1916 and 1918. It is perhaps worth observing in this connection, for example, that nearly all of the new biographies of Haig that have been published in the past ten years or so – including Gary Sheffield's own fine study, *The Chief* (2011) – portray Haig not as the principal 'butcher' or as a real-life General Melchett, but instead as a single-minded professional soldier with a profound sense of duty who, despite mistakes and setbacks, kept his head in the face of unprecedented challenges and presided over that very process of improvement that enabled the British Expeditionary Force to make a truly significant contribution to the ultimate Allied victory.

It is also worthy of note that Gary Sheffield's emergence as a recognised world authority on the Great War has almost precisely coincided with this wider acceptance of the 'revisionist' interpretation summarised briefly above. He can, indeed, justly claim to have played a key role in re-shaping our views of the 1914–1918 conflict. As the essays and papers which constitute this present volume clearly demonstrate, Professor Sheffield is more than capable of producing detailed operational and command studies on the one hand and illuminating strategic and historiographical overviews on the other. His chapters here on the difficult and demanding topics of morale, discipline and officer–man relations are equally perceptive and penetrating. On reading these essays again – over twenty years since their initial publication in some cases – I am particularly struck by the maturity of the earlier pieces. As a young scholar, Gary Sheffield undeniably 'hit the ground running' to an astonishing degree and he has more than matched those same high standards of scholarship ever since. The formidable breadth of his reading and his prodigious capacity for research, writing and presenting international conference papers are all reflected in this book.

As Professor Sheffield himself indicates in his Preface, I have a personal connection with some of the chapters in this volume. Gary and I first met when, as an eager young undergraduate, he came to the Imperial War Museum to seek advice about potential areas of research, and the availability of sources, relating to Kitchener's Army. I remember steering him towards a study of the 22nd Royal Fusiliers – the Kensington battalion – a topic which Gary later broadened into an MA dissertation for which I subsequently acted as his external examiner. During the same decade he became my successor as Secretary-General of the British Commission for Military History. In 1997 he was a valuable member of the team which I was allowed to select to represent this country at a joint Anglo-Australian historical conference held in both London and Canberra. The fourth chapter in the book, on the Australian performance at Pozières in 1916, was originally presented at that conference. In more recent years, we have both been associated with the MA programme in British First World War studies at the University of Birmingham. I have therefore maintained a close – almost paternal – interest in Gary Sheffield's career as an historian ever since that first meeting in the Reading Room of the IWM in the early 1980s. I feel privileged to be his friend and colleague and to have played some tiny part in his development as one of the leading, and most popular, scholars in his field.

Peter Simkins
December 2013

Preface

The origins of this book lie in the idea, which has been on my mind for some while, that I should bring together in one place some of the articles and book chapters on the First World War that I have written over the years. 2014, the centenary of the outbreak of the war, seemed an appropriate year to publish it. The oldest piece dates back to 1986, and is based on some postgraduate work I completed in 1984, while the newest was written especially for this book. So, *Command and Morale* consists of a series of snapshots of research spanning an academic career of, at the time of writing, almost thirty years.

The title of the book reflects my two principal research interests in the field of First World War studies. My work has been concerned with the top and the bottom of the British army of the First World War: with high commanders, especially Douglas Haig, Hubert Gough and, latterly, Henry Rawlinson; and with the ordinary soldier and regimental officer. I started reading adult military history books around the age of 10 or so, and although my initial interest was in the Second World War and, a little later, the Napoleonic Wars (two historical passions that remain with me still), I can remember reading A.J.P. Taylor's *Illustrated History of the First World War*. This was a book firmly in the 'lions led by donkeys' camp, although to be fair to Taylor, it was a good deal more subtle than its peers and remains worth reading for its insights into non-military aspects of the war. Not surprisingly, from this and other sources I picked up the standard narrative of military incompetence, 'futility', and 'disillusionment'. I was surprised to discover that any ground had been gained at all during the various offensives.

I had something of an epiphany when, at the age of 13, I read Martin Middlebrook's *The First Day on the Somme*. It changed my life by awakening my interest in the ordinary British soldier of the Great War, for it was the detail of the raising of Kitchener's Army, and the fate of the individual soldiers that Middlebrook discussed that captured my imagination, rather than the details of the fighting on 1 July 1916. One of the soldiers that featured heavily in the book was Private Richard Richardson ('Dick') King of the King's Own Yorkshire Light Infantry who was killed on that terrible day. As it happens, I often visit King's home village, Tickhill in Yorkshire, and I like to go to the village war memorial to pay my respects.

Arriving at the University of Leeds to read History in 1979, I was fortunate to be taught by Dr Hugh Cecil, the first of a series of mentors in my academic career. He ran a Third Year Special Subject on 'Britain and the First World War'. Taking this course broadened and deepened my interest in the war. I have Middlebrook's *First Day on the Somme* to thank for the broad choice of topic for my dissertation, but one very important by-product of this research was meeting Peter Simkins, then Senior Historian at the Imperial War Museum. He advised me to look at some archives on the raising of a battalion of Kitchener's Army, 22nd Royal Fusiliers (Kensington). Peter took this 20-year-old undergraduate seriously, and not only became another mentor but began a friendship which has lasted, to date, thirty-two years.

Moving on to postgraduate work, I took my exploration of the Kensingtons further, writing a 40,000 word thesis for an MA By Research.[1] I remained at Leeds, and my work was supervised by Hugh Cecil and another mentor, Edward M. Spiers; I was extremely fortunate in the quality of the people who influenced me early in my career. The thrust of my research was to look at the relationships between regimental officers and 'Other Ranks', and the influence that these Officer–Man Relationships (OMR) had on morale and discipline. My interest was sparked by an undergraduate essay on the morale of the British army of the Great War. I remember writing something to the effect that OMR showed the British class system at its best, much to the disapproval of a friend of pronounced left-wing views. Actually, what might be called my 'Downton Abbeyesque' views underwent significant modification in the course of my research, but the core of them remained intact. The culmination of my studies into the subject came with my PhD thesis, undertaken at King's College London, when I examined OMR, morale and discipline across the entire BEF. My work was supervised by Professor Brian Bond, another seminal influence.[2] My thesis was revised for publication in 2000 as *Leadership in the Trenches*.[3] Chapters 11 and 13 in this book are based on my MA thesis, and Chapters 9 and 10 reflect my doctoral work. A little later I was commissioned to write the authorised history of the Royal Military Police, which included a substantial section on the Great War.[4] This allowed me to explore another aspect of the discipline of the army of 1914–18, and I was a little surprised by my conclusions, which demonstrated the extent to which a group which had a number of vital roles had been demonised (see Chapter 12).

By the time I started on my part-time PhD, in 1986, I had already been working for a year as a Lecturer in the Department of War Studies and International Affairs at the Royal Military Academy Sandhurst. My time at Sandhurst was a wonderful apprenticeship as a military historian. Coming into regular contact with soldiers broadened my understanding of the culture of the British army – and I was frequently struck how much the army of the 1980s had in common with that of 1914–18 and 1939–45 – and I was privileged to work in a department that was packed with first rate military historians who took the trouble to take an interest in the work of a young scholar: Richard Holmes, Paddy Griffith, John Pimlott (all, sadly, no longer with us), and also Christopher Duffy, Nigel de Lee, Ian Beckett and Keith Simpson. Once again, I had fallen on my feet. In 1985–6 the Department was dominated by the rivalry of two 'big beasts', John Keegan and David Chandler. A series of ill-thought-out MOD 'reforms' destroyed the old WS and IA Department, and many of the big names left, but happily a new Department arose from the ashes, and is currently in rude health.

By the early 1990s my research interests were moving in the direction of the conduct of military operations in the First World War. This was crystallised by the publication of two seminal books: Robin Prior and Trevor Wilson's *Command on the Western Front* (1992) and Paddy Griffith's *Battle Tactics of the Western Front* (1994). Inspired by these books, and the informal school of historians of the BEF based around the British Commission for Military History, in 2001 I published *Forgotten Victory*, in which I attempted to put the case for a revisionist view of Britain and the British army on the Western Front.[5] While writing this book I became interested in the question of why the war came about and why Britain became involved, and also British strategy in the context of coalition warfare. Chapters 1 and 2 reflect these interests. Two years later I wrote a short book in which I was able to explore the Somme in greater depth, building on my arguments in *Forgotten Victory*.[6] In Chapter 7 I focus on the role of British forces in the iconic Canadian battle of Vimy Ridge, and more generally in the still remarkably under-researched Battle of Arras.

In 1997 it was through the good offices of Peter Simkins I was invited to go to Canberra to speak in an Anglo-Australian conference. I met a number of Australian military historians and developed an abiding interest in Australian military history, and have been fortunate enough to return there to research at regular intervals. Chapter 4 is the product of my Australian research in the late 1990s, and Chapters 2, 6 and 8 were originally papers written for Australian Chief of Army's history conferences organised in Canberra by the Army History Unit.

This new direction in my research was also much influenced by frequent participation in battlefield tours involving Sandhurst officer cadets. I learned a great deal from recces for battlefield tours, especially those to Normandy led by my Sandhurst colleagues Nigel and Martine de Lee. These tours were very different from most of those that I had previously experienced, which involved numerous visits to cemeteries and a great deal of emoting, but little attempt to relate tactical actions to the ground, let alone to put it into the wider operational and strategic context. At Sandhurst I learned what a valuable educational and research tool a properly conducted battlefield tour could be. I took this a stage further when, after leaving Sandhurst in 1999, I became Land Warfare Historian on the Higher Command and Staff Course at the Joint Services Command and Staff College. It was a privilege to work on the HCSC, the British military's senior operationally focused course, alongside military colleagues, teaching the next generation of high commanders of the Army, Royal Navy and Royal Air Force. Working on the Staff Ride, a sort of super battlefield tour, alongside Richard Holmes was one of the highlights of my career. He was erudite, kind and immensely entertaining, and I learned a huge amount from him. I was very much focused on high command in my teaching, and naturally my research drifted that way, resulting in work on Hubert Gough (see Chapter 5), my edition of Douglas Haig's papers co-edited with John Bourne, published in 2005[7] and then *The Chief*, my single-authored biography of the First World War British Commander-in-Chief.[8] I am now examining the career of Henry Rawlinson. Chapter 3 is a taster of what is to come.

By the time *The Chief* appeared I had moved to the University of Birmingham. This enabled me to work closely with John Bourne, a friend whose work I had admired for many years. Sadly, he had to take early retirement, which coincided with a change of regime. Suffice it to say that I was delighted to move up the road to the University of Wolverhampton in 2013, where, working with Stephen Badsey, John Buckley and Spencer Jones, we are very well placed to make a major contribution to military history, particularly First World War studies over the centenary years.

With one exception I have resisted the temptation to make major changes to the original text, instead silently correcting various minor things (one piece in particular had been butchered by a previous editor) and providing brief suggestions for further reading that takes more recent scholarship into account. In order to maintain the integrity of chapters, there is a little overlap in content. The exception is Chapter 5, on the generalship of Hubert Gough on the Somme, where I have added a case study taken from another source to my original chapter.

Gary Sheffield
Wantage and Wolverhampton, November 2013

Notes

1. G.D. Sheffield, 'The Effect of War Service on the 22nd (Service) Battalion Royal Fusiliers (Kensington), 1914–18, with Special Reference to Morale, Discipline and the Officer/Man Relationship' (MA (By Research) University of Leeds, 1984).
2. G.D. Sheffield, 'Officer–Man Relations, Morale and Discipline in the British Army, 1902–22' (PhD, King's College London, 1994).
3. G.D. Sheffield, *Leadership in the Trenches: Officer-Man Relations, Morale and Discipline in the British Army in the Era of the First World War* (Basingstoke: Macmillan, 2000).
4. G.D. Sheffield, *The Redcaps: A History of the Royal Military Police and its Antecedents from the Middle Ages to the Gulf War* (London: Brassey's, 1994).
5. Gary Sheffield, *Forgotten Victory: The First World War – Myths and Realities* (London: Hodder Headline, 2001).
6. Gary Sheffield, *The Somme* (London: Cassell, 2003).
7. Gary Sheffield and John Bourne (eds), *Douglas Haig: War Diaries and Letters 1914–18* (London: Weidenfeld & Nicolson, 2005).
8. Gary Sheffield, *The Chief: Douglas Haig and the British Army* (Aurum, 2011).

Acknowledgements

I would like to reiterate my thanks to the holders of copyright material who gave permission for their use in the original articles: precise acknowledgements are to be found in the endnotes of individual chapters. Crown Copyright material appears by kind permission of The National Archives and the Australian War Memorial. I am indebted to Mr Andrew Rawlinson for permission to quote material from General Lord Rawlinson's papers in Chapter 3. If I have inadvertently breached copyright, I hope I will be forgiven, and will rectify the situation in a future edition of this work.

Thanks are due to the following for permission to make use of material previously published as book chapters and articles:

- Exisle Publishing, for Chapter 1: 'Britain and the Empire at War, 1914–1918: Reflections on a Forgotten Victory'. In John Crawford and Ian McGibbon (eds), *New Zealand's Great War: New Zealand, the Allies and the First World War* (Auckland: Exisle Publishing, 2007), pp. 30–48.
- Dr Roger Lee, Army History Unit, for Chapter 2: '"Not the Same as Friendship": The British Empire and Coalition Warfare in the Era of the First World War'. In Peter Dennis and Jeffrey Grey (eds), *Entangling Alliances: Coalition Warfare in the Twentieth Century* (Canberra: Australian Military History Publications, 2005), pp. 38–52.
- Taylor and Francis, for Chapter 4: 'The Australians at Pozières: Command and Control on the Somme, 1916'. In David French & Brian Holden Reid (eds), *The British General Staff: Innovation and Reform* (London: Frank Cass, 2002), pp. 112–26.
- Pen and Sword, for Chapter 5: 'An Army Commander on the Somme: Hubert Gough', in Gary Sheffield and Dan Todman (eds), *Command and Control on the Western Front: The British Army's Experience 1914–18* (Staplehurst: Spellmount, 2004), pp. 71–95, and 'Hubert Gough' (co-author with Helen McCartney). In Ian F.W. Beckett and Steven Corvi (eds) *Haig's Generals* (Barnsley: Pen & Sword, 2006), pp. 75–96.
- Dr Roger Lee, Army History Unit, for Chapter 6: 'Haig and the British Expeditionary Force in 1917'. In Peter Dennis and Jeffrey Grey (eds), *1917: Tactics, Training and Technology* (Canberra: Australian Military History Publications, 2007), pp. 4–22.
- Wilfrid Laurier University Press, for Chapter 7: 'Vimy Ridge and the Battle of Arras: A British Perspective'. In Geoffrey Hayes, Andrew Iarocci and

Mike Bechthold (eds), *Vimy Ridge: A Canadian Reassessment* (Waterloo, Ont: Wilfrid Laurier University Press, 2007), pp. 15–29.

- Dr Roger Lee, Army History Unit, for Chapter 8: 'The Indispensable Factor: British Troops in 1918'. In Peter Dennis and Jeffrey Grey (eds), *1918: Defining Victory* (Canberra, Department of Defence, 1999), pp. 72–95.
- New York University Press, for Chapter 9: 'The Morale of the British Army on the Western Front, 1914–18: A Case Study in the Importance of the "Human Factor" in Twentieth-Century Total War'. In Geoffrey Jensen and Andrew Wiest (eds), *War in the Age of Technology* (New York: New York University Press, 2001), pp. 105–39.
- Pen and Sword, for Chapter 10: 'Officer-Man Relations, Discipline and Morale in the British Army of the First World War'. In Hugh Cecil and Peter Liddle (eds), *Facing Armageddon – 1914–18: the War Experienced* (Barnsley: Pen and Sword, 1996), pp. 413–24.
- Pen and Sword, for Chapter 11: '"A very good type of Londoner and a very good type of colonial": Officer–Man Relations, and Discipline in the 22nd Royal Fusiliers, 1914–18'. In Brian Bond *et al*, *'Look to your Front': Studies in the First World War* (Staplehurst: Spellmount, 1999), pp. 137–46.
- Taylor and Francis, for Chapter 12: 'The Operational Role of British Military Police on the Western Front'. In Paddy Griffith (ed.), *British Fighting Methods in the First World War* (London: Frank Cass, 1996), pp. 70–86.
- Maney Publishing, for Chapter 13, 'The Effect of The Great War on Class Relations in Britain: The Career of Major Christopher Stone DSO MC'. *War & Society*, Vol. 7, No. 1, May 1989, pp. 87–105.

A very large number of people had an influence, through inspiration and practical help, on pieces in this book. Dr Spencer Jones very kindly allowed me to reproduce images from his collection. Part of Chapter 5 originally appeared in a chapter co-written with Dr Helen McCartney, and I am grateful that she agreed to let me make use of it. In addition to those mentioned above I would like to thank Dr Niall Barr, Dr Tim Benbow, Alan & Mandy Bird, Dr Jonathan Boff, Valerie Clark, Professor Lloyd Clark, Pam Cooper, Professor Saul David, Dr Robert T. Foley, Professor David French, Dr Andrew Gordon, Dr Christina Goulter, Dr Adrian Gregory, Professor Jeffrey Grey, Dr Peter Grey, Dr Bryn Hammond, Peter Hart, Dr Tony Heathcote, Professor Brian Holden Reid, Geoff Inglis, John Lee, Dr Michael LoCicero, Dr Jenny Macleod, Ross Mahoney, Chris McCarthy, Dr Helen McCartney, Major-General Mungo Melvin, Michael Orr, Dr Linda Parker, General Sir Nick Parker, Professor Bill Philpott, Dr Steffen Prauser, Stephen Prince, Professor Robin Prior, Dr Chris Pugsley, Dr Andrew Richardson, Lieutenant-General Jonathon Riley Ph D, Dr Simon Robbins, Dr Andy Simpson, Richard Smith, Dr Mike Snape, William Spencer, Professor Peter

Stanley, Kathy Stevenson, Professor Sir Hew Strachan, Barbara Taylor, the late John Terraine, Dr Dan Todman, Professor Andy Wiest, Dr Craig Wilcox, Professor Trevor Wilson, Commodore Keith Winstanley RN and Professor Jay Winter. Thank you to Professor Peter Simkins for his very generous Foreword. My family, especially Viv, Jennie and James, know how much I owe them. Jamie Wilson commissioned this book for Praetorian Press, and thanks are also due to Rupert Harding and Sarah Cook. If I have missed anyone out I offer my apologies.

This book is dedicated to Dr Roger Lee of the Army History Unit in Canberra. He has been an enormously important influence on the development of military history in Australia, is a fine scholar and a very good friend. I am delighted to dedicate this book to Roger.

PART 1

CONTEXT

PART
CONTENT

Chapter 1

Britain and the Empire at War, 1914–1918: Reflections on a Forgotten Victory

> To this day the First World War remains contested territory; people still care passionately about it and hotly dispute its causes, its character, and its legacies.[1]

Perceptions of the First World War

On the eve of the centenary of the outbreak of the First World War, the debate over the role of Britain and the British Empire in the First World War showed no signs of ceasing. In the UK the conduct of the war on the Western Front lies at the heart of the controversies, while in Australia and New Zealand the Gallipoli campaign of 1915 dominates the debate.[2] The issue of whether Britain and the Empire should have become involved at all has been a source of controversy in recent years. The nature of the wartime relationship between the 'Mother Country' and the Dominions, and how it was changed by the First World War, has of course been a fruitful ground not only for historians, but also for journalists and politicians.[3] In 1998, on the eightieth anniversary of the Armistice, two influential books appeared: John Keegan's *The First World War* and Niall Ferguson's *The Pity of War*.[4] There is much to admire in both books. Keegan's was beautifully written, while Ferguson has some very interesting things to say about economics, and the nature of combat. However, on two key issues – the origins of the war and the combat performance of the British Expeditionary Force (BEF) – I found myself in profound disagreement with both Keegan and Ferguson. My 2001 book *Forgotten Victory: The First World War – Myths and Realities* was, in part, a response to their books.[5]

Forgotten Victory reflected, and is in large part a synthesis of, the research of the last two decades. Here I will reconsider two of my major themes. First, that far from being futile, the war was fought for the very highest of stakes. It was forced upon Britain, which was compelled to fight a defensive war that it could not afford to lose. Moreover, the war was popular in the sense of it being a total, 'people's war'; there was a broad national consensus that the war had to be fought and won. Second, that the British Army was not the incompetent set of 'lions led by donkeys' beloved of popular myth; rather, that it underwent a steep learning curve and emerged as a formidable force which took a leading role in defeating the German army on the battlefield in 1918.

To some, these 'revisionist' views appear to be heretical. For the New Zealand writer Maurice Shadbolt, 'Gallipoli had no more significance than a lethal bar-room brawl'.[6] This view is representative of a school of thought that sees the war as pointless. Some regard it as somehow 'outside' history, disconnected from the normal course of events, and only accessible through literature and art produced by veterans of the conflict. My approach, as part of an informal global historical school of English-speaking historians that has for the last thirty years been using archival research to reassess the war, is rather different. I locate the First World War firmly within the context of political and military history. This war was, like any other, fought over political issues, and can be treated by historians like any other conflict.

The truth is that it is impossible to treat the First World War like any other: the scars on the psyche run too deep. Even to attempt to distance one-self from the emotional baggage of the last century by viewing the First World War in Clausewitzian terms runs the risk of accusations of callousness, although, gratifyingly, one reviewer described the book as 'compassionate'.[7] One can turn the 'callousness' argument on its head. It is tragic that bereaved families have for so long been told, quite wrongly, that their loved ones died in vain. The 'One Million Dead' of the British Empire, their widows and orphans, and descendants, deserve at the very least a sober reconsideration of *why* and *how* the war was fought.

In New Zealand, Australia and Canada, the First World War is seen as an important step on the road of nation building.[8] Glyn Harper has argued that the war led to the recognition 'that New Zealand and New Zealanders were different and this difference did not imply inferiority. New Zealand national-ism and a sense of identity had been born.'[9] Tom Frame has commented that '25 April 1915 gave birth to several powerful and abiding myths which said more about Australian identity and hopes for nationhood than about a short military expedition concentrated in a place few Australians knew anything about'.[10] Perhaps much the same could be said about New Zealand, and, with appropriate adjustments and 'Vimy Ridge' substituted for 'Gallipoli', Canada too. In these countries the memory of the First World War has a positive aspect that sits alongside perceptions of waste, incompetence and futility.

This positive view is missing from the British national perception of the conflict. The dominant images are, in the words of one of the most influential writers on the First World War, A.J.P. Taylor, 'brave helpless soldiers; blun-dering obstinate generals; nothing achieved'.[11] Moreover, the war is viewed as being fought over trivial issues. This perception is brilliantly parodied in the influential BBC TV comedy series *Blackadder Goes Forth*, when the origins of the war were reduced to 'some chap called Archie Duke shot an ostrich because he was hungry'.[12]

Historians, especially since 1980, have explored the riches of private and public archives to produce a composite and multi-faceted picture of Britain during the First World War that is at odds with received wisdom. But little of this research has entered the public consciousness. Even some historians seem to find it difficult to let go of the 'lions led by donkeys' version. I was fortunate in that *Forgotten Victory* was widely reviewed, and the positive reviews dwarfed the number of bad ones.[13] As Brian Bond commented, 'Most military historians who have seriously studied this subject will be in general agreement with Gary Sheffield's standpoint.'[14] By contrast, the reaction of one or two critics reminded me of Alfred Duff Cooper's comments about Liddell Hart's critique of his biography of Haig: 'His article was a polemic rather than a review … He set out to prove that Haig had always been wrong and it therefore followed that anyone who sought to defend him must have written a book that was misleading and worthless.'[15] Certainly some criticism of *Forgotten Victory* seemed to be the product of emotion rather than cool analysis and knowledge of the subject.

Given the role that the First World War is perceived to have played in nation-building, that the conflict remains politically contentious in Australia and New Zealand is perhaps to be expected. The fact that it remains so in the UK is rather more surprising. For some writers on the Left, there is an assumption that revisionist historians must be pursuing a reactionary agenda. In his review of *Forgotten Victory*, Frank McLynn described me as 'a simple-minded right wing ideologist'. As I pointed out in a letter to the newspaper in which this review was published, my political sympathies happen to lie on the Left, not the Right, as do those, incidentally, of a number of other revisionists, while still others are Conservative in their politics or apolitical. Other critics further to the Left of the political spectrum continue to see the First World War in starkly ideological terms. One reviewer argued that the war 'was a battle for the right of British and French capitalists to continue to exploit the workers and peasants of Africa and Asia … The revisionists are as wrong now as … Douglas Haig and his gang were then. The popular view of the war is the right one, Blackadder and all.'[16] Under the interesting title of 'Misled (sic) attempt to justify bloody war', another review explicitly linked the First World War to the 2003 war in Iraq: 'The First World War raises the questions – how can … wars be stopped? Not by voting Labour! The Labour Party opposed the war, until it started and then backed it when it began – just as now.'[17]

Turning to writers on the Right, a maverick Conservative MP, the late Alan Clark, was one of Haig's fiercest critics. His 1963 book *The Donkeys*, although panned at the time and ever since – Michael Howard condemned it as 'worthless as history' – remains in print. Clark believed that Britain was wrong to have entered the war, as its national interests were not at risk. The war destroyed an idyllic society (which existed largely, in fact, in Clark's imagination) in which interclass harmony prevailed. Once Britain joined the war, it was a monumental error to fight on land as opposed to imposing a naval blockade: 'the sacrifice of a whole generation in Flanders was little more than a placebo to the mulish vanity of the general staff'. It is not surprising to find Clark in 1999 arguing against intervention in another Balkan war in which, he said, Britain had no interest; nor to discover that he entered politics out of a sense of duty, believing he had to make amends for the way that the elite had betrayed the masses in 1914–1918.[18]

In the 1990s the First World War became a vehicle for debate on Britain's role in the European Union. A Thatcherite historian, Niall Ferguson, argued the British decision to go to war in 1914 as 'the greatest error of modern history'. Through the medium of the European Union, he argued, Germany has achieved the economic leadership of Europe that it sought in 1914, despite Britain fighting a war to prevent it happening.[19] Similarly, John Charmley's 1999 work arguing that British intervention in 1914 was neither inevitable nor desirable is implicitly, and in one place explicitly, linked to current debates about Britain's place in Europe.[20] On the Left and Right, there is a consensus that Britain's involvement in the First World War was a disastrous mistake.

The Origins of the War

Britain fought the First World War essentially to uphold the balance of power,[21] and to keep Belgium, long regarded as the outer fortification of Fortress Britannia, from German occupation. Any assessment of Britain's decision to go to war must begin with a survey of the state of the debate on the origins of the conflict. In *Forgotten Victory* I argued that the notorious 'War Guilt' clause (article 231 of the 1919 Treaty of Versailles) was essentially correct in blaming the war on 'the aggression of Germany and her allies'.[22] Nothing that I have read since has caused me to change that view. There is a consensus among historians that the primary responsibility for bringing about the war rests with Germany and Austria-Hungary. The work of the distinguished German historian Stig Förster 'stresses that no serious historian today could be an apologist for German policy prior to August 1914'.[23] However, as Annika Mombauer has recently commented, 'there are still commentators who refuse to acknowledge Germany's large share of responsibility for the events that led to war'.[24]

It is clear that Austria-Hungary's aggression against Serbia 'plunged Europe into war'. Following the assassination of Archduke Franz Ferdinand, Vienna wanted a limited war in the Balkans, but was prepared to run the risk of a general war; the Austrian elite was astoundingly myopic as to the possible reaction of Russia. Germany's culpability is equally clear. On 5–6 July the Kaiser, in consultation with Bethmann Hollweg, his Chancellor, issued what became known as the 'blank cheque' of support for Austria-Hungary's military actions. Now, with German support, the Austrians could initiate military action. Without it, Vienna would have had to try another tack, 'something less punitive'. The German decision was taken in full knowledge of the possible consequences. In short, the German elite was prepared to risk war. Some, like General Helmuth von Mòltke the Younger, had been urging war for some 'time.[25]

Why was this decision arrived at? Some apologists for German actions in 1914 point to the emerging threat of Russia. After the defeat at the hands of Japan in 1904–5, the Russian armed forces were in a state of disarray. The Great Programme of October 1913 was intended to rebuild Russian forces, possibly to deter German action against Russia's ally, France. In August 1914 completion of the programme was some years off, and even when finished it would not have placed Russia in a position of military superiority.[26] There is little doubt that the implications of Russian rearmament alarmed Berlin and Vienna, and led to the view that war might be better 'sooner rather than later'.[27] This is not much of a defence for German policy in July–August 1914. How Russia would have behaved if the Great Programme had been completed in peacetime is, of course, unknowable, while the moral and political dilemmas involved in a pre-emptive conflict have been thrown into sharp focus in our own time.

During the July crisis, Russian policy was influenced by German and Austrian 'coercion' during the Bosnian crisis of 1908. Militarily weak, the Russian elite believed that if it stood by and allowed Austria a free hand over Serbia, Russia 'would no longer be seen as a great power'. Russia's policy in 1914 was essentially defensive in the face of Austro-German aggression. Although the fact that Russia mobilised first allowed the Germans to portray the war as a defensive one, Russian mobilisation did not equate to a declaration of war, as the German ambassador was repeatedly informed by Sazonov, the Russian Foreign Minister. The Russians needed up to sixteen weeks to put their forces in a position to fight, and this period, they believed, could be used for diplomacy. As far as culpability for the outbreak of the war goes, one inescapable fact is that 'Russia mobilized; Germany declared war'.[28]

Famously, Fritz Fischer claimed that Germany went to war in 1914 to achieve world power. In particular, he argued that at a 'War Council' on 8 December the Kaiser and his senior advisers decided to go to war about eighteen months hence. Historians still debate the meaning of this meeting, but at the very least the War Council provides powerful evidence of the willingness of the German elite to contemplate aggressive war. Some argue that Berlin seized on the Serbian crisis to create conditions for a war of conquest. In contrast, it has been argued that German decision-making during the 1914 July crisis was characterised by 'chaos and confusion rather than direction and design', and was concerned with the immediate crisis, rather than a Fischerite deliberate bid for world power.[29] Even so Bethmann Hollweg, supported, as we have seen, by the Kaiser, took the 'calculated risk' of seeking to split the Russian–French–British entente, without war if possible, but with war if necessary. Whether one sees Germany as deliberately starting (or risking) war in a bid for European hegemony and world power, or for some lesser stake, the finger of guilt points firmly at Berlin.

Jeremy Black has stressed that 'chance played a central role' in Britain entering the war in 1914. France and Russia were no longer regarded as threatening by Britain, in part because of the Russian defeat at the hands of Japan in 1905, thus leaving its ally, France, open to German diplomatic pressure. A few years earlier Germany had seemed a natural ally of the British.[30] This view has much to commend it, but it seems to me one should not underestimate the extent to which the Germans made the weather. German behaviour helped create the conditions in which the three colonial powers formed an entente. In 1870–1 Prussia/Germany had defeated France, and Britain had been able to live with the consequences. Germany's aims were essentially limited and German troops stayed out of Belgium. The old balance of power was destroyed, but a new one was created and while Bismarck remained Chancellor, Germany lived within it. In 1914, *pace* John Charmley,[31] things were very different, thanks to a decade and a half of German sabre-rattling, an unlimited approach to war, and an attack on Belgium.

One historian has recently described as 'very optimistic' the notion that a victorious Germany would have proved a benign influence. Rather, 'A continental hegemony exercised by a Hohenzollern supreme warlord flush with easy victory would probably have had little room for liberalism, democracy, or British trade.' Moreover, if Germany had chosen to expand its power beyond Europe, 'who could then have checked him'?[32]

Robin Prior and Trevor Wilson also locate Britain's entry into the war in terms of the most simple national interest: 'survival as an independent, self-respecting state'. It had to prevent an enemy from controlling continental Europe, seizing the Channel ports and mounting a serious challenge to the Royal Navy's domination of the seas. By 1914 the importance of overseas trade to the British economy and the problems of feeding Britain's population from domestic produce meant that the German threat 'came to surpass any menace it had confronted in the times of Philip II, Louis XIV or Napoleon'.[33]

Still, Ferguson's argument remains attractive. We, of course, know that the war that broke out in August 1914 lasted until November 1918, cost millions of lives, and jerked world history into a groove that led to Stalin, Hitler and the threat of nuclear annihilation. Anything, some say, would have been better than that. That seems to be the thinking behind Richard Schweitzer's argument in *The Cross and the Trenches*. He accepts the 'compelling case' made in *Forgotten Victory* that 'Britain's vital national security interests were at stake in August 1914' in the Low Countries. Nevertheless, he goes on partially to espouse Niall Ferguson's argument 'that Germany may have evolved into a benign hegemon ... the subsequent humanitarian disasters in Russia and

Germany, suggest that an early German victory in the war, may, depending on one's vantage point, have been preferable'.[34]

All of this seems to turn on the ability of the Hohenzollern leopard to change his spots. The historical record – of the German army's atrocities against civilians in 1914, a consequence of a 'Clausewitzian commitment to using the most ruthless means necessary to win victory';[35] the harsh treatment meted out to occupied territories in France, Belgium and Poland; the ruthless exploitation of captured resources, including the use of forced labour; the emergence of the Hindenburg/Ludendorff military dictatorship – none of this inspires confidence in the evolution of Imperial Germany into a 'benign hegemon'. The British decision-makers in August 1914 were not dealing with fantasies. They had to deal with *Realpolitik*, in the form of the gravest of threats to national survival. To imagine that Britain could stay out of the war in the face of Germany's drive to the west in 1914 is wishful thinking. As Colin S. Gray has written in a direct rebuttal of Ferguson's thesis, 'Britain had no prudent choice other than to join the anti-German coalition in 1914. Had Britain stood aside, Germany would have defeated France and Russia. Britain would then have been deservedly friendless, facing a hegemonic Germany with an undamaged – indeed probably augmented – High Seas Fleet.'[36]

This situation would have been similar to the bleak prospect that Britain had to face after Dunkirk, except that in 1940 the saving grace was that the *Kriegsmarine* had been severely damaged in the Norway campaign. In Gray's all-too-plausible scenario, Britain would have faced a Germany dominant on land and powerful at sea, and in the Anglo-German conflict that would have surely come, Britain's worst strategic nightmare would have come true. The reputation of Imperial Germany has benefited from what came after. Hitler's regime was certainly worse than that of the Kaiser, but the Kaiser's was decidedly unpleasant and dangerous. The First World War took on the character of a struggle between liberal democracies (for all their faults, and notwithstanding an alliance with Czarist Russia) and an anti-democratic, illiberal, militarist autocracy. This was the first of three such challenges in the twentieth century, the others being Nazi Germany and Marxist-Leninism during the Cold War. In August 1914, in choosing to go to war, Britain made a decision that, even in full knowledge of the carnage and suffering that was thus unleashed, remains the correct one.

'Someone else's war'?

Even if it is accepted as the correct decision for Britain to go to war in 1914, does it follow that the rest of the Empire should have followed suit? Dame Silvia Cartwright, New Zealand's Governor-General, in a speech delivered at Chunuk Bair on Anzac Day 2003 argued against this notion: 'New Zealanders had nothing to gain from the fight at Gallipoli. It was someone else's war. Turkey was not our enemy.'[37]

However, Cartwright's views do not reflect the views held by New Zealanders of the First World War generation. Not only was Turkey allied to the Empire's principal enemy, but it posed a threat to Imperial security. Cecil Malthus, a New Zealand veteran of Gallipoli and the Western Front, believed to the end of his life that the war was justified by the need to halt German aggression.[38] Those New Zealanders who did oppose the conflict did so on grounds other than 'it was someone else's war'.[39] In 1914 the overwhelming majority of New Zealanders, Australians, and Anglophone Canadians and South Africans regarded themselves as in some sense 'British', as loyal subjects of King George V and citizens of the Empire. Late in life, Stan Stansfield, a New Zealand veteran, speaking of his motives for enlisting, commented on the British Empire business [which] was at the zenith, the peak of its power and popularity'.[40] In order to envisage an Australia that stayed out of the war, historian Geoffrey Blainey had to postulate a counterfactual country of 1914 in which a sizeable proportion of the population were of German, Austrian and Turkish origin.[41]

Even if Imperial sentiment is set aside, there were compelling strategic reasons for Australia and New Zealand to become involved in the war. Australasian defence rested ultimately on British naval supremacy. If Britain had been defeated, and the Royal Navy's shield removed, Australia and New Zealand would have been effectively defenceless, and obliged to turn elsewhere, as in 1942. Dominion participation in Britain's imperial wars before 1914 contained a measure of self-interest. By proving themselves loyal, they increased the chance of Britain coming to their aid should they be menaced by another power – either Germany or Britain's ally, Japan. Similarly, participation in the war against Germany was squarely in the national interest of Australia and New Zealand.[42]

The argument about whether 1914–1918 was 'someone else's war' is a prime example of the continued politicisation of the subject. The British Empire is also deeply controversial in the UK. In 2003 a Rastafarian poet rejected the offer of an Order of the British Empire (OBE) 'as a legacy of colonialism'. A few months later a parliamentary committee recommended a change of name to 'Order of British Excellence' as the former title was 'now considered to be unacceptable, being thought to embody values that are no longer shared by many of the country's population'. This prompted one correspondent to the BBC to pose the question 'Why are we always ashamed and apologetic of the British Empire?'[43] With failed states pricking the world's conscience, a modified form of imperialism appears to be creeping back onto on the international agenda, reinforced by debates about the 'imperial' nature of the USA. Niall Ferguson's 2003 book and TV series, which emphasised the positive aspects of the British Empire, provoked fury in some quarters.[44]

Total War

Why, given the military stalemate and appalling casualties on the Western Front, was there no compromise peace?[45] Domestic support for the war in all the belligerent states remained remarkably high in the first years of the war. Not until 1917 was there substantial wavering of resolve, and even then only Russia was forced out of the war. Until 1917 there was little pressure from below for a compromise peace. This fact allowed governments on both sides to pursue far-reaching war aims that made a compromise peace impossible. This was a consequence of total war, and the mentalities it breeds. Moreover, fundamental war aims were utterly irreconcilable. Germany sought to achieve hegemony over Europe, eventually evolving geopolitical objectives that resembled those pursued by the Third Reich a generation later, while Britain, France, Russia and later the USA sought to prevent this from occurring. The campaigns of 1914 brought the Germans important gains in Belgium and eastern France, and allowed the German army to remain on the defensive in the West while concentrating on defeating Russia. As long as the Allied armies were unable to dislodge German forces from the Western Front, Berlin saw no reason to compromise. For the Allies to have consented to a peace that allowed Germany to retain her gains in the West would have left both French and British security gravely weakened. Only when one side inflicted a decisive series of defeats on the other – which happened between July and November 1918 – did diplomacy come back into play. Although the Germans tried to divide the Entente by appealing over the head of the British and French to President Woodrow Wilson in Washington, this ploy was in vain. The war ended on the terms dictated by the Allies. Although much vilified, they were, in truth, not unduly severe considering that Germany had initiated, fought and lost a total world war. Indeed, the terms seem almost moderate in comparison with the treatment that Germany meted out to defeated Russia in 1918 at the Peace of Brest-Litovsk. The severity of the settlement at the end of the First World War bears no comparison with that imposed on Germany in 1945.[46]

Between 1914 and 1918 Britain and the Empire mobilised for total war. Democracies cannot fight and win a total war without the consent and active involvement of the masses, and the creation of 'nations-in arms' was a remarkable achievement. The onset of war weariness in Britain was countered to a large extent by a 'remobilisation' in 1917–1918, involving the announcement of 'democratic' war aims and the implementation of social and political reforms. In all, 5,704,000 men served in the British Army during the First World War, split roughly equally between volunteers and conscripts.[47] The army of the First World War was larger by far than any other army raised by Britain, before or since. The birth of this huge army was paralleled by the creation of a war economy to support it. In December 1916 David Lloyd George became Prime Minister. The emergence of Lloyd George, a populist politician of humble origins who won a reputation as a 'man of push and go' at the Ministry of Munitions, is a striking symbol of Britain's transformation into a state geared for total war. The creation of a centrally directed war economy capable of supplying its huge armies with sufficient quantities of weapons, ammunition and all the other equipment it needed to fight a modern high-intensity attritional war was a considerable achievement of the British nation in arms. Without it, the victories of the BEF on the battlefields of France and Belgium would have been impossible.

There was a similar pattern in the Empire. Out of a population of 8 million Canada sent 458,000 men overseas, of whom 57,000 became casualties. The 5 million Australians sent 332,00, resulting in 59,000 casualties; for New Zealand the figures were 1.1 million, 112,000 and 17,000. India found 1.5 million volunteers. Moreover, in the last two years of the war about one-third of the BEF's munitions were produced in Canada.[48] Black Africa also made a substantial contribution. Some 40,000 carriers and porters died in the East African campaign, for example.[49]

The war put the social and political fabric of belligerents under tremendous strain. Total war made less of an impact on the Dominions than on Russia or Germany, but the stresses were still significant. In July 1916 New Zealand followed Britain in introducing conscription, the first Dominion to do so. Something in the order of 10 per cent of the total population of New Zealand served overseas.[50] Across the Empire, the question of conscription became entangled with war weariness. Even in loyal New Zealand, conscription proved divisive. In Canada these problems were hugely magnified. About 35 per cent of the population comprised French-Canadians, but this community provided only 5 per cent of the Canadian Expeditionary Force. By comparison, in Toronto over two-thirds of the men who were eligible volunteered.[51] In 1917 a prolonged conscription crisis, culminating in a bitterly fought election, widened the rift between Canada's Anglophone and Francophone peoples. Similarly, as the October 1915 election revealed, the whole question of South Africa's participation in the war divided the Afrikaaner community down the middle. In Australia attempts to introduce conscription were twice rejected in referenda that also proved deeply divisive.

One of the paradoxes of total war in the twentieth century is that liberal democratic states have had to adopt many of the trappings and methods of authoritarian states in order to defend their values against ideological enemies.[52] For Britain and the Dominions to emerge from the war with their democracy not only intact but in many ways enhanced was a substantial achievement.

Strategy, Operations and Tactics

In 1932 Basil Liddell Hart argued that between 1914 and 1918 Britain had abandoned her traditional 'way in warfare' of using naval power, and financial muscle to subsidise allies, with disastrous results.[53] Many critics have echoed his condemnation of British strategy, Alan Clark among them. In reality, British strategy in 1914–1918 had strong continuities with previous practice, not least in that it was a war fought in coalition with France and Russia. This simple fact severely limited Britain's strategic room for manoeuvre. As Lord Kitchener commented in August 1915, 'unfortunately we had to make war as we must, and not as we should like to'.[54] France and Russia needed far more than economic and naval contributions from Britain, vital as they were. They needed troops on the ground on the Western Front. That was where the war was won and lost.

In recent years the old idea of a crude division between 'Easterners' and 'Westerners' in the British decision-making elite has largely been discarded. Apparent 'Westerners' like Sir William Robertson were well aware of the necessity for campaigns away from France. These fell into various categories, including campaigns undertaken to ensure harmony within the coalition (Salonika, Italy), to uphold local Imperial interests (the capture of Germany's Pacific colonies) or to gain strategically significant territory (Palestine, Mesopotamia). The latter was seen as vital for the Empire's place in the post-war world vis-à-vis her wartime allies and even, it has been argued, to acquire bargaining chips for use should the war end in a peace of exhaustion.[55]

Such operations were undoubtedly important, but they contributed little to the defeat of Germany. The contribution of the Royal Navy, including economic blockade, was an essential component in the Allied victory, but by itself it was not enough to bring about even the minimum war aim of the withdrawal of German forces from Belgium and France. That was only accomplished by the defeat of the German army in battle, and that mighty undertaking could not have been achieved without the decisive contribution of the British Expeditionary Force, in which the ten Dominion divisions played a prominent role. British and Allied strategy in the First World War was on occasion wasteful and even incompetent, but ultimately it proved less wasteful and incompetent than that of Germany and the Central Powers. In the end, this was what mattered.

The change in warfare between 1914 and 1918 is graphically illustrated by examining the fate of the cavalry. In the initial, mobile stages of the 1914 campaign, British cavalry was highly effective in the roles of reconnaissance and screening the main body of the BEF, employing a mixture of mounted and dismounted action. When the front began to congeal into trench warfare, the limitations of mounted troops became clear. Major Lord Tweedmouth of the Royal Horse Guards (The Blues) recorded in his diary for 26 October 1914:

> Supposed to be a rest day. Turned out at 2 pm to support an advance by General Vaughan. Were stopped on the way and told to cover the retreat

of the 20th Bde and lined the woods on each side of the road. Situation changed again and we went off at a gallop to make a demonstration. C Sqn in advance. My sword carried away just as we got to the crest between Hugh Grovenor's trench and Gerry Ward's. We got the shrapnel pretty hot then and my horse was hit in the leg and I had to stop and get into Hugh's trench. Got out presently and shot my horse with my revolver and saved all my kit. Found the led horses of D Sqn and went back with them to Zillebeke. We were very lucky considering the fire we came in for and had men wounded, and lost over 20 horses killed and wounded, mostly in C Sqn.[56]

Contrary to received wisdom, horsed cavalry were effective on occasions on the Western Front during trench warfare. But the general experience of cavalry is neatly summarised by the historian of the 3rd Dragoon Guards: 'When the regiment left Egypt in 1914, nobody had any conception of the work which awaited the cavalry on the Western Front. By training and tradition all ranks expected to be used as mounted troops. Four years later they looked back on their campaigns, and found that only on rare occasions had they used their horses.' Instead, the regiment had carried out a variety of tasks, many 'strange and distasteful', ranging from infantry work in the trenches to burying corpses, although they had carried out a very successful mounted charge almost at the end of the war.[57]

The 3rd Dragoon Guards were caught up in static trench warfare. Although this form of warfare was far from new,[58] from October–November 1914 until the end of 1917 the peculiar circumstances of the Western Front dictated that the defensive had a temporary advantage. This situation gradually changed, as new weapons (notably the tank, artillery, aircraft and light machine gun) were introduced or improved, and, just as importantly, tactics were evolved to make best use of the new equipment.

A key development was the evolution of an all-arms weapons system, in which various pieces of technology, lethal and non-lethal, different troop types and effective command and control systems operated in a synergistic fashion. Striking visual evidence of the importance of this development is to be seen in central London to this day. The Foot Guards were a notoriously 'tribal' organisation, yet their First World War memorial includes a bas relief of an 18-pounder field gun in action and a signaller using a field telephone. The message is clear, and echoes a theme that runs throughout the divisional history: the Guards Division was an all-arms team that consisted of far more than socially elite infantry regiments.[59]

A parallel development – the emergence of three-dimensional, indirect artillery fire, an advance that was made possible by the use of aircraft for artillery spotting – was of the utmost importance. These two developments transformed the conduct of warfare in a Revolution in Military Affairs (RMA), the product of 'technological development', 'doctrinal and operational inno-vation' and 'organisational adaptation'.[60] The German breakthrough of March 1918 demonstrated that the pendulum had swung in favour of the attacker. However, the Hundred Days offensives of August–November 1918 demonstrated that it was the Allies, and specifically the forces of the British Empire, rather than the Germans, who had learned most effectively from the bloody battles of 1915–1917.

During the Hundred Days the higher command of the Allies demonstrated a grasp of what would today be called 'operational art', co-ordinating Army-level offensives across a wide front. Moreover, they chose to make shallow but logistically sustainable advances, covered by artillery fire, before switching the point of attack to a different sector to keep the enemy off-balance. This contrasted strongly with the German methods of the spring, when attacking forces made spectacular advances that outran their artillery and supply lines, leaving them vulnerable to counterstrokes. By this stage the Germans were rapidly exhausting their resources of men, horses and many other essentials. The BEF too was running short of men, but the British had the priceless advantage of being able to fight a 'rich man's war' with apparently limitless supplies of guns and munitions, and excellent logistic support. During the attack on the Canal du Nord in late September 62,813 tons of ammunition were fired in only three days. Whatever criticisms can be made of the BEF's operations in previous campaigns, during the Hundred Days it was playing to its strengths.[61]

The experience of the New Zealand Division offers some 'snapshots' of the BEF's tactical learning curve process. This division's action in the Battle of the Somme on 15–17 September 1916 demonstrates the immaturity of the BEF's style of warfare at that stage of the war. Generally, too much was expected of the tank on its debut; tactical co-ordination between the tanks and the infantry was rudimentary; the artillery fire-plan was flawed; and gunnery techniques left a lot to be desired. The New Zealand infantry followed a creeping barrage, but some betrayed their inexperience by advancing into the British barrage. Some troops were faced by intact barbed wire, and on occa-sions the barrage failed to materialise. Logistic problems were compounded by bad weather, and, in the words of the divisional historian, 'robbed the British of the fruit of their efforts'. Although the New Zealanders, who dis-played considerable élan and were well served by excellent battlefield leader-ship, did well, overall the attack of 15 September 1916 fell short of Haig's expectations.[62]

A year later much had changed. The New Zealand Division, like the rest of the BEF, had absorbed the lessons of the Somme, retraining in the new platoon tactics.[63] It had benefited from improved gunnery, and more efficient staff work and planning at all levels, in the battles of Messines on 7 June 1917 and Broodseinde on 4 October 1917. These battles were models of 'bite and

rawly

hold' tactics in which infantry advanced on limited objectives, supported by heavy fire power.[64] The division's attack on 12 October during First Passchendaele was, by contrast, a bloody failure. Brigadier General Herbert Hart of 4 NZ Brigade gave the reasons for the failure in his diary. He noted the difficulty of getting the guns forward over ground 'absolutely shattered, ploughed up & pockmarked by shellfire', a problem exacerbated by wet weather:

> Consequently the artillery preparation was incomplete. Uncut wire was met & was insurmountable under such conditions. Mud & wire prevented our men keeping up to the barrage. Hun machine gunners, protected in concrete pillboxes during the bombardment, came out with their machine guns after the barrage passed on, & shot down our men while still struggling to get through & over the mud & wire.[65]

Plumer's Second Army had delivered three bite and hold operations in rapid succession, on 20 and 26 September and 4 October. But the very success of the British artillery cratered the ground and made it increasingly difficult to get the guns forward for the next attack. In the wet and muddy conditions of Passchendaele, it proved impossible to sustain the operational tempo. As the subsequent success of the Canadian Corps demonstrated, even under these conditions bite and hold could be made to work, if time and substantial engineering resources were made available to prepare the battlefield.[66] However, this methodical approach ran the risk of losing the impetus of the initial advance.

By the time of the Hundred Days, matters had moved on again. Brigadier General Hart, by now commanding 3 New Zealand (Rifle) Brigade, recorded that:

> The battle [of Bapaume, August 1918] is entirely different to all earlier battles in France. Troops are not so densely packed, there is greater scope for initiative & leadership. Advances are deeper & on much wider frontages ...
>
> There are many tanks, whippets & armoured cars about, some going up for more work, some returning weary & battle scarred, & many derelict by the roadside ... Artillery was moving forward everywhere, lorry water tanks were particularly busy & overhead there was a constant overhead buzz from aeroplanes. The whole scene was very stirring & much less gruesome than the Somme, Messines or Passchendaele.[67]

The complexity of some operations in the Hundred Days is demonstrated by 3 Brigade's capture of Le Quesnoy on 4 November 1918. This involved barrages by field artillery and machine gun, trench mortar and Lewis Gun fire, the projection of burning oil and smoke by Special Companies of the

Royal Engineers, a sophisticated scheme of manoeuvre for the infantry and, of course, the use of scaling ladders.[68]

The New Zealand Division was an unusually effective formation, certainly one of the best in the BEF, and under the command of the formidable Major General Sir Andrew Russell it developed a distinctive style. However, the division needs to be placed into context of a BEF-wide process of learning and adaptation that, by the Hundred Days, resulted in the overall quality of Haig's army being very high. The term 'learning curve' should not be taken to mean that the process was a smooth upward course, and it encompassed logistics, command and staff work, and a host of other factors as well as tactics. But the learning curve was real enough, and it helped deliver victory on the battlefield.

Conclusion

The Allied victory of 1918 was a vital element in the relative peace and prosperity enjoyed by the West at the end of the twentieth century. The defeat of Germany preserved liberalism and democracy in Europe and delivered a check to a militarist, aggressive autocracy. The fact that Britain, the Dominions and their allies would find it necessary to engage in two further global conflicts against ideological enemies – one hot, one cold – does not detract from the importance of the war of 1914–1918 . The argument that the world in 1919 would have been a better place if the First World War had not taken place, or more parochially, if Britain and the Empire had not become involved, is a red herring. A German victory in that war would have produced a situation significantly worse than the imperfect 'real' world of 1919. The war waged by Britain and the Empire was tragic, destructive and wasteful – but it was not futile.

*   *   *

Afterthoughts

This essay was written in 2003–4 for a conference in New Zealand, hence the numerous NZ references. In recent years two influential books have appeared that have attempted to shift the blame for the war away from Berlin and Vienna. In *The Sleepwalkers* (London: Allen Lane, 2012) Christopher Clark focuses attention on Serbia and Russia; essentially, by arguing that no single state should be blamed for bringing about the war, he has turned the historiographical clock back to the 1930s. Sean McMeekin's *The Russian Origins of the First World War* (Cambridge, MA: Bellknap Press, 2011) argues that Russia's designs on the Ottoman Empire caused the war. Both books offer valuable perspectives on the 'Eastern' origins of the war, but neither, to my mind, convincingly absolves Germany and Austria-Hungary from un-leashing the war. Annika Mombauer's article 'The First World War: Inevi-table, Avoidable, Improbable Or Desirable? Recent Interpretations on War

Guilt and the War's Origins' (*German History*, vol. 25, no. 1, 2007), published before either of these books, gives an excellent review of the scholarly state of play at that time. I see no reason to dissent from her views about the culpability of decision-makers in Vienna and Berlin.

Acknowledgements
Thanks are due to the Household Cavalry Museum and the Army Museum, Waiouru, New Zealand, for permission to use material for which they hold the copyright.

Notes
1. 'Introduction' to Jay Winter, Geoffrey Parker, Mary R. Habeck (eds), *The Great War and the Twentieth Century* (New Haven, CT, and London: Yale University Press, 2000), p. 1.
2. J.M. Bourne, *Britain and the Great War 1914–1918* (London: Edward Arnold, 1989), p. vii; Jenny Macleod, *Reconsidering Gallipoli* (Manchester: Manchester University Press, 2004).
3. For an example tinged with Australian nationalism, see Jonathan King, *Gallipoli: Our Last Man Standing* (Milton, Qld: John Wiley, 2003).
4. John Keegan, *The First World War* (London: Hutchinson, 1998); Niall Ferguson, *The Pity of War* (London: Allen Lane, 1998).
5. Gary Sheffield, *Forgotten Victory: The First World War – Myths and Realities* (London: Headline, 2001).
6. Maurice Shadbolt, *Voices of Gallipoli* (Auckland: Hodder & Stoughton, 1988), p. 13.
7. David Horspool, The *Guardian*, 21 July 2001.
8. Jeff Keshen, 'The Great War Soldier as Nation Builder in Canada and Australia', in B.C. Busch, *Canada and the Great War* (Montreal and Kingston: McGill-Queen's University Press, 2003), pp. 3–4, 19–20.
9. Glyn Harper (ed.), *Letters from the Battlefield* (Auckland: HarperCollins, 2001), p. 14.
10. Tom Frame, *The Shores of Gallipoli: Naval Aspects of the Anzac Campaign* (Alexandria, NSW: Hale & Iremonger, 2000), p. 13.
11. A.J.P. Taylor, *The First World War An Illustrated History* (Harmondsworth: Penguin, 1966 [1963]), p. 140.
12. Richard Curtis *et al.*, *Blackadder The Whole Damn Dynasty* (London: Michael Joseph, 1998), p. 442.
13. For hostile reviews, see Frank McLynn in the *Independent*, 29 June 2001; Ian Ousby, the *Spectator*, 30 June 2001; John Keegan, the *Daily Telegraph*, 25 August 2001.
14. Brian Bond, *Times Literary Supplement*, 31 August 2001. See also Sir Michael Howard, *Journal of the Royal United Services Institute*, vol. 146, no. 5 (2001), 70. To his great credit, Niall Ferguson reviewed the book favourably: *Sunday Times*, 8 July 2001.
15. Alfred Duff Cooper, *Old Men Forget* (London: Rupert Hart-Davis, 1953), pp. 185–6.
16. *Socialism Today*, 74, April–May 2003.
17. *Morning Star*, 28 April 2003.
18. Alan Clark, 'Douglas Haig: The Greatest Betrayal', *Daily Express*, 11 November 1998; Alan Clark, letter to *Sunday Telegraph* quoted in Brian Bond, Editor's Introduction, in Brian Bond (ed.), *The First World War and British Military History* (Oxford: Clarendon, 1991), p. 11; Alan Clark, speech in House of Commons, reported on 13 May 1999 on news.bbc.co.uk/hi/english/uk_politics/newsid_341000/341713.stm; 'Alan Clark – a unique politician', news.bbc.co.uk/hi/english/ uk_politics/newsid_441000/441268.stm.
19. Niall Ferguson (ed.), *Virtual History* (London: Picador, 1997), ch. 4; Ferguson, *Pity of War*, pp. 457–62.
20. John Charmley, *Splendid Isolation? Britain and the Balance of Power 1874–1914* (London: Hodder & Stoughton, 1999), pp. x, 1–2, 7.

21. For a recent assessment, see T.G. Otte, '"Almost a Law of Nature"? Sir Edward Grey, the Foreign Office, and the Balance of Power in Europe, 1905–12' in Erik Goldstein and B.J.C. McKercher (eds), *Power and Stability: British Foreign Policy, 1865–1965* (London: Frank Cass, 2003), pp. 77–118.

22. Sheffield, *Forgotten Victory*, p. 33

23. Quoted in Annika Mombauer, *The Origins of the First World War: Controversies and Consensus* (London: Longman, 2002), p. 211.

24. Mombauer, *Origins*, p. 212.

25. Graydon A. Tunstall, Jr., 'Austria-Hungary', in Richard F. Hamilton and Holger H. Herwig (eds), *The Origins of World War I* (Cambridge: Cambridge University Press, 2003), pp. 136, 146; Annika Mombauer, *Helmuth von Moltke and the Origins of the First World War* (Cambridge: Cambridge University Press, 2001), pp. 283–9.

26. David Alan Rich, 'Russia', in Hamilton and Herwig, pp. 213–14.

27. David G. Hermann, *The Arming of Europe and the Making of the First World War* (Princeton, NJ: Princeton University Press, 1996), p. 209.

28. Rich, 'Russia', pp. 214, 223–5.

29. Holger H. Herwig, 'Germany', in Hamilton and Herwig, p. 183.

30. Jeremy Black, *Why Wars Happen* (London: Reaktion, 1998), p. 180.

31. Charmley, *Splendid Isolation?*, pp. 1–2.

32. J.P. Harris, 'Great Britain', in Hamilton and Herwig, p. 299.

33. Robin Prior and Trevor Wilson, *The First World War* (London: Cassell, 1999), pp. 23, 25–6.

34. Richard Schweitzer, *The Cross and the Trenches: Religious Doubt among British and American Great War Soldiers* (Westport, CT: Praeger, 2003), pp. 119–20.

35. John Horne and Alan Kramer, *German Atrocities, 1914: A History of Denial* (New Haven and London: Yale University Press, 2001), p. 424.

36. Colin S. Gray, *Modern Strategy* (Oxford: Oxford University Press, 1999), p. 66.

37. www.gg.govt.nz/media/speeches.asp?type=current&ID=235 (accessed 7 July 2004).

38. Cecil Malthus, *Armetières and the Somme* (Auckland: Reed, 2002), pp. 14–15.

39. Jock Philips, 'Was the Great War New Zealand's war'?, in Craig Wilcox with Janice Aldridge (eds), *The Great War: Gains and Losses – Anzac and Empire* (Canberra: Australian War Memorial, 1995), p. 69.

40. Nicholas Boyack and Jane Tolerton, *In the Shadow of War* (Auckland: Penguin, 1990), p. 25.

41. Geoffrey Blainey, 'If Australia had not participated in the Great War, what kind of society would have emerged?' in Wilcox and Aldridge, *The Great War*, p. 172.

42. For studies on this theme, see Chris Coulthard-Clark, 'Australian Defence; Perceptions and Policies, 1871–1919'; Craig Wilcox, 'Australian Involvement in the Boer War: Imperial Pressure or Colonial Realpolitik?'; Christopher Pugsley, 'At the Empire's Call: New Zealand Expeditionary Force Planning, 1901–1918', all in John A. Moses and Christopher Pugsley (eds), *The German Empire and Britain's Pacific Dominions 1871–1919* (Claremont, CA: Regina Books). See also Nicholas Lambert, 'Economy or Empire? The Fleet Security Concept and the Quest for Collective Security in the Pacific, 1909–1914', in Keith Nielson and Greg Kennedy, *Far Flung Lines* (London: Frank Cass, 1997), pp. 55–83.

43. The *Guardian*, 27 November 2003; bbc.co.uk/go/pr/fr/-/1/hi/uk_politics/3888581.stm (accessed 13 July 2004).

44. Niall Ferguson, *Empire. How Britain Made the Modern World* (London: Allen Lane, 2003).

45. For the diplomacy of the war, see David Stevenson, *The First World War and International Politics* (Oxford: Oxford University Press, 1988), and David Stevenson, 'War Aims and Peace Negotiations', in Hew Strachan (ed.), *The Oxford Illustrated History of the First World War* (Oxford: Oxford University Press, 1998).

46. For recent scholarship on Versailles, see Manfred F. Boemeke, Gerald D. Feldman and Elisabeth Glaser (eds), *The Treaty of Versailles: A Reassessment after 75 Years* (Cambridge: Cambridge University Press, 1998).

47. Peter Simkins, *Kitchener's Army* (Manchester: Manchester University Press, 1989), p. xiv.

48. Figures from Robert Holland, 'The British Empire and the Great War, 1914–1918', in Judith M. Brown and Wm. Roger Louis (eds), *The Oxford History of the British Empire vol. IV, The Twentieth Century* (Oxford: Oxford University Press, 1999), pp. 117–18.

49. Ross Anderson, *The Forgotten Front: The East African Campaign 1914–1918* (Stroud: Tempus, 2004), p. 296.

50. W. David McIntyre, 'Australia, New Zealand, and the Pacific Islands', in Brown and Louis, *Oxford History of the British Empire*, p. 671.

51. Holland, *The British Empire and the Great War*', p. 126; Ian Miller, '"A Privilege to Serve": Toronto's Experience with Voluntary Enlistment in the Great War', in Yves Tremblay (ed.), *Canadian Military History Since the 17th Century* (Ottawa: Directorate of History and Heritage, 2001), p. 151.

52. One example of this was the coercion of conscientious objectors. For the New Zealand experience, see Paul Baker, *King and Country Call: New Zealand, Conscription and the Great War* (Auckland: Auckland University Press, 1988), pp. 170–201.

53. B.H. Liddell Hart, *The British Way in Warfare* (London: Faber, 1932).

54. George H. Cassar, *Kitchener: Architect of Victory* (London: Kimber, 1977), p. 389.

55. See Brock Millman, *Pessimism and British War Policy 1916–1918* (London: Frank Cass, 2001).

56. TS diary, in War Diary, RHG, Household Cavalry Museum, Windsor.

57. H.P. Holt, *History of the 3rd (Prince of Wales's) Dragoon Guards 1914–1918* (Doncaster: D.P. & G., 2001 [1937]), p. 109.

58. I find the argument that Maori played a major role in inventing trench warfare is unconvincing. See James Belich, *The New Zealand Wars and the Victorian Interpretation of Racial Conflict* (Auckland: Penguin, 1998 [1986]), pp. 297–8, 315–18; Christopher Pugsley, 'Maori did not invent trench warfare', *New Zealand Defence Quarterly*, 22 (1998), 33–7.

59. See for instance Cuthbert Headlam, *History of the Guards Division in the Great War 1915–18* vol. I (London: John Murray, 1924), pp. 251, 255.

60. Jonathan Bailey, *The First World War and the Birth of the Modern Style of Warfare*, Occasional Paper 22 (Camberley: SCSI, 1996); James R. Fitzsimonds and Jan M. Van Tol, 'Revolutions in Military Affairs', *Joint Force Quarterly*, Spring 1994, 25–6; Robin Prior and Trevor Wilson, *Command on the Western Front* (Oxford: Blackwell, 1992), p. 309; G.D. Sheffield, 'Blitzkrieg and Attrition: Land Operations in Europe 1914–45', in G.D. Sheffield and Colin McInnes, *Warfare in the Twentieth Century: Theory and Practice* (London: Unwin-Hyman, 1988).

61. Ian Malcolm Brown, *British Logistics on the Western Front 1914–1919* (Westport, CT: Praeger, 1998), pp. 197–8.

62. H. Stewart, *The New Zealand Division 1916–1919: A Popular History Based on Official Records* (Auckland: Whitcombe & Tombs, 1921), pp. 73–90.

63. Stewart, *New Zealand Division*, p. 159.

64. See '4th NZ Infantry Brigade, Narrative of events ... October 4th 1917', Sir Herbert Hart Papers 1990.1026, Kippenberger Military Archive and Research Library [KMARL], Army Museum, Waiouru.

65. Diary, 12 October 1917, Hart Papers, 1990.1021, KMARL.

66. 'Administrative Report ... 1st Canadian Division at Passchendaele ...' 7 Dec. 1917, MG30 E54 vol. 2, file 15, Phelan Papers, National Archives of Canada.

67. Diary, 24 August 1918, Hart Papers, 1990.1021, KMARL.

68. '3rd NZ (Rifle) Brigade, Report on the Capture of Le Quesnoy, 21 Nov. 1918', Hart Papers, 1990.1047, KMARL.

Chapter 2

'Not the Same as Friendship':
the British Empire and Coalition Warfare
in the Era of the First World War

Writing in the aftermath of the Second World War, the British diplomat and politician Harold Nicolson stated that 'The basis of any Alliance, or Coalition, is an agreement between two or more sovereign States to subordinate their separate interests to a single purpose.'[1] As far as it goes, this statement is true enough, but 'military alliances', as Paul Kennedy reminds us, 'are not the same as a friendships'.[2] Still less are coalitions. A British soldier-scholar, Jonathon Riley, has defined a coalition as 'a partnership of unequals', a short-term grouping of powers

> born for the moment: the individual members may be very diverse in political structure, economic power and culture, but are brought together in the face of a single unifying threat or common goal. Military contributions are inevitably based on more short-term considerations, and the resulting structures for consultation and decision-making are inevitably *ad hoc*. This is not to say that they do not work ... the achievement of a common purpose can be a powerful spur indeed.[3]

Some actors in a coalition are more powerful than others, and power can shift within a coalition over time. All have their own interests, which they pursue if necessary at the expense of their partners, especially as the end of the war nears, whether defeat or victory beckons. The end of the threat that caused the formation of the coalition tends to lead to the break-up of the grouping.[4]

Previous Experience
The British were old hands at coalition warfare. From the late seventeenth century Britain had fought a long series of wars in coalition with other states. In the period 1688–1945 Britain fought twelve Great Power wars. All were fought in coalition, with the exception of two: the Anglo-Spanish War of 1726–1729, and the American War of Independence of 1775–1783. All ended in victory, except of course the latter, in which the British were defeated by a coalition of France, Spain and the rebellious colonies. Successive generations of British decision-makers drew the appropriate lesson. 'Meeting her security

needs by co-operating with other powers was the norm for Britain … both in peace and war ….'[5] Coalition building and sustaining were fundamental tasks for British politicians and military commanders over the last 300 years. This was the natural consequence of the central tenet of British foreign policy, pursuit of the balance of power, allied to British determination to keep the strategically vital Low Countries out of the hands of aggressors.

Some British leaders, such as Marlborough, Wellington, Castlereagh and Churchill, proved to be highly adept at this task. Even Lord Raglan, the British field commander in the Crimea in 1854–1855, who has generally had a bad press, deserves some credit for his performance as a coalition general. According to legend, Raglan habitually referred to his allies, the French, as the enemy, having spent his youth fighting the French in the Napoleonic Wars.[6] In reality, Raglan made this gaffe on only one occasion, at a public dinner, at which it provoked laughter.[7] This anecdote serves to underline the truth of the classic statement made by Raglan's contemporary, Lord Palmerston, that Britain had 'no eternal allies' nor 'perpetual enemies', but British 'interests are eternal and perpetual'.[8] Raglan in fact fully recognised the importance of maintaining the coalition, successfully maintaining good relations with his French and Turkish allies.[9]

By 1914 the British were somewhat out of practice at coalition warfare. Although there had been some minor combined operations (such as in China in 1900), the last major war fought in coalition had been the Crimean War of 1853–1856. The fundamental reason for this lack of coalition activity was the state of European politics in the second half of the nineteenth century. As no actor attempted to threaten the status quo sufficiently to alarm the British, London was able to adopt a policy of 'Splendid Isolation'.[10] The victories of Prussia/Germany over Austria in 1866 and France in 1870–1871 and the creation of Imperial Germany did, of course, alter the balance of power. Thanks to Bismarck's essentially limited objectives, this seismic shift in the structure of European power occurred without alienating the British. By the early years of the twentieth century, under the erratic rule of Wilhelm II, Germany was emerging as a threat. The British returned to the traditional practice of coalition building.

Coalition building and maintenance

Coalition building in peacetime has been defined as 'a range of activity expressly intended to secure foreign policy objectives not by threatening potential adversaries but by influencing the behaviour of allies and potentially friendly by-standers'.[11] The origins of the Entente coalition that was to fight in the First World War began with attempts to repair relations between Britain and France. This was not a conscious anti-German move. However, as tensions grew over the first decade of the twentieth century, the Entente took on more of the character of a defensive coalition, especially after Britain came to an understanding with France's ally Russia in 1907. However, the grouping remained very loose. Although sometimes referred to as an alliance,[12] this term is misleading. The debate within the British cabinet about whether Britain should enter the war in August 1914, and the fright that this gave the French, underlines the essentially fragile, temporary and *ad hoc* nature of the Entente.

The efficient functioning of coalition can be complicated by linguistic and cultural issues. Indeed, these factors can place barriers between allies that at times appear almost insuperable. An account by First Army commander General Sir Charles Monro of a meeting with Joffre in April 1916 is unconsciously revealing: 'Old Joffre came to lunch with us. Such a fine old boy, a very quiet taciturn old gentleman very unlike our estimate of a Frenchman. Unfortunately he does not speak a word of English and my French conversation is a very stunted vehicle so intercourse was not very easy.'[13] Perhaps linguistic problems could be overcome rather more easily than cultural prejudices that reached back centuries and were founded in a long record of conflict between the two states and peoples. They were certainly not confined to one side. French Anglophobia was real enough, and French suspicions of 'Perfidious Albion' were never far below the surface. For all that, in Philip Bell's words, 'it is remarkable that in 1914–1918 France and Britain held so well together at ... [a number of] different levels'.[14]

Once constructed, like buildings, coalitions need to be kept in good repair by constant maintenance. Three individuals in particular stand out as 'maintenance men': Lord Kitchener, Secretary of State for War from August 1914 to his death in June 1916; Sir Edward Grey, Foreign Secretary until December 1916; and Sir William Robertson, Chief of the Imperial General Staff from December 1915 to February 1918. In 1914 and 1915 the existence of an Eastern Front, and the Germans' decision to make their primary efforts there rather than in the West, bought Britain valuable time in which to mobilise for total war, to raise a large army and deploy it to France, and to avoid (with the exception of the Second Battle of Ypres in April 1915) major defensive operations. As Major General Callwell noted, in early 1915 Kitchener 'was constantly watching the Eastern Front with anxiety', fearing that 'Russian weakness' would enable the Germans to transfer substantial numbers of troops to the Western theatre.[15] From 1916 onwards, with a large BEF on the battlefield and Russia having suffered major defeats in 1915, the situation had changed as Britain grew more powerful *vis à vis* its allies, and Russian power declined. Russia nonetheless continued to be a significant factor in British strategy. The crumbling of the Russian army and the revolution in 1917 brought about a 'search for an alternative force' to 'keep the Eastern Front in being'.[16] Kitchener and Grey were keenly aware of the importance of Russia and the Russian army to Britain; one scholar has recently commented that Kitchener 'considered the Western and Eastern fronts to be indivisible' and that he was 'unflagging' in his efforts to provide Russia with munitions.[17]

There is no better example of the British government's attention to Russia than the decision taken, prior to the Dardanelles campaign, on the future of Constantinople. It was decided that should the operations prove successful, the Ottoman capital would be given to Russia. As the Foreign Office pointed out, this 'involv[ed] a complete reversal of the traditional policy of His Majesty's Government, and is in direct opposition to the opinions and sentiments at one time universally held in England and which have still by no means died out'.[18]

The very word 'jingo', meaning strident, popularist nationalism, originated with a music-hall song of the 1870s: 'We don't want to fight but by jingo if we do ... The Russian shall not have Constantinople.'[19] However, as Grey argued in defence of his policy, 'Solidarity with Russia in the first two years of the war was essential to avoid defeat in France', and it was necessary to allay Russian suspicion of British motives behind the Gallipoli campaign, and also the adherence of two potential Balkan rivals, Italy and Greece, to the Allied cause.[20] This decision was one akin to the British government's acceptance of becoming dangerously dependent on American finance to fight the war: the gravity of the immediate threat outweighed the possibility of deleterious long-term effects.[21] If Paris was worth a Mass, the coalition was worth Constantinople.

In a similar fashion, Britain became involved in the Salonika campaign, and conducted an offensive at Loos in September 1915, primarily for reasons of French domestic politics. There is a good case to be made that a timely Allied intervention in the Balkans in 1915 could have reaped substantial benefits for the Entente, but the expedition that landed in Salonika in October was 'a last minute expedient dictated above all else by considerations of French internal politics and undertaken with almost no technical evaluation of its strategic possibilities'. It was decided in Paris that a command away from the Western Front had to be found for General Sarrail, who seemed to offer a threat to Joffre's position. While British generals might rail against acquiescence in the scheme, the fear that the Sarrail affair might bring down the French government, and even lead to one under Joseph Caillaux which might contemplate a separate peace with Germany, led inexorably to British involvement in the Balkans. Even after Sarrail was dismissed by Clemenceau in November 1917, the campaign dragged on, not least because of Anglo-French competition for influence in the region.[22]

Similar considerations existed in the case of the Battle of Loos.[23] The French planned a large-scale offensive for September 1915, and called upon the British Expeditionary Force to participate by attacking in the area of Loos. There were good operational reasons why the British Army should not have fought in this battle.[24] Neither Field Marshal Sir John French (C-in-C

BEF) nor General Sir Douglas Haig (Commander First Army) was initially keen on the plan. The ground over which the BEF was to attack was extremely difficult, consisting of slagheaps, miners' cottages and winding gear. Kitchener planned to husband his troops until 1916, carrying out attrition by minor operations, rather than committing to a large-scale offensive in 1915. Divisions arriving in France from Britain were in need of additional training and the BEF was still short of artillery and other equipment. However, the British government, Kitchener in particular, became convinced in the summer of 1915 that defeatist sentiment was so widespread in France that, if Britain appeared not to be pulling its weight within the Coalition, this might lead to Alexandre Millerand being replaced by the 'pro-German sympathiser' Caillaux. This 'alarmist' view, which was grossly exaggerated, was largely based on the views of Lord Esher, a confidant of Kitchener. Esher was based in France and acted as an alternative source of information and advice to that provided by the British ambassador, Lord Bertie. The relationship was uneasy. Bertie's views on French morale were more sanguine and more accurate; he described Esher as 'most pessimistic morally, politically, militarily and financially'.[25] However, Esher had Kitchener's ear, and converted the field marshal from a sceptic into a reluctant advocate of Loos. As we have seen, the need to provide active support to Britain's other major coalition partner, Russia, which had suffered a series of serious defeats at the hands of the Central Powers in 1915, was also an important strand in Kitchener's thinking, and this influenced his views on the necessity of attacking at Loos.[26]

In the cases of both Salonika and Loos, British generals objected to British involvement, finding it difficult to discern how the British national interest would be served by participating in these ventures. Viewed narrowly, such views appeared reasonable. When placed in the context of British grand strategy, it was squarely in Britain's national interest to maintain relative harmony within the coalition. Salonika and Loos were judged to be prices that it was necessary to pay to maintain alliance cohesion.

The British decisions over Constantinople, Salonika and Loos were not taken out of any sense of friendship with Russia and France. On the contrary, Kitchener and others of the British elite remained highly suspicious of Russia and France, both major colonial rivals. Kitchener, the Imperial servant *par excellence*, had spent much of his adult life glaring suspiciously at France or Russia or both. He had, after all, commanded the British force that faced down Marchand's French expedition at Fashoda in 1898, an incident that brought the two states close to war. As Commander in Chief in India from 1902 to 1909, the threat to the Raj from Russia had been a primary concern of Kitchener's.[27] Suspicion of France and Russia, so recently potential enemies, now allies but still rivals, was a key factor in the insistence of the British government in the era of Asquith and Kitchener on the independence of the BEF from foreign, i.e. French, command. Kitchener had hoped that France and Germany would wear each other out on the battlefield and allow Britain, deploying her large war-raised armies, to dictate the peace. As Major General Sir Frederick Maurice argued, Kitchener 'did not wish our influence on the peace settlement to be diminished by putting ... [British military] power under foreign control'.[28]

We noted earlier that the balance of power can shift within a coalition. This was precisely what Kitchener expected to happen, and he planned to take advantage. In the event, his plans went awry, and it was the American Expeditionary Forces that enabled the United States in 1919 to play that role that Kitchener had intended for the British. The British CIGS, Sir Henry Wilson, was furious in October 1918 at the bilateral exchanges between Berlin and Washington about how to conclude the war.[29] As Harold Nicolson noted, 'the arrival of new partners is bound to introduce fresh claims and further complications' into a coalition. The 'later arrivals usually feel less exhausted and more righteous than the original combatants', and thus tend 'to press their claims with greater vigour than their war-wear[y]' allies.[30] The USA, having husbanded its resources until the end of the war, in 1918–1919 pursued its national interests irrespective of those of its allies – just as Britain would have done in the same position.

Case study: the Commanders of the BEF
The First World War, like all coalition wars, was a matter of conferences, negotiations and compromises. The *ad hoc* nature of the anti-German coalition meant that effective machinery for the management of the allied war effort did not exist in 1914 and evolved, painfully slowly, over the course of the war. One participant in an inter-Allied meeting in April 1915 recorded ruefully that 'The end of it all was that our military convention amounted to little more than an agreement that we were all jolly fine fellows, accompanied by cordial expressions of goodwill and of determination on the part of the four contracting Powers to do their best and to stick together.'[31]

At the strategic level, the Supreme War Council, which for all its many faults was a major step in the right direction, was not created until late 1917. On the Western Front a sensible command organisation did not emerge until spring 1918. In the absence of unity of command, much depended on relationships between individual commanders to make the coalition work.

When Field Marshal Sir John French took the BEF to war in 1914, Kitchener gave him instructions that were rich in ambiguities. They informed French that the BEF was to 'support and co-operate with the French Army against our common enemies', and that 'every effort must be made to coincide most sympathetically with the plans and wishes of our Ally'. However, 'your command is an entirely independent one, and that you will in no case come in any sense under the orders of any Allied General'. In reality, as Britain was the junior partner in the partnership, the commander of the BEF could only contemplate failing to accede to the wishes of the French under extreme circumstances. Here is not the place for a detailed discussion of Allied relations in 1914–1915. Suffice it to say that Sir John French generally did fall in with Joffre's plans, although he may not have been happy about it. On at least two occasions French proposed courses of action that alarmed his allies. During the retreat from Mons in 1914, Kitchener had to come to France to prevent French marching the BEF out of the line to refit. French was rattled, over-estimated the damage sustained by the BEF and had convinced himself that 'the force under my command is not in its present condition able to render effective support to our Allies, no matter what their position might be'.[32] A year later the Secretary of State for War again had to come out to France to order his fellow field marshal to 'co-operate vigorously' with the French offensive, resulting in what had been intended as an 'artillery demonstration' becoming the Battle of Loos.

If nothing else, the realities of the strategic situation generally forced Sir John French into close co-operation with his allies. In June 1915 he wrote to Kitchener:

> In spite of the large reinforcements which I have received since the beginning of the year my Army is not yet of such a size as to enable it to produce a decisive result independent of the French ... Every offensive operation which I have carried out has therefore been made in close co-operation with the French, and after being discussed with General Joffre.[33]

This was the bottom line. Whatever the personal views of the British C-in-C, however he might privately (or semi-publicly) complain about his Allies, the British Army was never of a size to allow it to 'produce a decisive result independent of the French'. In spite of their defects as coalition commanders – and there were many – neither French nor Haig ever entirely lost sight of this reality.

General Sir Douglas Haig, who succeeded to command of the BEF in December 1915, was a much more intelligent man than his predecessor, and was keenly aware of the coalition dimension to his job. Kitchener too, perhaps mindful of French's shortcomings in this area, issued Haig with an amended set of instructions that increased the stress on co-operation with allies. Working closely with the French was one of Haig's central tenets.

This conclusion may surprise the reader of Haig's diaries. It is easy to select a host of entries in which Haig is rude about the French – one reason why, when the first edition of the diaries was published in 1952, only twelve years after Dunkirk, it caused outrage in France. But we should judge his actions rather than his words. Although he used his diaries to sound off and release his frustrations, essentially Haig was a loyal and co-operative ally, who fully recognised the importance of working closely with the French. That is not to deny the existence of disputes over taking over line, over the strategy of the Somme, over the control of Second Army in the final offensives of 1918, and indeed over other issues. Haig could be an awkward partner. But on the big things that really mattered, he co-operated. In April 1917 the attitude of Haig's Chief of Staff, Kiggell, was described as 'that of cordially disliking & mistrusting the French, yet honestly trying to do them justice'. This also admirably summarises the approach of the British Commander-in-Chief.[34] In October 1916, for instance, Joffre pressed Haig for 'wide and deep offensive operations' towards specific objectives. Haig replied,

> Meanwhile to the utmost extent of the means at my disposal, and so far as weather conditions render possible, I will continue to co-operate with you in exploiting to the full the successes already gained. But I must remind you that it lies with me to judge what I can undertake, and when I can undertake it.

'It was the last sentence which had upset General Joffre's equilibrium,' wrote Haig in his diary. Here was Haig seeking to juggle the twin demands of co-operating with his Allies for the common good – for Joffre was the *de facto* Allied Commander-in-Chief – and asserting his independence. Haig continued:

> I told des Vallières [French liaison officer at GHQ] that it was most desirable for our good relations in the future that both General Joffre and his Staff should know that I could only receive orders from my Government. And I also told him that I knew as a fact that a certain number of French Statesmen were anxious that the British Army in France should be placed *under* Joffre's orders. This could never be, neither the people at home nor the British Army in France would submit to such a thing.[35]

Joffre seems to have realised that he had gone too far, and the subsequent meeting with Haig was successful. Haig clearly recognised that whatever his personal views – and given the growing criticism in London of his conduct of the Somme and rumours that plots were afoot to have him replaced, there were good reasons to halt the attacks in Fourth Army's sector – the disciplines of coalition warfare forced him to continue to attack alongside the French Sixth Army. However, what Haig would not do was accept direct orders from Joffre. Hints, suggestions and clearly expressed preferences, yes; orders, no.

It is clear that Haig, very aware of his position as an independent commander, was always going to be difficult to persuade of the virtues of true unity of command. What made the situation much worse was the ham-fisted conspiracy between Lloyd George and the French revealed in the ambush at the Calais conference in February 1917. If this plan had worked, Haig's power would have been severely curtailed and the BEF placed under the command of General Robert Nivelle, the newly appointed French Commander-in-Chief. Robertson and Haig were outraged, and the conference resulted in a compromise by which Haig was placed under Nivelle only for the duration of the forthcoming offensive. Moreover the British C-in-C was given what today is known as a 'national red card', with Haig given the right to appeal to his government if he felt national interests were being imperilled.

The consequences of the Nivelle affair were grave. It further poisoned the already poor relationship between Haig and Robertson on one side and Lloyd George on the other. Moreover, it further set back the prospects of unity of command. In November 1917, against the background of the creation of an inter-Allied Supreme War Council, a senior staff officer spoke to Haig and 'broached the subject of an Allied C-in-C, but found that Nivelle's experiment is still much too fresh in DH's & Kiggell's mind to allow them to look at it quietly'.[36]

The crisis of March 1918 was to force unity of command upon the Allies. To Haig's credit, he made the new situation work. Relations with General (later Marshal) Ferdinand Foch, the new Allied *generalissimo*, were by no means always smooth, but they were reasonably effective, an outcome that owed much to the common sense of both men and their joint awareness of the necessity of co-operation.

If Haig deserves some credit for his performance as a coalition commander on the Western Front, he showed less awareness of the importance of the coalition dimension at the grand strategic level. It was understandable that as a theatre commander Haig should focus on that theatre, but his single-mindedness led him to underestimate the importance of the other fronts in a multi-front war. On 18 July 1916, for example, when the BEF was heavily engaged on the Somme, the question arose yet again of sending guns and ammunition to Russia. Haig argued that 'I can see no doubt that the most patriotic and the wisest policy is to provide all that we require ourselves before we give to others.'[37]

From Haig's standpoint it was frustrating that his forces should be denied important resources at a time when it appeared that a substantial victory was possible on the Somme. The government had to take the wider view that it was essential to keep Russia in the war, and even using a narrower perspective a reinvigorated offensive on the Eastern Front was likely to have beneficial consequences for the BEF. Haig also tended to place the needs of his forces in Flanders over the necessity of keeping Italy in the war.[38] In 1918 Haig's breach with Robertson came over what Haig saw as Robertson's failure to maintain 'the policy of "concentration on the Western Front"'.[39] Whatever Robertson's personal preferences, the realities of coalition warfare and fighting a global war simply did not allow the CIGS to concentrate troops and resources in the West to the extent that Haig demanded. This is not a simple issue, for one would expect a theatre commander to fight tenaciously for priority in resources, and Haig's arguments in favour of the Western Front were powerful. Possibly if he had become Chief of the Imperial General Staff, as was suggested on occasion,[40] he would have taken a global perspective. But as a theatre commander, Haig's vision was distinctly more parochial.

The Empire as a coalition

There is one further level of coalition that must be considered. The Empire itself was something of a coalition. India acted as second power centre: the Mesopotamian campaign, for instance, was run from India, not London. By the end of the war the white Dominions, while loyal, could not be treated simply as extensions of Great Britain. The 'British' army that fought at Gallipoli and in the Middle East was actually a coalition force. So was the BEF, with ten of the sixty divisions being drawn from Canada, New Zealand and Australia; these were among the most effective formations at Haig's disposal. Recognition of the role of the Empire, partly but not entirely symbolic, came about with the establishment of the Imperial War Cabinet of 1917 and 1918. It was attended by Dominion Prime Ministers Borden (who tended to act as a spokesman for the Dominions when there was a collective view)[41], Smuts, Hughes and Ward. Smuts in particular became a powerful actor on the British political scene.

Their experiences on Gallipoli and the Western Front helped to build a sense of national identity for these forces and these nations, and the corollary of this was the emergence of Dominion military formations as something more than simply overseas contingents of the BEF. Monash, Currie and Russell became commanders of proto-national armies. This is something that Haig found difficult to comprehend. Famously, after a series of disputes about the determination of the Canadians to keep their divisions together, Haig complained that some Canadians saw themselves as 'allies rather than fellow citizens in the Empire!'[42] However, the attitude of British high commanders to the evolution of Dominion military nationalism was essentially pragmatic. Haig himself in 1917 referred to 'our "Imperial Army"' and the need for Dominions to have commanders and staffs for what he tellingly described as 'their portions of the Imperial Forces'.[43] This approach was undoubtedly facilitated by the demonstration of Dominion military excellence; had the Australians and Canadians combined demands for their recognition as national armies with inept combat performances, the British might have been rather less willing to compromise.

There were further layers of coalition within the Empire. Christopher Pugsley has written of the complexities of the Australia–New Zealand relationship in the First World War. New Zealand, as the smaller state, was inevitably the junior partner, and the British authorities tended – erroneously – to assume that the interests of the two Anzac countries and forces were identical.[44] 'Being heard', Pugsley argues, 'is the traditional problem for the junior partner', and it was certainly a problem for New Zealand in the First World War. Conversely, South African troops took the lead in the campaign in East Africa from 1916, boosting the profile of the Union and Jan Christian Smuts.[45]

To a very large extent, the Dominions judged their national interest as being identical with Britain's – hence the committal of troops to the Eastern Front and the Middle East. However, there were some distinct differences. The alliance of Britain with Japan in 1902 had caused unease in Australasia. A move that made good strategic sense in London looked rather different when viewed through an Australian or New Zealand prism, not least because it demonstrated that the 'Anglo-Japanese treaty took precedence over Australian interests'.[46] Worse, during the war Japan occupied some German Pacific islands, an event that proved to be permanent rather than temporary, and which Britain accepted as a *fait accompli*. Alarmed, Australia took a number of steps to safeguard its security, including the dispatch of a spy to report on the Japanese armed forces, and retained substantial citizen forces at home in Australia.[47] The ties between Britain and Australia were far closer than with Britain's European allies, being born of shared bloodlines, heritage and sentiment. Yet even here there was clear evidence that national interests prevailed over friendship. All this helped move Australia towards a stance more clearly independent from Britain.

Conclusion

A number of books on coalition warfare have titles – *Allies of a Kind*,[48] *An Uneasy Accord, Uneasy Coalition*[49] – that hint at the ambiguity of the whole business. The experience of the Entente coalition in the First World War underlines the truth that coalitions are not the same as friendships; rather, national interests prevailed. For all that, it was a successful coalition. Combined, the Allies drew upon vast resources of economic and military power, far beyond that available to individual states. United by a common enemy, they weathered the storms of 1914–1916; survived internecine struggles and shifts in the balance of power within the coalition, including the withdrawal of one of its principal members; and coped with the arrival of a new and powerful ally in the same year. The Empire coalition also survived, and indeed endured for at least another generation. The same was not true of the Entente. Like many coalitions in history, the Entente was the short-lived product of a specific circumstance that brought together disparate actors with diverse interests. Germany was the glue that held the coalition together, and the end of the German threat was followed by the break-up of the coalition. As Riley argues, 'coalitions, formed for adversity, seldom survive strategic success'.[50]

Further Reading

A version of this paper was given at the Australian Chief of Army's Conference in 2005. The contemporary context was 'Bush's Wars' in Afghanistan and Iraq, and it was striking how many themes in historical case studies resurfaced during the operations of the US-led coalition operations in the early twenty-first century. Important writings on the British experience of coalition warfare in 1914–1918 that have appeared since this paper was first published include two books by Elizabeth Greenhalgh, *Victory through Coalition: Britain and France during the Great War* (Cambridge: Cambridge University Press, 2005) and *Foch in Command: The Forging of a First World War General* (Cambridge: Cambridge University Press, 2011). Roy A. Prete, *Strategy and Command: The Anglo-French Coalition on the Western Front in 1914* (Montreal: McGill-Queen's University Press, 2009) is also useful, as is William Philpott, *Bloody Victory: The Sacrifice on the Somme and the making of the Twentieth Century* (London: Little, Brown, 2009), which emphasises the coalition dimensions of the Somme campaign. All these books stress the critical role of Foch as a coalition commander, as does my biography of Haig, *The Chief: Douglas Haig and the British Army* (London: Aurum, 2011). Finally, an important collection which contains much of relevance, including my commentary on pieces by Greenhalgh and Philpott, is Robert Tombs and Emile Chabal (eds), *Britain and France in Two World Wars: Truth, Myth and Memory* (London: Bloomsbury, 2013).

Acknowledgements

Material in the French Papers appears by kind permission of the Trustees of the Imperial War Museum. Material in the Clive Papers appears by kind permission of the Trustees of the Liddell Hart Centre for Military Archives.

Notes

1. Harold Nicolson, *The Congress of Vienna 1812–1822: A Study in Allied Unity* (New York: Harcourt Brace Jovanovich, 1974), p. 51.
2. Paul Kennedy, 'Military coalitions and coalition warfare over the past century', in Keith Neilson and Roy A. Prete, *Coalition Warfare: An Uneasy Accord* (Waterloo, ON: Wilfrid Laurier University Press, 1983), p. 3.
3. J.P. Riley, *Napoleon and the World War of 1813: Lessons in Coalition Warfighting* (London: Frank Cass, 2000), pp. 3, 438.
4. Riley, *Napoleon*, p. 436.
5. David French, *The British Way in Warfare 1688–2000* (London: Unwin Hyman, 1990), pp. xii, 234.
6. W. Baring Pemberton, *Battles of the Crimean War* (London: B.T. Batsford, 1962), p. 36.
7. I am grateful to Dr John Sweetman, Raglan's biographer, for this information.
8. Quoted in Gary Sheffield, *Forgotten Victory: The First World War – Myths and Realities* (London: Headline, 2001), p. 35.
9. John Sweetman, *Raglan: From the Peninsula to the Crimea* (London: Arms & Armour, 1993), pp. 291, 310, 344.

10. For an interesting critique of this concept that I nonetheless find ultimately unconvincing, see John Charmley, *Splendid Isolation? Britain, the Balance of Power and the Origins of the First World War* (London: Hodder & Stoughton, 1999).

11. Geoffrey Till, *Seapower: A Guide for the Twenty-First Century* (London: Frank Cass, 2004), p. 298.

12. Hew Strachan, *The First World War* (London: Simon & Schuster, 2003), p. 40.

13. Quoted in George Barrow, *The Life of General Sir Charles Carmichael Monro* (London: Hutchinson, 1931), pp. 106–7. Barrow claims that Monro actually 'spoke French well' (p. 107).

14. P.M.H. Bell, *France and Britain 1900–1940: Entente & Estrangement* (London: Longman, 1996), p. 64 (for linguistic and cultural problems, see pp. 15–22, 63–4, 92–112).

15. C.E. Callwell, *Experiences of a Dug-Out 1914–1918* (London: Constable, 1920), p. 223.

16. Keith Neilson, *Strategy and Supply* (London: Allen & Unwin, 1984) p. 305.

17. George H. Cassar, *Kitchener's War* (Washington DC: Brassey's, 2004), pp. xvi, 295.

18. F.O. Memo., 12 Mar. 1915, in C.J. Lowe and M.L. Dockrill, *The Mirage of Power* vol. III *The Documents* (London: Routledge, 1972), p. 512.

19. Andrew Roberts, *Salisbury: Victorian Titan* (London: Phoenix, 2000 [1999]), p. 178.

20. Grey of Fallodan, *Twenty-Five Years* (London: Hodder & Stoughton, 1928 [1925]), vol. III, p. 141; Lowe and Dockrill, *Mirage of Power*, vol. II, pp. 77–83.

21. David French, *British Strategy and War Aims 1914–1916* (London: Allen & Unwin, 1986), pp. 121–2, 228, 248.

22. David Dutton, '"Allies are a tiresome lot": Britain, France and the Balkan Campaign 1915–18', in David Dutton (ed.), *Statecraft and Diplomacy in the Twentieth Century* (Liverpool: Liverpool University Press, 1995), pp. 38, 47–51. See also David Dutton, *The Politics of Diplomacy: Britain and France in the Balkans in the First World War* (London: I.B. Tauris, 1998).

23. This discussion is based primarily on Rhodri Williams, 'Lord Kitchener and the Battle of Loos: French Politics and British Strategy in the Summer of 1915', in Lawrence Freedman *et al.* (eds), *War, Strategy and International Politics* (Oxford: Clarendon Press, 1992), pp. 117–32.

24. The fullest scholarly treatment of Loos is Nick Lloyd, *Loos 1915* (Stroud: Tempus, 2006).

25. Lady Algernon Gordon Lennox (ed.), *The Diary of Lord Bertie of Thame 1914–1918* (London: Hodder & Stoughton, 1924), vol. I, p. 192 (entry for 4 July 1915).

26. Lloyd, *Loos 1915*, pp. 41–4.

27. George H. Cassar, *Kitchener: Architect of Victory* (London: William Kimber, 1977), pp. 98–100, 139.

28. Sir Frederick Maurice, *Lessons of Allied Co-operation Naval Military and Air 1914–1918* (London: Oxford University Press, 1942), p. 174.

29. French, *British Strategy and War Aims 1914–1916*, pp. 24–5; Sheffield, *Forgotten Victory*, pp. 66–7, 70–2, 225.

30. Nicolson, *Congress of Vienna*, p. 52.

31. Callwell, *Experiences of a Dug-Out*, p. 283.

32. French to Kitchener, F.62, 31 Aug. 1914, French Papers, IWM.

33. French to Kitchener, 23 Jun. 1915, OAM 446, French Papers, IWM.

34. Diary, 17 Apr. 1917, G.S. Clive Papers, II/3/LHCMA (Liddell Hart Centre for Military Archives, King's College, London).

35. Haig diary, 23 Oct. 1916, in Gary Sheffield and John Bourne (eds), *Douglas Haig: War Diaries and Letters 1914–1918* (London: Weidenfeld & Nicolson, 2005), p. 246.

36. Haig diary, 15 Nov. 1917, Clive II/3, G.S. Clive Papers, LHCMA.

37. Haig to von Donop, 18 July 1916, in Sheffield and Bourne, *Douglas Haig*, p. 207.

38. See Haig diary entries for 4 Sept, 7, 10 Nov. 1917 in Sheffield and Bourne, *Douglas Haig*, pp. 321–2, 339–40.
39. Haig to Lady Haig, 4 Feb. 1918, in Sheffield and Bourne, *Douglas Haig*, p. 379.
40. Churchill to Asquith, 4 Oct. 1915, in M. Gilbert, *Winston S. Churchill*, companion vol. III, part 2, (London: Heinemann, 1972), p. 1196.
41. L.F. Fitzharding, *The Little Digger 1914–1952* (Sydney: Angus & Robertson, 1979), p. 322
42. Haig diary, 5 May 1918, in Sheffield and Bourne, *Douglas Haig*, p. 410.
43. Robert Blake (ed.), *The Private Papers of Douglas Haig 1914–1919* (London: Eyre & Spottis-woode, 1952), p. 214 (entry of 17 March 1917).
44. Christopher Pugsley, *The Anzac Experience: New Zealand, Australia and Empire in the First World War* (Auckland: Reed, 2004), pp. 25, 28, 37.
45. See Ross Anderson, *The Forgotten Front: The East African Campaign 1914–1918* (Stroud: Tempus, 2004).
46. Stuart Macintyre, *The Oxford History of Australia* vol. IV, *The Succeeding Age 1901–1942* (Melbourne: Oxford University Press, 1993), p. 180.
47. Chris Coulthard-Clark, 'Australian Defence: Perceptions and Policies, 1871–1919', in John A. Moses and Christopher Pugsley (eds), *The German Empire and Britain's Pacific Dominions 1871–1919* (Claremont, CA: Regina Books), p. 170.
48. Christopher Thorne, *Allies of a Kind: The United States, Britain, and the War Against Japan, 1941–1945* (New York: Oxford University Press, 1978).
49. Jehuda Wallach, *Uneasy Coalition: The Entente Experience in World War I* (Westport, CT: Greenwood, 1993).
50. Riley, *Napoleon*, p. 436.

PART 2

COMMAND

Chapter 3

Omdurman to Neuve Chapelle: Henry Rawlinson, Douglas Haig and the Making of an Uneasy Command Relationship, 1898–1915

This chapter was written especially for this book. It represents the first fruits of my research into General Sir Henry Rawlinson, which will eventually result in a volume of Rawlinson's First World War diaries and letters. My co-editor on this project is Dr John Bourne. I would like to thank Professor Peter Simkins and Professor Stephen Badsey for their comments on an earlier draft of this chapter.

Henry Rawlinson, later Baron Rawlinson of Trent, was one of the most significant British generals of the First World War. Commander of Fourth Army during both the Battle of the Somme in 1916 and the victorious Hundred Days campaign of 1918, 'Rawly' was thus intimately associated with both the darkest and finest hours of the British Expeditionary Force (BEF): the First Day on the Somme (1 July 1916) and the Battle of Amiens (8 August 1918). His relationship with Douglas Haig was central to Rawlinson's career on the Western Front. The two men were near-contemporaries (Haig was three years older), and from early 1915 onwards Rawlinson emerged as one of Haig's most important subordinates; on the Somme in 1916 Rawlinson was undoubtedly Haig's principal lieutenant. Although one historian has described Rawlinson as a 'loyal subordinate of Haig',[1] this was far from the case: their relationship was by no means an easy one. The two men had very different characters, and although both were well-connected politically and with the Royal Household, Haig and Rawlinson had different patrons and circles of influence within the army. Worse, in 1915–1916, Rawlinson developed a concept of operations that was very different from Haig's. In the planning for the Somme in 1916 and on the first day of the battle Rawlinson subverted his superior's intentions, with disastrous effects. The difficult relationship between Rawlinson and Haig was to play a significant role, for good and ill, in the fortunes of the BEF.[2]

Henry Seymour Rawlinson was born in Dorsetshire in 1864 (the 'Trent' in his title refers to his Dorset home). He had a family background of intellectual attainment. His father was Sir Henry Rawlinson, Bart (1810–1895), an army officer and political agent for the East India Company who became a noted Assyriologist.[3] The future general's uncle, Canon George Rawlinson, was Camden Professor of Ancient History at Oxford, and a translator of Herodotus.[4] Rawlinson's biographer, Major General Sir Frederick Maurice, claimed that he inherited his father's 'gift of quick accurate judgement'.[5] His contemporaries in the army also thought 'Rawly' to be clever, but this was not necessarily seen as a positive; he combined obvious intelligence with a reputation for deviousness and ambition. In about 1904 Ian Hamilton described Rawlinson and his great friend Henry Wilson as 'each in their own line as selfish and as cunning as foxes'.[6]

Young Henry attended Eton before going to the Royal Military College, Sandhurst in 1883. Rawlinson's background thus differed from that of Douglas Haig, who was born in Edinburgh in 1861, the son of a wealthy whisky manufacturer. He attended a less prestigious public school (Clifton College) before going up to Brasenose College, Oxford and then Sandhurst. Although Haig had undergone the essential educational rite of passage at a public school, and was indistinguishable from any other young man of the upper classes, background prejudice against his origins in 'trade' was present as late as the First World War.[7] Henry Rawlinson's background of old wealth contrasted with Douglas Haig's.

Rawlinson was commissioned in 1884 into a socially exclusive and expensive regiment, the 60th Rifles (formally, the King's Royal Rifle Corps) before transferring in 1892 into an even smarter regiment, the Coldstream Guards, in order to be closer to his recently widowed father. Rawlinson rapidly came to the attention of his father's friend Sir Frederick Roberts (later Earl Roberts of Kandahar), one of Victorian Britain's greatest military heroes and the leader of the eponymous 'Ring' or clique within the officer corps. 'Bobs' quickly grew to like young Rawlinson. Roberts' daughter described him as one of her father's 'inner friends to whom he always turned'.[8] 'Rawly' became one of the bright young officers that Lord Roberts accepted as protégés. Another was Henry Wilson, whom Rawlinson introduced to Roberts while the two younger men were at Staff College. When Roberts died in November 1914 at the age of 82 on a visit to the BEF in France, Rawlinson wrote 'Lord Bobs [sic] death was a heavy blow to us all and particularly to me who have been in such close touch with him for nearly 30 years.'[9]

Haig had a very different set of patrons. His early patrons included General Sir George Greaves and Field Marshal Sir Evelyn Wood, and Wood was a leading member of the Wolseley Ring – the opposite clique to Roberts'. From 1899 his principal mentor was his fellow cavalryman John French. Haig was never close to Roberts; indeed, they were on opposite sides in an acrimonious debate on cavalry doctrine after the Boer War. Haig, as a rather bumptious recent Staff College graduate serving under Kitchener in the 1898 Sudan campaign, was critical of the 'Sirdar' [Kitchener's title in Egypt], including in letters to Wood. However, while serving in India from 1903 to 1906 Haig and Kitchener made common cause against the Viceroy, Lord Curzon.[10] While relations between the two men were relatively good during the First World War, Haig retained his doubts about 'K of K's' methods.[11] Certainly, Kitchener's dealings with Haig were never as warm as those with Rawlinson, who became something of a protégé of Kitchener.

It is important to place the role of patron and protégé in the Victorian army into context. Maurice frankly admitted in his biography of Rawlinson that 'the general opinion' of the man during most of his career was that he was 'lucky ... the implication being that fortune and interest [i.e. patronage] had as much to do with his advancement as had merit'. Undoubtedly, Rawlinson's military career benefited from patronage, but, as Maurice correctly stated, he was helped by Roberts and Kitchener because he was recognised as having considerable potential.[12] The same was true of Haig and his patrons. Helping on such men was regarded in the army in a very different light to advancing the careers of the undeserving.

Rawlinson's early military career resembled Haig's in some ways, but not in others. Both served in India, where they were keen polo players. Both were professional, thinking officers in an officer corps not noted for those qualities, and thus attracted the attention of senior officers early in their careers. Interestingly, as both Haig and Rawlinson were independently wealthy (the latter succeeded to his father's baronetcy in 1895), neither needed to do this to gain advancement for financial reasons.

Haig seems to have entered the army determined to excel, and proved to be a conscientious regimental officer in the 7th Hussars in Britain and India, acquiring responsibility (becoming regimental adjutant) early on. He was marked out as a coming man, and he did extremely well at Staff College in 1896–97. Rawlinson too spent time in India, arriving in 1884 straight from Sandhurst, but unlike Haig he carried out regimental soldiering with his battalion (4/60th) for only a relatively short time before becoming Roberts' aide-de-camp in 1886. Rawlinson's 'dawn of ambition' came in 1885, at a time of tension between Russia and Britain over Afghanistan, when he found 'the determination to take his profession seriously'.[13] Rawlinson attended Staff College in 1892–1893, and did well, landing a coveted post as a brigade major at Aldershot. He excelled in that post, which cemented within the army his growing reputation for professionalism and competence. He also had considerable personal charm, as indicated by his familiar nickname, 'Rawly'. Winston Churchill, something of an expert in such things, later described him as 'a very good companion', while Major General Louis Spears wrote that 'Rawly had a way of floating over and away from his troubles'.[14] This contrasted with Haig's single-mindedness and oft-reported taciturnity and reserve, which could make him quite hard going. Peter Simkins has likewise favourably compared Rawlinson's relations with his foreign allies with Haig's, which were frequently 'tinged with prickly intolerance, contempt, suspicion and chauvinism'.[15]

At Staff College Rawlinson formed a firm friendship with Henry Wilson, an Irishman serving in the Rifle Brigade, whom he had previously met on active service in Burma. Like Rawlinson, Wilson was to climb high in the army, eventually becoming Chief of the Imperial General Staff (CIGS) in 1918. Rawlinson too was due to become CIGS but died unexpectedly as a result of an operation for appendicitis while serving as Commander-in-Chief in India in 1925.[16] Wilson was an intensely political soldier with an extrovert personality who had a somewhat chequered relationship with Haig. Rawlinson's friendship with Wilson was another reason for the somewhat reserved Haig to regard him with a degree of suspicion. One senior soldier wrote of Wilson and Rawlinson that they 'always hunted in couples, and no one could ever decide as to which was the cleverest',[17] and this not necessarily an expression of unalloyed admiration. An indication of the complex nexus of friendships, loyalties and rivalries in the Victorian army is that one of Rawlinson's contemporaries at Staff College was Launcelot Kiggell, who was Haig's friend and protégé. Kiggell was to be Haig's controversial Chief of Staff at General Headquarters (GHQ) on the Western Front. Others included Julian Byng (who was to receive preferment under Haig, rising to command Third Army in 1917–1918); Aylmer Haldane, a future corps commander who disliked Haig; and Alexander Hamilton-Gordon, another future Western Front corps commander whom Haig admired, but Rawlinson eventually sacked.[18]

Rawlinson's first taste of active service came during an anti-guerrilla campaign in Burma in 1886–1887. Haig had to wait until Kitchener's expedition to the Sudan in 1898, in which he commanded a squadron of Egyptian cavalry. Rawlinson served as Kitchener's ADC in this campaign. He seems not have pulled any strings to get this post, being in the right place at the right time, but the knowledge that he was Roberts' protégé could not have but smoothed Rawlinson's path. Rawlinson privately recorded his initial impressions of his new chief: 'I both like and admire him, but on some minor points he is as obstinate as a commissary mule.' His most important criticism was that 'this is too much of a one-man show'. Reluctant to delegate, Kitchener was at the centre of everything: 'If anything were to happen to the Sirdar there would be chaos.'[19] Haig's criticisms ran on similar lines.

The decisive battle of the campaign was Omdurman, fought on 2 September 1898. The Anglo-Egyptian army was attacked by the forces of the Mahdi, which were crushingly defeated, leaving about 10,800 dead on the field of battle, and a further 16,000 wounded. Kitchener's army suffered a paltry 48 dead and 382 wounded. Douglas Haig was very nearly numbered among them. Placed so as to screen the infantry, Haig's squadron came under fire and took casualties. As Kitchener's ADC, Rawlinson was sent with a message. He recorded that

> ... we could see our contact squadrons under Douglas Haig gradually withdrawing as the Dervishes advanced ... When I reached him he was within about 600 yards of the enemy's long line, and I noticed that his confident bearing seemed to have inspired his Fellaheen [i.e. the Egyptian soldiers], who were watching the Dervish advance quite calmly. It was a magnificent sight, those thousands of wild brave savages advancing to their destruction.[20]

It is not clear whether Rawlinson and Haig had met at this stage; the tone of Rawlinson's comments suggests that they had.

The formative event in the careers of both Rawlinson and Haig was the Second Boer War. Major Haig went to South Africa in 1899 as Chief of Staff to Major General John French, commander of the Cavalry Division. By the end of the war in 1902, Haig was an acting major general (shortly to be made permanent), having acquired both a wealth of staff and command experience, and an enviable reputation within the army. Rawlinson went out to South Africa in 1899 to serve as Deputy Assistant Adjutant General (DAAG) on the staff of General Sir George White, General Officer Commanding Natal. Colonel Ian Hamilton, the Assistant Adjutant General, had suggested that Rawlinson be appointed. Rawlinson was rapidly promoted to AAG to White's Chief of Staff, Sir Archibald Hunter. Haig's path crossed with Rawlinson's on 22 October 1899 when he briefed him on the recent fight at Elandslaagte.

Rawlinson was trapped inside Ladysmith during the siege. When it appeared inevitable that the town would be invested, he wrote to his wife, 'Things are looking rather fishy – we shall be invested and cut off here before very long but we have a strong position and plenty of supplies.' He was confident that all would be well, and was already seeing it in career terms: 'I shall hope to come out of it a full colonel and a V.C. – I place my faith in Him who looks after us and for your sake darling he will bring me out of it safe and sound.'[21] Ladysmith was relieved in late February 1900. In the aftermath, in his own words, Rawlinson 'kept up my practice of falling on my feet'.[22] Lord Roberts arrived to take command in South Africa, with Kitchener, now ennobled as Lord Kitchener of Khartoum, as his Chief of Staff. Rawlinson was appointed to the staff, and invited to live in Roberts' house. He was a hardworking and efficient staff officer, and he learned the lesson that the British army's staff system was defective.[23]

In December 1900, erroneously believing that the war was nearly over, Roberts handed over command to Kitchener and left for England. Rawlinson travelled with him, but was pleased to receive, shortly after his return home, a telegram from 'K of K' recalling him to South Africa. The conventional phase of operations had morphed into a guerrilla struggle. Rawlinson was back in theatre in March 1901, just over twelve months since Ladysmith had been relieved. Although one of the reasons for his return was that 'I don't hanker after an office-stool', initially Rawlinson was plunged back into staff work.[24] However, on 1 April he assumed command of a column of 1,500 mounted men together with artillery and carried out an anti-guerrilla sweep in Western Transvaal. This was not without danger. 'Surprised laager yesterday morning,' he telegraphed to his wife in April 1901. 'Captured one gun one pom-pom [.] My horse shot and I was taken prisoner for two minutes [.] Only then Boers bolted casualties slight hurrah.'[25]

By the time the war ended in May 1902 Rawlinson, just like Douglas Haig, had added a reputation as a field commander to his burgeoning standing as a competent staff officer. 'Rawlinson is doing very well in command of a column, & will I feel sure merit his Col[onel]cy when his time comes,' Kitchener informed Roberts in May 1901.[26] In January 1902 Ian Hamilton told Roberts that Rawlinson had been given command of a large column 'and we have certainly given him the pick of South Africa for troops'.[27] However, as his mentor Lord Roberts detected, Rawlinson was not entirely trusted among the wider officer corps. There was, as Roberts told Kitchener in April 1901, 'a feeling against him [Rawlinson] at the War Office' but nonetheless the Field Marshal was 'sure he is an officer well worth pushing on'.[28] A year later Roberts was hearing similar whispers: he told Ian Hamilton that 'It grieves me terribly to hear doubts about him.'[29] The cloud of distrust that surrounded Rawlinson did not, however, hamper the advancement of his career. At the end of the fighting in South Africa, Rawlinson was one of a select group of middle-ranking officers who had commanded columns – including Herbert Plumer, Julian Byng and Douglas Haig – and were marked out as high-flyers.[30] All four went on to command an army on the Western Front.

In the years between the end of the Boer War and the beginning of the First World War, however, Douglas Haig drew decisively ahead of the pack. A series of demanding posts culminated in him being appointed to the plum Aldershot Command in 1912. In August 1914 Haig took this force, transformed into I Corps of the BEF, to war. By an accident of timing, at this moment Rawlinson was on the sidelines. From June 1910 to May 1914 he had commanded 3rd Division, but spent the summer of 1914 unemployed and without a place in the BEF. It was a cruel blow to a man whose career had prospered up to that point.

As a substantive full colonel (he had achieved that part of his ambition, although not the Victoria Cross) in 1903 Rawlinson had been posted as Assistant Adjutant-General to the Department of Military Education and

Training at the War Office. There he worked with Henry Wilson on a new *Manual of Combined Training*. The experience frustrated Rawlinson, who wrote in October 1903 'This is a terrible place... I have never worked harder for six months with less result than I have here'.[31] Thought Roberts' good offices, Rawlinson moved on to become Commandant of the Staff College, with the rank of brigadier general. This was a much more congenial posting. Rawlinson was a reforming Commandant of Camberley. In the view of Brian Bond, the pre-eminent historian of the Staff College, Rawlinson 'could hardly have been a better choice' following General Herbert Miles, a rather lacklustre Commandant.[32] In 1907 Rawlinson moved on to take command of 2 Brigade at Aldershot. At this time he toyed with the idea of leaving the army, possibly to go to Canada, while continuing to soldier on in the auxiliary forces. However a growing conviction that war with Germany was likely, a view shared with his friends Henry Wilson and Lord Roberts, and also with Douglas Haig, influenced him to stay with the Regulars. As a result, he commanded 3rd Division, as a major general. He played a role in the Curragh Incident of spring 1914, supporting the Gough brothers's stand against Asquith's Liberal government. Rawlinson's behaviour, which can only have reinforced his reputation as an intriguer, contrasted with Haig's, who was careful to steer a middle course during the Curragh upheavals.[33]

Rawlinson believed that the failure to find a post for him in the BEF was down to the fact that Field Marshal Sir John French, 'was displeased with my handling of the 3rd Division at manoeuevres last year'. Maurice believed that Rawlinson was wrong about this.[34] While it is true that French, the Commander-in-Chief of the BEF, had been critical of the performance of other officers as well as Rawlinson, possibly the latter's views were not entirely wide of the mark. As French's biographer, Richard Holmes, put it, the Field Marshal 'had long regarded Rawlinson with considerable suspicion'.[35] Not even the presence on the BEF's staff of Henry Wilson, who acted as French's Sub-Chief of Staff and confidante (a remarkable turnaround from a decade before, when French had bracketed Wilson with Rawlinson as a pair to mistrust) could ease Rawlinson into the original Expeditionary Force.[36] 4 August 1914, the day Britain went to war with Germany, saw Rawlinson take up the mundane if important role of Director of Recruiting at the War Office.

Rawlinson finally got out to the Western Front in September 1914, as replacement for the injured Major General Thomas Snow, commander of 4th Division. He was rapidly promoted to command the newly formed IV Corps in a role, independent of the BEF, operating around Antwerp. IV Corps then fell back towards Ypres where it joined the BEF. Rawlinson fell foul of French (who added to his mental list of Rawlinson's misdeeds, real or imagined, resentment at his independence during the Antwerp foray) and was briefly sent back to Britain, but on 6 November 1914 he was back commanding IV Corps at Ypres. With the division of the BEF into two Armies at the end of 1914, Rawlinson came under the command of Lieutenant General Sir Douglas Haig's First Army.

Very early in the New Year of 1915 Rawlinson wrote to his friend Clive Wigram, a former army officer and Assistant Private Secretary to King George V. Rawlinson was far from unusual among senior officers in writing to the Palace, in the knowledge that his views would be passed on to the King. This letter is particularly interesting, as it sets out Rawlinson's views on the tactical situation. In strategic terms, as he had made clear a little earlier in a letter to Lord Derby, Rawlinson was an optimist:

> there is no manner of doubt that we are going to succeed in crushing the German Empire. It may be a war of exhaustion, it may take one, two or three years to complete but we shall do it, & as the war continues we shall be daily gaining wealth and strength, whilst Germany will be daily losing them.[37]

However, writing to Wigram, Rawlinson had a rather different view of the immediate prospects of tactical success:

> I doubt if we have either the ammunition or numbers yet to drive the enemy out of his present line of entrenchments. It is not until we can use an unlimited amount of ammunition that we can force our way forward without undue loss to the attacking infantry, for now a days a really heavy bombardment is the indispensable prelude to an infantry attack on a prepared position.

Rawlinson believed that the newly raised Kitchener Armies needed to be deployed in significant numbers, along with also more guns, 'and above all more good ammunition for our field & heavy ordnance for it is this trench warfare & this attack of fortresses which will tax our resource most whilst there seems little prospect of our being able to make much use of our Cavalry in which we excel'.[38]

Thus before the start of the 1915 campaigning season, Rawlinson had already come to several important conclusions about the character of operations on the Western Front. It was a form of siege warfare, akin to an 'attack of fortresses'. Artillery was the key. It was not merely a question of possessing a vast number of tubes (and he showed that heavy as well as field guns were required) but also that an inexhaustible supply of ammunition was necessary. Without effective artillery support, attacking infantry would suffer prohibitive losses and their assaults would fail.

This was an extremely perceptive analysis, and subsequent events were to show the wisdom of these views. However, in two respects Rawlinson's opinions were less accurate. First, in spite of this pessimism, Rawlinson thought that the task of driving 'the Germans out of France & Belgium' would be accomplished over 'the course of the next few months', although 'It will take time & a heavy expenditure of life to do this, but it will be done.'[39] This was to prove far too optimistic a view. Second, Rawlinson's dismissal of the utility of cavalry, and by extension, mobile operations, was too sweeping. Even under conditions of trench warfare, cavalry had its place under certain conditions;[40] arguably, those conditions were present on 10 March 1915, during the Battle of Neuve Chapelle. Rawlinson's concept of what was and was not achievable on the Western Front was repeatedly to bring him into conflict with his superior, Douglas Haig, over the next two years.

That the Rawlinson/Haig relationship on the Western Front was not to be a harmonious one became evident as early as February 1915, during the planning for the Battle of Neuve Chapelle, the first major British offensive operation undertaken under conditions of trench warfare. Haig's First Army was entrusted with the attack, and he asked his two corps commanders, Rawlinson and Willcocks (Indian Corps) for their plans.[41] Rawlinson's response was curious. He delegated planning to his subordinates, the commanders of 7th and 8th Divisions. This annoyed Haig, who seems to have thought that as commander of IV Corps, Rawlinson should have taken the lead. Haig also thought the plan put forward by Rawlinson's corps was overly complex, lacked detail, and was too focused on the immediate objective (Aubers Ridge) rather than the strategic picture – the advance on Lille that Haig envisaged after the crust of the German defences had been broken.[42] It is clear that Rawlinson did not share Haig's optimism. It was not until 6 March, a mere four days before First Army's attack, before he sought his divisional commanders' views on exploitation after Neuve Chapelle village had been taken, and gave them a leisurely 24 hours to submit their views.[43]

Rawlinson's tactical opinions clashed directly with Haig's more optimistic vision that at least a measure of mobility could be restored to the battlefield, and it was worth planning to take advantage of such opportunities that presented themselves. Haig's *modus operandi* as a high commander was to set overall objectives, call for plans from subordinate formations, and then (along with the relevant staffs) to engage in debate with his lieutenants to shape those plans until he was happy with them. This approach sat uneasily with Rawlinson's conception of the corps level of command as what Andy Simpson has described as a 'postbox',[44] passing on instructions from higher authorities to his subordinate divisions.

Haig's eve of battle message to the First Army declared 'At no time in this war has there been a more favourable moment for us, and I feel confident of success.'[45] Pre-battle preparations were thorough, and included the systematic photographing of German positions by the Royal Flying Corps: an innovative use of the fledgeling air arm. On 10 March, following a 35-minute bombardment by the Royal Artillery, the attack began. The initial phase achieved some measure of surprise and was largely successful, and the village of Neuve Chapelle quickly fell to the advancing British infantry, who penetrated to a maximum depth of 1,100 yards. According to the plan, reserve units were to have passed through the assault troops, who were ordered to consolidate their gains.

However, the attack bogged down as a series of delays occurred. These were largely due to simple friction of war, especially difficulties in communicating on the battlefield. Although pressed by 7th Division's commander, Major General Tommy Capper, Rawlinson, relying as he was on fragmentary information, was cautious. He refused to release his reserves until 1.15pm, by which time he was sure that they could get forward. Willcocks would not move until IV Corps was in place, and so the order for a general advance was only issued at around 2.50pm. Delays in implementing the orders meant that the battalions began their attacks as late as 5.30 or even 6pm. By then the Germans had recovered from their initial setbacks, rushed up reserves and plugged the gaps. First Army's attacks were, unsurprisingly in hindsight, failures. Although the omens seemed propitious when viewed from higher headquarters, further assaults over the next two days were also bloodily repulsed.[46]

The aftermath of Neuve Chapelle saw a sharp deterioration in the relationship between Haig and Rawlinson. In his official report the First Army commander stated, in effect, that Rawlinson had sacrificed an opportunity for a substantial advance on 10 March. In private correspondence, Haig was forthright about his subordinate's failings: 'if Rawlinson had only carried out his orders and pushed on from the village at once, we would have had quite a big success'.[47] While Haig was justified in blaming Rawlinson and Willcocks for failing to obey his orders and to exploit the initial success, such was the chaos of the battlefield that not even prompt action by his corps commanders could have delivered the success that Haig believed was within his grasp.

In trying to cover his tracks, Rawlinson resorted to the underhand stratagem of attempting to scapegoat Major General F.J. ('Joey') Davies, the commander of 8th Division, for the failure on 10 March. This manoeuvre backfired spectacularly on Rawlinson and almost ended his military career. Davies, clearly outraged by this behaviour, gathered evidence in his defence, which he sent to Rawlinson. Rawlinson wrote to Haig, accepting 'all responsibility for the having delayed the advance from the village until 3.30pm'. Haig, who had initially supported the removal of Davies, was annoyed: 'I am afraid that Rawlinson is unsatisfactory in this respect, loyalty to his subordinates!' Haig consulted with the C-in-C, who of course was an enemy of Rawlinson's, and then informed Rawlinson in person of 'Sir J. French's views ... and told him to take it as a warning from Sir John, and that next time he will lose his Corps'.[48] According to Rawlinson's diary, Haig personally assured him that he would 'fight my battles for me'. Rawlinson, in his relief that he was not to be Stellenbosched, wrote that 'I am certain I have a good friend and staunch ally ... I feel quite sure that I should get justice in DH's hands'.[49] This might have been thought to put Rawlinson firmly in Haig's camp, as he owed his professional survival to the First Army commander's intervention.[50] However, the next two years were to show that Rawlinson remained distinctly independently minded.

Although in his diary Rawlinson denied that he 'had been trying to sacrifice him [Davies] in order to save myself',[51] it is clear that the Davies affair became common knowledge among the higher echelons of the army, which can only have damaged Rawlinson's reputation. Major General Henry Horne, commander of 2nd Division, commented in July 1915 that Davies had done '*very* well at Neuve Chapelle. It was a higher person than he that was blamed & it was wrong to try & put it on Davies'.[52] Rawlinson tried to 'spin' the incident, writing to the Adjutant General to the Forces, 'We are not going to lose Joey Davies after all for on going into the question of the delay in pressing on the first day I found that it was as much my fault as his.' If this shows a less-than-admirable side of Rawlinson's character, the very next sentences in the letter show him at his best, attempting to discern the lessons of the battle:

> It is easy to be wise after the event but if I had to do it again I would keep the Troops detailed to carry on the advance, entirely separate from those engaged in the first assault so that there would be no possibility of their being drawn into the fighting until the moment arrived for their push forward. On this occasion the reserve b[riga]de was absorbed in the assault of the front line of trenches so that when required to go on it took time to collect it & it was in consequence late.[53]

Rawlinson also explained to his highly placed contacts his concept of how operations under conditions of trench warfare ought to be conducted. In a letter to Wigram, which he could be confident would reach the attention of the King, Rawlinson set out his ideas:

> Yes, the experience of Neuve Chapelle has taught us all a great deal and I hope that next time we have enough ammunition to undertake a similar enterprise that we shall remember what experience has taught us. The losses are the feature most to be deplored. The great majority occurred on the 2nd and 3rd days in attacking the enemy's defended pivots and houses. These might all have been avoided if we had been content with the capture of the village itself instead of persisting in pressing on in order to get the cavalry through. I confess that this idea does not appeal to me. The cavalry will I fear do no good when they do get through for they are certain to be held up by wire & trenches in whatever direction they may attempt to go. The enemy are not yet sufficiently demoralised to hunt them with cavalry. We must wait for several months before that

happy state of affairs supervenes. However, both Sir John & Douglas Haig are confident that we might be able to do something with our cavalry even now & I devoutly hope that they are right but my opinion is that the time is not yet.

What we want to do now is what I call 'Bite & hold'. Bite off a piece of the enemy's line like Neuve Chapelle & hold it hard against all counter attack. The Bite can be made without much loss & if you choose the right place & make every preparation to put it quickly in a state of defence there ought to be no difficulty in holding it against the enemy's counter attacks & inflicting on him at least twice the loss that we have suffered in making the bite ... but it of course entails the expenditure of a good deal of Art[iller]y ammunition which we have not got ...

The second paragraph, concerning 'bite and hold', has often been quoted by historians, but the previous paragraph has received much less attention. It indicates that Rawlinson was not opposed to the use of cavalry *per se*, but that he believed that they were only useful in the pursuit. He made a similar point in a letter to Kitchener, written a little later: 'When the enemy infantry is defeated of course the cavalry will have great success but the German infantry is not yet sufficiently shaken to warrant you charging them with the cavalry.'[54] While this is a more nuanced view of cavalry than that sometimes attributed to Rawlinson, it shows a surprising lack of understanding of the capabilities of the 'hybrid' cavalryman of 1915. Haig was a leading advocate of this type of cavalry, which combined expertise in the traditional shock charge with the ability to fight effectively on foot.[55] This lack of understanding, or possibly a simple lack of faith in the reformed cavalry, was to have serious consequences on the first day of the Battle of the Somme, when Rawlinson was Haig's principal operational commander.

As we have seen, even before the battle Rawlinson had shown that he was sceptical that substantial advances were possible under conditions of trench warfare. The experience of the next battle, a straightforward defeat at Aubers Ridge (9 May 1915) reinforced Rawlinson's thinking. In a letter to the Adjutant General, he stated his belief that victory was to be gained by attrition at every level from the strategic to the tactical:

I don't see at the moment how we are going to force the enemy back to their own frontier except by the very slow process of seige [sic] operations or the attrition of the hostile personel [sic] caused by the pressure which is being & will be brought upon Germany by all sides. What we really want to is to kill the greatest possible number of Germans in the shortest possible space of time. Up to the present the idea of gaining ground has been too prominent and the idea of causing heavy losses to the enemy has not formed a sufficiently important element in the schemes that have been devised. I have always advocated the policy of 'bite & hold' ... I think these ideas are now beginning to prevail at G.H.Q. but it has taken a long time & cost many lives to convince Sir John that his high flown optimistic schemes of great successful movements are not practical propositions at present though they may become so later on ... [bite & hold] is the class of operations which must now become the rule of all of us [i.e. British and French] until the enemy become really demoralised & decimated. I do not expect this till the autumn at the earliest.[56]

Haig understood the importance of attrition, but he combined this with a belief that a breakthrough was possible under conditions of trench warfare. Certainly, in contrast to Rawlinson, he was in favour of taking advantage of local conditions to gain ground. As Haig's operational thinking evolved, he was in favour of bite and hold, but using mobile forces (including but not limited to cavalry) to enlarge the bite, rather than waiting for an ideal breach to be opened.[57] While Rawlinson had one plan to which he stuck, fairly rigidly, Haig had a more flexible approach.

Rawlinson commanded IV Corps at the Battle of Loos in September 1915. He was not convinced by Haig's ambitious plan for a breakthrough and would have preferred a slower, more methodical approach. However, in Nick Lloyd's damning phrase, while Rawlinson was 'one of the most tactically astute commanders in the BEF, he proved sadly deficient in using his insights about artillery and the [sic] "bite and hold" to conduct operations effectively'.[58] Interestingly, Rawlinson would argue that a great opportunity for a substantial advance had been thrown away by Sir John French's failure to hand over the operational reserves to First Army. In this his views coincided with Haig's.[59] It seems that Rawlinson had believed that he would have reserves in hand on the morning of the first day of the battle. Robin Prior and Trevor Wilson have suggested that his views may have been motivated by the desire to help remove French from the position of Commander-in-Chief. Rawlinson certainly contributed to the whispering campaign against his old adversary.[60] But on balance it appears that Rawlinson genuinely believed that a major success had been sacrificed by French's obduracy.

The fundamental mismatch between Haig's and Rawlinson's respective approaches to operations was to come to a tragic head at the beginning of the Battle of the Somme in 1916. In spite of their disagreements, and the Joey Davies affair, Haig promoted the career of Henry Rawlinson. When he assumed the position of Commander-in-Chief at the end of 1915, Haig made it clear that he would not be influenced in his choices of personnel by faction or personal likes and dislikes.[61] In was in this spirit that Haig recommended Rawlinson for promotion to army commander. Rawlinson 'was not a sincere man', Haig reflected in his diary, 'but he has brains and experience'.[62] As commander of Fourth Army, Rawlinson cannot have been unaware that he was a potential Commander-in-Chief in waiting, should Haig slip up. Rawlinson was entrusted with the principal attack on the Somme. His views on bite and hold had not altered since 1915 and during the planning phase there was substantial divergence between his concept of operations and Haig's. In the end Haig's idea of using all-arms mobile forces to exploit opportunities was sabotaged by Rawlinson. On 1 July 1916 the chance of achieving an advance of several miles on the southern flank (which in the context of the time would have been a substantial achievement) went begging. Not only did Rawlinson ignore the opportunity but he actually stood down the reserves that could have taken advantage of the fleeting opportunity at midday, just before they became necessary.[63]

Subsequently, as after Neuve Chapelle, Rawlinson attempted damage limitation, claiming that Haig had only wanted mobile reserves to be used 'should we be successful all along the line in gaining the whole of the objectives for the first day'.[64] The evidence suggests otherwise. Rawlinson remained as Fourth Army commander throughout the Somme offensive, but his performance was not always to Haig's satisfaction. Sidelined by Haig in 1917, Rawlinson was given a field command after Hubert Gough was sacked in March 1918. This was a decision over which his friend Henry Wilson, by then Chief of the Imperial General Staff, had much influence.

One of the most vicious attacks on Henry Rawlinson's character was launched in July 1916 by the recently ennobled Viscount French. He criticised Haig's use of Rawlinson on the Somme: 'The command of so big an operation should have been entrusted to a man who enjoyed the confidence of officers and men. None really trusts or believes in Rawlinson.' By this time French was a bitter and disappointed man, and he had reason to hate both Haig and Rawlinson.[65] Yet although his criticism was emotionally driven and exaggerated, it does reflect the fact that many people were suspicious of Rawlinson.[66] To some degree, Douglas Haig was one of them.

Henry Rawlinson was an intelligent man, who in 1918 proved to be an excellent battlefield commander. But in 1915–1916 his relationship with Haig was a rocky one. Coming from dissimilar backgrounds and cliques within the army, and possessing very different personalities, the two men were not natural friends and allies. This problem was exacerbated by the fact that Rawlinson was caught out in his attempt to scapegoat a subordinate after Neuve Chapelle, and, especially, because the two men had fundamentally different views on how to conduct operations. Far from subordinates not daring to criticise Haig, as is sometimes claimed, Rawlinson frequently argued with him, and did not hesitate to subvert his superior's plans. In spite of everything, the relationship was underpinned by a degree of mutual admiration as fellow professional soldiers. During the climatic Hundred Days campaign in

1918, Rawlinson became one of Haig's most reliable and trusted army commanders. But the road from Omdurman to Amiens ran via Neuve Chapelle, and it was strewn with boulders.

Notes

1. Mark Jacobsen (ed.), *Rawlinson in India* (Stroud: Sutton Publishing for Army Records Society, 2002), p. xix.
2. Unless otherwise stated, biographical details are drawn from Sir Frederick Maurice, *The Life of General Lord Rawlinson of Trent* (London: Cassell, 1928) and Gary Sheffield, *The Chief: Douglas Haig and the British Army* (London: Aurum, 2011).
3. R.W. Ferrier and Stephanie Dalley, 'Rawlinson, Sir Henry Creswicke', *Oxford Dictionary of National Biography* (*ODNB*), http://www.oxforddnb.com/view/article/23190?docPos=1 (accessed 28 Oct. 2013).
4. Ronald Bayne, *rev.* M.C. Curthoys, 'Rawlinson, George', *ODNB*, http://www.oxforddnb.com/view/article/35689?docPos=5 (accessed 28 Oct. 2013).
5. Maurice, *Rawlinson*, p. 6.
6. Quoted in John Lee, *A Soldier's Life: General Sir Ian Hamilton 1853–1947* (London: Macmillan, 2000), p. 87.
7. Sheffield, *The Chief*, p. 10.
8. Maurice, *Rawlinson*, pp. xii–xiii.
9. Keith Jeffery, *Field Marshal Sir Henry Wilson: A Political Soldier* (Oxford: Oxford University Press, 2006), p. 20; Rawlinson to Kitchener, 18 Nov. 1914, Rawlinson Papers, 5201-33-17, National Army Museum (NAM).
10. See Sheffield, *The Chief*, pp. 21, 23, 29–30, 33, 55.
11. See e.g. Haig manuscript diary, 14 Nov. 1915, in Gary Sheffield and John Bourne (eds), *Douglas Haig: War Diaries and Letters* (London: Weidenfeld & Nicolson, 2005), pp. 110–12, 170.
12. Maurice, *Rawlinson*, p. xii.
13. Maurice, *Rawlinson*, p. 10.
14. Churchill to Henry Wilson, 4 Apr. 1920, in Keith Jeffery (ed.), *The Military Correspondence of Field Marshal Sir Henry Wilson 1918–1922* (London: Bodley Head for Army Records Society), p. 159; Spears, quoted in Peter Simkins, 'For Better or For Worse: Sir Henry Rawlinson and his Allies in 1916 and 1918', in Matthew Hughes and Matthew Seligmann, *Leadership in Conflict 1914–1918* (London: Leo Cooper, 2000), p. 16.
15. Simkins, 'For Better or For Worse', p. 14.
16. Jacobsen, *Rawlinson in India*, p. 189.
17. Quoted in Jeffery, *Henry Wilson*, p. 20.
18. Maurice, *Rawlinson*, p. 25.
19. Quoted in Maurice, *Rawlinson*, p. 31.
20. Quoted in Maurice, *Rawlinson*, p. 389.
21. Rawlinson to wife, 17 Oct. 1899, Rawlinson Papers, 2011-11-18-1, NAM.
22. Quoted in Robin Prior and Trevor Wilson, 'Rawlinson, Henry Seymour', *ODNB*, http://www.oxforddnb.com/view/article/35690?docPos=2 (accessed 28 Oct. 2013).
23. See Rawlinson's comments from April 1900, quoted in Maurice, *Rawlinson*, pp. 62–3.
24. Quoted in Maurice, *Rawlinson*, p. 67.
25. Rawlinson to wife, 15 Apr. 1901, Rawlinson Papers, 2011-11-18-3, NAM.
26. Kitchener to Roberts, 24 May 1901, in André Wessels (ed.), *Lord Kitchener and the War in South Africa 1899–1902* (Stroud: Sutton Publishing for Army Records Society, 2006), p. 120.
27. Hamilton to Roberts, 1 Jan. 1902, in Wessels, *Lord Roberts*, p. 219.

28. Roberts to Kitchener, 19 Apr. 1901, in Wessels, *Lord Roberts*, p. 173.

29. Roberts to Hamilton, 27 Mar. 1902, quoted in Stephen Badsey, *Doctrine and Reform in the British Cavalry 1880–1918* (Aldershot: Ashgate, 2008), p. 124.

30. Lawrence James, *Imperial Warrior: The Life and Times of Field-Marshal Viscount Allenby 1861–1936* (London: Weidenfeld & Nicolson, 1993), p. 42.

31. Ian F.W. Beckett, 'Henry Rawlinson', in Ian F.W. Beckett and Stephen J. Corvi, *Haig's Generals* (Barnsley: Pen & Sword, 2006), p. 166; quotation from Maurice, *Rawlinson*, p. 83.

32. Brian Bond, *The Victorian Army and the Staff College* (London: Eyre Methuen, 1972), pp. 196–7.

33. Ian F.W. Beckett (ed.), *The Army and the Curragh Incident 1914* (London: Bodley Head for the Army Records Society, 1986), pp. 5, 21, 28.

34. Maurice, *Rawlinson*, p. 98.

35. Richard Holmes, *The Little Field Marshal: Sir John French* (London: Jonathan Cape, 1981), p. 243.

36. Holmes, *Little Field Marshal*, p. 127.

37. Rawlinson to Derby, 24 Dec. 1914, Rawlinson Papers, 5201-33-17, NAM.

38. Rawlinson to Wigram, 3 Jan. 1915, Rawlinson Papers, 5201-33-17, NAM.

39. Rawlinson to Wigram, 3 Jan. 1915, Rawlinson Papers, 5201-33-17, NAM.

40. For this general argument, see David Kenyon, *Horsemen in No Man's Land* (Barnsley: Pen & Sword, 2011). Unfortunately, Kenyon skips over the spring 1915 battles, beginning his analysis of 1915 at Loos.

41. Haig manuscript diary, 15 Feb. 1915, Acc.3155, N[ational] L[ibrary] of S[cotland].

42. Haig manuscript diary, 23 Feb. 1915, Acc.3155, NLS; Robin Prior and Trevor Wilson, *Command on the Western Front* (Oxford: Blackwell's, 1992), pp. 27–32.

43. Prior and Wilson, *Command*, pp. 31–2.

44. Andy Simpson, 'British Corps Command on the Western Front, 1914–18', in Gary Sheffield and Dan Todman (eds), *Command and Control on the Western Front: The British Army's Experience 1914–18* (Staplehurst: Spellmount, 2004), p. 98.

45. Haig, 'Special Order', 9 Mar. 1915, WO 95/2, T[he] N[ational] A[rchives] of the UK.

46. Sheffield, *The Chief*, pp. 107–9.

47. 'First Army weekly report of operations', [10 Mar. 1915] WO 95/2; Haig manuscript diary, 11 Mar. 1915, Acc.3155, NLS; Haig to Kiggell, 2 Apr. 1915, quoted in Sheffield, *The Chief*, p. 110.

48. Haig manuscript diary, 16, 17 Mar. 1915, in Sheffield and Bourne, *Douglas Haig: War Diaries and Letters*, pp. 110–12.

49. Rawlinson, diary, 17 Mar. 1915, RWLN 1/1, C[hurchill] A[rchives] C[entre], Churchill College, Cambridge.

50. Prior and Wilson, *Command*, p. 71.

51. Rawlinson diary, 16 Mar. 1915, RWLN 1/1, CAC.

52. Horne to wife, 4 July 1915, in Simon Robbins (ed.), *The First World War Letters of General Lord Horne* (Stroud: History Press for Army Records Society, 2009), p. 123.

53. Rawlinson to General Sir Henry Sclater, 21 Mar 1915, Rawlinson Papers, 5201-33-17, NAM.

54. Rawlinson to Kitchener, 1 Apr. 1915, quoted in Badsey, *Doctrine and Reform*, p. 255. Badsey correctly points out that it is incorrect to see Rawlinson's 'bite and hold' comments to Wigram as representing his 'definitive contribution to this doctrinal issue' (p. 255).

55. See Badsey, *Doctrine and Reform*, *passim*.

56. Rawlinson to Sclater, 13 May 1915, Rawlinson Papers, 5201-33-17, NAM.

57. Sheffield, *The Chief*, p. 121.

58. Nick Lloyd, *Loos 1915* (Stroud: Tempus, 2006), pp. 50, 216.

59. Rawlinson to Derby, 29 Oct., 27 Nov., 1915, 27/20, Derby Papers, Liverpool Record Office.
60. Prior and Wilson, *Command*, pp. 130–4.
61. Haig manuscript diary, 14 Dec. 1915; Sheffield, *The Chief*, p. 138.
62. Haig manuscript diary, 12 Dec. 1915, quoted in Sheffield, *The Chief*, p. 168.
63. See Sheffield, *The Chief*, pp. 165–75.
64. Rawlinson, circular letter, 18 July 1916, quoted in Sheffield, *The Chief*, p. 168.
65. French, diary, 5 July 1916, quoted in Holmes, *Little Field Marshal*, p. 328.
66. James, *Imperial Warrior*, p. 88, gives Rawlinson's nickname as 'Cad'. The reference is unfortunately unfootnoted.

Chapter 4

The Australians at Pozières: Command and Control on the Somme, 1916[1]

The first action of the Australian Imperial Force (AIF) on the Somme has an evil reputation. At Gallipoli the Australians lost about 23,000 officers and men in eight months in 1915. At Pozières and Moquet Farm in July–August 1916 Australian divisions lost approximately similar numbers in only six weeks.[2] Private J.T. Hutton of 17th Battalion (2nd Australian Division) recorded his impressions of the battle in a series of terse diary entries: 'Its just like hell pure & simple'; 'Murder bloody murder'; 'Wipe the scenes away they are awful.'[3] Charles Bean, the war correspondent and Australian official historian, was convinced that the shelling at Pozières was worse than at the Third Battle of Ypres in 1917.[4] The commander of 6 Australian Brigade wondered whether the losses of the summer fighting would have the same impact in Australia as the initial news of the casualties at Gallipoli, and bring in more volunteers for the AIF.[5] In short, Pozières was, in Bean's words, 'one vast Australian Cemetery'.[6]

Some Australian soldiers looked upon these operations as worthwhile. 'Australia is keeping her name up & doing exceptionally good work,' noted one Other Rank.[7] 'Pozières', a piece of doggerel written by 'Fray Bentos' that appeared in a trench journal, concluded by emphasising that the battles had taught 'these haughty Prussians' a lesson.[8] Yet the verdicts of historians on these operations have been harsh. One states that the operations around Pozières and Mouquet Farm were 'ill-conceived in the extreme'. The commanders of Reserve and Fourth Armies 'hardly ever co-ordinated their attacks'. Moreover, 'the fronts of attack were too narrow; and the inability of the artillery to perform tasks essential to any advance was never taken into account by the command. The ground captured proved to be of little importance to the overall campaign, although the Germans were impressed by the tenacity of the Australian attacks.'[9] These are powerful indictments of commanders and staff work, both British and Australian. This chapter examines Australian command and staff work during the operations on the Somme in July–August 1916, seeking to place the Australian experience into the wider context of that of the British Expeditionary Force (BEF) on the Western Front.

The divisions of the Australian Imperial Force (AIF) arrived in France from Egypt in March 1916. The first major Australian battle on the Western Front was 5th Division's bloodily abortive attack at Fromelles on 19 July. The Battle of the Somme began on 1 July, and on 23 July 1st Australian Division attacked the village of Pozières. This was vital ground. Pozières was perched on one of the highest points on the ridge on which the German Second Line was located, and sat astride the Roman road that ran from Albert to Bapaume. From Pozières windmill to the rear of the ruined village the defenders could look north-east to the fortress of Thiepval, a British objective of 1 July that was still firmly in German hands, and east to High Wood, a major wood in the southern sector of the Somme battlefield. Possession of Pozières would be an important step towards allowing the British to attack Thiepval from the rear, while a relatively small advance in the south would make a considerable part of the German Second Line untenable, at a time when the German Third Line was still under construction. Both sides realised the importance of Pozières.

1st Australian Division's attack on 23 July was successful.[10] By 25 July the village had fallen and the line had been advanced 1,000 yards. However, the ferocious German bombardment cost the division 5,285 casualties. The next major series of attacks around Pozières would be carried out by 2nd Australian Division. The initial assault, on 29 July, failed. A second attempt was rather more successful, but in all 2nd Australian Division's operations cost 6,848 casualties. Beginning on 9 August, 4th Australian Division entered the battle, attacking towards Mouquet Farm, in the direction of Thiepval. A series of attacks was carried out in this area by 4th, 1st and 2nd Australian Divisions, the last on 3 September. Three were outright failures; four resulted in gains. Then the Australians were sent to another sector, away from the Somme – for the moment. Mouquet Farm finally fell to the British 11th Division on 26 September.

After the war Lieutenant General Sir John Monash, commander of the Australian Corps in 1918, claimed that the key to success in battle was to develop a carefully choreographed plan like a musical score.[11] Recent scholarship lends some weight to this view, at least as far as the Western Front was concerned. Such an approach rests very largely on competent command and, especially, efficient staff work. With this in mind, it is important to examine the upper echelons of the AIF in July 1916.

Before the war Australia had a small number of permanent soldiers and a sizeable militia, backed by compulsory military training for youths (or 'Boy Conscription').[12] Eventually, Australia was to put five infantry divisions into the field, together with mounted forces in the Middle East and a number of other troops. Like the BEF as a whole, the AIF faced the problem of finding higher commanders and staff officers for a force on a scale far beyond anything planned for prior to 1914. The senior officers of the AIF were a mixture of British and a few Australian Regulars, and Australian Militia officers. Places at the British Army staff colleges at Camberley and Quetta had been made available to Australian officers in 1905. In all there were eight *psc* officers, two of them seconded from the British Army, available to Australian forces in 1914.[13] They included Australian Regulars such as Thomas Blamey, Cyril Brudenell White and John Gellibrand (the latter was an Australian who had served with the British Army, retiring to Tasmania in 1912).[14] There were a few other Australians who could claim to be staff trained or who had staff experience: John Laverack, an Australian officer whose Camberley course was interrupted by the outbreak of war; J.G. Legge, who had served as Australian representative on the Imperial General Staff in London from 1912 to 1914; and W.T. Bridges, the first Australian to reach general officer rank. Bridges was the first commandant of the Royal Military College Duntroon, which opened in 1911 with the aim of providing Australia with staff officers, but in 1914 Duntroon graduates were used for regimental duties.[15] Moreover, during the war talented Australians were sometimes given posts in the wider BEF, the most prominent being White, who followed General Sir William Birdwood to Fifth Army in 1918 to become its chief of staff,[16] but also E.C.P. Plant, who served on Fourth Army Staff in 1918, and S.G. Savige, who ended up in Persia as part of Dunsterforce.[17]

A number of very high quality ex-Militia officers came to hold command and staff positions in the AIF, including William Glasgow, James Cannan, H.E. 'Pompey' Elliot, J.J. Talbot Hobbs, and, of course, John Monash. The latter was one of a number of Militia officers who benefited from the 'War Courses' begun by Bridges in 1908, which gave at least a smattering of staff training.[18] Hobbs took a military science course at the University of Sydney in 1909. By no means all Militia officers took their hobby so seriously but such men, like some of their Territorial Force counterparts in Britain, clearly did. Indeed, one historian has suggested that Monash was not 'handicapped educationally' by his non-attendance at Staff College, but that diligent personal study, his engineering background and his everyday work as a Militia officer compensated for lack of a *psc*.[19] Clearly, Monash was an exceptional soldier, and the wider question of the effectiveness of staff training at Camberley and Quetta lies outside the scope of this chapter.[20] However, it is fair to say that the best Militia officers had some training and experience that proved valuable on active service.

Tim Travers has demonstrated that the Edwardian British Army was 'strangely personalized', the upper echelons being marked by factionalism.[21] The fledgling Australian forces also had their fair share of cliques and feuds. In part this was related to nationalistic tensions. In July 1916 a number of key posts, including command of I and II ANZAC Corps, commanded by Birdwood and Godley respectively, and 1st and 4th Australian Divisions (led, respectively, by Walker and Cox) remained in the hands of British or Indian Army officers. In early 1916 Birdwood and White, his chief of staff, were sometimes suspected of preferring British officers to Australians, although

Bean claimed that, if anything, Birdwood was 'always prepared to try an inferior Australian officer rather than a British officer who he knows to be more capable'.[22] There is certainly evidence that Birdwood was keen to promote Australian talent,[23] but this had to be balanced against the need for trained staff officers, as senior Australian commanders recognised.[24] Australian officers were, however, by no means a band of brothers. There were clashes of personalities, frustrated ambitions and tensions between Militia and Regular officers: all of these factors were involved when Elliot was passed over by White for command of 3rd Australian Division in favour of Gellibrand.[25] Perhaps the most controversial Australian commander was Legge (2nd Australian Division) who had a number of enemies within the AIF.[26] There were tensions between White and Gellibrand, whom the former may have perceived as a potential rival in 1914–1915.[27] In 1918 Bean and another journalist, Keith Murdoch, opposed Monash's appointment to command of the Australian Corps and carried out a 'sordid intrigue' to replace him with White.[28]

Pozières had been attacked several times by British formations before 23 July. Why did 1st Australian Division's attack succeed, while previous attacks had failed? One study of the battle concludes that the key factor was 'the quality of the troops used in the assault'. 1st Australian Division was fresh, well trained, and experienced (it had served on Gallipoli).[29] There is undoubtedly much in this explanation, but it does not go far enough. Several other factors must also be taken into account.

The first relates to staff work.[30] 1st Australian Division drew upon the hard-won lessons learned by British formations in the first three weeks of the Somme battle. In his official history Bean discusses this in general terms[31] but it is worth devoting more attention to this subject. On 14 July (that is, nine days before the first Australian assault on Pozières) Lieutenant Colonel T.A. Blamey, the chief of staff of 1st Australian Division, issued General Staff Memorandum No. 54. This consisted of a series of lessons learned from recent fighting passed on by the British 7th and 19th Divisions. Blamey had taken the trouble to discuss with his opposite numbers in nearby British divisions their tactical experiences.[32] Blamey's choice of divisions consulted is interesting. It may have been chance, or it may have been because both formations had been conspicuously successful. 19th Division, a New Army formation, was in reserve on 1 July but had taken La Boisselle on 2 July, using a feint 'Chinese' barrage against Ovillers to divert attention from the real target, followed by a rush across No Man's Land that took the Germans by surprise.[33] 7th Division, a Regular formation, had attacked on 1 July and captured the fortified village of Mametz. It then participated in the successful dawn assault of 14 July on Bazentin Ridge. C.T. Atkinson, the perceptive author of the division's history, summarised the reasons for success on 1 July as: effective use of artillery in wire cutting and accurate barrages; all arms co-operation, the product of 'careful and systematic training'; and the 'lessons' taught by the GOC and the staff.[34]

These lessons were enshrined in Blamey's memorandum of 14 July, and in the No. 56 issued four days later; the latter may have drawn on the experience of other British divisions. Blamey instructed that attacks should not be launched from more than 200 yards from the enemy line. If No Man's Land was wider, a 'jumping off place' needed to be established, or troops should 'form up under cover of darkness within this distance'. Rather than simply advancing as far as they could, 'definite objectives' were to be set for the infantry. Each phase of the battle was to be 'covered in turn by an artillery barrage'. Particular attention needed to be paid to mopping up enemy positions, 'P' smoke bombs being recommended for dealing with dugouts. Blamey also offered practical advice on what to do once a position was captured, on matters such as delivery of rations and ammunition, and the need to equip some troops with picks and shovels for the consolidation of captured positions, and to send forward parties of sappers and pioneers as soon as possible. Lewis Guns were to be pushed forward, in part to give the infantry cover while they were consolidating. Finally he stressed the importance of communications; of contact patrols by the RFC; and of providing an officer to liaise between brigade HQ and divisional HQ, as well as forward units, who was to actually go forward and see for himself the situation on the ground.[35] All of this was excellent advice, much of which 1st Australian Division was to put to good use on 23–26 July.

The attack on 23 July, although successful, revealed several tactical limitations. Two British battalion commanders of 48th Division commented that the 1st Australian Division crowded their trenches, leading to unnecessary casualties.[36] Despite the insistence of their British tutors on the importance of consolidation, and Blamey's memos on the subject, in their excitement some attacking infantry threw away their picks and shovels – evidence, apart from anything else, of poor battle discipline. More positively, 1st Australian Division's papers reveal them struggling to come to terms with one of the major problems of trench warfare – command at low levels. In July and August 1916 the Australians were fighting 'bite-and hold' or 'step by step' operations: that is, limited battles, dominated by artillery, which aimed not to break through the enemy positions and reopen mobile warfare at one fell swoop but to inflict heavy casualties on the enemy in taking a piece of key ground from which to launch another similar attack. This was the most appropriate method for the BEF to use in 1916, given its level of training and experience, the strength of the German defenders, and the absence of a usable instrument of exploitation. However, on at least two occasions in the first two weeks of the Battle of the Somme rigid application of the bite-and-hold approach, or diffidence about exploiting enemy weaknesses, led to the missing of important opportunities to make significant advances. The first came on

1 July, when the success of Rawlinson's right flank gave the British a golden opportunity to, at the very least, seize and occupy the woods behind Montauban ridge. These woods – High Wood, Delville Wood and the rest – were to cost the BEF dearly in casualties over the next few months. Similarly, after the success of the dawn assault of 14 July, High Wood was there for the taking, but delays in following up the initial assault allowed the Germans to reinforce their positions in the wood. It is against this background that we should assess Blamey's General Staff Memorandum No. 59 of 1 August 1916, which examined the lessons of the recent actions at Pozières.

This document stressed the need for thorough preparation before each successive advance, and that troops must have specific objectives, and not advance beyond them but consolidate captured positions (this included reorganising the assaulting troops). Pressing on must be left to follow-up waves. This was of some importance, because it seems that 'many' of the attacking infantry did not understand that the attack was essentially limited, and dictated by the pace of the artillery barrage: some men said that the 'artillery did not lift quickly enough for them to get on'. 'Numerous' casualties resulted.

However, sticking to pre-arranged objectives had to be balanced against the seizing of opportunities – such as taking terrain features abandoned by the enemy. Patrols were to be pushed forward, but, in Blamey's words, the 'principle' to be observed was for the captured position to 'be made strong against counter-attacks while no opportunity must be lost for want of initiative. It is to be noted that the initiative, if uncontrolled and if based on hope as to what the enemy may be doing, may easily become dangerous. A subordinate commander who pushes forward without having thoroughly examined the situation by means of patrols incurs a grave risk.'

Of great importance was the need to report on actions taken, and to tell neighbouring units so that they might co-operate with the additional forward move.[37]

This document shows 1st Australian Division groping towards the principles of devolved command, known today as 'mission command'. If 'top down' command was applied rigidly, it could stifle initiative and sacrifice tactical opportunities. Conversely, lack of 'grip' by commanders could lead to newly captured positions being left too weak to resist the inevitable counter-attack that formed an integral part of German tactical doctrine, and to Australian troops advancing into their own barrage.

Blamey's efforts at collating and disseminating tactical advice should be placed in the context of the BEF's culture of innovation and improvisation. The creation of doctrine was a dynamic process. Units at all levels examined operations to try to learn lessons, and such information went up to higher levels of command,[38] and came back down in the form of doctrinal pamphlets and semi-informal notes, often issued when operations were still in progress. Before Pozières, 2nd Australian Division issued a 'lessons learned' document on raids, and Australian units received 'primers' on subjects such as the use of artillery and infantry tactics.[39] The 4th Australian Division issued a 'lessons learned' report after its operations in the Pozières area,[40] and I ANZAC Corps issued its own summary of lessons at the end of the Somme campaign.[41] These documents reflect similar debates in formations across the BEF, and played their part in the reshaping of tactical doctrine at the beginning of 1917 that made the BEF a more effective force during the battles of that year than it had been on the Somme.[42]

Robin Prior and Trevor Wilson's seminal *Command on the Western Front* has established something of a new orthodoxy that the correct use of guns was a vital factor in achieving success on the Western Front.[43] For the attack on 23 July 1st Australian Division and 48th Division, attacking on its immediate left, were supported by a substantial concentration of artillery. In addition to organic divisional artillery, the assault was supported by the artillery of 25th Division, whose infantry had been pulled out of the line, and 'the bulk of the X Corps medium and heavy guns'. XLV Heavy Artillery Group, consisting of the British 36th and 108th Siege Batteries, and the Australian 55th Siege Battery armed with 9.2-inch howitzers, was 'at the direct call of 1st Australian Division from 21st July'.[44] 1st Australian Division's Operation Order No. 31 of 21 July also mentioned the heavy artillery of Reserve Army assisting the attack.[45] This was a powerful concentration of artillery on a limited front.

The mere possession of large numbers of guns did not guarantee success, but clearly the artillery support for the attack of 23 July was very effective. 'The systematic bombardment' of the village commenced on 19 July at 2.00am, reducing it to rubble.[46] Counter battery fire was good. In his after-action report of 3 August, Major General Harold 'Hooky' Walker, the commander of 1st Australian Division, noted that the heavy artillery 'responded quickly' to requests for aid: 'on each occasion the enemy's fire diminished steadily and the infantry obtained a respite'. As for the attack itself, Walker recorded that 'The barrages were most effective', and praised the 'accurate shooting' of his divisional guns, stating that the infantry had pushed up to within 50 yards of the barrage in the assault.[47] A feint Chinese barrage to the west of Pozières attempted to deceive the defenders as to the direction of the assault.[48]

On 23 July the use of artillery compared favourably to that provided for previous attempts to seize Pozières. An unsuccessful attack was carried out on 14 July by 'strong patrols' of 34th Division, in the mistaken belief that the defenders were pulling out. But as 'three different artillery staffs [III Corps, X Corps, 34th Division] were issuing orders for it [the preliminary bombardment], much difficulty was found in ensuring that the barrage should fall clear of attacking troops'.[49] On the following day 34th Division attacked Pozières in greater strength on two occasions. Although Rawlinson believed that the seizure of Pozières should be accomplished with relative ease,[50] according to the British official historian the assaulting troops believed that 'the artillery preparation and support were quite inadequate'. The second bombardment, while visually impressive, was a case of too little, too late. Although the divisional artillery fired from 5pm to 6pm, with 100 heavy guns (40 from X Corps, Reserve Army) adding their voice at 5.30pm, the bombardment failed to suppress the German machine gunners, who were observed by a British airman emerging from shelters and sprinting for their machine guns. The British attackers were not following the barrage closely enough, and thus lost the race to the wire. Yet another attack by 34th Division, this time on 17 July, also failed, in part because machine gun fire was not suppressed.[51] A report of a reconnaissance carried out by a X Corps staff officer on the following day stated that the trenches contained unburied dead.[52]

These earlier attacks had obvious benefits for Walker's men on 23 July. They enjoyed the cumulative effects of the bombardment on the German positions at Pozières in terms of destruction, and, perhaps more importantly, the gunners supporting the Australians had the benefit of knowing where their targets actually were. This was particularly significant when one examines a primary reason for the failure of Fourth Army's attacks on 22/23 July: that they were assaulting a position located largely on a reverse slope. This meant that extensive aerial reconnaissance was needed to allow the artillery to register its guns. However, the weather in the days leading up to the attack was poor, making aerial observation difficult. In sharp contrast to the artillerymen supporting 1st Australian Division's attack, Fourth Army's gunners had precious little time to register their pieces. The accuracy of the bombardment – and subsequently the attacking divisions – suffered as a result. Another spin-off of the poor weather was the delay of the general assault, which gave the Germans time to prepare to be attacked.[53]

Another of Prior and Wilson's major themes is that narrow front attacks usually failed, not least because it allowed the defenders to concentrate their artillery fire against a single target. There was a third advantage enjoyed by Walker's division that was denied to previous attackers of Pozières. The Australians attacked not on a narrow, one or two divisional front, but, in theory, as part of a simultaneous, broad front attack that stretched from the left of Pozières across the inter-Army boundary right across to the extreme right flank of Fourth Army. In reality, the six participating divisions attacked at four different times, lessening the impact of a concerted push. However, on the left flank there was a simultaneous assault in the Pozières area, although it must be admitted that this was more through luck than judgement. The two Reserve Army divisions – 48th and 1st Australian – attacked at 12.30am. The left hand formation of Fourth Army, the British 1st Division, also attacked at this time to conform to the assault on Pozières. However, 19th Division had been ordered to attack an hour later, at 1.30am, but when a new German position (Intermediate Trench) was belatedly discovered in No Man's Land, through RFC reconnaissance, Fourth Army ordered this position to be attacked at 12.30am before the main assault was launched at 1.30am. 51st (Highland) Division would also have attacked Intermediate Trench at 12.30am had the order to do so been received. As it was, four divisions attacked, simultaneously, side by side.[54]

Intermediate Trench was a major factor in the failure of 19th Division's attack. Allocating a mere 60 minutes to its capture was a hopelessly optimistic decision by Fourth Army. It was later claimed that Corps and Army headquarters at first refused to believe reports of Intermediate Trench's very existence, and it was therefore omitted from the artillery fire plan. More generally, lack of preparation (19th Division was still trying to locate the exact front line on the 21st), the absence of surprise – sacrificed by the preliminary bombardment, which then failed to do its job – and unsuppressed machine guns put paid to 1st and 19th Divisions' attacks.[55] The comparison with 1st Australian Division's well-prepared attack, supported by an effective bombardment, is all too stark.

The attack of 2nd Australian Division on 29 July likewise offers a sad contrast with that of Walker's division. Brigadier General Philip Howell, a senior staff officer of II Corps (another Reserve Army formation) wrote in his diary: 'Last night's attack by Australians on trenches E of Pozières reported a ghastly failure: too rushed: inadequate preparation & reconnaissance: attempting too much at once.'[56] This verdict is fair. The attack was not mounted as part of a concerted, broad front attack. Instead, it was a classic example of 'penny-packeting'. On the left flank one battalion of 12th Division tried, and failed, to take a position on the flank of 23rd Australian Battalion, which as a result was left out on a limb. On the right, a single battalion of 23rd Division made a successful attack; elsewhere, there were minor operations by 5th and 51st Divisions. The artillery support for the attack was substantial – once again 25th Divisional Artillery added its weight, as did the heavies of II Corps (which had just relieved X Corps), I Anzac Corps and Reserve Army. But the heavy guns dispersed their fire, shelling not only targets around the OG Lines at Pozières, but also Mouquet Farm and Courcelette, thus dissipating the effect of the bombardment.

It may also be relevant that there is no evidence of Blamey's tactical memoranda, or their equivalent, in the war diary of Legge's 2nd Australian Division. The suspicion that 2nd Division did not have the benefit of tactical advice offered by experienced formations is strengthened by a terse note of a conference held later on the 29th, presided over by Birdwood and attended by White, Legge and his chief of staff: 'Decided to repeat the attempt to capture enemy's position in OG1 and OG2 after more thorough preparation had been made and all details worked out … Trench to be dug within 200 yards of enemy's line as a jumping off place. OG1 and OG2 to be subjected to heavy bombardment under Special programme.'[57]

If it is indeed the case that Legge's staff had failed to seek out tactical advice, this reflects poorly on 2nd Australian Division, but the failure to share information also raises questions about staff work in 1st Australian Division and I ANZAC Corps. It is perhaps significant that the commander of 4th Australian Division, Major General H.V. Cox, made a point of consulting with other formations before his division was committed to battle. On 18 July he spoke to Horne, the commander of XV Corps, which had enjoyed some success in the battle thus far, and then, like Blamey, he visited the head-quarters of 7th Division 'and got much information'. After 1st Australian Division's successful attack on Pozières he lunched with Walker 'and talked to him about the battle', and on 31 July he talked with Legge and the com-manders of 23rd and 12th Divisions. 4th Australian Division successfully cap-tured trenches around Mouquet Farm in operations on 9 and 12/13 August. After the first operation, Cox met Walker and Blamey. Clearly, Cox, like Blamey, believed in consultation and learning from the success and failures of other formations, and this seems to have been a factor in his division's achievements.[58]

One of the most controversial aspects of the entire battle concerned the respective roles of the commanders of Reserve Army and I ANZAC Corps, Hubert Gough and William Birdwood. The story of Gough's behaviour before 1st Australian Division's attack on 23 July is reasonably well known. According to Bean, on arriving at Reserve Army's front on 18 July Walker was told by Gough, 'I want you to go into the line and attack Pozières tomorrow night!'[59] Walker was appalled at what he described in his diary as 'Scrappy & unsatisfactory orders from Reserve Army', going on to write 'Hope shall not be rushed into an ill-prepared ... operation but fear I shall.'[60] I ANZAC Corps headquarters had not yet arrived, and clearly, little more than a day was hopelessly insufficient time for preparation. Walker and White successfully argued against Gough and dissuaded him from ordering what would almost certainly have been a premature attack that would have been a bloody failure. Apparently this was not the only battle Walker had fight against Gough before the 23 July attack. In 1928 Walker recorded how he had to seek more artillery, as the initial allocation was insufficient, and only succeeded in being allowed to attack from the south-east, rather than the south-west, the route of the unsuccessful pushes launched in the past, by taking 'Moses' Beddington, a Reserve Army staff officer whom Gough trusted, up to the front to show him the ground. Walker's verdict on Gough was scathing: 'the very worst exhibition of Army commandship (sic) that occurred during the whole cam-paign, though God knows the 5th army was a tragedy throughout'.[61]

Gough angrily rejected this version of events when he was shown a draft of Bean's Australian official history, in which Bean claimed that Gough was 'temperamentally' inclined towards rushed attacks: 'I can hardly believe a word of this story about my meeting with General Walker,' Gough wrote in 1927. 'I was not "temperamentally" addicted to attacks without careful reconnaissances and preparation ....'[62]

This is not the place for a full-scale assessment of Hubert Gough's role as commander of Reserve Army on the Somme.[63] There is, however, a considerable body of evidence that suggests that Gough was a prescriptive, 'hands-on' commander. This was a rather different approach from that favoured by Rawlinson, commander of Fourth Army, who was inclined to set broad objectives and then leave corps and divisional commanders to get on with it. Indeed, if Gough can be criticised for breathing down the necks of his subordinates, Rawlinson stands condemned for lack of 'grip'. Gough's approach caused a good deal of friction between Reserve Army headquarters and subordinate commanders. At the end of the Somme campaign Reserve Army's chief of staff Neill Malcolm issued a memorandum in which he condemned the 'marked tendency to disregard, or to dispute the advisability of order[s] issued from Army Headquarters', and went on to defend the issuing of such orders.[64]

What impact did Gough's command style have on Australian operations on the Somme? It has been suggested that as an Army commander Gough disliked having a level of command between him and the battlefield.[65] Therefore it is possible that on 18 July 1916 Gough was keen to get Walker to attack before Birdwood and I ANZAC Corps headquarters arrived to, from Gough's point of view, complicate matters. In fact, I ANZAC Corps did not take over responsibility for 1st Australian Division's sector until noon on 23 July – that is, after the attack had been launched.[66] The fact that Gough dispensed with I ANZAC Corps headquarters on 23 July was, in one sense, not necessarily a bad thing, since the artillery support that a Corps headquarters would normally have co-ordinated was present in abundant measure. Even after the Corps headquarters was in place, Gough continued to exercise direct control of operations.[67]

Our knowledge of the role played by Birdwood in the operations at Pozières is tantalisingly incomplete. There is no record of his reactions to the planning for the attack of 23 July.[68] While Birdwood wrote descriptions of the battle in letters to Lord Derby and the Australian Governor-General in which his choice of words 'we' and 'my boys' implies responsibility for the victory, his input into 1st Australian Division's attack appears to have been minimal.[69] The occasion on which he (and White) did seem to have an influence was in obtaining a delay in the attack, when they were, in Bean's words, 'most courteously consulted' by Reserve Army.[70] However, Bean stressed that Walker and White were primarily responsible for dissuading Gough from his original plan.

This was not the only occasion on which Gough pressurised Australian commanders. When Brigadier General Howell of II Corps met Legge, after 2nd Australian Division's unsuccessful attack on 29 July, he found him 'furious with the [Reserve] army: at least 1000 men lost for nothing'.[71] After the war Legge himself stated that 'Any apparent haste' he had shown in attacking 'should be properly ascribed to the daily pressure of the Reserve Army Commander'.[72] There is little doubt that Gough pressurised Legge into attacking on 29 July before preparations were fully complete.[73] In the official history Bean blamed Legge for buckling under, and said that White blamed himself for not standing up to Gough. Bean's verdict was followed by Peter Charlton in his 1986 study of Pozières.[74] However, one should take this with a pinch of salt. White and Legge had fallen out in early 1916, and Bean was not an impartial witness. As one Australian historian has noted, a 'schoolboy sense of hero-worship was never far from Bean', and Bean described White as 'the greatest man it has been my fortune intimately to know'.[75] To place the blame on Legge is, C.D. Coulthard-Clark has argued, 'grossly unfair'. I ANZAC Corps in the shape of White and Birdwood did not specifically oppose 2nd Division's operation against Pozières on 29 July and therefore gave it 'tacit endorsement'.[76] Whatever Legge's abilities as a commander,[77] to put a mere divisional commander up against an Army commander – particularly one with Gough's abrasive and bullying style – was not a fair competition. I ANZAC Corps should have acted as a buffer zone between Reserve Army and the subordinate formations.[78]

Bean believed that in 1916 2nd Australian Division's 'general staff was weak'. Gellibrand considered that Legge's chief of staff, Lieutenant Colonel A.H. Bridges, gave poor service.[79] However, this was not the only occasion on which Australian staff work in this period came in for criticism. To pick just one, minor, example, a Grenadier Guards subaltern was scathing about the way an Australian battalion carried out a relief,[80] but the most serious criticism can be levelled at the staff work of I ANZAC Corps. Birdwood leaned heavily on White, whom he praised in September 1916 as 'one of the best officers it has ever been my good fortune to have with me'.[81] This compliment appeared in the context of an explanation of why Birdwood considered it more important to keep White at I ANZAC Corps HQ than to put him in command of a division. White was privately critical of Birdwood, resenting the heavy burden of staff work placed upon him.[82] However, Eric Andrews has highlighted White's weaknesses as a staff officer during the Bullecourt fighting in 1917, and Bean's role in glossing over his hero's frailties.[83] Similar criticisms can be made of I ANZAC Corps staff work in 1916. Philip Howell was critical, implicitly or explicitly, of Birdwood and White on several occasions, while Gellibrand believed that I ANZAC Corps should have provided Legge with an effective staff.[84] Rawlinson was similarly unimpressed on occasions by I ANZAC Corps staff work.[85] Similar criticism could be levelled at many British formations at this period; in general, the BEF's staff work was to undergo a distinct improvement in 1917–1918.

If there was indeed a question mark over Australian staff work in 1916, this puts one of Haig's comments in a new light. Following the failure of 2nd Australian Division's attack on 29 July, the British Commander-in-Chief criticised the preparations and bluntly told Birdwood and White, 'You're not fighting Bashi-Bazouks now – this is serious, scientific war, and you are up against the most scientific and most military nation in Europe.' Haig clearly feared, with some reason, that the experience of Gallipoli had not been good preparation for the rigours of the Western Front. Earlier, on 22 July, he had worried whether Gough had given 1st Australian Division a straightfor-ward job. Unlike Walker and Blamey, Legge's staff had made serious errors in the preparation for their attack. According to Bean, White, stung by Haig's 'Bashi-Bazouk' comment, stood up to the Commander-in–Chief. He had earlier failed to take such a strong line against Gough.[86]

During the Hundred Days offensive of 1918 the five division Australian Corps emerged as an elite force. Bean's explanation for the impressive perfor-mance of Australian troops in 1918 amounted to the fact they were superior soldiers, emerging from a democratic, egalitarian frontier society very differ-ent from that of Britain, that encouraged the soldierly virtues of 'determin-ation, endurance, and improvisation'.[87] In recent years this 'Anzac myth' has been challenged.[88] Current scholarship, while not denying the excellence of the 'battle culture' of the Australians, has placed it within the context of a BEF-wide improvement in command, staff work, the emergence of the all-arms battle, and the application of scientific methods of warfare, particularly as regards gunnery, to tactics.[89] Edmonds criticised Bean for being 'inclined to write as if the Australian divisions were in 1916, when they arrived in France, the perfect instrument they were in August 1918, and to attribute their earlier failures in 1916 to British generals'.[90] This comment contains a measure of truth. While Gough's performance as a general must be taken into account when assessing I ANZAC Corps' operations on the Somme, it is clear that Australian formations went through the same steep 'learning curve' as their British, and for that matter other Dominion, counterparts. 1st Australian Division, which was well led and experienced, with the benefit of good advice from other divisions, performed more effectively than 2nd Australian Divi-sion, which lacked these advantages but learned from its mistakes. Many com-parisons could be made with British divisions. On 8 August 55th Division, a Territorial formation from West Lancashire, made a number of elementary mistakes in their first, unsuccessful, attack on the Somme. 55th Division too learned from its mistakes and, indeed, became an elite 'storm' formation later in the war.[91] Australian divisions in 1916 were no better, and no worse, than comparable British formations. Operational effectiveness was the product of factors such as training, leadership and artillery support, not national origin.

We have seen that in 1914 the AIF had a very small pool of trained staff officers on which they could draw. Arguably, the situation was not very much better for the British Army, which in August 1914 had 908 active officers with the *psc* qualification. By the beginning of 1916 ninety of these men had been killed. Given that the BEF had increased from six infantry divisions in 1914 to about sixty in 1916 – not forgetting other units and formations on other fronts – it can be seen that trained staff officers had to be spread very thinly indeed.[92] In July 1916 Australian and most British divisions suffered from a common lack of trained and staff officers and commanders accustomed to operating at the appropriate level. Over the next two years Australian and British commanders and staff alike were to acquire more experience, in the process of which a rough meritocracy emerged from the personalised pre-war armies. Many commanders were 'degummed' – deprived of command – *en route*: Legge, for example, returned to Australia in 1917. During these years Australians progressively replaced British officers in Australian formations. Monash implied that this enhanced the efficiency of staff work within the Australian Corps.[93] By 1932 Edmonds had come to believe that the staff work of Australian formations was better than the rest of the BEF. Interestingly, he excluded 2nd Australian Division from this compliment, even though this formation's seizure of the Mont St Quentin position on 31 August 1918 surely rates as one of the finest feats of arms in the entire war.[94] The historical spadework necessary to substantiate, qualify or refute these assertions has yet to be undertaken.[95] However, one might with confidence assert that the most important factors in the success of Australian staff work were experience and competence, regardless of the national origin of individual staff officers, and the crucial fact that the Australian Corps always had the same divisions under command, enhancing teamwork between higher and lower formations. Moreover, in contrast to the situation with Birdwood in 1916, in 1918 the Australian Corps was more obviously a national army. Monash was prepared to fight his corner against higher command, and was perhaps held in higher regard by his superiors. British corps did not enjoy these advantages. As Edmonds wrote to Bean in 1928, it might have been more efficient if 'Haig had kept British divisions permanently in corps ... But don't try to persuade the Australian public that in 1916 the Australian Corps was the fine instrument it was in 1918'.[96]

Further Reading
The only book solely dedicated to Australian operations at Pozières that has been published since my piece first appeared is a popular account: Scott Bennett, *Pozières: The Anzac Story* (Brunswick, Vic.: Scribe, 2011). Curiously, this author's research did not extend to the original of this chapter, and does not really mark an advance on Peter Charlton's 1986 popular book. In a different league is Robert Stevenson, *To Win the Battle: The 1st Australian*

Division in the Great War, 1914–1918 (Melbourne: Cambridge University Press, 2012). This is an excellent study that includes, among much else, a brief analysis of Pozières. If I was writing this piece today, it would be greatly enriched by having access to Stevenson's deep research into the organisation, administration, training and staff work of the division. Meleah Hampton, a historian on the staff of the Australian War Memorial, is completing an Adelaide University Ph. D on Pozières and Moquet Farm that will undoubtedly prove definitive.

Acknowledgements

Material in the Bean and Birdwood Papers appears by kind permission of the Australian War Memorial. Material in the Howell Papers appears by kind permission of the Trustees of the Liddell Hart Centre for Military Archives. Material in the Hughes and Hutton Papers appears by kind permission of the State Library of New South Wales.

Notes

1. I would like to thank Helen McCartney and Niall Barr for reading and commenting on this piece, and the Australian Army for awarding me a grant that enabled me to undertake archival work in Australia.
2. Peter Dennis *et al*, *The Oxford Companion to Australian Military History* (Melbourne: Oxford University Press, 1995), p. 655.
3. J.T. Hutton diary, 27, 28, 31 July 1916, MML MSS 1138, M[itchell] L[ibrary], S[ydney]. See also W.V. Wright diary, 22, 23 July 1916, ML MSS 1012, MLS.
4. Bean to Edmonds, 18 Apr. 1934, Bean Papers, 3 DRL 7953, item x34, A[ustralian] W[ar] M[emorial].
5. J. Gellibrand to W. Gellibrand, 12 Oct. 1916, 3 DRL 6541, item 2, AWM.
6. Quoted in G.D. Sheffield, '"One Vast Australian Cemetery": The battle for Pozières, July 1916', *Wartime: Official Magazine of the Australian War Memorial*, 7 (Spring 1999), p. 22.
7. G.B. Hughes, diary, 26 July 1916, ML MSS 3923, MLS.
8. *The Oh Pip* Somme issue, A2771, MLS.
9. Dennis, *Oxford Companion*, p. 655. See also Peter Stanley, 'Gallipoli and Pozières: A legend and a memorial', *Australian Foreign Affairs Record*, vol. 56, part 4 (April 1985), pp. 285–7.
10. For narratives of the fighting, see C.E.W. Bean, *The Official History of Australia in the War of 1914–1918*, vol. III, *The A.I.F. in France: 1916* (St. Lucia: University of Queensland Press, 1982 [1929]), pp. 448–862; Wilfred Miles, *Military Operations France and Belgium, 1916*, vol. I (London: Macmillan, 1938), pp. 115–16, 141–56, 208–28, 282–5; Peter Charlton, *Australians on the Somme Pozieres 1916* (London: Leo Cooper, 1986).
11. John Monash, *The Australian Victories in France in 1918* (London: Imperial War Museum, 1993 [1920]), p. 56.
12. Jeffrey Grey, *A Military History of Australia* (Cambridge: Cambridge University Press, 1990), pp. 80–1; Christopher Coulthard-Clark, 'Formation of the Australian armed services, 1901–14', in Michael McKernnan and Margaret Browne (eds), *Australia: Two Centuries of War & Peace* (Canberra: Australian War Memorial in association with Allen & Unwin Australia, 1988), pp. 128–30.
13. Peter Sadler, *The Paladin: A Life of Major-General Sir John Gellibrand* (Melbourne: Oxford University Press, 2000), p. 56.
14. Biographical details are drawn, unless otherwise stated, from Dennis, *Oxford Companion*.
15. C.D. Coulthard-Clark, *A Heritage of Spirit: A Biography of Major-General Sir William Throsby Bridges* (Melbourne: Melbourne University Press, 1979), p. 116.

16. Through this chapter the functional title 'chief of staff' is used in preference to more formal titles such as 'Brigadier General General Staff'.
17. For Gough's views on the desirability of using Australians on the staffs of British formations, see Malcolm to Birdwood, 17 May 1917, AWM 25 515/1, AWM.
18. Coulthard-Clark, *Heritage*, p. 116; P.A. Pedersen, *Monash as Military Commander* (Melbourne: Melbourne University Press, 1992 [1985]), pp. 27–8.
19. Pedersen, *Monash*, pp. 37–8.
20. For these topics, see Brian Bond, *The Victorian Army and the Staff College, 1854–1914* (London: Eyre Methuen, 1972); Brian Holden Reid, *War Studies at the Staff College 1890–1930* (Camberley: Strategic and Combat Studies Institute, 1992).
21. Tim Travers, *The Killing Ground: The British Army, the Western Front and the Emergence of Modern Warfare 1900–1918* (London: Allen & Unwin, 1987), pp. xxi, 3–36.
22. Bean notebook, Feb.–March 1916, pp. 49, 54, 3 DRL 606, item 40(2), AWM.
23. But see E.M. Andrews, *The ANZAC Illusion: Anglo-Australian relations during World War I* (Cambridge: Cambridge University Press, 1993), p. 113.
24. Birdwood to Sir R. Munro-Ferguson (Governor-General), 3 Oct. 1915, 3 DRL 3376, item 31, AWM; same to same, 23 Jan., 18 May 1916, Birdwood Papers, 3 DRL 3376, item 32, AWM.
25. J.M. Bourne, 'The BEF's generals on 29 September 1918: An Empirical Portrait with Some British and Australian Comparisons', in Peter Dennis and Jeffrey Grey (eds), *1918: Defining Victory* (Canberra: Army History Unit, 1999), p. 104.
26. Birdwood to Munro-Ferguson, 31 Dec. 1916, Birdwood Papers, 3 DRL 3376, item 32, AWM. For Legge, see C.D. Coulthard-Clark, *No Australian Need Apply: The Troubled Career of Lieutenant-General Gordon Legge* (Sydney: Allen & Unwin, 1988).
27. Sadler, *Paladin*, pp. 54–6.
28. P.A. Pedersen, 'General Sir John Monash: Corps Commander on the Western Front', in D.M. Horner (ed.), *The Commanders: Australian military leadership in the twentieth century* (Sydney: Allen & Unwin, 1984), p. 103.
29. Charlton, *Australians on the Somme*, p. 139.
30. Blamey asserted that the plan was 'chiefly mine'. See D. Horner, *Blamey: The Commander-in-Chief* (St. Leonards: Allen & Unwin, 1998), pp. 43–5 for a discussion of this claim, and some criticism of 1st Australian Division's staff work.
31. Bean, *A.I.F.* vol. III, pp. 452–4. See OA 256, 16 July 1916, in War Diary [WD], Reserve Army General Staff, WO 95/518, The National Archives. This memorandum, on the importance of infantry keeping close to the artillery barrage, was sent from GHQ to Reserve Army and subsequently circulated. Bean seems to refer to it in *A.I.F.* vol. III, p. 453.
32. Reports on lessons were also sent to Fourth Army, arriving on 19 July: File 47, 'Notes on Somme', Montgomery-Massingberd Papers, L[iddell] H[art] C[entre] for M[ilitary] A[rchives].
33. Everard Wyrall, *The History of the 19th Division* (London: Arnold, nd), p. 42.
34. C.T. Atkinson, *The Seventh Division* (London: John Murray, 1927), pp. 276–7.
35. Appx 7 & 9 to July 1916, WD, GS, 1st Australian Division WO 95/3156, TNA.
36. White to Walker, 28 July 1916, AWM 27 354/35, AWM. For this lesson, see document on lessons learned (n.d. but *c*. June 1917), Gellibrand Papers, 3 DRL 1473, item 101a, AWM.
37. Appx 2 to August 1916, WD, GS, 1st Australian Division, WO 95/3156, TNA.
38. See Files 47 and 48, 'Notes on Somme', Montgomery-Massingberd Papers, LHCMA. This consists of a number of reports from divisions and corps, based in turn on material from subordinate units, solicited by Fourth Army while the battle was in progress. Similar material was gathered by Fifth Army at the end of the Somme: WO 158/344, TNA.

39. 'Report on Minor Enterprise ...', issued by 2nd Australian Division, 7 June 1916; 'Notes on Artillery' nd but *c.* June 1916; No. S 309, issued by HQ I ANZAC Corps, 20 June 1916, all in Monash Papers, 3 DRL 2316–22, AWM.
40. Issued by HQ 4th Australian Division on 14 August 1916, Monash Papers, 3 DRL 2316–22, AWM.
41. I ANZAC Corps General Staff Circular No. 38, 16 Dec. 1916, Monash Papers, 3 DRL 2316–23, AWM.
42. John Lee, 'Some Lessons of the Somme: the British Infantry in 1917', in Brian Bond *et al*, *'Look to Your Front': Studies in the First World War* (Staplehurst: Spellmount, 1999), pp. 79–87.
43. Robin Prior and Trevor Wilson, *Command on the Western Front* (Oxford: Blackwell's, 1992).
44. Wilfred Miles, *Military Operations*, vol. II, p. 142; 21 July 1916, WD, GS, I ANZAC Corps, WO 95/980, TNA.
45. Appx 19 (sic) to July 1916, WD, GS, 1st Australian Division, WO 95/3156, TNA.
46. Bean, *A.I.F.*, vol. III, p. 491.
47. Appx 19 to July 1916, WD, GS, 1st Australian Division, WO 95/3156, TNA.
48. Miles, *Military Operations*, vol. II, p. 142.
49. Bean, *A.I.F.*, vol. III, pp. 458–9.
50. Rawlinson diary, 16 July 1916, CC/1/5, Churchill College, Cambridge.
51. Bean, *A.I.F.*, vol. III, pp. 460–1, 467; Miles, *Military Operations*, vol. II, pp. 97–8; H.A. Jones, *The War in the Air*, II (Oxford: Clarendon Press, 1928), p. 232.
52. X Corps to Reserve Army, 18 July 1916, AWM 45 [35/7], AWM.
53. Miles, *Military Operations*, vol. II, p. 112; Prior and Wilson, *Command*, p. 212; Jones, *War in the Air*, vol. II, p. 237.
54. Prior and Wilson, *Command*, pp. 211–12.
55. Wyrall, *19th Division*, p. 54; Miles, *Military Operations*, vol. II, p. 138.
56. Diary, 29 July 1916, Philip Howell Papers, IV/D/13, LHCMA.
57. 29 July, WD, G.S., 2nd Aus Div, WO 95/3254, TNA.
58. H.V. Cox, diary, 18, 25, 31 July, 5, 11 Aug. 1916, 1 DRL 0221, AWM.
59. C.E.W. Bean, *Two Men I Knew* (Sydney: Angus & Robertson, 1957), p. 134.
60. Walker to Bean, 13 Aug. 1928 (quoting diary entry of 18 July 1916), 3 DRL 7953, item 34, Bean Papers, AWM.
61. See note 60 and Bean, *Two Men*, p. 134; P.A. Pedersen, 'The AIF on the western front: the role of training and command', in McKernan and Browne, *Two Centuries*, p. 173; T.H.E. Travers, 'From Surafend to Gough: Charles Bean, James Edmonds, and the making of the Australian Official History', *J[ournal] of the A[ustralian] W[ar] M[emorial]*, 27 (October 1995), p. 19.
62. Edmonds to Bean, 16 Nov. 1927, enclosing 'General Sir Hubert Gough's remarks', 3 DRL 7953, item 34, Bean Papers, AWM.
63. See Chapter 5 and I.F.W. Beckett, 'Hubert Gough, Neill Malcolm and Command on the Western Front', in Bond *et al*, *'Look To Your Front'*, pp. 1–12.
64. Memo, Malcom to Corps, 16 Nov. 1916, WD, A&Q Reserve Army, WO 95/523, TNA.
65. Anthony Farrar-Hockley, *Goughie* (London: Hart-Davies, McGibbon, 1975), p. 188.
66. Bean, *A.I.F.*, vol. III, p. 530. For speculation on the form that Gough's directives took, see Bean to Edmonds, 28 April 1928, AWM38, 3 DRL 7953, item 34, AWM.
67. Pedersen, 'AIF on the western front', p. 174.
68. J.D. Millar, 'A Study in the limitations of command: General Sir William Birdwood and the A.I.F., 1914–1918' (Ph. D, University of New South Wales, 1993), p. 143.
69. Birdwood to 'Eddy' [i.e. Derby], 15 Aug. 1916, Birdwood Papers, 3 DRL 3376, item 16; Birdwood to Munro-Ferguson, 15 Aug. 1916, 3 DRL 3376, item 32, both AWM.
70. Bean, *A.I.F.*, vol. III, p. 483.

71. Diary, 29 July 1916, Howell Papers, IV/D/13, LHCMA.
72. Legge to Bean, 25 May 1934, 3 DRL 7953, item x34, AWM. Legge appears to be referring to the August fighting.
73. Gellibrand, however, believed that Legge preferred to attack rather than take casualties while remaining static in the trenches. Gellibrand to Bean, 26 Jan. 1934, 3 DRL 7953, item x34, AWM.
74. Coulthard-Clark, *No Australian*, pp. 147–8; Charlton, *Australians on the Somme*, pp. 174–8, 189.
75. Lloyd Robson, 'C.E.W. Bean: A Review Article', *JAWM*, No. 4 (April 1984), 56; Bean, *Two Men*, p. xi.
76. Coulthard-Clark, *No Australian*, pp. 147–8.
77. Coulthard-Clark, *No Australian*, pp. 159–61; Pedersen, 'AIF on the western front', p. 174.
78. For further examples of Gough's pressure on the Australians for hasty action, see diary, 1, 5 Aug. 1916, Howell Papers, IV/D/13, LHCMA.
79. Bean to Edmonds, 18 Apr. 1934, 3 DRL 7953, item x34, AWM; Sadler, *Paladin*, p. 93.
80. Lieutenant B. Lawrence, letter, Nov. 1916, in Ian Fletcher (ed.), *Letters from the Front* (Tunbridge Wells: Parapress, 1993).
81. Birdwood to Hutton, 30 Sept. 1916, Sir E. Hutton Papers, Add Mss 50 089, vol. XII, excerpt in White Papers, PR 85/83, AWM.
82. White to wife, 24 Apr., 22 July, 21 Sept. 1916; White to Gellibrand, 8 June 1917; all quoted in Rosemary Derham, *The Silence Ruse: Escape from Gallipoli* (Armadale: Cliffe Books, 1998), pp. 44, 49, 51, 53.
83. E.M. Andrews, 'Bean and Bullecourt: Weaknesses and Strengths of the Official History of Australia in the First World War', *Revue Internationale d'Histoire Militaire*, No. 72 (Canberra: Australian Commission for Military History, 1990), pp. 25–47.
84. See, for example, diary, 8 Aug. 1916, Howell Papers, IV/D/13, LHCMA; Sadler, *Paladin*, p. 95.
85. Rawlinson diary, 11, 24 Dec. 1916, 13 Feb. 1917, RAWLN 1/7, Churchill College, Cambridge. See also E.M. Andrews and B.G. Jordan, 'Second Bullecourt revisited', *JAWM*, No. 15 (October 1989), p. 43.
86. Bean, *Two Men*, p. 137; Haig diary, 22 July 1916, in Robert Blake (ed.), *The Private Papers of Douglas Haig 1914–1919* (London: Eyre & Spottiswoode, 1952), p. 155.
87. C.E.W. Bean, *The Official History of Australia in the War of 1914–1918*, vol. VI, *The A.I.F. in France: May 1918 – The Armistice* (St. Lucia: University of Queensland Press, 1983 [1942]), p. 1079.
88. This has engendered a considerable literature. For a sample of the arguments, see Andrews, *ANZAC Illusion*, pp. 60–3, 144–7, 214–15.
89. S.F. Wise, 'The Black Day of the German Army: Australians and Canadians at Amiens, August 1918', in Dennis and Grey, *1918: Defining Victory*, pp. 25–96.
90. 'Report on work of Historical Section, 1st December 1927 to 30th November 1928', CAB 103/6, p. 4, TNA. (I owe this reference to Dr Jenny Macleod.)
91. 'Notes from Recent Operations' [issued by 55th Division], 21 Aug. 1916, WO 95/2900, TNA (I owe this reference to Michael Orr); Anon, *The War History of the 1/4th Battalion the Loyal North Lancashire Regiment 1914–18* (privately published, 1921), pp. 80, 107.
92. John Hussey, 'The Deaths of Qualified Staff Officers in the Great War: "A Generation Missing"?', *Journal of the Society for Army Historical Research*, 75 (1997), pp. 250, 253–5.
93. Monash referred to Blamey, his chief of staff in 1918 as a 'Staff College graduate, but not on that account a pedant'(!); Monash, *Australian Victories*, pp. 295–6.
94. Edmonds to Bean, 14 Nov. 1932, 3 DRL 7953, item 34, AWM.
95. As Roger Lee recognises in his pioneering study, 'The Australian Staff: The Forgotten Men of the First AIF', in Dennis and Grey, *1918: Defining Victory*, pp. 115, 129.
96. Edmonds to Bean, 27 June 1928, Bean Papers, 3 DRL 7953, item 34, AWM.

Chapter 5

Hubert Gough: An Army Commander on the Somme and Ancre

In Hubert Gough's 1931 memoir, *The Fifth Army*, ghosted by the novelist Bernard Newman, we find this passage: 'No subordinate was ordered to attack before he was ready, if the reports of his unreadiness reached Army Headquarters. On the contrary, many attacks by subordinates were prevented or postponed by the Army because the preparations were not complete, the front too narrow, or the numbers engaged inadequate.'[1] This passage, and several others, seems to be a direct rebuttal of C.E.W. Bean's criticisms of his conduct of operations involving Australian forces on the Somme in 1916 (*see* Chapter 4). Bean's 1916 volume of the Australian official history had appeared in 1929. Gough's omissions in *The Fifth Army* are equally interesting. He says nothing about the argument with Walker on 18 July, and in a passage which praises several Australian officers, including divisional commanders, omits any mention of Walker.[2]

Gough's alleged behaviour at Pozières is a microcosm of the charge-sheet against his performance as an Army commander. He was a 'thruster', prone to launch hasty, ill-prepared attacks, often on a narrow front; he bullied his subordinates; and the staff work in Fifth Army was deficient. Gough, and Fifth Army, stands in sharp contrast to the commander of Second Army, General Sir Herbert Plumer, and his staff. They became renowned for the methodical and successful conduct of operations under the conditions of trench warfare, and earned a favourable reputation among officers and men quite at odds with Gough's.

Yet Gough also had his defenders. Beddington, in summing up the Somme campaign, referred to Gough as 'a great commander'.[3] Much more surprising was the verdict of Basil Liddell Hart, that scourge of Great War generals. Liddell Hart, who was instrumental in reconciling Gough and Lloyd George in the 1930s,[4] stated that Gough 'was unlucky' in that the First World War cramped his 'dynamism and acute sense of mobility'. In an earlier war, or in the Second World War, Gough might have emerged as 'one of the outstanding figures in military history ... Even under the extraordinary cramping conditions of the Western Front ... his performance was a lot better than was generally recognised.'[5] A more moderate view was the verdict of Sir Charles Bonham-Carter, the respected head of GHQ's training branch in 1917–1918.

He opined that Gough 'had greater qualities than any of the other Army Commanders if the conditions of war suited him ... If only he had had a good staff he might have done great things. He was too impatient and did not realise that infantry attacks took time to prepare.'[6] These are views that cannot be ignored.[7] This chapter examines Gough's career, and especially his performance as an Army commander on the Somme, in an attempt to discover the accuracy of such judgements.

Hubert Gough's Career

Hubert de la Poer Gough was born in London in 1870, of a distinguished Irish military family. Both his father and uncle had won the Victoria Cross, as did John Edmond Gough, Hubert's younger brother. 'Johnnie's' contemporary, General Sir George Barrow, described him as 'one of the most soldierly-minded men I have ever come across and a twentieth-century Chevalier Bayard ... Had he lived he might have gone to the top of the Army'.[8] Hubert was educated at Eton and the Royal Military College Sandhurst and was commissioned into the 16th Lancers in 1889. He saw service in one colonial 'small war', the Tirah expedition of 1897–1898. In January 1899 he went to the Staff College, Camberley, as a student. Following the outbreak of the Second Boer War, Gough went out to South Africa at the very end of 1899. On the whole he was an effective regimental officer and commander, and the high point of his war was leading the party that relieved Ladysmith in February 1900.[9] The nadir came on 17 September 1901, when he led a composite mounted regiment, without adequate reconnaissance, towards a tempting target of Boers at Blood River Poort, only to find that they were merely the advance guard of a numerically far superior body, which promptly captured Brevet Lieutenant Colonel Gough and his entire force. In his sympathetic biography, General Farrar-Hockley commented that Gough 'had made a judgement and a decision that led to the death, injury or capture' of his command.[10] Lord Anglesey, a leading authority on British cavalry, attributes the incident to 'A combination of vague intelligence and youthful impetuosity (or, as some might say, a misapplication of "the cavalry spirit") ...'.[11] However, Gough emerged from this fiasco with his reputation more-or-less intact. Kitchener expressed his 'deepest sympathy'. Farrar-Hockley is probably correct to surmise that the excess of zeal displayed by Gough at Blood River contrasted favourably with the timidity that had characterised most previous defeats in South Africa. To his credit, Gough treated this episode at some length in his memoirs.

In 1904 Gough was posted as an instructor to the Staff College, Camberley. He took over command of his regiment, 16th Lancers, at the end of 1906. In 1911 Gough was promoted to command 3rd Cavalry Brigade, and he took this formation to war in August 1914. Thereafter his rise was swift. Gough commanded, as a major general, 2nd Cavalry Division at the First Battle of

Ypres. In spring 1915 he took over 7th Infantry Division, and in July I Corps. Gough was appointed in March 1916 as commander of the Reserve Corps for the imminent operation on the Somme. His force was renamed Reserve Army in May 1916, although at the beginning of the Somme offensive Gough was effectively under the command of Rawlinson's Fourth Army.

Relations with Fellow Officers

The pre-war officer corps was a small body, divided into the inevitable cliques. By the time war broke out in August 1914, Hubert Gough had already established relationships, for good or ill, with many of the men with whom he would work at the highest level of command on the Western Front. When Gough was instructing at the Staff College, the Commandant was Henry Rawlinson, who was to command Fourth Army on the Somme in 1916. Gough's fellow instructors included Richard Haking and John du Cane, who both became Corps commanders during the First World War, and 'Tommy' Capper, whom Gough succeeded in command of 7th Division in 1915.[12] When Johnnie Gough was a student, another instructor was Launcelot Kiggell, later Haig's chief of staff at GHQ. In later life Gough was to describe Kiggell, not without reason, as a weak and indecisive man.[13]

In 1914 the Curragh Incident divided the army. Many officers, with those of 3rd Cavalry Brigade, based at the Curragh Camp near Dublin, in the vanguard, threatened to send in their papers rather than face the possibility of being used to coerce Protestants into accepting Home Rule for Ireland. The Gough brothers were prominent among the protesters. 'Wully' Robertson, a future Chief of the Imperial General Staff (CIGS), gave support of a less strident nature.[14] A number of officers were on the other side, including Field Marshal Sir John French, and Major Philip Howell of 4th Hussars, who we will meet later in these pages. French was subsequently denounced by Gough, who was glad when French was sacked as Commander-in-Chief (C-in-C) British Expeditionary Force (BEF) at the end of 1915, as 'an ignorant little fool'.[15]

Perhaps the most significant breach in the Gough brothers' personal relationships over the Curragh was with Henry Wilson. Their former friend played an 'equivocal' role in the affair.[16] In October 1916 Wilson, as commander of IV Corps, came under the orders of Gough's Reserve Army. Gough, no doubt with some relish, 'haul[ed] him over the coals' because Wilson's 'show had been so badly organised'. In later life Hubert Gough blamed 'his own ill-repute' and his scapegoating for the Third Battle of Ypres on 'stories spread by Henry Wilson'.[17] Gough's resentment against Wilson did not diminish with time. He devoted a chapter of his memoirs to denouncing Wilson, and as late as 1963, shortly before his death, Gough lambasted Wilson in a television interview: 'Had him under my command once. Out-and-out crook. Never did a stroke of work. Sat in his office writing to his lady friends in high places.'[18] But in comparison to Henry Wilson, one of the most 'political' soldiers that the British Army has ever produced, Hubert Gough's skills as a political in-fighter were limited. In March 1918, by which time he had leap-frogged Gough to become CIGS, Wilson had his revenge.

Three future Army commanders, Gough, Byng and Birdwood, worked together in the South African War in 1900. At this time Gough wrote in an uncomplimentary fashion about Julian Byng in his diary. This led Byng's biographer later to comment on Gough's 'prickly and suspicious nature', which made it difficult for him to become friends with his peers.[19] Certainly, the view that Gough was jealous of Byng seems to be borne out by some views expressed privately some years after the First World War. Byng's strength, Gough insisted, lay in 'appealing to colonials' (a reference to the former's successful command of the Canadian Corps in 1915–1917) but he lacked 'military ideas' and had 'no brain'.[20] As Third Army commander, Gough opined, Byng's conduct of the 1918 March Retreat was 'damned incompetent'.[21] In 1916 Byng's Canadian Corps had served under Gough's command on the Somme, and the relationship was not particularly happy.[22] Brainless or not, Byng's conduct of the attack on Vimy Ridge in April 1917 was highly successful, and his handling of operations in 1918, although not immune from criticism, was sound enough. Byng's successes led to honours, financial rewards and the governor-generalship of Canada, which in the 1920s must have been wormwood and gall to the disgraced Gough.[23]

Gough had an equivocal relationship with another cavalryman and future fellow Army commander, 'the Bull', Edmund Allenby. Gough and Allenby shared the characteristic that they frightened their subordinates; John Bourne has described them as 'demanding tyrant[s]'.[24] Gough served under Allenby before the war, and while he admired the man's character he had no great respect for his brains. Gough claimed that on the Western Front Allenby 'would apply orders rigidly without reasoning'. However, Allenby was 'very just – never bore malice against subordinates who disagreed'. At least Allenby came off better than another contemporary who achieved success as a cavalryman in the First World War, Philip Chetwode, whom Gough denounced as a 'crawler' and a 'funk'.[25] Moreover, Anglesey judges Gough's criticism of Lord Dundonald, his superior in South Africa, as 'probably unfair'.[26]

As Gough admitted, his rapid promotion at a relatively early age (an Army commander at 46; Rawlinson was seven years older) caused him problems. He bridled when Kitchener made what Gough (at the time a Corps commander) perceived as a sneering reference to his youth.[27] One is tempted to apply a little amateur psychology and see Gough's bullying managerial style as an attempt to compensate for his lack of years when dealing with subordinates who were his contemporaries or who were older. In fairness, one should mention that a junior officer recorded that on the Western Front he met Gough while out riding and they 'talked very civilly, which I appreciated'.[28] While Gough's post-war comments should be seen in the light of his disappointment and anger at being removed from command in 1918, the overall picture that emerges is not an attractive one.

Gough and Haig

Unquestionably the major figure in Gough's rise was General Sir Douglas Haig, the commander of I Army in 1915, who became C-in-C BEF in December 1915. Haig and Gough had served together as far back as the Boer War, and again at Aldershot. Haig was deeply affected by the death of Johnnie Gough, his Chief of Staff, in January 1915. Hubert to some degree replaced his brother as Haig's 'confidant and sounding-board'.[29] Clearly mutual respect was high. Haig's views of Gough's qualities are indicated by a remarkable passage in a book co-authored by Lieutenant Colonel J.H. Boraston, Haig's private secretary. Boraston's views can safely be assumed to reflect those of his chief, who gave 'tacit approval' to the project.[30] This passage amounts to a spirited defence of both Gough and Haig's championing of his subordinate. Boraston argued that Gough's 'fine record of service' in 1914–1915 made him the obvious man for the job of commander of Reserve Army. Gough's performance on the Somme 'amply justified the selection of this young but brilliant general', and in the semi-mobile fighting of February–March 1917 Gough 'showed a mastery of tactical manoeuvre, and of the skilled use of ground and artillery in support of infantry attack, which, it is submitted with respect, would establish his right, had he no other claim, to rank among the most able of the many competent generals that the war brought into positions of high command'.[31]

Before the Somme, Reserve Army was under the control of Haig's GHQ. The details of the scheme for its employment are still fairly obscure, but in the opinion of Stephen Badsey, who has pieced together the evidence, the formation's 'training and structure clearly suggest that the embryo Reserve Army plan was for 25th Division to exploit any success by Fourth Army, closely followed by two or more of the [three available] cavalry divisions ... and then by the infantry of [three division–strong] II Corps following up'. In the event, Rawlinson's breakthrough did not occur; in any case, the Fourth Army commander subverted the whole concept.[32] Thus Gough never had the opportunity of open warfare in which Liddell Hart believed he would excel.

Gough's elevation may also have owed something to Haig's relationship with Rawlinson. Earlier, in April 1915, Haig had appointed Gough to command of a division in Rawlinson's IV Corps. In doing so, to use modern political parlance, Haig briefed Gough against Rawlinson. Haig may have seen Rawlinson as a rival.[33] Possibly Haig's appointment of Gough to take over part of Fourth Army's front on the second day of the Somme offensive owed something to his desire to use his protégé as a counterbalance to the well-connected Rawlinson.[34] In terms of age, seniority (at the beginning of the Somme Gough was a lieutenant general, Rawlinson a general) and in function Gough was the junior Army commander on the Somme. The Gough–Haig–Rawlinson triangle would repay more research.

Gough emerged from the Somme with his reputation riding high. In March 1917 Lord Bertie, the British ambassador in Paris, noted that Gough was being 'mentioned in French quarters as a possible successor to Haig'. Nivelle seems to have been the instigator of this notion.[35] Nevertheless, Rawlinson rather than Gough (or Plumer) was Haig's initial choice in January 1917 to lead the forthcoming 'big push' in the Ypres salient.[36] By July 1917 things had changed. Gough was placed in command of the main assault at the beginning of the Third Battle of Ypres. However, in late August, after disappointing results, Haig gave Plumer responsibility for the main part of the battle. Even after Gough's sideways move he retained much of Haig's confidence.

The German breakthrough on Fifth Army's front on 21 March 1918 fatally undermined Gough's credibility. Foiled in his desire to remove Haig, Lloyd George 'chose to move against Derby [the Secretary of State for War and a Haig supporter, pushed sideways to become Ambassador to France in April 1918] and Gough ... [who] became the army's sacrifice to appease the government's critics'. Passchendaele had already undermined Gough's position with the government, if not with Haig.[37] The CIGS, Henry Wilson, was not unwilling to wield the knife. On 26 March, at the Doullens inter-Allied conference, Wilson 'discussed removal of Gough, and told Haig he could have Rawly, and Rawly's old Fourth Army staff from Versailles, to replace Gough'.[38] Haig tried to retain Gough's services. He ignored the suggestion of Lord Derby, who wrote to Haig on 5 March recommending that Gough be appointed Governor of Gibraltar.[39] On 24 March, three days after the beginning of the German offensive, Bertie noted that 'the Army wanted General Gough to be "ungummed" [sent home] and that Haig saved him'. Three days after that Bertie wondered whether there would have to 'be a scapegoat for the disaster', and that 'if Haig cover [sic] Gough', whether both men would have to go.[40] Indeed, on 26 March and 3 April Haig argued with Lloyd George on Gough's behalf.[41] Ultimately, Haig realised that if Gough did not go, his own position was under threat, and Haig said privately, 'I was conceited enough to think that the army could not spare me.'[42] Haig had sympathy for Gough's plight after his dismissal but advised him not to make a fuss; Byng took a similar view.[43] This has been interpreted as Haig 'cold shoulder[ing]' Gough from selfish motives,[44] but a more generous reading is possible. Gough might have suffered an injustice, but the efficient conduct of the war at a crucial moment was more important than one man's reputation. An Army commander could be sacked without too many reper-cussions. The removal of Haig might have created more problems than it solved.

Reserve Army's Operations on the Somme

By the evening of 1 July 1916 Haig had recognised that the frontage held by Fourth Army was too big for one headquarters and commander to handle. Gough, on 2 July, took command of X and VIII Corps under Fourth Army, and on 3 July Reserve Army formally assumed command of the northern sector of the Somme battlefield.[45]

A major and valid criticism of British operations on the Somme was that they were often characterised by lack of co-ordination between formations, and that forces were used in inadequate numbers or 'penny-packets'. Too often, attacking on a narrow front allowed the Germans to concentrate their fire on a limited sector, with devastating effects. By contrast, an attack on a broad front could force the enemy to split their artillery fire, thus reducing its effect.[46] However, Gough told Birdwood (commander I Anzac Corps) in July that Reserve Army had attacked often, in modest numbers, to keep the Germans 'off balance'. 'Once we allow him to get his breath back,' said Gough, 'we shall have to make another of these gigantic assaults by which time all the German defences will have been repaired and strengthened. I think our way keeps down casualties and brings the best results.'[47] Such a view was not unreasonable in July, when it appeared that the German defences might be on the point of crumbling. They make less sense in August, when it was clear, as Haig pointed out to his Army commanders at the beginning of the month, that the Germans had 'recovered to a great extent from the dis-organisation' of early July and their positions could not be attacked 'without careful and methodical preparation'.[48]

Gough did not have a completely free hand in carrying out operations on the Somme. For most of the campaign, Reserve Army's operations were subsidiary to the main effort being undertaken by Fourth Army. Moreover, in 1916 the shell shortage was by no means over. To feed the enormous bom-bardments on Fourth Army front, there was a need to economise on other sectors. These two factors restricted Gough's freedom of manoeuvre from the outset.

In discussions on 2 July Rawlinson and Haig agreed that Gough should attack with two brigades towards the Schwaben Redoubt, where survivors of the previous day's assault were believed to be holding out. Kiggell reported that Haig wanted Gough to 'damp down his operations to the lowest limit in order to secure that result', and clearly Rawlinson was of a similar mind. Gough, however, wanted to attack an enemy salient south-east of Thiepval with two divisions (32nd and 49th). When he met Kiggell on the evening of

2 July, Gough agreed to use six battalions (i.e. less than two brigades) 'early' on the following day. Ominously, Gough 'said that he could not guarantee success with that force, but thought the prospects good enough to justify the attempt'.[49] Gough thus came up against the realities of his position, that his role was subordinate to Rawlinson's. He also showed his willingness to gamble, by committing small forces to carry out a difficult and demanding operation.

In the event the attack was a complete shambles. It was originally timed for 0315 to coincide with an attack on Ovillers, but at 2.55am Gough contacted III Corps to tell them that Reserve Army's attack had had to be postponed until 6.00am. Even this extended preparation time was hopelessly unrealistic for the two brigades of 32nd Division (14 and 75 Brigades, the latter attached from 25th Division) to prepare. Messages were delayed in reaching subordinate commanders and artillery support was grossly deficient. This was partly because batteries did not receive news of the new start time until they had already begun the preliminary bombardment for the 3.15am attack, using up precious ammunition. It was also because 32nd Division's frontage of attack was increased from 800 to 1,400 yards. The attack was thus carried out on an objective nearly twice as long as that originally envisaged with only half of the anticipated artillery ammunition available. Not all of this was Hubert Gough's fault: Haig, Rawlinson and X Corps bore a share of the blame, and the attack bore the hallmarks of the chaos that typified the beginning of the Somme campaign. But it was an inauspicious start to Gough's command on the Somme.[50]

Gough's attempt to expand the scope of operations in his sector can perhaps be seen as an attempt to flex his muscles as an Army commander. If so, it was unsuccessful, and Kiggell on behalf of GHQ laid out the parameters of future Reserve Army operations. In a 'Note' of 4 July Gough was instructed to keep in touch with units of Fourth Army, and to pin the enemy on Reserve Army's front by threatening attacks. These objectives were, however, dependent on the availability of ammunition. Reserve Army's supply of shells was finite and would not be replenished.[51]

Haig still envisaged a wider role for Gough should Fourth Army make substantial progress. On 15 July, the day after the successful dawn attack on Bazentin ridge, Third Army was informed that when Rawlinson had seized the Ginchy–Flers–Le Sars line, Reserve Army would then strike north from the Ancre valley, attacking from the south the enemy on Third Army's front.[52] Three days later, Haig's optimism had somewhat diminished and, in view of Fourth Army's difficulties in getting forward, the assault on Pozières was entrusted to Reserve Army (*see* Chapter 4).[53] This was the first time that Gough had been given anything approaching a starring role.

Haig's instructions of 2 August to Gough and Rawlinson designated the struggle on the British right flank as the main effort, along the boundary with the French. Once again, Reserve Army was assigned a subsidiary role, to make 'careful and methodical progress' in the Pozières–Mouquet Farm–Ovillers area 'with as little expenditure of fresh troops and of munitions as circumstances will admit of'.[54]

The BEF's attack of 15 September 1916 was intended by Haig to achieve a breakthrough and have decisive consequences. On 28 August Gough submitted to GHQ a fairly ambitious plan for operations on his front, including the capture of Courcelette. However, on 4 September Kiggell told Gough that Haig was opposed to large-scale operations on Reserve Army front 'for the present'. Instead, Gough was to stick with his previous methods. For the 15 September offensive, Gough was to 'secure' Fourth Army's left flank and hold the Germans on Reserve Army's front 'by the usual means', which precluded a major attack. Courcelette should not be attacked until Martinpuich – which Rawlinson did not regard as a primary objective – was attacked by Fourth Army. Kiggell went on to say that if Fourth Army did well, it would be able to threaten Thiepval from the rear. If Fourth Army did not succeed in this, there was unlikely to be a 'further decisive attack this autumn' and men and guns would 'probably' be sent to Gough to take Thiepval 'so that we can establish ourselves there for the winter'.[55] In issuing appropriate orders, Reserve Army informed Corps commanders that they 'were free to undertake any minor operations for the improvement of their positions and, whenever possible, they will dig forward towards the enemy'.[56]

In fact, Reserve Army was given a more active role in the attack of 15 September. On the afternoon of the previous day Haig intervened to order that Martinpuich was to be captured as soon as Flers fell, which would allow Gough's army 'to come into action with full effect at the earliest possible moment'. Reserve Army was to be ready to attack Courcelette on the afternoon of 15 September, and 'directly Courcelette and Martinpuich were in British hands both Armies should begin a combined advance northward'. As the Official Historian commented, Gough 'had, in effect, anticipated the eleventh-hour instructions' issued by Haig.[57] In the event, Reserve Army secured its objectives but Fourth Army's limited progress did not permit this northbound push to occur.

On 26 September Reserve Army began its biggest operation so far: the Battle of Thiepval Ridge. Fourth Army on the previous day had mounted another major and fairly successful push, and Gough used four divisions of Canadian and II Corps on an attack frontage of 6,000 yards, from Courcelette to the Schwaben Redoubt. Haig hoped that following successful operations by Gough, Third Army should attack at Gommecourt to protect Reserve Army's left. In the event, although Thiepval, an objective of the 1 July assault, was taken on 27 September, the offensive became bogged down, with fighting continuing well into November. The British Official History's comments on the situation at the end of September are, for all their measured tone, damning of the higher command of Reserve Army:

> The attack was not conducted as an operation of semi-siege warfare, so all depended upon infantry *elan* allied with the usual destructive bombardment and creeping barrage; yet on the slopes of the ridge in the confused fighting along trenches and around shell-craters and dug-outs, it was often impossible for the artillery to provide close support to the assaulting troops. In the later attacks, a greater degree of co-ordination along the whole front might have increased the prospects of success.[58]

Although attacking on a larger scale, Reserve Army soon reverted to penny-packeted, narrow front attacks. On 28 September Gough ordered that Stuff and Schwaben Redoubts were to be taken by the following day. Yet on 29 September very small numbers of troops were used. 3rd Canadian Division used only one battalion, which co-operated with three companies of a battalion of 11th Division to capture Hessian Trench. 18th Division, probably wisely, cancelled a proposed attack by an exhausted battalion, 7/Queen's, while another battalion became involved in a fierce bombing fight. This was the sum of Reserve Army units in action that day. Stuff Redoubt was not captured in its entirety until 9 October, and the Schwaben on the 14th.[59]

Haig entrusted Gough with the BEF's last major attack on the Somme.[60] Gough's offensive was launched on either side of the River Ancre on 13 November. This area had not been heavily fought over since 1 July, with the result that the terrain, although sodden and muddy, had not been as heavily shelled as that in the southern part of the battlefield. Thus supplies could be brought forward over relatively short distances on roads superior to those in Fourth Army's sector. Gough's plan was essentially limited, with the assaulting troops given realistic objectives. He was able to field a respectable concentration of artillery, including 282 heavy guns, and a moderately complex creeping barrage was designed to support the infantry. The staff work, planning and preparation for the attack was of a generally high standard, and the assaulting troops were able to draw upon the hard-won tactical lessons of the previous five months of fighting. There were failures, but the battle, fought in two phases, was a modest success, the villages of Beaumont-Hamel and Beaucourt being the most notable gains. Gough had forced the Germans out of some strong defences, and gained good positions for launching subsequent operations. As Haig went to the inter-Allied conference in Chantilly with a victory under his belt, he might have reflected that Gough had amply repaid his confidence.

Gough's Command Style

However, the C-in-C's high opinion of Gough and Fifth Army was not widely shared in the rest of the BEF.[61] Gough's biographer placed much of the blame for the unpopularity of Fifth Army on its chief of staff, Major General Neill Malcolm. According to Farrar-Hockley, while Gough went round jollying his commanders along, Malcolm 'exceed[ed] his powers' by verbally beating them up, and some thought that this was a variation on the 'nice policeman, nasty policeman' routine beloved of interrogators. More-over, Farrar-Hockley argues that these problems mostly occurred in 1917, after Beddington had left Reserve Army staff.[62] Beddington had acted as a buffer state, for instance in relations with the BGGS of V Corps, who always rang Beddington rather than Gough or Malcolm.[63]

This gives only a part of the true picture. Certainly Malcolm was disliked; by October 1917 Haig had got to hear of Malcolm's unpopularity.[64] In the following month Major General G.S. Clive discussed the 'unpopularity of the Fifth Army command' with Malcolm. Clive noted that Malcolm 'is only beginning to hear of it, although it has been common talk for perhaps three months'. Malcolm claimed that '"doubtful" officers' were dispatched to Fifth Army in the belief that Gough would sack them if they were not up to their job.[65] Beddington, if his memoir is to be believed, in December of that year told Malcolm to his face of his unpopularity, although Malcolm does not mention it in his diary.[66] After the war Gough – no doubt eager to shift the blame – privately admitted the truth of some of the complaints, saying that although Malcolm had a 'good brain, he had not been an ideal chief of staff[;] too impatient with those who are slow, and showed it'. He also admitted that he had been wrong in having Malcolm accompany him on trips to corps and divisions, because this stopped his subordinates from frankly discussing their problems with Malcolm, a view he also aired publicly in *The Fifth Army*.[67]

But as Michael Howard commented in his review of Farrar-Hockley's biography, there was more to Fifth Army's 'malaise' than just that.[68] There is a considerable body of evidence of problems in Gough's command during the Somme.

Command in the BEF can be characterised as an only partially successful version of what today would be described as *Auftragstaktik* or 'mission command'. In principle, this means higher commanders setting objectives but then giving their subordinates the latitude to work out the best methods of achieving those objectives. On some occasions on the Western Front this 'hands off' approach was ineffective because of a combination of insufficiently trained subordinate commanders, the British Army's lack of a culture of *Auftragstaktik*, and the inclination of higher commanders to interfere in operations. There is certainly some truth in this picture, although it can be over-drawn. In Gough's case things were rather different. He was a prac-titioner of the opposite of prescriptive, 'top-down' command. His 'hands-on' approach is reflected by Reserve Army's dealings with Corps.

In 1916 the Corps level of command had several main roles. Thanks to its static position in the line, it could perform an administrative function, it controlled artillery, and it planned operations. During the Battle of the Somme Rawlinson's Fourth Army devolved much power and responsibility to Corps in allowing them to conduct battles. By contrast, Gough used a highly prescriptive approach, using Corps as little more than 'postboxes' – that is, as methods of passing down to divisions detailed orders drawn up by Army, orders that were far more detailed than those issued by Rawlinson's Fourth Army.[69]

Farrar-Hockley argued that Gough liked to miss out the Corps level of command.[70] Michael Howard suggested that Gough was quite simply over-promoted, and he certainly seems to have been happiest while commanding, some times by remote control, low-level formations.[71] Gough's almost personal control of 32nd Division during the Ancre fighting is a case in point.[72]

During the fighting on the Ancre in October-November 1916, Gough issued a memorandum 'written by the Army Commander for the guidance of Divisional and Infantry Brigade Commanders'.[73] Gough, in effect, went over the heads of his corps commanders and told his subordinates at divisional and brigade level how to do their jobs. Gough's 'hands-on' approach was an attempt to master the dilemma well expressed by Malcolm two days before the opening of the Somme battle. Malcolm identified the problems inherent in issuing orders that would cover all eventualities in the complex operations ahead. Subordinate commanders needed to be allowed to exercise initiative, but Army had to be able to direct operations. Unfortunately, events were to prove that Malcolm's view that Reserve Army had struck the right balance was inaccurate, as this formation's style of command and control caused a good deal of friction between Gough and his subordinates.[74]

Clearly, Gough believed that an Army commander was more than a mere co-ordinator of the activities of subordinate formations: he should actually command. On 6 July, writing of the preparations for the battle for Ovillers, Malcolm noted that at Corps level there was a propensity to regard Gough's interventions as meddling. Gough firmly believed that his job was to command, and Malcolm had no doubt that the Army commander would win the battle of wills.[75] However, if his post-war comments are to be believed, Gough believed in a collegiate style of command. In 1936 he commented that GHQ 'left [Army Commanders] alone and rarely came to see them. It should have treated the Army Commanders as a battalion commander treats his four company commanders, conferring with them regularly, and thrashing out questions in discussion.'[76] Not only is the accuracy of this observation dubious – Haig did visit his Army commanders regularly[77] – but Gough's wartime behaviour suggests he did not really practise what he preached. In August 1916 Malcolm again noted that commanders serving under Reserve Army chafed at Gough's hands-on style of command.[78]

Gough believed that commanders should grip their formations. Unfortunately, his over-enthusiastic espousal of this practice at Army level made it difficult for his subordinates to command troops in the field. Sir Aylmer Hunter-Weston, commander of VIII Corps, although initially admiring of Gough, was glad to leave Reserve Army after a month of being under its command. In a letter to his wife he hinted that he disliked Gough's micromanagement, and in a conversation with Philip Howell he criticised Gough's 'impetuosity' and 'optimism'.[79] Gough was a hard taskmaster. Demands directed to subordinate commanders for 'An explanation in writing' why something did or not happen was part of his arsenal.[80]

Resentment at Gough's methods was clearly widespread. It led to a clash with Lord Cavan, XIV Corps commander, over Reserve Army's interference with a planned operation at Beaumont Hamel.[81] An argument between Gough and the commander of 48th Division, Major General R. Fanshawe, brought the latter to the verge of resignation.[82]

One of the most serious clashes was with Brigadier General Philip Howell, chief of staff in Lieutenant General Claud Jacob's II Corps. This formation replaced Morland's X Corps in the line in late July 1916. Gough had a low opinion of Morland, who had not performed particularly well on 1 July or, in Gough's view, subsequently.[83] Jacob, by contrast, was a capable commander whom Gough later described as 'the soundest soldier in the British Army'.[84] Malcolm recorded on 28 August 1916 that II Corps did not understand orders had to be obeyed. He principally blamed Howell for the notion that the planning of operations was a dialectical process involving Army and Corps, with discussion of options and perhaps even the eventual rejection of Army plans. Malcolm recognised that, given that Gough's views were diametrically opposed to Howell's, a clash was inevitable.[85] Indeed, in a private letter of 23 September 1916 Gough called Howell 'a great thorn' who 'always tries to argue, he produces the most complicated schemes, he always wants to avoid fighting, & he never loyally carries out his orders'.[86]

Howell was not an impartial witness. Apart from being on opposite sides of the Curragh controversy, Howell was an intellectual, something of a Bohemian, and a political radical, while Gough was politically conservative.[87] Both men, however, enjoyed the trust of Douglas Haig. Howell conceded that Gough was 'very loveable in many ways', but at one stage he professed to doubt Gough's sanity.[88] On joining Reserve Army, Howell expressed an 'instinctive feeling of mistrust' for Malcolm as an Army chief of staff, and his feelings hardened over the coming weeks.[89] A letter written by Howell in August offers some support for Farrar-Hockley's views on Fifth Army's malaise: '[Gough is] really quite a child & can be managed like one if treated as such & humoured. M is at the bottom of half the mischievous ideas & mischief making ...'.[90] Even allowing for his obvious biases, Howell was an astute observer, and his diary and letters give a clear picture of the problems involved with Gough's 'hands-on' style of command, as seen from Corps level.

On taking over from X Corps in July, Howell was told by the outgoing staff that 'relations with Reserve Army very strained: much interference with details & questions [&] criticism'. Certainly, 'All seem rather fed up with undue interference in details from above'. This was partly a turf fight. Gough had centralised Reserve Army artillery under Brigadier General Tancred, a move which removed control of an important function from Corps level, which seems to have been especially resented by the gunners of X Corps.[91] Very early in II Corps' tour in the front line, on 25 July, Gough arrived at II Corps headquarters 'to direct our minor enterprises'.[92]

Clearly, as time went on Howell became less and less tolerant of Reserve Army's methods of command. On 11 August Howell noted that he had drafted a plan 'in the full knowledge that Army will interfere in all the execution details'. Sure enough, later 'Army upset the barrage arrangements'. Howell recorded that in an attack by 12th Division on 2 August Reserve Army took 'direct control of 4 machine guns!'. Malcolm and Gough certainly spent the day with Major General Scott, the commander of 12th Division, and Malcolm's diary entry suggests that they had been prodding him to take action.[93] On this occasion Howell had a disagreement with Malcolm. When Malcolm suggested 'that all previous failures [were] due to inadequate control [being] exercised by [Gough]', Howell retorted that it was 'still more due to army commander jumping to conclusions & overruling the man on the spot'.[94] Here, in a nutshell, is the clash between two different philosophies: Reserve Army's prescriptive, top-down command, versus II Corps' devolved, decentralised version.

At almost the very end of the Somme campaign Malcolm issued an extra-ordinary confidential document to Corps. Gough had noticed, it began, that

> in certain Corps there is a marked tendency to disregard, or to dispute the advisability of, order [sic] issued from Army Headquarters, and to consult their own convenience rather than the good of the Army as a whole. [Orders were] not issued without due consideration of their effect and constant objection to their execution adds greatly to the burden of command.

Gough recognised that a 'spirit of discipline and loyal co-operation' should not 'hamper legitimate initiative', for 'Every commander is glad to listen to useful suggestions for the common good'. Indeed, sometimes it was right for subordinates to tell commanders that orders could not be carried out, but 'The justification or condemnation of such objections lies entirely in the spirit in which they are made'.[95]

This memorandum might seem to be aimed directly at Howell, but he had been killed by shellfire in September. It perhaps reflects the fact that around this time Malcolm came to realise that Gough had created a culture in which his subordinates were unwilling to say what they really thought. Afraid of the consequences, they carried out orders even if they disagreed with them. While not blind to the drawbacks of Gough's command style, Malcolm was convinced that often the Army commander did indeed know best.[96]

Thus it seems that Gough recognised, at least in theory, the importance of low-level initiative – although it is interesting that Malcolm's memorandum is couched almost entirely in negative terms, referring to objections to Reserve Army orders. However, Gough interpreted such objections as personal criticism. Gough's prickly personality and his bullying nature, combined with his prescriptive style of command and the strong personalities of some of his subordinates, inevitably led to friction.

Hubert Gough's style of command was certainly different from that of his fellow Army commander Henry Rawlinson, and was clearly disliked by a number of his subordinates. What, if any, difference did it make to the success of operations?

In the case of 2nd Australian Division's first attack at Pozières on 29 July, Gough's 'direct control of operations' seems to have led to disaster.[97] This division relieved 1st Australian Division after the latter's assault had captured most of the village. Although there were tactical reasons for 2nd Australian Division's failure, there is little doubt that Gough pressurised Major General J.G. Legge, the divisional commander, into attacking before preparations were fully complete.[98] Bean blamed Legge, not entirely fairly, for buckling under to Gough's demands, and said that Brudenell White blamed himself for not standing up to Gough. In later years White wrote of Gough's 'impulsiveness and hastiness'.[99] The truth is that Legge should have had greater support from his superiors at Corps levels. It was not a fair competition to pit a divisional commander (especially a 'colonial' from outside the charmed circle of the British Regular army) against an Army commander. A comment of Bean's seems entirely apt in the context of Pozières: Gough's 'impetuosity is hard to stem and leads him to press schemes of his own upon subordinate units'.[100]

Can Bean's comment be related more generally to Gough's conduct of operations? At Blood River Gough's tendencies towards impetuosity and attacking without adequate preparation were demonstrated for the first time. This was a pattern that was to recur throughout his career. On learning of the German retirement in February 1917, Gough happened to be visiting 91 Brigade HQ. He ordered an immediate pursuit, but the brigade commander, H.R. Cumming, pointed out that 'such a move was impossible before daylight on account of the nature of the ground' and the exhaustion of the troops. After a little argument, Cumming got his way, but, as he recalled, Gough's departure 'with many injunctions to press on as early and as fast as possible' allowed the brigade staff to get on with the 'thousand and one details essential to the morrow's operations'. It seems that Gough overlooked the importance of detailed planning.[101]

An episode in April 1917, when Gough ordered, over the protests of Anzac commanders, a hasty, ill-prepared and ultimately disastrous attack at Bullecourt, must also be entered on the debit side of the ledger.[102] Later in 1917 Gough was responsible for the early stages of the Third Battle of Ypres (or 'Passchendaele') and his handling of these operations has been criticised along similar lines.[103] Yet the Battle of the Ancre would suggest that Gough *was* capable of conducting a carefully prepared setpiece attack. It is perhaps of relevance that this offensive was delayed by poor weather, creating time for preparations to be completed. Bonham-Carter's comments on Gough, cited above, appear apposite in this connection. Perhaps if Gough had been served by a chief of staff with a different temperament, one who was prepared to rein in his boss's enthusiasm, Gough might have emerged as a more rounded and successful commander. Haig also deserves criticism for not exercising greater 'grip' over his subordinate.

Gough as a Tactician

In early October 1916 Reserve Army issued over the signature of Neill Malcolm a 'memorandum of attacks ... written by the Army for the guidance of Divisional and Infantry Brigade Commanders'.[104] This document repays study, as it sheds much light on Gough's views on tactics, and also, indirectly, on his performance as an Army commander. As early as the spring of 1915 some British commanders were beginning to experiment with the idea of bite-and-hold operations. This involved carrying out fairly limited attacks with strong artillery support, aimed at seizing a portion of the enemy line, the idea being to smash up enemy counter-attacks with artillery and machine guns, before repeating the process. A leading exponent of this broadly attritional method was Henry Rawlinson, commander of Fourth Army, operating on Reserve Army's flank. Rawlinson's forces achieved a number of successes using this process, including the seizure of Bazentin Ridge on 14 July and Delville Wood on 27 July. As John Lee has noted, however, Hubert Gough was in the opposite camp, 'fear[ing] that opportunities for exploitation would be lost if every unit was obliged to stop at a pre-determined line, dictated by the artillery plan'.[105]

As Gough's October 1916 memorandum made clear, he favoured substantial advances into enemy positions rather than a more limited approach, envisaging troops attacking up to five separate consecutive objectives. Recognising that considerable depth of attacking troops was 'often' desirable, he recommended that brigades attack with two battalions 'up' and two in the second line, making a total of eight waves, perhaps with the last four waves in 'small columns' for speed of movement. Gough advocated a sort of conveyor-belt approach, in which successive waves were dispatched under a set of standard operating procedures (SOPs), each wave having been '*previously* and *definitely* detailed to their objectives', along with timetables for the advance and artillery barrages. He argued that some attacks had failed because brigade and battalion commanders had held troops back as a general reserve, waiting for firm information about where and when to commit them, and thus opportunities had not been exploited.[106]

Much of this tactical advice is sensible. Gough was fully apprised of the importance of the infantry following the artillery barrage,[107] and of 'mopping-up' parties behind the assault waves. Gough's thoughts on command were an intelligent attempt to cope with a major challenge. In stressing the need for precise timetables, Gough took some of the elements of the bite-and-hold approach. Yet his insistence on the need to keep pushing on was the antithesis of bite-and-hold. Gough envisaged divisions attacking with two brigades in the front line and the third in reserve. Two battalions would take the first objective, the other two would 'follow as closely as possible, pass through, and take the second objective'. When this had been achieved, the brigadiers should 'reorganise their battalions on the first objective ... detailing only sufficient men to consolidate and hold the position (this should not require very much)'. The third objective was to be assaulted by the third brigade; he judged that to wait until the troops of the first two brigades had reorganised would be to waste time. However, such troops would be available to attack the fourth objective, although fresh troops would be needed for an attack on a fifth. As Gough accurately observed, 'The art and difficulty of command lies in maintaining communications, knowing the position of your troops and their tactical situation, and thus being in a position to control them and to form a sound plan based on the actual facts.'[108]

As well as the adoption of SOPs, Gough believed that a partial solution to the problem lay in getting brigade and divisional commanders forward when their troops advanced. He stressed the importance of 'moving forward with their wires' – that is, maintaining telephone contact with superiors and subordinates – although he appears to have believed that it was best for commanders to be forward even if their electronic communications failed. At the centre of Gough's tactical memorandum was the idea of exploitation of apparent opportunities to advance. In discussing command procedures, Gough made a revealing comment: 'When cut off from advanced troops, it is no use sending officers to reconnoitre and report before coming to a decision. Valuable time is lost, and by hesitation the decision is left to the enemy. Only the immediate energetic employment' ... [of troops] in large force [could rectify the situation].'[109]

It is easy to be critical of such a comment, which seems to underline Gough's reputation for impetuosity and hasty attacks. Yet it is undoubtedly true that fleeting opportunities did go begging because of a commander's hesitation – after the capture of Bazentin Ridge on 14 July 1916, for instance. However, it is difficult to avoid the conclusion that, given the state of training and experience of both infantry and artillery in 1916, Gough was asking too much of his men. He implicitly underplayed the importance of artillery, relying instead on infantry. But as successful operations on the Somme, at Arras and at Third Ypres were to demonstrate, under the trench warfare conditions of 1915–1917 effective use of artillery was the key to success on the battlefield.

Gough's principles of attack were over-ambitious. Even successful attacks left assaulting formations weakened; quite apart from casualties sustained, men had to be used to consolidate positions, mop up pockets of resistance and the like. Those who were theoretically available to renew the assault would have been tired. Gough's assumption that sufficient troops could be organised from the two assaulting brigades to attack a fourth objective seems over-optimistic. It paid too little attention to the realities of Clausewitzian friction on the battlefield. The important tactical manual SS144, 'The Normal Formation for the Attack', promulgated in February 1917, incorporated the experience of the Somme. As Lee comments, SS144 is a compromise that reflects both a modified version of Gough's way of thinking and the opposite, which asserted that each wave should take and consolidate only one objective, with other units leap-frogging through the wave in front to advance on the next objective. The events of 31 July 1917 cast doubt on the wisdom of Gough's approach. On this, the opening day of the Third Battle of Ypres, units of Gough's Fifth Army, having obtained 'early success', took advantage of their liberty to 'push ahead' – with, as Lee comments, 'less than happy results'.[110] It is worth noting that by this time the lessons of the Somme had been absorbed, codified and disseminated; artillery and infantry tactics were considerably more advanced than a year earlier; and troops were more experienced and better trained.

Case Study: The Ancre, November 1916

The Battle of the Ancre in November 1916 was perhaps Gough's finest hour as an offensive general. It resulted in the capture of Beaumont Hamel and Beaucourt, and ensured that the Somme offensive ended with a victory, albeit a limited one that took ground that was supposed to have fallen on 1 July. Haig and GHQ took a particularly close interest in this attack for several reasons. Whereas Fourth Army's operations had generally taken precedence earlier in the battle, on this occasion Gough's attack was the BEF's 'main effort'. The offensive had wider ramifications in a European context, to pin down German troops that might otherwise have been sent to the campaign in Rumania, to influence Russian opinion on the efforts of their Anglo-French Entente partners, and to demonstrate to the Germans that the BEF had every intention of continuing to bring pressure on the Somme front. Even more importantly, it represented the last chance for the BEF to achieve a substantial success before Haig went to the inter-Allied conference at Chantilly, and Gough's success strengthened Haig's hand. Moreover, as Gough later noted, by November 1916 the first 'murmurs' against Haig were beginning to be heard. Indeed, Gough himself was later to be mentioned as a possible successor to Haig, although on hearing this rumour Brigadier General Home of the Cavalry Corps remarked in his diary that it was 'too comic as I don't think they could ever make him do what they wanted'.[111] It is small wonder that Haig wrote in his diary at the end of the first day of the battle, 'The success has come at a most opportune moment'.[112]

Fifth Army's success was due to a number of factors. Throughout the battle Army and Corps had been drawing and disseminating lessons,[113] and many were applied on the Ancre.[114] An attack in this sector had several logistic advantages, the planning and staff work were generally sound and the assaulting divisions were supported by a respectable weight of artillery, far superior to that employed on 1 July. The operation also benefited from being planned and prepared over a period of weeks, rather than being a hasty attack. The original, ambitious plans devised by GHQ in October had to be reduced in scope as a consequence of poor weather, which turned the battlefield to a muddy morass. The assault had to be postponed on several occasions and the weather was so bad that the entire enterprise remained in doubt almost to the last minute. Haig on 2 November told Gough 'To have patience, and not to launch the main attack until the weather was better and the ground dry. It was better to wait than to start a series of small operations which would not have the same decisive results ...'.[115] On 6 November Haig repeated his instruction that the attack should not begin until the ground was sufficiently dry 'for the infantry to advance freely', and when there was the likelihood of two days of 'fair weather'.[116]

There were frequent contacts between GHQ and HQ Fifth Army, and between Gough and his Corps commanders, in the preparatory period. Haig dispatched Kiggell, his Chief of Staff, to Fifth Army HQ on 8 November to explain the political background of the attack, although, as a memorandum by Malcolm stressed, Haig did not 'desire to press Sir H. GOUGH into an action where the prospect of success was not sufficiently good to justify the risk'. Gough then consulted with his Corps commanders, Jacob (II), Edward Fanshawe (V) and Congreve (XIII) on 10 November, and the attack was settled for the 13th 'unless there was more heavy rain'. According to Malcolm, at the meeting, held at 10am at Senlis, Fanshawe and Congreve argued to extend the range of the attack, pushing for deeper objectives. 'General JACOB, whose task was lighter, was ready to conform with either decision.' The final decision was to go for deeper objectives.[117]

Still, the question of the state of the ground and the weather placed a question-mark over the attack. 'Staff officers and patrols' went out every day to check on the ground, and it is clear that there was no consensus among senior commanders. However, Gough decided, on the morning of 11 November, to attack on 13 November as planned. He then consulted several divisional and brigade commanders, to find that there was '[s]till some difference of opinion', however 'the ground [was] undoubtedly improving fast'. That afternoon, Fanshawe of V Corps visited Army HQ and the time of the attack was debated; the question was whether a night or dawn attack was preferable, given the 'state of the moon'. Eventually, after further consultation with Jacob and the divisional commanders, the decision was made to attack at 5.45am.[118]

On 12 November, the day before the attack, Kiggell was sent by Haig to ascertain Gough's opinion of the prospects for success. Gough weighed up the impact on the morale of the troops of a further delay, and concluded that

> the time had come when we must either attack on Monday or make up our minds to withdraw and rest the bulk of the troops. Further postponement would have a very bad effect, and should not be considered. There had been no rain for four days – although there has been heavy fog – and similar conditions are likely to maintain throughout tomorrow. We can hardly hope for anything more favourable during the winter months.[119]

Two decades later Gough recalled the loneliness of the commander having to make a weighty decision:

> It seemed to me that the responsibility placed on my shoulders was a very heavy one. I can remember our sitting at a small deal table in my poorly furnished room that I used as a bed-sitting room . . . in a farm[,] . . . and as Kiggell gravely elaborated the great issues at stake, and my mind turned over the tactical situation of my troops and that of the enemy, I gazed out of the poky little window looking on the dull and dirty courtyard, and considered what my decision should be.[120]

He eventually consulted with subordinate commanders before reporting to Haig. The C-in-C visited Gough's HQ at 4pm that afternoon, and ordered the attack to go ahead on 13 November, if weather conditions remained favourable.

It is interesting that, in spite of the political capital riding on a successful attack, Haig was insistent that it should not go ahead unless it was likely to be successful, and he paid close attention to the preparations. It was by no means certain that the battle would be launched until Haig took the decision on the afternoon of 12 November. It is probable that Haig regarded a failed battle as worse than no battle at all; that while a successful attack would strengthen his hand at the forthcoming conference, another failure would weaken it. This interpretation differs from Robin Prior and Trevor Wilson's recent argument that Gough read between the lines of Haig's instructions that the C-in-C was so desperate for a success – any success – in reality he had no alternative to attack unless the weather made it absolutely impossible.[121] While Haig was undoubtedly an optimist, he also had a strong streak of pragmatism in his make-up. While the capture of Beaumont Hamel – a 1 July objective – was 'nice to have', it was essential to avoid a highly visible failure. Moreover, since at least mid-October Haig had been aware (from Major General F.I. Maxse, who had heard from his brother Leo, editor of the *National Review*) that there was a plot, centred around F.E. Smith, the Attorney General, to sack him from his post.[122] Significantly, in his diary for 12 November, while Haig noted 'I am ready to run reasonable risks', he also stated 'the necessity for a success must not blind our eyes to the difficulties of ground and weather. Nothing is as costly as failure!'[123]

This episode also throws some interesting light on command relations. Haig's relationship with Gough seems to have been rather closer than his dealings with the other Army commander on the Somme, Rawlinson. However, the degree of supervision of the preparations for this attack suggests that Haig was not blind to his protégé's faults. As for Gough's relations with commanders further down the chain of command, in the words of the Official Historian he 'consulted his subordinate commanders freely'.[124] The extent to which corps, divisional and brigade commanders actually felt able to speak their minds is, of course, another matter. Simon Robbins, citing the evidence of post-war letters by G.D. Jeffreys (commander of 57 Brigade, 19th Division, II Corps) and G.M. Lindsay (Brigade Major, 99 Brigade, 2nd Division, V Corps) to Edmonds, argues that Gough launched the battle over 'the protests of various Corps and divisional commanders and staff who pointed out the appalling conditions and the exhaustion and disorganisation of his troops'. Haig decided in favour of the attack because Gough was 'so keen and confident'.[125]

Gough was only partially satisfied with the results of the attack. A good deal of ground was taken in some sectors, Beaucourt and Beaumont Hamel falling to the 63rd (Royal Naval) and 51st (Highland) Divisions respectively. Beddington took an officer of the 63rd Division to dinner with Gough, who listened to his account and paid the division a handsome compliment.[126] However, at Serre in the north there was little success. As befitted a 'hands-on' interventionist commander, on hearing of problems in this sector at 2pm on 13 November, Gough intervened, going 'at once' to V Corps to order fresh attacks to support 31st Division in the Serre area. By early evening Gough had decided, in the light of further evidence, to switch V Corps' effort to seize 'the Yellow Line from Beaucourt to the ridge North of Beaumont Hamel'.[127] Encouraged on the morning of the following day by optimistic reports from Fanshawe at V Corps, Gough approved a scheme to take Munich and Frankfort Trenches as a preliminary to attacking Serre.[128] This initiated a vicious localised struggle.

As Peter Simkins has commented, all too often on the Somme 'the set-piece phase' of an assault resulted in culmination, and 'subsequent attacks became piecemeal, hastily-organised affairs which lacked both weight and co-ordination'.[129] This was certainly true of V Corps' operations on the Ancre after 13 November. While there were compelling tactical reasons to seize the remainder of the high ground on V Corps' front after the partial success of the first day of the attack, this was always going to be an operation fraught with difficulties. The very factors that had led to much success on 13 November – careful preparation and a heavy artillery bombardment – were largely absent in the succeeding days. In Paris on 14 November Haig was informed of Gough's far-reaching plans and was far from happy, telephoning GHQ 'to the effect that the Commander-in-Chief did not wish the Fifth Army to undertake any further operations on a large scale until after his return from PARIS'. Haig was, no doubt, worried that a setback would negate, or at least reduce the impact of, the success of 13 November. Gough did not hear of Haig's views until 9am on 15 November, at the exact time that two divisions of V Corps (2nd and 51st) were crossing the start line. Again Gough conferred with his corps commanders and obtained consensus that the attack should go ahead. Following consultation with Kiggell, Haig that afternoon retrospectively approved the offensive. At 9am on 16 November Gough again met Jacob and Fanshawe. His optimism had declined, and a more limited assault was substituted for the ambitious plan to capture ground as a staging post for an attack on Serre.[130]

The post-13 November operations of Fifth Army indicate that Gough repeated many elements of his earlier command style. He was optimistic and aggressive, to the extent that even Haig became concerned about the ambition of Fifth Army operations. However, Haig remained generally indulgent of his protégé. Fifth Army's attacks bore a distinct resemblance to the narrow-front, penny-pocketed attacks around Pozières and elsewhere in the summer, with the added complication of appalling weather. Moreover, there is clear evidence of Gough's use of what the modern British forces call a 'long screwdriver' to interfere with the actions of subordinate formations.

Gough's frequent intervention in the command of 32nd Division in the fighting for Frankfort Trench from 18 November onwards has been noted by several historians.[131] According to Lieutenant Colonel E.G. Wace, the division's GSO1, Gough's decisions on even minor matters were relayed to Major General W.H. Rycroft, the divisional commander, 'who was terrified of Gough', via Corps. Gough complained to Haig about Rycroft. It seems that the C-in-C also had little time for him, and had already earmarked a successor, and Rycroft was sacked.[132] It should be noted that Wace was also removed shortly after the battle, which probably coloured his views passed on to Edmonds in the 1930s, but clearly there is a good deal of substance to his charges.

Less familiar is Gough's treatment of the commander of V Corps, Lieutenant General E.A. Fanshawe. Fifth Army on 16 November demanded a report from V Corps on recent operations, which was forwarded on 21 November.[133] Some of Gough's comments on Fanshawe's report, issued over Malcolm's signature, fairly scorch the page:

> V Corps Order G.267 of 15th November. This order puts too much on to the divisional commanders and does not exercise sufficient control over the operation. The want of strict Corps control is evident in several respects, e.g.
>
> No mention is made of the capture of MUNICH TRENCH ...
>
> The orders to the artillery are not clear. It appears from divisional orders that the barrage was to be on MUNICH TRENCH until Zero +6', when the infantry was to take the trench. No mention of this is made in Corps orders. Were there no Corps Artillery orders beyond those in the telegram G.267?

In the copy in V Corps War Diary, there are some marginal notes, presumably by Fanshawe. Against these criticisms he noted, in obvious frustration:

> They do not understand that I am at the end of a telephone in touch with both Divisions and Brigade, who arranged for the MUNICH TRENCH in combination with me, but my order went in before. To arrange the time of [artillery] lift ie zero +6 off MUNICH TRENCH took a long time, but was not put in the order.

To the question of whether further artillery orders were issued by V Corps, Fanshawe scribbled 'No. None were considered necessary. The CRAs worked together.'[134] There is much more of this sort of thing, of Gough posing questions that Fanshawe was compelled to answer. Some of Gough's points are fair, if harshly expressed, but others are not; some were based on factual inaccuracies. All this suggests a commander who had an incomplete grasp of the realities of the battle. They also offer supporting evidence for the idea that Gough developed a climate of fear among his subordinates, perhaps even employing a policy of divide and rule. This is the obvious interpretation of Gough's deliberate humiliation of Fanshawe in front of the latter's subordinates, an event that could only have undermined the Corps commander's authority. Against the information that copies of Gough's remarks had been sent to Fanshawe's subordinates, the commanders of 2nd and 51st Divisions, the V Corps commander scrawled a heart-felt 'I hope not all of them'. Unlike Rycroft, however, Fanshawe retained his post.

The fighting on the Ancre witnessed a clash of command philosophies: Gough desired to exercise direct control over subordinate formations, while they preferred to be given greater latitude to plan and execute operations. On 16 November, when the battle was still in progress, Gough's frustration was displayed in the 'confidential memorandum' issued by Malcolm to the Corps (see above) that attacked criticism of Fifth Army's orders.[135] This hints at the extent to which relationships had broken down between Corps and Army.

Conclusion

Gough's finest moment might have come in the Hundred Days campaign of 1918, when the BEF took the offensive under conditions of open warfare. By then, however, Gough had been removed from his command, although, as many historians acknowledge, he had demonstrated a good deal of skill in his conduct of the March retreat. Gough's military vices outweighed his virtues. Whatever his talents for mobile warfare, he was not the right man to command an Army during the Battle of the Somme. Douglas Haig's choice of subordinates was by no means as bad as some would claim. However, in the case of Hubert Gough Haig promoted and sustained a man beyond his level of competence.

Further Reading

Farrar-Hockley's biography of Gough is extremely dated, and we badly need a replacement. Gough's great rival Henry Wilson has fared much better: see Keith Jeffrey, *Henry Wilson: A Political Soldier* (Oxford: Oxford University Press, 2006), which also provides important contextual material on Gough's Irish background. William Philpott, *Bloody Victory: The Sacrifice on the Somme and the making of the Twentieth Century* (London: Little, Brown, 2009) contains some useful, if brief, material on Gough.

Acknowledgements
Material in the Clive, Howell and Liddell Hart Papers appears by kind permission of the Trustees of the Liddell Hart Centre for Military Archives.

Notes
1. Sir Hubert Gough, *The Fifth Army* (London: Hodder & Stoughton, 1931), p. 133.
2. Gough, *Fifth Army*, pp. 129, 143.
3. E. Beddington, *My Life* (privately published, 1960), p. 103. Quotations are from a copy in the author's possession; there is another in the L[iddell] H[art] C[entre] for M[ilitary] A[rchives], King's College, London.
4. B.H. Liddell Hart, *Memoirs*, vol. I (London: Cassell, 1965), p. 364. The former prime minister used his new-found friend as an additional stick with which to beat Douglas Haig, claiming, for instance that Haig used Gough as a scapegoat to divert attention from his (Haig's) own failings in March 1918. David Lloyd George, *War Memoirs*, abridged version, vol. II (London, Odhams, *c*.1938), pp. 1741–2, 2019.
5. Liddell Hart to Arthur Barker, 19 Sept. 1954, L[iddell] H[art] P[apers], 1/323/16, LHCMA.
6. 'Talk with Gen. Sir Charles Bonham-Carter', LHP, 11/1935/114, LHCMA.
7. For a cautiously favourable assessment of Gough set in the wider context of the British Army, see I.F.W. Beckett, 'Hubert Gough, Neill Malcolm and Command on the Western Front' in Brian Bond *et al*, *'Look To Your Front: Studies in the First World War'* (Staplehurst, Spellmount, 1999), pp. 1–12.
8. G. de S. Barrow, *The Fire of Life* (London: Hutchinson, 1942), p. 19.

9. The Marquis of Anglesey, *A History of the British Cavalry*, vol. IV, *1899–1913* (London: Leo Cooper, 1986), pp. 122, 186, 264.
10. Anthony Farrar-Hockley, *Goughie* (London: Hart-Davis, MacGibbon, 1975), pp. 65–8; Hubert Gough, *Soldiering On* (London: Arthur Barker, 1954), pp. 83–9.
11. Anglesey, *British Cavalry*, vol. IV, p. 264.
12. F. Maurice, *Rawlinson of Trent* (London: Cassell, 1928), pp. 85–6.
13. 'Talk with Sir Hubert Gough', 9 Apr. 1935, LHP, LH 11/1935/72, LHCMA; Tim Travers, *The Killing Ground* (London: Unwin-Hyman, 1987), p. 104.
14. David R. Woodward (ed.), *The Military Correspondence of Field-Marshal Sir William Robertson, Chief Imperial General Staff December 1915–February 1918* (London: Bodley Head for Army Records Society, 1989), p. 7.
15. Letter from Gough, 29 Jan. 1916, quoted in Richard Holmes, *The Little Field Marshal* (London: Jonathan Cape, 1981), p. 1. In later life Gough was somewhat more charitable: *Soldiering On*, p. 127.
16. Keith Jeffrey, *The Military Correspondence of Field Marshal Sir Henry Wilson 1918–1922* (London: Bodley Head for Army Records Society, 1985), editor's introduction, pp. 9–10.
17. 'Talk with Sir Hubert Gough', 9 Apr. 1935, LHP, LH 11/1935/72, LHCMA.
18. Gough, *Soldiering On*, pp. 171–3; review of *Tonight* programme by Maurice Richardson, in *The Observer*, 24 March 1963, LHP, LH 1/323/44, LHCMA. For the view that Wilson was more sinned against than sinning, see Basil Collier, *Brasshat: A Biography of Field-Marshal Sir Henry Wilson* (London: Secker & Warburg, 1961), pp. 214–15.
19. Jeffery Williams, *Byng of Vimy* (London: Leo Cooper, 1992 [1983]), pp. 36–7.
20. 'Talk with Lloyd George and General Sir Hubert Gough (at the Athenaeum)', 28 Nov. 1935, LHP, LH 11/1935/107, LHCMA.
21. Gough to Liddell Hart, 22 Sept. 1954, LHP, LH 1/323/17, LHCMA.
22. Williams, *Byng*, p. 139.
23. Williams, *Byng*, p. 236.
24. J.M. Bourne, 'British Generals in the First World War', in G.D. Sheffield (ed.), *Leadership and Command: The Anglo-American Military Experience since 1861* (London: Brassey's, 1997), p. 109.
25. 'Talk with Lloyd George and General Sir Hubert Gough (at the Athenaeum)', 28 Nov. 1935, LHP, LH 11/1935/107, LHCMA.
26. Anglesey, *British Cavalry*, vol. IV, p. 75.
27. Gough, *Soldiering On*, p. 125.
28. Charles Carrington, *Soldier from the Wars Returning* (London: Hutchinson, 1965), p. 104.
29. Ian F.W. Beckett, *Johnnie Gough, V.C.* (London: Tom Donovan, 1989), pp. 206, 208; Peter Simkins, 'Haig and the Army Commanders', in Brian Bond and Nigel Cave (eds), *Haig: A Reappraisal 70 Years on* (Barnsley: Leo Cooper, 1999), p. 88.
30. Keith Simpson, 'The Reputation of Sir Douglas Haig', in Brian Bond (ed.), *The First World War and British Military History* (Oxford: Clarendon Press, 1991), p. 145.
31. George A.B. Dewar assisted by J.H. Boraston, *Sir Douglas Haig's Command* (London: Constable, 1922), pp. 184–5. This chapter is initialled 'JHB'.
32. Stephen Badsey, 'Cavalry and the Development of Breakthrough Doctrine', in Paddy Griffith (ed.), *British Fighting Methods in the Great War* (London: Cass, 1996), pp. 153–5.
33. Farrar-Hockley, *Goughie*, pp. 152–3.
34. I owe this suggestion to Professor Stephen Badsey. See also Chapter 3.
35. Lady Algernon Gordon Lennox (ed.), *The Diary of Lord Bertie of Thame* (London: Hodder & Stoughton, 1924), p. 114 (diary entry, 10 Mar. 1917); David R. Woodward, *Lloyd George and the Generals* (Newark, NJ: University of Delaware Press, 1983), p. 51.
36. Robin Prior and Trevor Wilson, *Command on the Western Front* (Oxford: Blackwell, 1992), p. 268.

37. David French, *The Strategy of the Lloyd George Coalition, 1916–1918* (Oxford: Clarendon Press, 1995), pp. 232–3.

38. C.E. Callwell, *Field-Marshal Sir Henry Wilson*, vol. II (London, Cassell, 1927), p. 78.

39. French, *Strategy*, p. 233.

40. Lennox, *Bertie*, pp. 287, 289.

41. Haig diary, 26 Mar., 3 Apr. 1918, Haig Papers, N[ational] L[ibrary] of S[cotland].

42. Beddington, *My Life*, pp. 173–4.

43. Haig to wife, 16 June 1918 and Haig to Gough, 6 July 1918, Haig Papers, NLS; Williams, *Byng*, p. 236.

44. Gerard J. DeGroot, *Douglas Haig 1861–1928* (London: Unwin-Hyman, 1988), p. 383.

45. 2 and 3 July 1916, 'Extracts from War Diary of G.S. Reserve Army', AWM 45 30/1–30/11, Australian War Memorial [AWM].

46. See Prior and Wilson, *Command*.

47. Farrar-Hockley, *Goughie*, p. 190.

48. O.A.D. 91, 2 Aug. 1916, in Wilfred Miles, *Military Operations, France and Belgium, 1916*, vol. II, (London: Macmillan, 1938), Maps and Appendices, Appx 13.

49. O.A.D. 36, 'Note of interview at Fourth Army Headquarters … at mid-day, 2nd July, 1916'; O.A.D. 43, 'Note' by Kiggell, 4 July 1916; O.A.D. 39, 'Confirmation of telephone conversation between the C.G.S and the G.O.C. Fourth Army. 7.10pm 2/7/16; all AWM 252 [A116], AWM.

50 Miles, *Military Operations*, vol. II, pp. 10–15.

51. S.G. 59/0/1, 'Proposed Scheme for the Capture of Courcelette and Formation of a Defensive Flank', 28 Aug. 1916, AWM 252 [A131], AWM; O.A.D. 44, 'Notes of arrangements made verbally with Sir. H. Gough on 2nd and 4th July, 1916', AWM 252 [A116], all AWM.

52. O.A.D. 68, Kiggell to Third Army, 15 July 1916, AWM 252 [A116], AWM.

53. Miles, *Military Operations*, vol. II, p. 102.

54. O.A.D. 91, 'The Commander-in-Chief's Instructions to the Fourth and Reserve Armies, 2nd August', in Miles, *Military Operations*, vol. II, Appendices, p. 35.

55. O.A.D. 137, 5 Sept. 1916, 'Note of Interview with Sir H. Gough, on 4th September, 1916', AWM 252 [A116], AWM. See also O.A.D. 116, 'G.H.Q. Plan for a mid-September Offensive', 19 Aug. 1916, in Miles, *Military Operations*, vol. II, Appendices, pp. 46–7.

56. S.G. 21/0/32, memo from Reserve Army, 5 Sept. 1916, AWM 45 [35/9], AWM.

57. Miles, *Military Operations*, vol. II, pp. 301–2.

58. Miles, *Military Operations*, vol. II, p. 422. The last sentence is also implicitly critical of Haig.

59. Miles, *Military Operations*, vol. II, pp. 420–1, 453–4.

60. See Miles, *Military Operations*, vol. II, pp. 476–524.

61. Philip Gibbs, *Realities of War* (London: William Heinemann, 1920), p. 389; Brian Bond and Simon Robbins (eds), *Staff Officer: The Diaries of Lord Moyne 1914–1918* (London: Leo Cooper, 1987), pp. 162–4; Beckett, 'Hubert Gough', pp. 2–4.

62. Farrar-Hockley, *Goughie*, pp. 226–9.

63. Farrar-Hockley, *Goughie*, pp. 228–9; Beddington, *My Life*, p. 102.

64. Haig, diary, 5 Oct. 1917, 9 Dec. 1917, NLS.

65. Diary, 25 Nov. 1917, Major General G.S. Clive Papers, CAB 45/201/3, TNA.

66. Beddington, *My Life*, pp. 121–2; Neill Malcolm, diary (I am grateful to Captain Dugald Malcolm for giving me access to this diary).

67. 'Talk with L[loyd] G[eorge] and Hubert Gough', 27 Jan. 1936, LHP, LHCMA; Gough, *Fifth Army*, p. 134.

68. Review by Michael Howard, LHP, LH 1/323/48, LHCMA.

69. See Andy Simpson, 'British Corps Command on the Western Front, 1914–1918', in Gary Sheffield and Dan Todman (eds), *Command and Control on the Western Front: The British Army's Experience 1914–18* (Staplehurst: Spellmount, 2004).

70. Farrar-Hockley, *Goughie*, p. 188.
71. Review of *Goughie* by Michael Howard, LHP, LH 1/323/48, LHCMA.
72. E.G. Wace to J.E. Edmonds, 30 Oct. 1936, CAB 45/134, TNA; Peter Simkins, 'Somme footnote: the Battle of the Ancre and the struggle for Frankfort Trench, November 1916', *Imperial War Museum Review*, No. 9, pp. 96–100, and also see below.
73. Memo, 5 Oct. 1916, WO 95/518, TNA.
74. Malcolm diary, 29 June 1916.
75. Malcolm diary, 6 July 1916. He made a similar comment on 13 July 1916.
76. 'Talk with L.G. and Hubert Gough', 27 Jan. 1936, LHP, LH 11/1936/31, LHCMA.
77. Simkins, 'Haig and his Army Commanders', pp. 95–6.
78. Malcolm, diary, 18 Aug. 1916.
79. Hunter-Weston to wife, 1, 12 July, 3 Aug. 1916, Hunter-Weston Papers, British Library, no. 48365 (I owe these references to Andy Simpson); diary, 16 July 1916, Philip Howell Papers, IV/D/13, LHCMA.
80. e.g. WO 95/851, G.S. 406/49, Reserve Army to X Corps, 3 July 1916, TNA.
81. XIV Corps note, 3 Aug. 1916, WO 95/910, TNA.
82. Malcolm, diary, 25 Aug. 1916; diary, 25 Aug. 1916, Howell Papers, IV/D/13, LHCMA.
83. Diary, 22 July 1916, Howell Papers, IV/D/13, LHCMA; Howell to wife, 22 July 1916, IV/C/3/324, Howell Papers, LHCMA; Haig, diary, 23 July 1916, in Blake, p. 155. For a positive view of Morland by a junior regimental officer, see Anthony Eden, *Another World* (London: Allen Lane, 1976), p. 124.
84. Gough, *Soldiering On*, p. 132.
85. Malcolm, diary, 28 Aug. 1916.
86. Beckett, 'Hubert Gough', p. 8.
87. [R. Howell], *Philip Howell: a memoir by his wife* (London: Allen & Unwin, 1942), p. 42; Gough, *Soldiering On*, pp. 1–2, 70.
88. Howell to wife, 12 Aug. 1916, Howell Papers, IV/C/3/332a, LHCMA.
89. Howell to wife, 15 July 1916, IV/C/3/319a, 29 July 1916; same to same, IV/C/3/327; same to same, 7 Aug. 1916, IV/C/3/330; all Howell Papers, LHCMA.
90. Howell to wife, 2 Aug. 1916, IV/C/329, Howell Papers, LHCMA.
91. Reserve Army memos G.339, 13 July 1916, and S.G.3/1/7, 24 July 1916, AWM45 30/1–30/11, AWM; diary, 23, 24 July 1916, IV/D/13, Howell Papers, LHCMA.
92. Diary, 25 July 1916, IV/D/13, Howell Papers, LHCMA.
93. Malcolm, diary, 3 Aug. 1916. 12th Division's history, co-authored by Scott, perhaps unsurprisingly makes no mention of Gough's intervention, although it does cite a complimentary order issued by Reserve Army when the division passed out of his command later in August. A.B. Scott and P.M. Brumwell, *History of the 12th (Eastern) Division in the Great War* (London: Nisbet, 1923), pp. 63–4, 73–4.
94. Diary, 2 Aug. 1916, IV/D/13, Howell Papers, LHCMA.
95. Confidential memo. from Fifth Army to Corps, 16 Nov. 1916, WO 95/518, TNA.
96. Malcolm, diary, 21–22 Nov. 1916.
97. Pederson, 'The AIF', p. 174. For a fuller discussion of this attack, see Chapter 4.
98. Diary, 29 July 1916, Howell Papers, IV/D/13, LHCMA.
99. White to Bean, 19 Sept. 1927, Bean Papers, 3 DRL 7953, item 4, AWM.
100. Bean to Edmonds, 28 Apr. 1928, Bean Papers, 3 DRL 7953, item 34, AWM.
101. H.R. Cumming, *A Brigadier in France* (London: Naval & Military Press, n.d., [1922]), pp. 44–5.
102. For Bullecourt, see E.M. Andrews, 'Bean and Bullecourt: Weaknesses and Strengths of the Official History of Australia in the First World War', *Revue Internationale d'Histoire Militaire*, No. 72 (Canberra, 1990), pp. 25–47; J Walker, *The Blood Tub: General Gough and the Battle of Bullecourt, 1917* (Staplehurst: Spellmount, 1998).

103. See Andrew A. Wiest, 'Haig, Gough and Passchendaele', in Sheffield, *Leadership and Command*, pp. 77–92.
104. Reserve Army S.G.43/0/5, WO 95/1293, TNA.
105. John Lee, 'Some Lessons of the Somme: The British Infantry in 1917', in Bond *et al, Look to your Front*, p. 86.
106. Reserve Army S.G.43/0/5, WO 95/1293, TNA.
107. Reserve Army issued a memorandum that consisted of a note from GHQ (O.A.D. 256, 16 July 1916) on the importance of the creeping barrage, with an endorsement by Gough: S.G.31/3/1, 17 July 1916, AWM252 [A133], AWM.
108. Reserve Army S.G.43/0/5, WO 95/1293, TNA.
109. Reserve Army S.G.43/0/5, WO 95/1293, TNA.
110. Lee, 'Some Lessons', p. 84.
111. Gough, *Fifth Army*, p. 155; Archibald Home (Diana Briscoe, ed.), *The Diary of a World War I Cavalry Officer* (Tunbridge Wells: Costello, 1985), p. 126.
112. Haig, diary, 13 Nov. 1916, in Gary Sheffield and John Bourne (eds), *Douglas Haig: War Diaries and Letters 1914–1918* (London: Weidenfeld & Nicolson, 2005), p. 255.
113. See e.g. Loch Papers, II Corps G. 1266, 'Notes on the Attack', 12 Sept. 1916, Imperial War Museum [IWM]; Reserve Army S.G. 66/56, 12 Oct. 1916 (points on infantry and tank tactics for forthcoming operations), TNA.
114. For instance, a mine was blown near Beaumont Hamel simultaneously with the commencement of the artillery barrage. This produced a greater effect than the blowing of a mine in the same area 10 minutes before the attack commenced on 1 July 1916: AWM 41/1–41/7, O.A. 247, Butler to Armies, 5 Dec. 1916, AWM.
115. Haig, diary, 2 Nov. 1916, in Sheffield and Bourne, *Douglas Haig*, p. 250.
116. Miles, *Military Operations*, vol. II, p. 462.
117. 'Memorandum on Operations', 13 Nov. 1916, Fifth Army S.G. 72/81, TNA.
118. WO 95/518 'Memorandum', 13 Nov. 1916, TNA.
119. WO 95/518 'Memorandum', 13 Nov. 1916, TNA.
120. Gough, *Fifth Army*, p. 156.
121. Robin Prior and Trevor Wilson, *The Somme* (Yale: Yale University Press, 2005), p. 293.
122. Haig, diary, 16 Oct. 1916, in Sheffield and Bourne, *Douglas Haig*, p. 241.
123. Haig, diary, 12 Nov. 1916, in Sheffield and Bourne, *Douglas Haig*, p. 254.
124. Miles, *Military Operations*, vol. II, p. 476.
125. Simon Robbins, *British Generalship on the Western Front 1914–18* (London: Cass, 2005), pp. 20–1.
126. Royal Marines Museum, ARCH 7/17/5 (1), Maj. J Montagu to a friend, 20 Nov. 1916; Beddington, *My Life*, pp. 102–3.
127. WO 95/518, Fifth Army S.G. 72/84, 13 Nov. 1916, TNA.
128. WO 95/518, Fifth Army S.G. 72/90, 16 Nov. 1916, TNA.
129. Simkins, 'Somme footnote', p. 94.
130. WO 95/518, Fifth Army S.G. 72/90, 16 Nov. 1916, TNA.
131. Travers, *Killing Ground*, p. 189; Simkins, 'Somme footnote', pp. 96–7; Robbins, *British Generalship*, pp. 32–3.
132. CAB 45138, Wace to Edmonds, 30 Oct. 1936, TNA; National Library of Scotland, Acc.3155, Haig Ts diary, 21 Nov. 1916.
133. WO 95/747, V Corps GX.8325, 21 Nov. 1916, TNA.
134. WO 95/747, Fifth Army S.G. 72/86, 25 Nov. 1916, TNA.
135. WO 95/518, Fifth Army to Corps, 16 Nov. 1916, TNA.

Chapter 6

Haig and the British Expeditionary Force in 1917

The most awful phase of the War for the British Army [was] – the nightmare-like Flanders offensive of 1917 ... Time scatters the poppies of oblivion over most things, but the lapse of twelve years has not effaced the impressions of sordid horror and melancholy which this period of the War engraved on the mind ... the effort and sacrifice demanded of our Army – and willingly given – is scarcely credible ... when one compares the results with the dogged tenacity of infantry, gunners and transport men under loathsome nerve-wracking conditions and the utterly prodigal expenditure of munitions and technical resources of every kind, one feels resentful of the doctrinaire fanaticism which kept the machine driving on at top-pressure, month after month, as though the gain of each few yards of water-logged craters was worth every sacrifice.[1]

So wrote Capt D.V. Kelly in a book published in 1930. Elsewhere in the book Kelly, who had served with 6/Leicesters (21st Division), was by no means hypercritical of GHQ. This makes his condemnation of Passchendaele particularly powerful. Kelly presents the images of the British Expeditionary Force (BEF) in 1917 that have come to dominate the memory of that year, at least in the United Kingdom: the offensive at Passchendaele, or the Third Battle of Ypres, to give it its proper name.[2] British, Australian, New Zealand, South African, Canadian, French and German soldiers battling in the mud, under appalling conditions that pushed them to the very limits of endurance; huge losses incurred for minor gains of territory; an uncomprehending and uncaring High Command. Indeed, when you add in the failures and bloody attrition that all too rapidly succeeded the early promise of the first days of the Battle of Arras (April 1917); the false dawn of the tank attack at Cambrai in November, which caused the bells to be rung for victory at home, only for the German counter-offensive to throw the attackers back; the near-defeat in the First Battle of the Atlantic; the mutinies in the French army; the revolutions that effectively removed Britain's ally Russia from the war; and the catastrophic Italian reverse at Caporetto – 1917 does indeed appear to have been a grim year for the Entente in general, and the British Empire in particular.

But shake the kaleidoscope, and let the pieces assume another pattern. Another interpretation of 1917 is that the BEF, effectively 'deskilled'[3] in

1914–1915, had undergone its major baptism of fire on the Somme in 1916, and in 1917 showed considerable evidence of the success of its 'reskilling'. It applied the hard-won experience of 1916 and at Arras showed how much it had learned – but also how much there was still to learn. The growth in the competence of the BEF was mirrored by the rapid development of a war economy that supplied the many and various tools that the army needed to fight. The morale of the army was severely tested, but it did not break. Although at Passchendaele the BEF did not achieve its ambitious aims, it did succeed in several important ways – not least in pinning down the German army, and inflicting heavy attritional losses (as German sources make clear, the defenders also suffered appallingly) – and came tantalisingly close to inflicting a major operational defeat on the Germans that could have had important strategic consequences. At Arras, Passchendaele and Cambrai the units of the BEF demonstrated their increasing tactical sophistication, and commanders and staffs too showed that they had improved since the Somme. At Cambrai especially the BEF gave a foretaste of the weapons system that was to prove so effective in the following year. As one ally, Russia, departed the war, another, in the shape of the USA, took its place. Undoubtedly 1917 was a grim time, but the British survived it.

These pictures of 1917 are not mutually exclusive. All of them contain a measure of truth, and to create an accurate portrait one needs to reflect, to a greater or lesser degree, all of the above factors. One's interpretation ultimately depends on whether one views the glass as half empty or half full. The more I study the BEF in 1917, the more I am convinced that one should see it as half full.

To see the full extent of the achievement of the BEF in 1917 we must go back to the beginning of the war. The BEF of 1914 was well trained and well equipped, but it was of a size that was simply inadequate for the scale and intensity of warfare to which it would be committed; this problem was exacerbated by heavy losses, especially in experienced officers and NCOs, during the fighting in the early months of the war. Lord Kitchener, Secretary of State for War, once demanded rhetorically, 'Did they remember, when they went headlong into a war like this, that they were without an army, and without any preparation to equip one?'[4] – 'they' of course referring to the politicians. The result of this lack of preparation was the need for improvisation on a truly heroic scale. The creation of the mass volunteer army that bore Kitchener's name, matched of course by the raising of citizen forces in the Dominions, was the result. The few available experienced officers and NCOs were spread very thinly indeed across new battalions; the same was true of staffs at every level. Commanders from the Commander in Chief of the BEF downwards found themselves with responsibilities vastly greater than anything they had experienced before, and for which their pre-war training and preparation ranged from the scant to the non-existent. And this expansion took place against a profound change in the conduct of warfare, while fighting – usually carrying out offensive operations – against a skilled and determined enemy. The wonder is that the BEF achieved as much as it did in 1917, given the very low base from which it started.

Arras

A body of important new work has stressed that the BEF examined its experiences in 1916, extracted lessons and applied them to its fighting methods.[5] The Battle of Arras in April 1917 demonstrated the fruits of this learning process. The British high command did not want to launch a major offensive at Arras, but found themselves committed to it, as a result of the machinations of Lloyd George and Nivelle, in order to support the French attack on the Chemin des Dames. In some ways 9 April 1917, the first day of the first major British offensive since the Somme, was comparable with 1 July 1916.[6] The frontage was roughly similar, as was the number of attacking divisions. But some things were very different. Staff work was of an all-round higher quality in April 1917. The creeping barrage had become standard practice, while the density of heavy guns was about three times greater on the first day of Arras than on the first day on the Somme, and there was more ammunition. However, we should note that the BEF's divisions each deployed twenty pieces of heavy artillery, which was only half the number available to the French divisions. But the improved performance of the artillery was not just down to sheer numbers of guns. Near Vimy Ridge the flash spotters and sound rangers of 1st Field Survey Company discovered 86 per cent of the locations of enemy batteries, and generally most German batteries were neutralised (if not actually destroyed) in the initial stages of the British attack, lavish use being made of chemical weapons.[7] A machine gun barrage and forty tanks supported the attacking infantry, who showed that their training in the tactics enshrined in the SS135 and SS143 manuals issued in early 1917, incorporating the lessons of the Somme, had been put to good use. In fact, 9 April 1917 was the BEF's best day since the beginnings of trench warfare.

Rightly, the capture of Vimy Ridge by Canadian (and a number of British) troops is viewed as the highlight of the day, but there was plenty of success elsewhere.[8] Two British formations, 4th Division and 9th (Scottish) Division, achieved the longest single advance since trench warfare began, about 3½ miles. German mistakes undoubtedly aided the BEF's success, but defensive errors alone cannot explain the success of 9 April 1917. What Arras demonstrated was that by spring 1917 the BEF had mastered the set-piece bite-and-hold battle: a philosophy of limited battle that involved 'biting' a chunk out of an enemy position and holding it against counter-attack. This method combined some of the advantages of the attackers, especially gaining the initiative, with those of the defender, digging in and using artillery and machine guns to break up enemy assaults. Subsequent operations were to show that conducting an effective mobile battle was beyond them. On 10 and 11 April the British advance lost vigour as tiring troops met German reserves. Allenby, deprived of air reconnaissance because of bad weather, ordered his forces to commence the pursuit, but the result was the congealing of the front; the BEF had failed to turn its victorious 'break-in' into a 'break-through'. The very success of British artillery on the first day inevitably led to the ground becoming shattered. Given time, engineers and pioneers would build roads and tracks that would enable the guns to move to new positions, to begin the process of hammering at enemy strongpoints as a preliminary to another major attack. Prior to 9 April, the attacking formations had made excellent use of the generous allocation of time before the assault. But lengthy pauses between attacks are the enemy of maintaining operational tempo. Thus on 11 April the British infantry found themselves up against uncut wire, with the 18-pounder guns that should have been cutting that wire still struggling forward to get into range. This was not the last time that the limitations of the bite-and-hold approach was to be revealed in the year 1917.

Messines

The Arras methods were repeated, with variations, at Messines in June. This battle, a preliminary to Haig's main Flanders offensive, was entrusted to the ultimate safe pair of hands, General Sir Herbert Plumer, whose methods were described by Tim Harington, his Chief of Staff, as being underpinned by three Ts: 'Trust, Training and Thoroughness'.[9] Second Army's preparations were typically meticulous, not least in the use of nineteen mines detonated beneath the German positions. But even before the mines were blown, the British gave themselves a crucial advantage by dominating the artillery battle. The Germans were outnumbered by a factor of 2 to 1 in heavy guns, and 5 to 1 in lighter pieces, and about half of the defenders' guns were lost before the attack went in on 7 June.

It is fair to point out that the mines at Messines made the battle a unique and effectively unrepeatable operation. But the mines were the icing on the cake. The basic artillery-dominated, set-piece battle was not dependent on mines for success. But it could only get an army so far. Haig has often been criticised for delaying the main assault against the Ypres salient until six weeks after the Messines attack. As Ian Malcolm Brown has demonstrated, logistic problems made it impossible to switch forces rapidly from the Messines operation to mount a new offensive against the Gheluvelt plateau.[10] Once again, harsh logistic realities prevented prompt exploitation of tactical success.

Passchendaele

The beginning of the Third Battle of Ypres on 31 July 1917 sent mixed messages. At a local tactical level, careful preparations, such as those carried out by the Guards Division in the Boesinghe sector, and good all-arms co-operation produced some advances of up to 3,000 yards. But at the operational level there was failure. Gough, the Fifth Army commander, had wanted an advance of 6,000 yards, intended to take the British troops to the German Third Position as a preliminary to breaking out of the Ypres salient in a further series of operations. Gough's plan proved too ambitious, not least because it played into the hands of the Germans, who were employing flexible defensive tactics based around counter-attack formations that struck the attackers as they became over-extended. As Harington put it, 'The further we penetrate his line, the stronger and more organised we find him ... [while] the weaker and more disorganised we are liable to become.'[11] The weather broke, and in awful muddy conditions the Battle of Langemarck (16–18 August) degenerated into piecemeal attacks that made minor gains at the cost of heavy losses.

The BEF returned to form when Gough was sidelined and Plumer's Second Army was handed the main effort. After a three-week period of intense preparation, the Battle of the Menin Road commenced on 20 September. A combination of thoroughly rehearsed infantry, massed artillery support, and objectives set only 1,600 yards or so ahead, so that the attackers would stay within range of their own artillery and machine guns, proved to be highly effective. The German official history bemoaned that the counter-attack formations, ready to intervene in the battle at 8.00am, could not get into action 'until the late afternoon; for the tremendous British barrage fire caused most serious loss of time and crippled the thrust power of the reserves'.[12] It was a bloody battle for the attackers, and Prior and Wilson have argued that the success of Menin Road has been exaggerated and that the praise heaped on Plumer was the product of 'the diminishing expectations accompanying the campaign'. Gough had promised much but failed to deliver, while Plumer's more modest endeavour lived up to lower expectations.[13] A fair point, but Menin Road had a more profound impact on the Germans than the operations of 31 July. On that day German defence-in-depth tactics worked successfully. At Menin Road they did not, and the battle heralded a run of British offensives that brought the Germans close to defeat.

The basic methods of 20 September were repeated at Polygon Wood (26 September) and at Broodseinde (4 October). Faced by mounting casualties (159,000 men by this stage) and a precipitous decline in morale, in mid-October one faction in the German high command advocated a limited withdrawal to force Haig to redeploy his artillery. Crown Prince Rupprecht, the local Army Group commander, even began to prepare for 'a comprehensive withdrawal' that would have entailed giving up the Channel ports – which, of course, would have fulfilled one of the major British objectives of the campaign at a stroke.[14]

But on 4 October the weather broke again, and the problems experienced at Arras of the very success of artillery-driven bite-and-hold attacks destroying the ground and making it difficult to get the guns forward began to manifest themselves. Preparations for the Battle of Poelcappelle (9 October) were feeble in comparison with previous operations (although it still caused heavy damage to the Germans), because the preparations were far from complete. In appalling conditions produced by heavy rain, inadequate numbers of engineers and pioneers struggled to build and maintain wooden plank roads under shellfire. Infantry reached the start line for the attack only after an exhausting journey along duckboard tracks 'which eventually petered-out into waist-deep mud'. Among their many tasks, the sappers had to build gun platforms, otherwise artillery pieces could not fire. First Passchendaele (12 October) saw more of the same. But bite-and-hold could still work. Heroic and extensive engineering by the Canadian Corps produced conditions in which the capture of Passchendaele Ridge was achieved in four stages, culminating in the attack of 10 November.

The problem was not at the tactical level. Official historian Cyril Falls once commented that 'Tactics were seldom more skilful' than at Third Ypres.[15] The problem lay with bite-and-hold as an operational method, a problem that was exacerbated, but not caused, by the terrible conditions. In order to achieve anything approaching a decisive success, the attacker had to land a continuous stream of heavy blows, giving the enemy no time to recover. But the very nature of a steady advance on a relatively narrow front so churned up the ground that it effectively guaranteed a law of diminishing returns, as the longer operations continued, the more difficult it was to bring the guns forward.

The Battle of Cambrai in November gave a glimpse of the way out of the dilemma. It added several more elements to the BEF's weapons system which gave a tantalising hint that mobility was returning to the battlefield; indeed, that the tactical pendulum was starting to swing towards the attacker. The innovations at Cambrai were twofold: the mass use of 476 tanks, including 98 support tanks loaded with supplies; and the use of a 'predicted' artillery bombardment, made possible by advances in gunnery technique by which gunners no longer had to sacrifice surprise by firing preliminary ranging shots.

In the words of General Byng, Cambrai was initially intended as a tank raid to 'put the wind up the Boche'.[16] It rapidly evolved into a more ambitious plan, perhaps leading to a breach of the Hindenburg Line or the capture of the key rail junction of Cambrai itself. Initially the attack of 20 November 1917 went well, except on 51st Highland Division's front. It was an example of another mostly successful bite-and-hold operation with a new element in the shape of the mass tank attack. However, as we have seen, Cambrai was a more ambitious offensive than those of earlier in the year. The cavalry – still the only useable instrument of exploitation – were supposed to exploit through the gap created by the initial assault. By the time the attackers reached the St. Quentin Canal it was getting dark, and the cavalry operations were limited in scale and achieved little. A sobering fact is that of the 476 tanks that began the operation, only 297 were still 'runners' at the end of the day. The majority of the mechanical casualties had broken down rather than been disabled by enemy fire.

The battle rapidly degenerated into an attritional struggle. Worse, on 30 November the Germans launched a counter-offensive that prefigured the methods which were to be used with great effect in their 1918 spring attacks: surprise, a short artillery bombardment, stormtroops, low-flying aircraft. The British were pushed back, losing much of the ground captured in the initial assault. The Battle of Cambrai was a clear sign that both the British and German armies had developed a weapons system that under the right conditions was capable of breaking the tactical deadlock.

Into 1918

Sometimes the battles and campaigns of the First World War are viewed in isolation. I believe that they should be set in the context of the war as a whole, and in this case it is instructive to look back from the end of the war to see how the BEF's methods developed in 1917. This is not to use hindsight in a crude fashion, but rather to recognise that there was a learning process going on, and the battles of 1917 represented an important stage in the BEF's development. Here I should say that I played a hand in the popularisation of the term 'learning curve', which has been criticised recently as not reflecting the reality that sometimes the process involved backward steps and, one might add, blind alleys.[17] This is absolutely fair comment: the phrase was nothing more than a handy if strictly inaccurate piece of shorthand developed in the early 1990s in the Two Eagles pub, just around the corner from the Imperial War Museum in London, where some wonderful informal seminars took place over pints and cheese doorstops. The learning process was not a simple upward progression. However, it is important to recognise that battles were analysed and the perceived lessons influenced, to varying degrees, doctrine, training and the conduct of future operations.

There are many reasons why the BEF of August 1917 – an army capable of achieving effective bite-and-hold operations – was transformed into the BEF of August 1918 – an army able to conduct a form of mobile warfare. Here I will concentrate on three. The first is the improvement in the quality of commanders and staffs, an improvement largely due in my view to additional experience. Quite simply, good staffs cannot be improvised overnight, and the British Army suffered particularly badly from the need to spread its available expertise very thinly indeed across a range of staffs. A number of bloody failures in 1916 and 1917 can be attributed to attack orders being issued from higher formations, which left insufficient time for lower level staffs and commanders to prepare plans, issue orders and brief the troops that would carry them out. Compare this with the Hundred Days in 1918. The history of the Royal Artillery comments that under conditions of mobile warfare 'It soon became practice for infantry brigadiers to organise their own fireplans with their own artillery commanders, the C[ommander] R[oyal] Artillery co-ordinating, stiffening (sic) and confirming them'.[18] As Chris McCarthy has observed, the 'flash to bang' time for operations was often drastically reduced, and yet commanders and staffs were able to cope: for example by taking the initiative by issuing verbal preliminary orders that anticipated final orders.[19] This showed the high degree of trust that had developed between commanders and staffs, the staff officers mostly being young men who had learned on the job; one, the future Prime Minister Anthony Eden, had been a schoolboy on the outbreak of war but became the youngest brigade major in the British Army. All this helped to increase the rate of operational tempo.

The second and arguably most important factor is that by the summer of 1918 the BEF had more guns and better logistic support than had been the case a year earlier. In 1917 the BEF had insufficient guns for two concurrent major offensives, or even for one major battle and a sizeable feint.[20] Problems were caused by guns wearing out, and the appalling conditions in the latter stages of Third Ypres meant that the Royal Artillery struggled to keep even the nominal number of guns available in the field. In June 1917 restrictions were placed on the use of artillery in quiet sectors 'to preserve the lives of the guns'. Three weeks before the opening of Third Ypres 7.7 per cent of 18-pounders, 4.8 per cent of 60-pounders and no less than 23.1 per cent of the BEF's 6-inch guns were unusable.[21] The Canadian Corps was allocated 227 heavy and medium guns and howitzers for its attack at Passchendaele on 26 October, but in reality only 139 guns came into action.[22] As we have seen, moving guns even from Messines to an adjacent battlefield was a time-consuming business. The lack of guns and the lack of mobility meant that the BEF could land only one major blow at a time, leading to the temptation to exploit any success in that sector to its utmost, even though experience showed that pushing on rarely brought success. In truth, there was little else that could be done if the aim was to capitalise on initial advances.

In 1918 the situation had been transformed. To understand how this was made possible, we need to look at the impressive development of the British war economy since 1914. It stands alongside the development of the mass citizen army as one of the most significant achievements of the British state in the twentieth century. John Bourne has drawn attention to the Box Repair Factory, located at Beddington to the south of London. This was one of numerous factories set up by the Ministry of Munitions. Opened in late 1916, it started repairing bomb and grenade boxes in early 1917, just in time for Arras.[23] The implications of the Box Repair Factory are highly significant. This was an economy dedicated to supplying the most obscure needs of the armed forces. It demonstrated impressive attention to detail and efficient organisation. It denoted a war economy that was overcoming the teething problems of earlier years. To use Bourne's phrase, it was an economy that, in 1918, allowed the BEF to fight a 'rich man's war': a war in which *materiel* was virtually unlimited. This was particularly true of artillery.

In 1914 only 91 guns were produced. By 1917 production per year had risen to 6,483, and in 1918 no fewer than 10,680 guns appeared from the factories. Thus in the last year of the war the supply of guns began to keep pace with demand. It is significant that a plan of December 1916 for expansion of the BEF's field artillery was only completed with the arrival of the last 18-pounder and 4.5-inch howitzer units in March and April 1918 respectively.[24] Supply of ammunition, by contrast, had caught up with demand by 1917.[25] By 1918 the BEF's artillery park was of such a size that it could absorb heavy losses of guns (859 in the first week of the German spring offensive).[26] Whereas in their offensives in the first half of 1918 the Germans had relied on a 'battering train' of artillery being moved up and down the front, and were running badly short of horses to move the guns, the BEF had enough guns to provide a strong core of artillery integral to formations, and sufficiently flexible logistics to move guns relatively swiftly from sector to sector. So, following the suspension of the Battle of Amiens on 11 August 1918, eleven field and heavy brigades were transferred from Fourth to Third Armies in time for the launching of a fresh offensive in the Bapaume area on 21 August.[27] The time taken to transfer the guns and complete Third Army's logistic preparations for battle can be profitably compared with the six weeks that elapsed between Messines and the opening of Third Ypres the year before.

The flexibility that sufficient guns, ammunition and effective logistics gave the BEF enabled it to conduct a series of operations, both concurrent and sequential, which allowed it to place enormous pressure on the German defenders. It enabled the tactically effective bite-and-hold techniques of Messines and Menin Road at long last to have operational significance. Eschewing the attempt to achieve a breakthrough that had often characterised British operations in previous years, as well as those of the Germans in the spring, in the Hundred Days the BEF fought limited, attritional battles but rapidly switched the point of attack from sector to sector, thus keeping the defenders off-balance and continually on the back foot. In combination with the other Allied armies – and the importance of Foch as overall co-ordinator should not be underestimated – the BEF used these methods to defeat the German army. It was a triumphant vindication of the methods of 1917, but it took the developments of 1918 to allow them to fulfil their potential.

Morale

One shrinks from the attempt to describe the conditions that prevailed in the Ypres salient. No part of it was ever at rest ... day and night the guns sprayed the trenches, the roads, the duckboard paths, with shrapnel and H.E., the grim resolve to kill dominating every other thought or desire … Guns sank axle-deep in the mud – Napoleon's *fifth* element – and were salved under deadly fire … The period at Ypres ended on a note of depression. One felt that the Division was beginning to doubt its ability to achieve the impossible … [The conditions] combined to awaken a vague, inarticulate protest against the cruelty and futility of war … The men were glad to quit the Ypres salient, but they did not leave it in a happy frame of mind. Every one felt that the Division was not at its best; and that it was capable of better things had opportunity been given.

This is a quotation, not from a disillusioned officer war poet, but from the history of 42nd (East Lancashire) Division, a book that in other places was written in a distinctly upbeat fashion. The quotation brings out the sheer nastiness of fighting in the salient in 1917 – although the author is also careful to point out that it was even worse for the Germans – but above all, the impression is of frustration: of enduring and fighting, but making little apparent progress.[28] One should be careful about generalising from the experience of a single division – 42nd Division's experience was of trench holding and minor operations – but there is plenty of evidence that the conditions during the Third Battle of Ypres placed a peculiar degree of strain on combatants.

However, one should be cautious before assenting to the oft-expressed opinion that Passchendaele was uniquely ghastly. I am not sure how one can compile a hierarchy of horror. Charles Bean, the Australian official historian, believed that the shelling at Pozières in July 1916 was worse than that at Passchendaele.[29] Thanks in part to David Lloyd George's *War Memoirs*, Passchendaele became known as 'the campaign [or battle] of the mud', but some veterans believed that the mud in the latter stages of the Somme offensive in 1916 was worse.[30] If horror is reduced to the statistics of the daily loss rate, Passchendaele was not the worst battle of the war – it wasn't even the worst battle in 1917. That dubious honour belonged to Arras, which had the heaviest daily loss rate (4,076). This was followed by the 1918 Hundred Days offensive (3,645) and the Somme in 1916 (2,943). Third Ypres, with a daily loss rate of 2,323, rated as the fourth most deadly experience endured by the BEF. In absolute terms, the Somme (141 days, 420,000 losses), followed by the Hundred Days campaign (which actually lasted 96 days, and resulted in 350,000 casualties) were the bloodiest battles. Third Ypres, at 105 days and 244,000 casualties, rated as the third bloodiest.[31]

Whichever way one looks at it, statistically Passchendaele was not the worst battle of the war. And yet it acquired a reputation of unique horror. As I have argued elsewhere, many British soldiers in the Second World War, who were engaged in fighting some pretty horrific battles of their own, in Burma or

Monte Cassino or Normandy, measured their experiences against the Western Front – often Passchendaele – and usually concluded that, as bad as things were for them in 1944, things had been worse for their fathers and uncles in 1917. The truth of the matter was a separate issue. I suspect that often they were seeking to cheer themselves up by persuading themselves that things could have been worse.[32]

The most important point to make about the morale of the BEF in the second half of 1917 is that although it dipped, it did not break. There clearly was a decline, as revealed by the postal censorship, supported by anecdotes and various other pieces of evidence, but this decline was neither terminal nor permanent. The ultimate test of the morale and cohesion of a military unit is its willingness to obey orders. I am unaware of major examples of combat refusals at Passchendaele, and the response of the BEF to the German offensives that began in March 1918 demonstrate that any damage to morale was not lasting.[33]

There was, of course, the rather famous mutiny at Étaples base camp in September 1917, but this was a military version of an industrial strike as soldiers protested against poor working (and living) conditions. It is noteworthy that these men were separated from their units, where good leadership by NCOs and officers and the benefits of belonging to a cohesive organisation helped to mitigate some of the harsher conditions of warfare on the Western Front. The Étaples mutiny, although it caused some short-lived alarm in the upper echelons of the BEF – this was, after all, the year of the Russian revolution, and the French mutinies had occurred a few months before – was certainly not insurrectionary in nature, nor did it mark a point at which the loyalty of the troops could no longer be relied upon. It has been well described as 'collective bargaining in khaki'.[34]

One of the best, although rather strange and mystical, Canadian memoirs of the First World War is Will Bird's *Ghosts Have Warm Hands*. Bird served with 42nd Battalion, The Black Watch of Canada. He wrote of the aftermath of battle: 'We had little drill, but rested and slept and had good food until finally we were more like human beings. But every man who had endured Passchendaele would never be the same again, was more or less a stranger to himself.'[35] Bird was clearly traumatised by the experience of Passchendaele, but it is surely an exaggeration to say that *everyone* who fought there was affected to such an extent. Many simply got on with life. And it is instructive to read in Bird's account, both overtly and between the lines, how the battalion was rebuilt, how the survivors put the terrible experience behind them, returned to trench duty and eventually participated in the Battle of Amiens. Passchendaele is proof that human beings can endure extraordinary levels of stress and strain. Collectively, the men of Haig's army in France were pushed close to the abyss – but they did not fall into it.

Douglas Haig

The generalship of Douglas Haig remains highly controversial. While some of the sillier charges against Haig have been rebutted, there is still a case to answer.[36] Here, given the limitations of space, I will confine my comments to some of the issues associated with the most contentious action of 1917, the Third Battle of Ypres.

Why fight at Ypres at all? There were real strategic objectives around Ypres, and Haig had long wanted to fight in this sector.[37] One only needs to stand on Passchendaele Ridge, to look back towards Ypres and over to the open ground beyond, for the military importance of this position to become clear. An advance out of the Ypres salient offered real strategic objectives, not least the Channel ports. One of the major reasons for Britain entering the war in August 1914 had been the concern that Belgium, and especially the Belgian ports, should not fall into hostile hands. The naval situation in 1917 caused grave concern to the Admiralty and the War Cabinet. When, on 20 June, Jellicoe burst out that it was 'no good discussing plans for next Spring – we [i.e. Britain] cannot go on' because of the submarine threat, he was exaggerating, as Haig understood.[38] Nonetheless, the First Sea Lord's opinion could not be ignored. Neither could his well-founded view that there was no single simple solution to the naval crisis. Part of a more complex solution was for the army to capture the Channel coast. Only a minority of U-boats were based in the major Belgian ports, as Britain's senior sailors knew, but occupation of the Flanders coast would bring other important advantages, including neutralising German surface raiders. As Geoffrey Till explains, 'The more the general U-boat threat sucked the [Royal] Navy's light forces out of the Channel, the more vulnerable would the Army's supply lines be to local German attack.'[39] No one believed that the capture of the coast would prove to be decisive, but it would be a very useful step in the right direction. It would be wrong to claim that concern for the naval position was foremost among Haig's motives for launching the Third Battle of Ypres. It would be equally misguided to underestimate it as a factor.

The question of coalition politics can be dealt with briefly. The idea that Haig had to fight Passchendaele to keep the pressure off the French army recovering from mutiny is not wholly convincing. Senior French commanders were opposed to the battle, wanting instead limited battles.[40] However, it is clear that Haig did not trust the French army. On 19 September, for example, he recorded in his diary 'Pétain's opinion [that] its discipline is so bad that it could not resist a determined German offensive'.[41] Whether this was true or not is a different matter. Haig believed it to be true, and it was undoubtedly a factor in his thinking.

Following the Allied break-out from the Ypres salient, the Germans began to retire from the coast, allowing Ostend and Zeebrugge to be captured in rapid succession. Three days after a British naval force under Sir Roger Keyes seized Ostend, the Germans evacuated the entire Belgian coastline. The previous sentences are not an excursion into the currently fashionable genre of alternative history (or 'allohistory'); it actually happened in October 1918. The circumstances were very different from a year earlier, but nonetheless demonstrate what Haig was seeking to achieve at Third Ypres. Haig has been criticised for planning for a breakthrough and a decisive offensive, rather than for opting to fighting a series of bite-and-hold battles.[42] There is an alternative view. For the attacker, limited victories did not always produce limited casualties, as the losses at Menin Road, Polygon Wood and Broodseinde in September–October 1917 were to demonstrate. To fight battles that captured little ground and brought the Allies no nearer ending the war but incurred large losses in the process was politically unattractive. John Terraine argued that in the aftermath of Arras GHQ had a crumb of comfort: 'Allenby's initial success had confirmed the belief that the enemy's line could be broken; it remained to be seen whether the British Army could make a better job of exploitation than the French.' Moreover, there was a belief that the success at Messines had not been exploited to its full extent.[43] Haig was out in his timing. In fact, it took another six months or so of tactical development before the breakthrough battle once again became possible. This was not immediately obvious in June–July 1917. Against this background, the choice of the thruster Gough over the methodical Plumer to command the main blow at Ypres becomes explicable. Haig made the wrong choice – Gough's shortcomings as a general were to become all too apparent in July–August 1917 – but the decision was not inherently unreasonable.

After the victory of Broodseinde on 4 October Haig chose to fight on. In retrospect we know that this represented the high point of the offensive, but given the circumstances of three rapid victories achieved in less than two weeks, it is not surprising that he took this decision. As one commentator argued, 'Three-quarters of the all-important Gheluvelt–Passchendaele Ridge had been won; should Faint Heart now take his hand from the plough, when "one more push" seemed likely to push the enemy off the dominating ridge which appeared to mark the boundary of the Promised Land?'[44]

At first sight, it is less easy to understand Haig's decision to prolong the battle after the battles of Poelcappelle (9 October) and First Passchendaele (12 October) had shown that the opportunity of breaking through had vanished. The decision becomes more explicable when we consider that once the Third Battle of Ypres began, like all offensives it gathered momentum of its own. In mid-October Haig was faced with three possibilities, none of them especially attractive.

The first option was to halt the campaign and let the BEF establish a line short of the high ground of the Passchendaele Ridge. While superficially promising, in reality this option was not realistic. As the Second Army Chief of Staff, General Tim Harington, later stated,

> ... after the capture of Broodseinde and the subsequent advance and hold up at Bellevue, close under Passchendaele, there was no place where the Army could have stopped for the winter and been maintained.
>
> I asked, in my *Life of Lord Plumer*, if anyone could suggest a line on which we could have stopped; I have never seen a reply. I had personally reconnoitred all the ground under the most appalling conditions and I feel sure that if he had been with me on the Gravenstafel Ridge, the most violent critic of Passchendaele would not have voted for staying there for the winter, or even for any more minutes than necessary.[45]

The second option was to fall back to a tenable position closer to Ypres, abandoning the territorial gains that had been made. This would be to accept the logic of a pure battle of attrition – that ground was unimportant, but Passchendaele was never just an attritional battle. To give up the ground so recently captured at such heavy cost was psychologically and politically impossible, just as, after the losses incurred in the fighting around Ypres in 1914 and 1915 it was impossible to abandon the salient and fall back to a more defensible position, although in purely military terms it would have been sensible to do so. In April 1918, under a completely different set of circumstances, Plumer was quietly to abandon the Passchendaele Ridge in the face of a German offensive. It hurt Plumer deeply to have to issue such 'heart-rending' orders.[46]

The final option was to fight on to secure the Passchendaele Ridge and there to establish a line on which the BEF could remain for the winter. It would also serve as a jumping-off position for a spring offensive – a factor that is often ignored, but it appeared to be a real possibility. This option would, it was clear, involve hard and bloody fighting in terrible conditions. Haig was convinced that the Ridge could be captured. He was right, although the efforts involved and the loss of human life were prodigious. Given the unattractive nature of the alternatives, it is not surprising that the decision was taken to fight on.

There were, of course, other factors that influenced Haig's determination to continue the offensive. The effect of his over-optimism on his generalship has been convincingly demonstrated.[47] Brigadier General John Charteris, the BEF's head of intelligence, has often been blamed for feeding Haig over-optimistic information. Certainly, the positive nature of Charteris's intelligence reports influenced Haig's decision-making.[48] However, Jim Beach, in his authoritative study of British intelligence on the Western Front, has argued that Charteris offered reinforcement of Haig's views, but did not create them. According to Beach, the intelligence picture that Haig received in October was encouraging, but did not in itself justify continuation of the offensive.[49] Neither Haig nor Charteris can be exculpated, but the system within which they operated was also at fault. Charteris was Haig's protégé, increasingly dependent on the C-in-C's support as he became less popular within the army. Haig was loyal to Charteris. In many contexts loyalty is an admirable trait, but there is no doubt that Haig was blinded to Charteris's shortcomings. The latter's treatment after his fall from grace – threatened with exile to Mesopotamia and regarded, in Haig's words, 'as almost a sort of Dreyfus' – suggests why he would want to keep on the right side of his Chief.[50] It would have taken a very strong man consistently to give the C-in-C messages he did not want to hear, even if Charteris did not deliberately manipulate the evidence. Yet a good intelligence system should give the commander robust, independent information and analysis. Haig needed cautious and sober intelligence assessments to balance his optimism. Charteris simply failed to provide what was necessary. The situation was to improve somewhat in 1918 after Charteris was replaced by Brigadier General Edgar Cox.

Conventional intelligence was not the only factor that informed Haig's decision-making. His memories of how close his I Corps had come to defeat during First Ypres in 1914, if only the Germans had pressed their attacks, were undoubtedly influential.[51] Haig's soldier's instinct told him that the enemy was in distress, and what we know from the other side of the hill suggests that he was not totally wrong. This helps to explain Haig's fury when General Macdonogh from the War Office provided a pessimistic intelligence assessment. Haig's notorious outburst, when he accused Macdonogh of relying on 'tainted' Roman Catholic sources, was not simply an example of bigotry; it referred to the belief that the Pope, by launching a peace initiative in August 1917, had taken a pro-German stance.[52] It also probably reflected Haig's frustration that a 'Base Wallah' in London should implicitly question the judgement of the 'man on the spot' so beloved of contemporary British doctrine.

In his 1917 despatch, and implicitly in his Final Despatch, Haig laid emphasis on the attritional impact of Passchendaele on the German army.[53] Even while the war was continuing, Haig's critics alleged that he tried to have it both ways: to seek breakthroughs and, when they did not materialise, to claim that the battle was really about attrition.[54] There is something in this. In the case of Third Ypres, the objective of the battle varied between the renewal of open warfare and attrition according to the circumstances of battle. However, the attrition argument will not go away. Haig's post-war explanation of it being part of the 'great engagements' that 'wore down the strength of the German Armies' and made possible the victories of 1918[55], has often been assailed. Because it contains an irreducible minimum of truth it has yet to be refuted convincingly, even if during the war Haig did not hold such a clear vision as laid out in his Final Despatch.

Let the last word on Passchendaele go to an opponent. As with any opinions expressed after the event, one must take care in using this as evidence, but it is nonetheless a most interesting perspective from a senior German officer at Passchendaele. Writing after the war, General Hermann von Kuhl, Chief of Staff to Crown Prince Rupprecht's Army Group, paid tribute to the BEF's 'courage' and obstinacy in attacking in Flanders, while denying there was any prospect of a breakthrough. However, given the strategic context – Russian and Italian weakness, the state of the French army, and the embryo state of the US commitment to the Western Front – the BEF was the

> only [Allied] army capable of offensive action ... If they had broken off their offensive, the German army would have seized the initiative and attacked the Allies where they were weak. To that end it would have been possible to withdraw strong forces from the east after the collapse of the Russians. For these reasons the British had to go on attacking until the onset of winter ruled out a German counter-attack.
>
> Today, now that we are fully aware of the critical situation in which the French army found itself during the summer of 1917, there can be absolutely no doubt that *through its tenacity, the British army bridged the crisis in France*. The French army gained time to recover its strength, the German reserves were drawn towards Flanders. The sacrifices that the British made for the Entente were fully justified.[56]

Further Reading

The collection in which this piece originally appeared contains a number of relevant articles: Peter Dennis and Jeffrey Grey (eds), *1917: Tactics, Training and Technology* (Canberra; Australian History Military Publications, 2007). Mark Connelly, *Steady the Buffs! A Regiment, a Region & the Great War* (Oxford: Oxford University Press, 2006) includes an excellent assessment of the combat performance of battalions of the Buffs, the East Kent Regiment. *Shock Troops: Canadians Fighting the Great War 1917–1918* (Toronto: Viking Canada, 2008), volume II of Tim Cook's excellent study of Canadian soldiers in the First World War, is essential reading. At the level of high command, two biographies of Haig give very different takes on the man: my own *The Chief: Douglas Haig and the British Army* (London: Aurum, 2011) and J.P. Harris, *Douglas Haig and the First World War* (Cambridge: Cambridge University Press, 2008).

Notes

1. D.V. Kelly, *39 Months with the 'Tigers' 1915–1918* (London: Ernest Benn, 1930), p. 73.
2. For brevity, the term 'BEF' is used to refer to all British Empire troops serving under Haig's command, not just those from the British Isles.
3. I owe this apt description to Dr John Bourne.

4. Lord Kitchener, quoted in John Hussey, '"Without an Army, and Without any Preparation to Equip One": The Financial and Industrial Background to 1914', *British Army Review*, 109 (1995), p. 76.
5. e.g. Andy Simpson, *Directing Operations: British Corps Command on the Western Front 1914–18* (Stroud: Spellmount, 2006), pp. 61–70; Alistair Geddes, 'Solly-Flood, GHQ, and Tactical Training in the BEF, 1916–1918', (MA, University of Birmingham, 2007).
6. Here and elsewhere I am drawing upon work previously published in my book *Forgotten Victory: The First World War – Myths and Realities* (London: Headline, 2001).
7. Peter Chasseaud, *Artillery's Astrologers* (Lewes: Mapbooks, 1999), pp. 263, 285.
8. For recent scholarship on this battle, see Geoffrey Hayes, Andrew Iarocci and Mike Bechtold (eds), *Vimy Ridge: A Canadian Reassessment* (Waterloo, Ont: Wilfrid Laurier University Press, 2007).
9. Sir Charles Harington, *Plumer of Messines* (London: John Murray, 1935), p. 79.
10. Ian Malcolm Brown, *British Logistics on the Western Front 1914–1919* (Westport, CT: Praeger, 1998), p. 164.
11. Second Army 'Notes on Training ...', 31 Aug. 1917, Monash papers, 3 DRL 2316, item 25, Australian War Memorial [AWM], quoted in Sheffield, *Forgotten Victory*, p. 173.
12. J.E. Edmonds, *Military Operations France and Belgium 1917*, vol. II (London: HMSO, 1948), p. 277.
13. Robin Prior and Trevor Wilson, *Passchendaele: the Untold Story* (New Haven and London: Yale University Press, 1996), p. 123.
14. Heinz Hagenlucke, 'The German High Command', in Peter H. Liddle (ed.), *Passchendaele in Perspective: The Third Battle of Ypres* (London: Pen & Sword, 1997), p. 53.
15. Cyril Falls, *The First World War* (London: Longmans, 1960), p. 286; Andy Simpson, *The Evolution of Victory* (London: Tom Donovan, 1995), ch. 6.
16. Quoted in Sheffield, *Forgotten Victory*, p. 181.
17. Christopher Duffy, *Through German Eyes: The British and the Somme 1916* (London: Weidenfeld & Nicolson, 2006), p. 323.
18. Sir Martin Farndale, *History of the Royal Regiment of Artillery: Western Front 1914–18* (London: Royal Artillery Institution, 1986), p. 293.
19. Chris McCarthy, 'Queen of the Battlefield: The Development of Command, Organisation and Tactics in the British Infantry Battalion during the Great War', in Gary Sheffield and Dan Todman (eds), *Command and Control on the Western Front: The British Army's Experience 1914–18* (Staplehurst: Spellmount, 2004), p. 191.
20. Edmonds, *Military Operations, 1917*, vol. II, p. 386.
21. Brown, *British Logistics*, p. 167.
22. Edmonds, *Military Operations, 1917*, vol. II, p. 348.
23. http://www.firstworldwar.bham.ac.uk/notes/A%20List%20of%20National%20Factories%20Controlled%20by%20the%20Ministry%20of%20Munitions.doc.
24. Farndale, *Royal Artillery*, pp. 341, 349.
25. Brown, *British Logistics*, p. 168.
26. Brown, *British Logistics*, p. 190.
27. Farndale, *Royal Artillery*, p. 292.
28. Frederick P. Gibbon, *The 42nd (East Lancashire) Division 1914–1918* (London: Country Life, n.d. but c.1921), pp. 99, 100, 103, 104–5.
29. Bean to Edmonds, 18 Apr. 1934, Bean papers, 3 DRL 7953, item34, AWM.
30. John Hussey, 'The Monsoon in Flanders, 1917', *Journal of the Society for Army Historical Research*, 74 (1996), pp. 246, 249.
31. Jonathan Nicolls, *Cheerful Sacrifice: The Battle of Arras 1917* (London: Leo Cooper, 1990), p. 211.

32. G.D. Sheffield, 'The Shadow of the Somme', in Paul Addison and Angus Calder, *Time to Kill* (London: Pimlico, 1997).
33. See Chapter 9.
34. Julian Putkowski, letter to editor of the *Guardian*, 26 Sept. 1986.
35. Will R. Bird, *Ghosts Have Warm Hands* (Ottawa: CEF Books, 2002 [1968]), p. 65.
36. The best single defence of Haig's generalship remains John Terraine, *Douglas Haig: The Educated Soldier* (London: Hutchinson, 1963). See also Brian Bond and Nigel Cave (eds), *Haig: A Reappraisal 70 Years On* (London: Leo Cooper, 1999); and 'Introduction' to Gary Sheffield and John Bourne (eds), *Douglas Haig: War Diaries and Letters, 1914–1918* (London: Weidenfeld & Nicolson, 2005). For a revisionist view of cavalry, see D. Kenyon, *Horsemen in No Man's Land: British Cavalry and Trench Warfare, 1914–1918* (Barnsley: Pen & Sword, 2011).
37. Haig, diary, 10 Dec. 1916, Acc. 3155, National Library of Scotland.
38. Haig, diary, 20 June 1917, in Sheffield and Bourne, *Douglas Haig*, p. 301. These words do not appear in the original manuscript version of the diary, only in the later typescript version; they are, however, fully consistent with the original entry.
39. Geoffrey Till, 'Passchendaele: The Maritime Dimension', in Liddle, *Passchendaele*, p. 77.
40. Elizabeth Greenhalgh, *Victory through Coalition* (Cambridge: Cambridge University Press, 2005), p. 153.
41. Haig, diary, 19 Sept. 1917, in Sheffield and Bourne, *Douglas Haig*, p. 329.
42. Prior and Wilson, *Passchendaele*, p. 197. For an interesting critique and suggested alternatives to Third Ypres, see M.G. Dougal, 'The attack of 12 October 1917 in the Third Battle of Ypres: Some reflections on relevant political and military factors', in C. Addis and J. Hayne (eds), *Seaford House Papers* (London: Royal College of Defence Studies, 1990), pp. 16–24.
43. J.A. Terraine, 'Passchendaele and Amiens – I', *Journal of the Royal United Services Institute*, 104 (1959), p. 177.
44. Alfred H. Burne, '"The Pitiful Tragedy" of Passchendaele', *Fighting Forces* (April 1949), 29.
45. Sir Charles Harington, *Tim Harington Looks Back* (London: John Murray, 1940), pp. 63–4.
46. Harington, *Plumer*, p. 161.
47. e.g. Nick Lloyd, '"With Faith and Without Fear": Sir Douglas Haig's command of First Army during 1915', *Journal of Military History*, 71 (2007), pp. 1051–76.
48. Nigel Steel and Peter Hart, *Passchendaele: The Sacrificial Ground* (London: Cassell, 2000), p. 60.
49. James Beach, 'British Intelligence and the German Army, 1914–1918' (Ph. D, University College London, 2004).
50. Haig, diary, 24 Aug. 1918, in Sheffield and Bourne, *Douglas Haig*, 449. It seems that Haig intervened to halt Charteris's posting to the Near East. I owe this information to Dr Jim Beach.
51. Haig, diary, 31 Oct. 1914, Sheffield and Bourne, *Douglas Haig*, p. 76.
52. Haig, diary, 15 Oct. 1917, in Sheffield and Bourne, *Douglas Haig*, pp. 336–7.
53. J.H. Boraston (ed.), *Sir Douglas Haig's Despatches (December 1915–April 1919)* (London: J.M. Dent, 1979 [1919]), pp. 133–5, 319–20.
54. See e.g. Lovat Fraser to Josiah Wedgwood MP, 28 Nov. 1917, J.C. Wedgwood, 1st Baron Barlaston papers, PP/MCR/104, Imperial War Museum.
55. Boraston, *Haig's Despatches*, p. 320.
56. Quoted in Jack Sheldon, *The German Army at Passchendaele* (Barnsley: Pen & Sword, 2007), pp. 315–16.

Chapter 7

Vimy Ridge and the Battle of Arras: April–May 1917

Introduction

In the Britain of the early twenty-first century most of the battles of the First World War are forgotten by all but specialist military historians. Vimy Ridge is an exception. In part this reflects the fact that the name, like 'the Somme' or 'Passchendaele', has remained in the British folk memory. It is suggestive that in the 1971 Disney children's film *Bedknobs and Broomsticks*, set on the southern coast of England in 1940 and featuring mainly British actors, a mention of Vimy Ridge (where the father of one of the principal characters had fought) is used early to establish the continuity of the Second World War with British battles of earlier eras.[1] The capture of Vimy Ridge is generally regarded in the UK as a solely Canadian affair, the Canadians succeeding where the French and British had failed (although in reality the latter had not actually made a serious attempt to capture the feature prior to April 1917). The symbiotic relationship between the Canadian Corps and the British Expeditionary Force (BEF) of which it formed a part is commonly misunderstood, and the key role played by British units and formations and individual British officers in the 9 April attack is forgotten.

The high visibility of the battle in the UK has been aided by the fact that Vimy Ridge lies just off a major highway much used by British tourists. Indeed, the Canadian memorial can be seen from the road. The First World War is a popular topic in British schools. Many schools regularly take parties of children on educational trips to visit Vimy Ridge, attracted especially by the artificially preserved trenches. There, through tours of Grange tunnel conducted by Canadian students, and views of the impressive Vimy memorial, pupils are exposed to a Canadian perspective. Most British teachers are ill-equipped to put the battle into its wider context or point out the contribution that non-Canadians made to the battle.

Needless to say, the Arras campaign, of which the Vimy action formed a part, comes firmly into the category of forgotten battles. This is strange, given that the Battle of Arras (9 April–17 May 1917) was a major offensive that, as we have seen, cost 159,000 British and Empire casualties – a daily loss rate of 4,076, which was higher than for any other major battle. Indeed, it has been calculated that had Arras continued at the same intensity for 141 days (the length of the Somme offensive in 1916), the losses would have been in the order of 575,00, which would have made it by far the bloodiest British offensive of the war.[2] Moreover, the strategic consequences of Arras were profound, and the battle marked an important stage in the BEF's operational and tactical learning curve. On 9 April, for instance, two British divisions, 4th and 9th (Scottish), achieved the longest advance up to that point by a British unit under conditions of trench warfare – some 3½ miles. The importance of the Arras campaign belies the lack of attention it has received from historians.

A survey of the literature published in Britain is instructive. The publication of anecdotal histories based on the writings and reminiscences of participants has become something of a boom industry in recent years, yet to the author's knowledge Jonathan Nicholls's *Cheerful Sacrifice* is the only popular history of Arras to have been published in the UK.[3] In Britain the phrase 'Battle of Arras' is more likely to be associated with the minor British armour/ infantry counter-attack against advancing German forces on 21 May 1940. Astoundingly, one book on European battlefields edited by a noted military historian included an entry on the 1940 action but ignored the major battle of 1917 altogether.[4] All this contrasts with the publication in Britain of at least five popular histories of Vimy Ridge in which the Canadians take centre stage, including books by Canadian authors Herbert Fairlie Wood and Pierre Berton.[5]

Scholarly attention is patchy; the only major study of the battle is the relevant volume of the British official history, published as long ago as 1940.[6] There are some short treatments on specific parts of the Arras campaign.[7] There is, however, an excellent recent study of the Bullecourt operations on Fifth Army's front by a British author, Jonathan Walker, and the Australian angle of this battle has also been covered by several authors.[8] Surprisingly, neither Tim Travers nor Robin Prior and Trevor Wilson covered Arras in any detail in their influential books on command in the BEF.

A common theme is that the capture of Vimy Ridge was somehow 'decisive', or a 'turning point' in the First World War.[9] It is not easy to see how this claim can be substantiated. The ridge was certainly an important position, and its capture improved the local tactical situation. Vimy Ridge had potential as a jumping-off point for a future offensive, but subsequent gains in the days and weeks that immediately followed were modest. For many reasons the principal Allied efforts for the rest of 1917 took place elsewhere. The real fruits of the capture of Vimy Ridge did not become apparent until almost a year later, when it proved an invaluable defensive position during Operation *Mars*, the German offensive of 28 March 1918, which took place only seven days after the dramatic German breakthrough south of the Somme. In the Vimy/Arras area the British VI, XVII and XIII Corps won a highly significant defensive victory. The German attack was stopped dead, derailing Ludendorff's plans, with major consequences for the future development of the German offensive.

It is difficult to avoid the conclusion that if Vimy Ridge had been captured by a British or French formation instead of the Canadian Corps, this action would not enjoy its current celebrity. While the Canadian Corps undoubtedly achieved a fine feat of arms on 9 April 1917, 'Vimy Ridge' resonates largely because of its role in the growth of Canadian nationalism. A similar point can be made about Gallipoli if Anzac forces had not been involved. It is likely that a folk memory of that campaign would have survived in the UK, if only because it was an important stage in the career of Winston Churchill, and, however misguidedly, the operation is commonly regarded as a great 'missed opportunity' to shorten the First World War. There is no doubt that the enduring fascination of Gallipoli is primarily a product of the status it has assumed in the national mythologies of New Zealand and Australia. In the case of both Australia and Canada, a more logical choice of battle to celebrate would be Amiens on 8 August 1918, an action that was genuinely a turning point in the First World War.

Three general points emerge from this preliminary survey. There is a failure to understand the 'Imperial' nature of the force that captured Vimy Ridge; the importance of the Canadian Corps' capture of Vimy Ridge has been exaggerated; and the significance of the wider Battle of Arras has been underrated.

The strategic background to the battle
Given freedom of choice, the Commander-in-Chief of the BEF, Field Marshal Sir Douglas Haig, would not have fought at Arras and Vimy in April–May 1917. When the Somme campaign was halted in November 1916 he fully intended renewing the battle early in the New Year, as a preliminary to shifting his forces to Flanders and launching a major offensive to capture the Belgian coast. This was an operation that was seen as vital if the U-boat menace was to be mastered. Haig's plans were thrown out of gear by the fall from power of Marshal Joffre in December 1916. 'Kicked upstairs', Joffre was replaced by General Robert Nivelle. The latter, boasting of new tactical techniques that had indeed produced success on a small scale at Verdun, ditched Joffre's plans and produced a scheme to achieve a decisive breakthrough.

Nivelle's objective was the 'destruction of enemy main forces on the western front'. He envisaged a 'prolonged battle' to break the enemy front; the Allies would then 'defeat' the German reserves and the exploitation phase would follow. The main blow would be launched by the French in Champagne, while British and French forces would attack to pin German divisions in the Arras–Somme area to prevent them reinforcing Champagne. Specifically, the BEF was to 'pierce' the enemy positions, advance to take the Hindenburg Line in rear, and then advance in the direction of Valenciennes–Louvain, and ultimately to Mons, Tournai and Courtrai. Further to the north

British Second Army was to exploit German weakness in Flanders and push forward.

In practice, the BEF had to relieve French formations to allow Nivelle to build up a strategic reserve, and Haig had to abandon his planned operations, agreed with Joffre at Chantilly in November 1916. On 25 December Haig 'agree[d] in principle' to Nivelle's plans and over the next few weeks the precise details were thrashed out. The result was that Haig committed the BEF to the holding offensive, 'but not to an indefinite continuation' of the battle; he had no wish to be sucked into a Somme-style attritional struggle. Moreover, if Nivelle's *attaque brusquée* failed to achieve decisive results, Haig would launch his Flanders offensive. Haig was essentially a loyal ally, but not one who could be pushed around.[10]

Nivelle won over David Lloyd George, British Prime Minister since December 1916, who harboured deep suspicions of Haig and General Sir William Robertson, the Chief of the Imperial General Staff. At the Calais conference in February 1917 Lloyd George attempted to bounce Haig and Robertson into subordinating the BEF to Nivelle.[11] Although the achievement of unity of command on the Western Front, Lloyd George's stated aspiration, was both sensible and desirable, if his Calais coup had succeeded it would not have brought this about. Simply placing the BEF under the French army would have been an abdication by the Cabinet of British national interest, although in practice Nivelle's freedom of action would have been trammelled by interference from London.

Irrespective of the merits of the proposal, the underhanded way in which Lloyd George sought to bring it about caused lasting damage to his already difficult relationship with Haig and with Robertson. In the event, an uneasy compromise was reached by which Haig was subordinated to Nivelle only for the duration of the forthcoming offensive, with the right of appeal to London. The Calais conference was a serious blunder that was surprising coming from such an accomplished politician as Lloyd George. Arras was fought under the shadow of one of the most serious civil-military clashes of the entire war.

In the event, although the BEF landed a very heavy blow on 9 April, it was unable to carry out the more ambitious parts of Nivelle's plan. Haig on 12 April assured Nivelle that in spite of the bad weather his forces were still driving towards Cambrai, but German reinforcements were being brought up and the BEF was adopting a more methodical approach, although hampered by the difficulties of moving artillery forward. In reality, the moment for a breakthrough had passed, and the BEF was locked into the attritional battle Haig had originally wanted to avoid. The Champagne offensive began on 16 April and achieved limited success, but had nothing of the decisive character that Nivelle had promised. Haig had to keep attacking to aid the French. In any case, he was sufficiently encouraged by the successes of the first ten days of the fighting to argue in favour of the continuation of the battle. The context was hints from Paris and London, triggered by the failure of Nivelle to achieve the quick victory he had promised, that offensive operations should be suspended until the arrival of the Americans and the revival of the Russians. This was something that Haig judged was unlikely to occur until the spring of 1918.[12]

Douglas Haig had learned from his time at Staff College in the 1890s that battles fell into a number of stages, including phases of attrition, break-through and exploitation. 'Great results are never achieved in war', Haig wrote on 18 April 1917, 'until the enemy's resisting power had been broken'; in the present circumstances it was 'a matter of time and hard fighting'. To halt now would be to discourage the BEF and give the Germans time to recover 'and to seize the initiative either in this theatre or in another'.[13] In spite of his earlier reservations, and his desire to fight in Flanders, Haig saw Arras as a part of the process of wearing out the enemy.

On 23 April the BEF launched another major attack, which pushed the line forward about a mile. This was disappointing in comparison to 9 April, but compared very favourably with the Somme. Knowing that the French might go onto the defensive, Haig intended the BEF to advance to a good defensive line and then consolidate to wait on events.[14] The final major act of the Battle of Arras came on 3 May. Haig's assessment was that the Germans had been weakened, but not sufficiently for a 'decisive blow'. Nivelle's problems, Haig believed, stemmed from a misjudgement of the 'guiding principles' from 'time immemorial' of the structured battle, 'and the remedy now is to return to wearing-down methods for a further period the duration of which cannot yet be calculated'.[15] The attack was a bloody fiasco, but it brought the curtain down on the Battle of Arras. Haig could now turn his attention to Flanders. For the time being, the French army was wrecked as an offensive instrument, and the BEF would have to shoulder the burden of the Allied offensive.

Operational aspects of the battle

An Army Commander held no independent Command, the fronts and flanks of Armies were rigidly tied down, the Army gains were won by hard frontal fighting, almost as mechanical as the movements of a parallel ruler: the art of strategy was almost completely denied to their operations, and these were of necessity methodical rather than brilliant.

The author of these words was Hastings Anderson, who, as a major general, served as chief of staff to General Sir H.S. Horne at First Army in 1917. As Hastings went on to argue, the fact that the Canadian Corps formed 'the backbone' of First Army, and the 'just fame' of the Canadians (and, one might add, their commanders) 'tended to obscure the part played by Lord Horne as an Army Commander'.[16] Hastings was correct. While Edmund Allenby, commander of Third Army at Arras, is well known, albeit primarily for his later campaigns in Palestine, Henry Horne remains in obscurity. And yet First Army's role in the battle was by no means negligible.

Horne was a Scot with a background in the Royal Horse Artillery, and was something of a protégé of Douglas Haig. He commanded XV Corps on the Somme before being promoted to command First Army. Vimy was his first battle as an Army commander. Initially he reserved judgement, but the successful performance of First Army staff in this operation won Horne's confidence. Haig had issued a warning order for First Army to prepare to assault Vimy Ridge on 17 November 1916, and on 2 January 1917 GHQ issued formal orders. At an early stage Byng, the Commander of the Canadian Corps, was informed of the impending offensive. Army issued a general plan, while Corps prepared a detailed 'scheme of operations'.[17] The actual attack of 9 April, the Canadian Corps claimed, 'was only the culminating phase of a prolonged and insistent offensive' of raids and artillery during the winter.[18]

Horne and First Army had a supporting but vital role in the Vimy success. They were responsible for 'directing, guiding, and combining [the Canadians] with the work of other Corps'.[19] This was a role for which Horne was well suited, for he had 'a consultative command style, encouraging discussion [and] explaining the overall plan of operations'.[20] One example of this came during a conference with his Corps commanders on 29 March, when he emphasised the importance (previously stressed by Haig) of co-ordinating with corps on the flanks when creating a line of resistance. On 15 April Horne, needing the information for a forthcoming conference of Army commanders, asked his Corps commanders how quickly they could get ready for a new attack. Perhaps the highest tribute to the role Horne played at Vimy came in a letter written by Byng to his wife on the same day: 'Horne has been more than helpful and backed me up in everything.'[21]

First Army also played an important role in providing the logistic arrangements that were key to the capture of Vimy Ridge. Horne's concern for the state of roads in the rear area was clear, when he took pains to clear up potential confusion about where responsibilities lay between Army and Corps. At the same conference he drew upon his own experience as a gunner to give some important advice on artillery matters, including the apparently mundane matter of care for artillery horses. In fact, given the difficulty of moving guns forward over No Man's Land after the success of 9 April, this point was far from trivial.[22]

The logistic achievements of First Army were considerable. The strength of First Army in April 1917 was approximately 320,000 men and 75,000 horses. On the 3½-mile attack frontage, in a 24-hour period, 7,200 tons of ammunition was expended of the 40,300 tons accumulated in front of railheads. Similarly, 828,000 full-day rations for men and 100,000 for horses had been stockpiled for First Army. Before the attack began, the problem of inadequate roads in the Vimy sector was a serious one, and the Royal Engineers were clearly proud of their road-building activities during the battle. One mile of plank road was constructed between Neuville St Vaast and Tilleuls in three days, using three RE Field Companies and an additional labour company: 3,000 men were used during 24 hours, working three shifts of six hours each.[23]

The relationship of the Canadian Corps to First Army and the wider BEF was symbiotic in other ways. The heavy artillery support at Vimy consisted of two Canadian and seven British Heavy Artillery Groups. Moreover the field artillery of three Canadian divisions was supplemented by two British units serving as 4th Canadian Division's artillery, and another eight British Royal Field Artillery brigades. Whereas the Canadians and Anzacs concentrated for the most part on producing elite 'teeth arm' formations, the British did not have that luxury, having to provide everything else needed by a modern army. They also produced, of course, infantry divisions. Moreover, some key players in the Canadian Corps were British, including Byng and Major Alan Brooke (the future Field Marshal Lord Alanbrooke), chief of staff to the Canadian Corps Artillery commander, as were a proportion of the fighting troops. British 13 Infantry Brigade, part of 5th Division, was attached to 2nd Canadian Division for the Vimy operation. The Canadian Corps occupied a slightly uncomfortable position both as a proto-national army, and a component, albeit an unusual one, of the wider BEF. While it developed its own, highly effective style of war fighting, it was never hermetically sealed from the other divisions, both 'Imperial' and Dominion, on the Western Front.[24]

The Learning Curve

Over the last twenty or so years the image of the BEF as 'lions led by donkeys' portrayed by popular writers such as Leon Wolff and Alan Clark has been comprehensively discredited. Instead, from the work of a number of scholars has emerged a nuanced view of the transformation of the BEF from a small, colonially orientated force into a large, sophisticated, technologically advanced and highly effective army. The Battle of Arras marked something of a 'half-way house' in this process. The bloody Somme offensive had been a salutary experience that yielded all manner of lessons on everything from minor tactics to high command. While many had been absorbed and applied while the fighting was in progress – the creeping barrage is an obvious example – the winter of 1916/1917 allowed a period of more considered reflection. At the end of the battle the Counter-Battery Staff Office was formed, which gave the BEF a 'corps-level ... centralised staff of artillery personnel dedicated to the suppression of the enemy's batteries through the analysis and tactical application of intelligence'.[25] In February 1917 important tactical changes were enshrined in two key doctrinal pamphlets, SS143, 'Instructions for the Training of Platoons for Offensive Action', and SS144, 'The Normal

Formation for the Attack'. Essentially, the platoon was turned from being a sub-unit of four rifle sections into a much more flexible force, consisting of one section each of riflemen, Lewis gunners, rifle grenadiers and bombers. This change was prompted in part by developments in the French army: the Canadian Corps was influenced by a visit paid by Arthur Currie to Verdun. However, more important were the lessons that had been learned the hard way by British Empire units. Just how effectively these lessons had been learned and applied became clear on 9 April 1917.

Fourteen British and Canadian divisions went over the top on 9 April 1917. The attack frontage was 25,000 yards, 2,000 yards less than on the Somme on 1 July 1916. There were more heavy guns at Arras, 963, or 1 per 21 yards, as opposed to 455, or 1 per 57 yards, and also more ammunition was available. The Arras attack was supported by poison gas, tanks and a massed machine gun barrage. 'The task before us is a difficult one,' opined the GOC 34th Division in an order to his troops, 'but in many respects, especially with regard to the weight of our Artillery Support, it is easier than that allotted to our Division in the early days of July last year when it won for itself a reputation for gallantry and determination second to none in the British Army.'[26] This must have been cheering news for veterans of 1 July, when 34th Division had sustained horrendous losses for meagre gains.

Almost everywhere the attack was successful. 'Owing to the fact that the whole attack from ZERO until the moment that the 4th Division passed through the 9th Division was carried out exactly to the timetable previously arranged', reported the compiler of 26 Brigade's narrative of operations, 'there is very little comment on the whole operation.'[27] 28 Brigade complained that the pace of the creeping barrage (100 yards in four minutes) was 'too slow for eager men assaulting a trench system that has been treated to thorough Artillery preparation' and that men ran into their own barrage on 9 April and suffered casualties as a result.[28] Conversely, 12th Division, which attacked up Observatory Hill, believed that a creeper that advanced 100 yards in six minutes would have been more realistic. This division's attack fell behind schedule but was still successful, not least because of effective gunnery: 'The infantry are loud in the praises of the artillery supporting them.'[29] British 13 Brigade, serving under the Canadian Corps on Vimy Ridge, listed four factors in their success on 9 April: the 'perfect steadiness' of the troops, 'despite being under a barrage'; 'the initiative and dash of Co[mpan]y and Platoon Commanders'; 'the intensity and accuracy of the barrage put up by the Canadian artillery;' and 'previous practice over the taped course, which all Commanders state was of immense assistance'.[30]

In some places there were local setbacks. 34th Division reported 'very feeble resistance' being put up by the enemy and the subsequent capture of objectives on time on all but the left of the left-hand brigade, which imposed delays and casualties. 34th Division had to complete the capture of its objectives on the following morning.[31] Overall, however, the results were impressive. About 9,000 prisoners were taken. Third Army formations advanced between 2,000 and 6,000 yards; the Canadian Corps captured Vimy Ridge; and VII Corps took some advanced positions of the Hindenburg Line. As Haig wrote to King George V at 3pm on 9 April, 'Our success is already the largest obtained on this front in *one* day.'[32]

The first day of the Arras offensive demonstrated that given careful preparation and staff work, massed artillery and well-trained and motivated infantry, the BEF was capable of capturing strong positions. The second and subsequent days of the battle, however, were to show that while since July 1916 the BEF had learned how to break *into* an enemy position, it had yet to master the art of breaking *out* and fighting a more mobile battle. On 10 and 11 April the advance of the weary troops slowed while German reserves began to reach the battlefield. The British official historian rightly commented that while the gains of 10 April were considerable achievements, they were seen as disappointments given the optimism caused by the success of the previous day.[33] The poor weather limited the aerial reconnaissance that the RFC could carry out, yet on 10 April, according to his biographer, the commander of Third Army, Allenby, 'was in a state of high excitement, certain that the decisive breakthrough was within his grasp'. On the following day he put out an order declaring that 'Third Army is now pursuing a defeated enemy and that risks must be freely taken'.[34] In fact, by this time the German troops arriving on the Arras battlefield amounted to a fresh force that had to be defeated anew. Allenby's breakthrough did not materialise, and the battle bogged down into an attritional struggle.

On 9 April the BEF seized the initiative, but over the next couple of days was unable to maintain a high operational tempo ('the rate or rhythm of activity relative to the enemy').[35] A major reason for this was, ironically, that the stupendous bombardment that had made the success of 9 April possible cratered the ground and reduced the moving forward of artillery to a slow and laborious process. Given time, engineers and pioneers would build roads and tracks which would enable the guns to advance to new positions. But to take time is to slow the tempo of an operation. As a result, British infantry on 11 April were too often committed to battle with insufficient artillery support, and came up against uncut wire. The 18-pounder guns that should have been used for wire-cutting were still struggling forward to get into range.

This problem had not been entirely resolved two weeks later. On 23 April British 5th Division, still serving with the Canadian Corps, launched an attack. Covered by a creeping barrage, the assault troops reached the enemy position without difficulty but then discovered the German wire was poorly cut. 'The necessity of filing through gaps in the wire had led to the parties that had penetrated the hostile positions becoming considerably broken up' and the Germans launched counter-attacks. 'Overwhelmed by weight of numbers', and lacking reinforcements, which could not be got forward, most of the attacking troops were forced to fall back to their own lines.[36] Artillery shortcomings, the failure of wire-cutting, the barrage moving too fast, machine guns not being suppressed: these factors were directly responsible for the debacle. Denied the long period of preparation available prior to the beginning of the offensive, this attack and others underlined the limitations of the BEF in semi-open warfare in early 1917.

Quite apart from artillery, there were other areas in which BEF formations struggled to adjust to the changed conditions. 12th Division attacked at 03.45 on 3 May, but parties dedicated to the mopping-up role overlooked shell-holes in the dark and failed to clear them out. The result was that German troops were able to assemble in Devil's Trench to the rear of the advanced waves of 12th Division and form a centre of resistance. The 'obscurity of the situation' and fear of hitting their own forces prevented an artillery bombardment of Devil's Trench. Major General A.B. Scott, the divisional commander, attributed the failure to, in addition to the failure to mop up, 'The start in the dark to cover such a depth of ground where objects were not well defined', and the 'absolute impossibility during daylight of movement over the open spurs, and then the want of any definite information and inability to use supports'.[37]

A sober assessment by 34th Division's staff on the operations of 28–29 April encapsulated many of the problems faced by the BEF in the latter stages of the Battle of Arras. The 'features' to which they drew attention included:

- The novelty of the operations as compared with those of 9th April for which the troops had been trained and for which time for preparation and reconnaissance had been ample.
- The rapidity in [sic] which plans had to be made, reconnaissances carried out and orders issued.
- The inexperience and lack of training of the greater proportion of the troops – mostly new drafts.
- The weakness of the artillery barrage owing possibly to lack of time for reconnaissance and casualties to materiel and personnel.
- The necessity for time for training in order that a division can 'pull its weight' and the necessity for Brigade and Battalion Commanders to anticipate orders and be prepared to move and attack at short notice.[38]

This assessment speaks eloquently of the shortcomings of an army that had learned how to conduct successful set-piece operations, but lacked the skills to fight a mobile, or even semi-mobile, battle. Over the next eighteen months the BEF was to acquire those skills. During the Hundred Days campaign of August to November 1918, the BEF was able to fight the high tempo, mobile battles that were simply beyond its capability in April 1917. More experienced commanders and staff; greater flexibility in command and control; more artillery; logistic excellence – all of these factors were important.[39] None of them was achieved overnight, and Arras, like the Somme before it, was an important point on the learning curve of the BEF.

Conclusion

One particular action during the Arras campaign – the attack on Vimy Ridge – has achieved and retained popular fame largely through three factors: the nationality of the troops selected to capture it; the proximity of Vimy to England; and the building of a visitor- (and especially pupil-) friendly memorial, complete with artificially preserved trenches. Canadian nationalism has led to an exaggerated sense of the importance of the capture of Vimy Ridge, and the British elements of the force that fought in the battle have been airbrushed out of popular memory. This is not to minimise the skill of the troops engaged in the battle, or its significance in terms of the 'learning curve' of the BEF. However, Vimy cannot be divorced from the wider context of the Battle of Arras. It was an offensive that had profound strategic consequences, and marked an important stage in the tactical and operational development of the BEF. Despite this, Arras is a campaign that has been neglected by popular memory and historians alike. It deserves a full-scale scholarly reassessment.

Further Reading

We are still waiting for the modern, scholarly work on Arras that I called for in 2007. The collection on which the original version of this piece appeared contains much of use, although for obvious reasons it is heavily weighted to the Canadian experience: Geoffrey Hayes, Andrew Iarocci and Mike Bechtold (eds), *Vimy Ridge: a Canadian Reassessment* (Waterloo, Ont: Wilfrid Laurier University Press, 2007). Two important books by Simon Robbins shed light on Henry Horne, commander of First Army. The first, an edited collection of *The First World War Letters of General Lord Horne* (Stroud: The History Press for Army Records Society, 2009), is supplemented by *British Generalship during the Great War: The Military Career of General Sir Henry Horne (1861–1929)* (Farnham: Ashgate, 2010).

Acknowledgements

I would like to thank Chris McCarthy for his advice on the Battle of Arras. Crown Copyright material in The National Archives appears by permission of HM Stationery Office.

Notes

1. The film depicts the repulse of a German amphibious raid by magically animated suits of armour and manikins dressed in uniforms of bygone ages. Possibly Vimy Ridge was chosen because, unlike a battle such as the Somme, it is regarded as a victory.
2. Jonathan Nicholls, *Cheerful Sacrifice: The Battle of Arras 1917* (London: Leo Cooper, 1990), p. 211.

3. In addition, there are several relevant volumes in the mass-market but highly specialised *Battleground Europe* series published by Pen & Sword.
4. David Chandler (ed.), *A Traveller's Guide to the Battlefields of Europe* (Wellingborough: Patrick Stephens, 1989 [1965]).
5. Herbert Fairlie Wood, *Vimy!* (London: Corgi, 1972); Pierre Berton, *Vimy* (London: Penguin, 1987); Alexander McKee, *Vimy Ridge* (London: Pan, 1968); Kenneth Macksey, *The Shadow of Vimy Ridge* (London: William Kimber, 1965); Kenneth Macksey, *Vimy Ridge 1914–18* (London: Pan/Ballantine, 1973).
6. Cyril Falls (ed.), *Military Operations: France and Belgium, 1917*, vol. I (London: Macmillan, 1940).
7. See the useful chapter on Gavrelle in Christopher Page, *Command in the Royal Naval Division: A Military Biography of Brigadier General A M Asquith DSO* (Staplehurst: Spellmount, 1999).
8. Jonathan Walker, *The Blood Tub: General Gough and the Battle of Bullecourt, 1917* (Staplehurst: Spellmount, 1998). For a good example, see Peter Sadler, *The Paladin: A Life of Major-General Sir John Gellibrand* (Melbourne: Oxford University Press, 2000).
9. An essay posted on the Internet by a military history enthusiast is wholly typical in this respect:http://www.planetmedalofhonor.com/features/articles/usersubmitted/article0027.shtml (accessed 21 February 2006).
10. Nivelle's directive, 4 Apr. 1917, WO 256/17, TNA; Nivelle to Haig, 21 Dec. 1916, and Haig to Nivelle, 6 Jan. 1917, in Falls, *Military Operations*, Appendices 2 & 7, pp. 4–6, 13–15; John Terraine, *Douglas Haig the Educated Soldier* (London: Hutchinson, 1963), p. 252.
11. For a recent treatment of this episode, see Andrew Suttie, *Rewriting the First World War: Lloyd George, Politics and Strategy 1914–18* (Basingstoke: Palgrave Macmillan, 2005), pp. 99–119.
12. Haig, diary, 18 Apr. 1917, in G. Sheffield and J. Bourne (eds), *Douglas Haig: War Diaries and Letters 1914–1918* (London: Weidenfeld & Nicolson, 2005), p. 285.
13. Haig to Robertson, O.A.D. 405, 19 Apr. 1917, WO 256/17, TNA.
14. David French, 'Who Knew What and When? The French Army Mutinies and the British Decision to Launch the Third Battle of Ypres', in L. Freedman, P. Hayes and R. O'Neill (eds), *War, Strategy and International Politics* (Oxford: Clarendon Press, 1992), pp. 141, 144; Report of conference of Haig and Army Commanders, O.A.D. 433, 30 Apr. 1917, WO 256/17, TNA.
15. Haig, diary, 1 May 1917, in Sheffield and Bourne, *Douglas Haig*, p. 289.
16. Hastings Anderson, 'Lord Horne as an Army Commander', *Journal of the Royal Artillery*, vol. LVI, No. 4 (January 1930), pp. 416–17.
17. Falls, *Military Operations*, pp. 302–3.
18. 'Canadian Corps report on operations …', c.1917, WO 106/402, TNA.
19. Anderson, 'Lord Horne', p. 417.
20. Simon Robbins, 'Henry Horne', in I.F.W. Beckett and Steven J. Corvi (eds), *Haig's Generals* (Barnsley: Pen & Sword, 2006), p. 102.
21. Quoted in Jeffery Williams, *Byng of Vimy* (London: Leo Cooper, 1992 [1983]), p. 165.
22. 'Report on conference …', 29 Mar. 1917; 'Minutes of conference of Corps commanders … 15 Apr. 1917';'Weekly summary of operations … 6/4/17 to 13/4/17', WO 95/169, TNA.
23. 'First Army (Vimy)' statistics; 'RE Services (A) Forward Roads'; both in WO 95/169, TNA.
24. See G.D. Sheffield, 'How even was the learning curve? Reflections on British and Dominion Armies on the Western Front 1916–1918', in Yves Tremblay (ed.), *Canadian Military History since the 17th Century* (Ottawa: Department of National Defence, 2000), pp. 125–31.
25. Albert P. Palazzo, 'The British Army's Counter-Battery Staff Office and the Control of the Enemy in World War I', *Journal of Military History*, 63 (January 1999), pp. 56–7, 73.

26. 'Special Order by Major General C.L. Nicholson', 4 Apr. 1917, WO 95/2433, TNA.
27. 26 Brigade account, 9 Apr. 1917, p. 1, WO 95/1738, TNA.
28. 28 Brigade account, 9 Apr. 1917, p. 6, WO 95/1738, TNA.
29. 'Report by GOC 12th Div. to VI Corps', 20 Apr. 1917, WO 95/1824, TNA.
30. 13 Brigade report on operations, 18 Apr. 1917, WO 95/1514, TNA.
31. 'Summary of War Diary, 34th Division for April 1917', WO 95/2433, TNA.
32. Haig to George V, 9 Apr. 1917, in Sheffield and Bourne, *Douglas Haig*, p. 278.
33. Falls, *Military Operations*, p. 253.
34. Lawrence James, *Imperial Warrior: The Life and Times of Field Marshal Viscount Allenby 1861–1936* (London: Weidenfeld & Nicolson, 1993), p. 101; Falls, *Military Operations*, p. 259.
35. John Kiszley, 'The British Army and Approaches to Warfare since 1945', in Brian Holden Reid (ed.), *Military Power* (London: Cass, 1997), p. 180.
36. WO 95/1514, 23 Apr. 1917, TNA.
37. Report by GOC 12th Div. to VI Corps, 13 May 1917, WO 95/1824, TNA.
38. 'Summary of War Diary, 34th Division for April 1917', WO 95/2433, TNA.
39. Andy Simpson, 'British Corps Command on the Western Front, 1914–1918', in Gary Sheffield and Dan Todman (eds), *Command and Control on the Western Front: The British Army's Experience 1914–18* (Staplehurst: Spellmount, 2004), p. 114.

Chapter 8

The Indispensable Factor: British Troops in 1918

On 11 November 1918 Field Marshal Sir Douglas Haig noted in his diary: 'The Armistice came into force at 11a.m.'[1] Haig's characteristic lack of emotion, which was not shared by all British senior commanders, belied the fact of a remarkable military victory over a formidable enemy, the Imperial German army.[2] This victory was won by a coalition, in which the forces of the British Empire played the leading role.[3] Yet in Great Britain, the very fact of a military victory in 1918 has largely been forgotten. In the summer of 1998 Professor Sir Michael Howard published a letter in *The Times* reminding people that we were approaching the 80th anniversary of the Hundred Days. Sir Michael suggested that the commemoration of this, the greatest series of victories in British military history, should match those for the 80th anniversary of the disastrous first day of the Somme.[4] Needless to say, 8 August 1998 did not see a repetition of the wall-to-wall media coverage that occurred on 1 July 1996.[5] Moreover, those who have remembered the Hundred Days have tended to downplay the role of 'British' as opposed to 'Dominion' troops. Of the sixty active divisions in the British Expeditionary Force (BEF) under the command of Field Marshal Sir Douglas Haig in November 1918, all but ten were British. Yet while the achievements of the Canadian and Australian Corps have been, rightly, celebrated, with a couple of exceptions the no less remarkable activities of many British troops have received scant attention. Rather, the alleged disgraceful defeat at the hands of the German *Kaiserschlacht* has been highlighted by popular authors. One, the journalist William Moore, used the catchpenny title *See How They Ran* for his book.[6] Martin Middlebrook's book on 21 March 1918, while well researched and objective, may give the unwary an unbalanced view by concentrating on one day of apparent defeat to the exclusion of later developments.[7]

Besides the volumes of British official history,[8] there are some other books on 1918 that give a balanced account of the activities of British forces. In this category I would include Major General H. Essame's *The Battle for Europe 1918* (1972), Gregory Blaxland's *Amiens 1918* (1968) and John Terraine's *To Win a War: 1918, The Year of Victory* (1978).[9] These books are still worth reading but they were largely based on published sources, and belong to an older historiographical tradition. Three more recent books have reinvigorated the debate on 1918. Tim Travers' *How the War Was Won* (1992) is a very well researched analysis of 1918, but his views on the British Army troops have proved somewhat controversial in revisionist historical circles in the United Kingdom. Robin Prior and Trevor Wilson's *Command on the Western Front*, also published in 1992, and Paddy Griffith's *Battle Tactics of the Western Front* (1994) are among the most important books ever published on the Western Front.[10] Both give a rather more positive view of the activities of British forces in 1918 than has been customary.

Unfortunately, books are still being published that contain unwarranted sideswipes at the performance of British troops in 1918, usually by means of unfavourable comparisons with Dominion troops.[11] This tendency has led to some of the revisionist school of British historians of the Western Front to refer ironically to Dominion troops as 'colonial supermen'. Of course, this is quite unfair. Recently, historians from the Dominions have placed 'Colonial' military excellence into a proper perspective.[12] However, we still lack a fully-fledged comparative study of British and Dominion troops.[13] This chapter can do no more than review the main issues, but hopefully it will provide a starting point for future research.

The British Army of January 1918 had little in common with its tiny, professional predecessor of August 1914.[14] Equally, it was a very different creature from the mass volunteer army that made its debut on the Somme in July 1916,[15] and it was to undergo further changes in character by the time of the Armistice in November 1918. Just over half (50.3 per cent) of all enlistments into the wartime British Army occurred after the introduction of conscription.[16] By January 1918, although many wartime volunteers and even a few pre-war Regulars and Territorials remained with the colours, the British Army was a largely conscript force. It was an army that contained a disproportionately large number of men taken from white collar occupations. There were a number of reasons why this should be so. One was the simple fact that, given the manpower problems faced by a state fighting a total war, clerks could be more easily spared for the army than industrial workers. Nevertheless, as John Bourne has reminded us, wartime British casualties – and hence British soldiers – 'were overwhelmingly working class'.[17]

In January 1918 the BEF contained a mixture of experienced and inexperienced soldiers. The heavy losses at Passchendaele (some 250,000) were replaced to some extent by recruits, and the tactical experience and wisdom passed on by the hard core of survivors of Third Ypres compensated to some extent for the casualties – at least in a military sense. The manpower crisis at the beginning of 1918 led to the drastic step of reducing the number of battalions in British brigades from four to three, thus reducing twelve battalion divisions to nine battalions. Battalions were disbanded, amalgamated and shuffled from division to division; thus 31st Division, a Kitchener division of Pals battalions unkindly known to some historians as the 'Thirty-Worst', received three battalions of Foot Guards. This process was traumatic. It involved the destruction of communities, of soldiers' emotional 'homes', and led in some cases to bitterness and depressed morale. It also meant that some tactical practices, based on the four-battalion brigade, had to be re-thought. This was far from the end of the trauma. At the end of the German offensives, some divisions underwent further radical restructuring, thus the infantry of the 34th were reduced to cadre before being reconstituted. More-over, most of the replacements that arrived at the front during the latter part of 1918 were extremely youthful and lacking in military experience.

The case of 19th (Western) Division, a Kitchener formation, illustrates this point. Making its debut on the Somme in 1916, it earned a reputation as a good fighting division. Committed to battle on the afternoon of 21 March 1918, it had incurred 3,800 casualties by the 26th. A large number of 'boys' arrived as replacements but there was no time to 'absorb' them properly into the division before it was sent north to Messines. There, on 10 April, 19th Division was thrown into the Battle of the Lys, suffering 4,346 casualties. By May the division 'was now composed almost entirely of new drafts, many of whom were not fully trained'. Sent to the south, 19th Division became involved in the latter stages of IX Corps' defensive battle on the Aisne. Between 21 March and 19 June the division suffered 13,000 casualties – 'or about 90 per cent of the strength of the Division'.[18]

In July 1918 the division received more drafts, but still the 'majority of the men were young soldiers with no experience' and only partially trained. However, 'Good progress was made and ... [by 7 August when 19th Division returned to the front line] the men had been through a course of short but fairly intensive training.' 19th Division then experienced a spell of active trench warfare, including a successful divisional-sized operation in the Neuve Chapelle area on 3 September. Its next major offensive action came during the successful Battle of the Selle in October. The losses incurred during these actions were replaced by 'considerable number of young soldiers with no previous experience of the war and very little time in which to train them'.[19] The division's final action was an attack on 6 November 1918. In the last week of the war it advanced 18 miles. 19th Division's total casualties since 21 March 1918 amounted to about 16,000. Its record of achievement, in its twelve opposed assaults during the Hundred Days, was an impressive 100 per cent.

The net result of the organisational changes and heavy casualties of 1918 were that for many, if not most, British divisions, the continuity of command and personnel of their constituent units was severely disrupted. Moreover, compared to the Canadian Corps and the New Zealand Division (the latter was the strongest division in the BEF), British divisions were weak.[20] Indeed, as Shane Schreiber has pointed out, in terms of manpower and firepower a

Canadian division 'resembled a British Corps'.[21] As has often been noted, the Australian and Canadian Corps had the great advantage over British corps of being permanent organisations, with all that implies for common doctrine, with staffs and commanders of various constituent parts becoming used to working together. Compare this with the complaint of a British divisional staff officer on hearing his division was about to come under the command of a different corps: each corps has its own methods 'and one has to get into new ways'.[22] The wonder is, given these problems, that so many British formations performed as well as they did.

And, as Peter Simkins' research demonstrates, British divisions *did* fight well during the Hundred Days. Simkins analysed British and Dominion divisions' offensive operations and concluded that while Dominion formations indeed performed well, the success rate of many British divisions was equally impressive. His statistical evidence, which he places into context by discussing factors such as divisional freshness and numbers of days in battle, offers compelling evidence that 'the British divisions in the "Hundred Days", in spite of the crises they had experienced earlier in the year ... made a very weighty contribution to the Allied victory'. He identifies the Guards, 9th, 16th, 18th, 19th, 24th, 25th, 34th, 38th and 66th as statistically the ten most successful British divisions. From these figures 'one could infer ... that, in general, ten British divisions performed at least as well as – and in a few cases possibly better than – the leading six or seven Dominion divisions'.[23]

This is not to claim that all British divisions fought brilliantly on all occasions. Clearly, some divisions did not perform well during the German offensives of March to July 1918. On 8 August 1918 a British gunner officer ungenerously complained that III Corps 'made a hopeless mess of their part' in the Battle of Amiens,[24] although we should note that it attacked under peculiarly difficult circumstances not of its own making. However, successful operations by British units greatly outnumbered failures, a fact that attests to the high level of competence to be found throughout the BEF. The example of 46th (North Midland) Division, a Territorial formation that performed spectacularly badly at Gommecourt on 1 July 1916 but carried out one of the outstanding feats of the war in storming Riqueval bridge and thus breaking the Hindenburg Line on 29 September 1918, is relevant here. Simon Peaple argues that by autumn 1918 the level of competence in the BEF was such that even an unexceptional formation like the 46th could display considerable competence, both in gunnery and infantry fighting.[25]

'Peaceful Penetration' was not solely an Anzac activity. 19th Division, which called it 'nibbling', was not committed to a major action from July to mid-October 1918. During this time the division carried out a programme of bombardments, patrols, raids and small attacks (up to and including brigade and divisional strength) that took ground from the enemy and wore down his strength and morale.[26] Simkins has referred to the importance of the 'relent-less pressure'[27] brought to bear on the Germans during the Hundred Days. The effect of this pressure on the Germans was intensified because Foch and Haig began to put into practice the rudiments of what we would today call 'operational art': treating the entire Western Front as a single battlefield, and switching the point of main effort from one sector to another, to keep the enemy 'on the back foot'. The closing down of the Amiens offensive on 11 August and switching the main attack north to Third Army's front sector is an obvious example. Constant attrition, as well as the more obviously spectacular advances, played a major part in bringing about the Allied victory in 1918.

There are some other aspects of British military performance in 1918 that were vital to the Allied cause. First is the performance of British troops during the German offensives. As Simkins has demonstrated, the harsh criticism levied by Monash and others of British efforts during Villers-Bretonneux in April was undeserved.[28] More generally, British troops deserve credit for their dogged performance during the German spring offensives. German 'stormtroop' tactics did not come as a complete surprise to the British high command[29] and in the first three months of the year divisions undertook con-siderable training in defensive measures, albeit under less than perfect condi-tions.[30] In spite of the tactical reverse suffered on 21 March, the German offensives in Picardy in March and on the Lys in April ended as British strategic victories, albeit defensive ones, that prevented the Germans from reaching their operational goals and eroded German manpower and morale.

Second, we should not forget the vast number of British troops who were not organised into divisions. The British Army had to spread its resources quite thinly. It could not concentrate its resources in 'teeth arm' units, nor could it focus on one main theatre of operations. Britain had to provide a full range of troops, all over the globe, from infantrymen and field gunners to the man who was described in his confidential report for 1918 as a 'good hard-working officer very well up in his special subject – boots'.[31] On 1 August 1918, for instance, some 548,780 men were serving in the Royal Artillery. On the Western Front the gunners had 19 Royal Horse Artillery, 415 Royal Field Artillery, 148 anti-aircraft, 77 Trench Mortar, 58 Royal Garrison Artillery Heavy and 331 Siege batteries.[32] A British RGA siege battery might just as well be used to support a Dominion as an English or Scottish division. The artillery support for the Australian Corps at Amiens on 8 August 1918 con-sisted of divisional batteries of the five Australian divisions: III (Aus.), VI (Aus.), XII (Aus.), plus numerous British artillery units: XIV, XXIII, 189, 298 Brigades RFA, XVI (Army) Brigade RHA; and no fewer than nine RGA brigades.[33] Thus the majority of the artillery that played such a crucial role in the Australian success was British: the credit for the Australian victory belongs to the British gunners as well as to the Antipodean infantry. The same basic point applies to British logistic and combat support units. 216 Army Troops Company Royal Engineers, a specialist bridging unit raised in the English Midlands town of Nuneaton, served for some time in 1918 in support of the Australian Corps.[34]

Let us now turn to look at various aspects of the performance of British troops in 1918. I will confine my comments to the following areas: morale; logistics; tactics and training; and leadership, command and control. I have recently written elsewhere on the subject of morale, so here I will limit myself to a few general points.[35] British military morale – in the sense of soldiers' willingness to fight – remained sound throughout the First World War. It certainly was in a trough in spring 1918, but had the morale of Gough's Fifth Army really collapsed, as some have claimed,[36] the Germans would have won the First World War. Surrenders of British soldiers and losses of guns notwithstanding, vastly more soldiers remained with their units and fought on than capitulated. Many of those who did surrender only did so after they had resisted for some time and the situation was clearly hopeless. Such a soldier was Private O.G. Billingham of 2/6 Manchesters (66th Division). He endured four and a half days of fighting, suffering a 'most awful time', resisting until the enemy had almost encircled his small party before he surrendered.[37] Official reports, based on the censorship of soldiers' letters, confirm that British morale remained basically sound during the spring offensives.[38]

Military victory brought with it higher morale. Apparently in response to a 'gloomy' letter from his father, in early June 1918 an officer of 9/East Surreys (12th Division) reported that soldiers at the front were rather more optimistic.[39] When the Allies finally seized the initiative, and the Germans were being pushed back, soldiers of all ranks began to sense that victory was near: 'These are great days for all of us and I pity anyone who isn't on the spot, and who has been through all the labour and heat of the day only to miss the reward at the end. Everyone is in fine form and confident to a degree not known hitherto.'[40]

A number of soldiers are credited with the aphorism 'amateurs talk tactics, professionals talk logistics'. Effective logistics is certainly the hallmark of a professional army. In its handling of supply and administration, as in so many other things, by January 1918 the BEF had come a long way from July 1916, let alone August 1914. This is clear from Ian Brown's 1998 monograph on the subject.[41] The *ad hoc* approach of the early war years was replaced by a much larger and more soundly based system by the time of the March Retreat. The Army Service Corps (ASC) grew from 498 officers and 5,933 other ranks in August 1914 to 10,477 officers and 314,693 men four years later.[42] Turning from transport to ordnance, by late 1917 the Armourers' Shop at the major base at Calais could repair 1,000 rifles per day, and the Bootmakers' Shop, claimed to be the biggest in the world, employed 500 soldiers and 100 French civilians who could repair 30,000 pairs a week.[43] The preparations for the

Somme offensive included putting the supply of water to the front line on a firm footing, and planning to get water forward quickly if a rapid advance should ensue.[44] Light tramways were constructed in forward areas to ease transportation problems.[45]

But in the spring of 1918 to some individuals it must have seemed as if the logistic system that had served the needs of trench warfare so well had broken down. A member of the Frolics concert party wrote that on 23 March:

> we had to make a hasty retreat with all our worldly possessions – every road out of the village was crowded with rushing traffic – lorries, limbers, G.S. waggons, great caterpillar-tractors with immense guns behind them, all were dashing along in an uninterrupted stream – and men, half-running, with portions of their kit dropping from them as they ran – for it was said that the enemy cavalry were through and were nearly in the village ... I never thought in the days when we looked with disdain on 'bully' and biscuits I should ever long for them and cherish a bit of hard, dry biscuit as a hungry tramp cherishes a crust of bread.[46]

Seen in a wider perspective, the British logistic system proved remarkably resilient under the enormous strain of the German offensives. British logisticians certainly made mistakes. The history of the Army Ordnance Services, published in 1929, candidly admits that in the build-up to the German offensive more should have been done to 'reduce or render more mobile' the various logistic workshops, dumps and the like. In the event, among other logistic catastrophes, a 'great part' of Fifth Army's 'central workshop was ... lost'.[47] However, the triumphs of the British logisticians far outweighed their disasters. Between 20 March and 30 April 1918 the British lost 816 18-pdrs and 280 4.5-in. howitzers. Yet during the period 26 March–9 May Fifth Army's artillery park alone, despite the need to move location several times as the enemy advanced, issued 585 guns and 2,941 machine guns.[48] A combination of the effectiveness of the BEF's logistics, and the inability of the Germans to advance further than they did to cut the British lines of communication (which was in part a product of German logistic problems), gave the fighting troops of the BEF a firm base upon which to fall back, regroup and prepare to take the offensive.

Unfortunately, neither Brown's new monograph nor the volume of the British Official History that deals with transportation goes into very much detail about the logistics of the Hundred Days.[49] The evidence suggests that the logistic system came under severe strain but was as flexible in the advance as it had been resilient in the retreat. The demands on combat support and logistic units were very different from those of trench warfare. Assault river crossings, in which bridge-building engineers played a vital role, were a feature of operations such as the Battle of the Selle and the crossing of the River Lys (both in October 1918). For instance, the Royal Engineers between the beginning of the war and August 1918 had constructed 180 steel bridges; in the three months after 8 August 1918 they built 330.[50] Success brought its own problems. Most fundamental of all, the logisticians had to struggle to keep advancing troops in supply. One of the most perceptive historians of the war, Cyril Falls, who served with 36th (Ulster) Division, discussed the logistic problems faced by II Corps when it broke out of the Ypres salient at the end of September: 'Batteries in an advance go forward only. The limbers which feed them, the lorries which feed the limbers from the train, must go forward and backward. Therein lay the real trouble. The roads were choked.'

The next phase of the offensive, on 14 October, was delayed until sufficient artillery was amassed for the assault. The attack was successful: Courtrai fell, and 36th Division continued to advance. By this stage, Falls judged, the chief obstacle to final victory was not the Germans but logistic problems. Wagons and lorries had to make their way across 'the terrible roads of the devastated area'. By 'good organisation and industry' and, not least, sheer hard work and dedication, the Army Service Corps 'scored a triumph',[51] as did the rest of the support services, including the provost branch, who wrestled with the problems of traffic control. The Ulster Division's experiences were far from untypical.[52] By improvisation and strenuous exertion the BEF's logisticians kept the advance going, but it was a near run thing. One can scarcely fault the performance of these British troops.

Nowhere was the British Army's learning curve more apparent than in the field of tactics. This is not the place for a detailed discussion of the implementation of tactical 'good practice' in the BEF between mid-1916 and the end of 1917.[53] Suffice it to say that the BEF took advantage of new technology as it became available – Lewis Guns, gas, trench mortars, the 106 fuse, tanks, wireless, aircraft and the like – and by trial and error developed effective tactics to harness it. The British battalion of August 1918 had far fewer men than its counterpart of two years earlier: about 500, compared to 1,000. However, its firepower was much more formidable. The four Lewis Guns per battalion of 1916 had grown to thirty, plus eight light trench mortars and sixteen rifle-bombers.[54] As we have seen, as early as the spring of 1917 the lessons of the Somme had been absorbed, resulting in the platoon organisation being changed from four rifle sections to one rifle section plus a section each of Lewis Gunners, bombers and rifle grenadiers.[55] Moreover, the division now included a Machine Gun battalion as a tactical unit, with the battalion commander in a position 'analogous' to that of the 'C[ommander] R[oyal] A[rtillery]' of a division concerning the artillery'.[56] Although Tim Travers has argued for the essential conservatism of officers who relied on infantry and artillery centred methods (as opposed to tanks), by 1918 the BEF was at the forefront of military technology.[57] Put in simple terms, the 106 artillery fuse probably made a greater contribution to the Allied victory than the tank.[58]

Tactical good practice could only be implemented by successful training. As we have seen, during 1918 time for training was at a premium, to be fitted in when operations permitted.[59] Yet the comments of the historian of the Welsh Guards were as applicable to 1918 as to earlier years: 'Training never ceased during the war. The hardened veteran, out of the line for a rest, joined the young recruit, who had just arrived in France for the first time, and trained.'[60]

The learning process continued while operations were in progress in 1918. As early as 5 April, during the first phase of the German offensive, GHQ issued the first of a long series of *Notes on Recent Fighting* in which an analysis of the lessons of 21–22 March were 'issued down to brigades'.[61] *Notes* No. 7, issued two weeks after the opening of the battles of the Lys, stressed the importance of holding the flanks of an enemy breakthrough and thus enfilading the enemy and helping to contain his advance, a lesson drawn from the dogged actions of 55th and 40th Divisions on the flanks of the German breakthough on 9 April.[62] When the Allies seized the initiative from the Germans, official publications disseminated the lessons of offensive war.[63] Other higher formations issued their own documents. In late August Horne's First Army issued a document that recognised that some divisions had greater expertise at fire and movement tactics in open warfare than others. It stressed the need for better training of troops acting as advance guards when not actually in contact with the enemy, who had a tendency to move 'in general lines' rather than concentrate in small bodies.[64] Such 'high level' tactical advice was in addition to the numerous studies produced by divisions or even lower level formations for use by units under their command. An important step was the appointment of Ivor Maxse, by reputation one of the finest trainers in the British Army, as Inspector General of Training in 1918.[65] His inspectorate issued a large number of 'Training Leaflets', which covered topics such as 'Sample of a Day's Training for a Company' and 'Attack Formation for Small Units' in a straightforward, accessible fashion. These leaflets were issued in vast numbers. Of the two mentioned above, by February 1919 39,426 were issued of the first and 41,496 of the second.[66] Clearly in 1918, as in previous years, the British high command was making strenuous efforts to analyse and disseminate tactical lessons of recent actions, and as a result commanders were receiving a great deal of useful tactical advice and information, which was integrated into training.[67]

The reality of the tactical learning curve was made explicit in an account of the attack on Beaulencourt carried out by 21st Division on 1 September 1918. This account was written in 1919 by Captain D.V. Kelly of 6/Leicesters, whose views on Passchendaele were quoted in Chapter 6.

> [This attack] gave a striking proof of the enormous advance made by the new British Army in the technique of warfare, for it was a small masterpiece achieved with one tenth of the casualties it would assuredly have

cost us in 1916. The long western-front of the village, which appeared the main line of approach, was defended by numerous well-concealed pits for riflemen and machine guns, and had we been attacking in the 1916 method the course of events would probably have been as follows. A tremendous artillery bombardment, perhaps for two days, would have annihilated the village and churned up the ground, and at zero hour our troops would have advanced in waves across the belt of land commanded by the various posts, who, as our barrage passed on behind them, would have opened a murderous direct fire on them and taken an enormous toll of casualties. Very possibly we should never have reached the village, but consolidated a line of shellholes a few yards beyond the starting-point, from which a fresh attack would have been delivered perhaps several days later.

By September, 1918, however we had acquired an improved technique. The Western side of the village was left severely alone, and the attack was arranged for the northern movement and assembly by night that would have been difficult for inexperienced officers. The artillery fired numerous periodic 'crashes', and their support at zero was arranged to appear merely a repetition of one of these and did not specially indicate the time or direction of the attack. Under cover of complete darkness the village was rushed and the defences taken in the rear, the whole affair being a complete surprise ... It is very important to remember that the artillery had improved their technique just as had the staffs and the infantry: in 1916 one could hardly have relied on the accuracy and exact synchronization, which one had now learned to expect, required for such an operation.[68]

About 130 Germans were captured, in addition to a number of weapons. The two assaulting battalions, 1/Wiltshires and 6/Leicesters, suffered only five killed and fifty wounded.[69]

Among the reasons for success mentioned by Kelly were sophisticated artillery techniques and good co-ordination between the gunners and the infantry, good staff work, and good regimental leadership: these factors made it possible to achieve surprise. While his description of the '1916 methods' was perhaps a little harsh, in broad terms it was correct. Kelly's description of the tactics of 1918 was applicable to many other formations: 21st Division was a very competent formation but it was far from unique. The tactical expertise of 1918 was, I would suggest, the product of hard-won experience gained on the Somme in 1916, at Arras and the Third Battle of Ypres in 1917, and good training.

British junior leadership in 1918 has had a bad press. The roots of the belief that British regimental officers behaved poorly in 1918 can perhaps be traced back to Brigadier General Sir James Edmonds' comments in the British official history.[70] However, it was also held during the war by some British Regular officers,[71] and it seemed to be an article of faith with many Australians.[72] I take issue with these views at length elsewhere,[73] and here it will suffice to say that by 1918 the selection process for British officers was very similar to that for Australians. By the last year of the war the British officer corps was a broadly meritocratic body in which leadership ability counted for vastly more and social status for much less than before the war. Most officers were by 1918 commissioned from the ranks, and something like 40 per cent of officers demobilised at the end of the war came from lower middle-class and working-class backgrounds.

There is much to be said that for the view that by the summer of 1917 the 'war was becoming more than ever a platoon commander's war, for it would be on their initiative and determination that success would depend'.[74] The Hundred Days was probably the finest hour of these meritocratic temporary officers. The quality of their leadership was a vital component of British military success in 1918. On 30 March 1918, on the sixth day of 20th (Light) Division's retreat, Major R.S. Cockburn came across some exhausted stragglers, lacking training and discipline, who seemed to have given up all thought of soldiering. However, their officers, who were themselves inexperienced, showed good leadership in halting the retreat by explaining to them why no further retreat was possible.[75] Leaders did not have to be officers. The minor counter-attack by Lewis gunners of 24/Royal Fusiliers (2nd Division) led by Company Sergeant Major 'Rosy' Read and Sergeant Roland Whipp during the March Retreat are typical of the countless number of similar operations instigated by NCOs.[76]

Good junior leadership was just as vital during the advance; low-level initiative and improvisation became increasingly important as the Allies pushed forward. Long periods for the preparation of assaults were not always available or even necessary.[77] This new tactical situation demanded excellence from staff officers and junior commanders. A gunner subaltern noted in his diary that orders for an assault to be made at 1.30am on 23 October only arrived 'soon after 9pm. Meant an unholy rush and consequently no sleep during the night.' However, the attack was a great success.[78] This can profitably be compared both to the rushed and frequently unsuccessful attacks on the Somme in 1916, and also to the 'minute preparations' and extensive practice carried out before many 1917 operations.[79] According to the commander of 5th Division's artillery, the 'outstanding feature' of operations in the Hundred Days 'was the way in which batteries pushed on and took advantage of the tactical situations as they developed. On many occasions batteries were commanded by quite junior subalterns with remarkable success, in spite of the fact that they were entirely new to open warfare conditions.'[80]

In late September the high command stressed that, while the barrage remained vital, it was also important to use 18-pdrs as 'weapons of opportunity' in direct support of the 'leading infantry', which required the closest liaison between the infantry and the guns. Guns were also to be used to engage enemy guns holding up the advance of tanks.[81] Not just field artillery, but guns as big as 60-pdrs, were to be 'pushed up ... boldly'.[82]

While the importance of the creeping barrage and counter battery work has been well covered in recent years,[83] the role of the infantry has perhaps received less attention than it deserves. The advice issued by Brigadier General James Jack to 'All Ranks 28th Infantry Brigade' of 9th (Scottish) Division on 27 September 1918 concisely encapsulates much of the tactical wisdom of the Hundred Days, which was based on the experience of 1916 and 1917:

- Brigadier has heard of your gallantry, has seen your smartness, and prays you use your wits.
- Keep as close as you can to 18pdrs (pipsqueak) barrage. Its their, [sic] so don't go into it. Never mind your dressing.
- Reply at once to any enemy small arm [sic] fire. Fire at once at any enemy you see in range – slowly and accurately from the quickest position, lying, standing, or kneeling.
- Don't crowd, the loose order will save you casualties if you use your wits.
- Watch your flanks and draw them back if necessary.
- If held up reply steadily to the fire whilst your comrades get round.
- If necessary help your comrades on flank by cross fire.
- Surround pill-boxes and Machine Guns. They can only fire one or two ways.
- Don't have more than about 100x [yards] between sections. Don't scatter from your sections, file is best for advancing, a few paces interval for firing.
- Push steadily forward in your little groups, using slow covering fire where necessary, and stick roughly to your own line of ADVANCE.
- Good luck.[84]

Such tactics were simple enough to be taught quickly and effectively to the vast numbers of inexperienced 18-year-olds arriving as reinforcements for the BEF in 1918.[85] Combined with effective support from the guns and some-times tanks and aircraft, such tactics were good enough to inflict defeat after defeat on the Germans.

In the last few weeks of the war, as the fighting moved into untouched countryside and into intact villages, towns and cities, on some occasions the importance of the artillery diminished: on 5 November, for example, a gunner officer noted that the enemy were retreating 'at such a rate as to render the H[eavy] A[rtillery] useless'.[86] Under such conditions the fighting abilities of the infantry made the difference between success and failure, victory and defeat.

The open warfare conditions of 1918 called for the learning of new skills. As an officer of 20th Division commented, with a slight degree of exaggeration, the British citizen army had trained for offensive action, but not how to withdraw under attack.[87] In fact, British divisions learned how to conduct a fighting retreat remarkably quickly and effectively. When the tide turned in favour of the Allies, they developed yet another approach to warfare. *Pace* those who believe that cavalry was completely redundant on the Western Front,[88] the mobility of mounted troops, which had been a useful asset in the days of trench warfare, now became a priceless one. During the Hundred Days there was a shortage of horsemen, and, tactically, 'the absence of mounted troops was severely felt'.[89] In September 19th Division formed a 'Divisional Mounted Detachment' that in October had a skirmish with German cavalry.[90] In early October the infantry divisions of I Corps were reorganised to facilitate rapid pursuit of the enemy. Infantry brigades were divided into an advanced guard and a main body. Each brigade commander was allotted an all-arms mobile body (one section of cavalry, one section RE, one 18-pdr battery, one section each of 4.5-in howitzers and medium trench mortars, one company of machine gunners, part of a Field Ambulance, and an 'Investigation Party' of men from a Tunnelling Company). This reorganisation 'proved very suitable to the circumstances'.[91]

The command and control (C2) of the BEF has been something of a blind spot for historians. Two of the most influential studies, by Martin Samuels and Martin van Creveld, concentrate on the beginning of the Somme campaign and do not analyse the situation in 1918, giving a one-sided view.[92] Samuels compares the situation at Thiepval on 1 July 1916 with German C2 on 21 March 1918, a case of comparing apples with bananas rather than apples with apples if ever there was one. Tim Travers in two very influential books painted a bleak picture of the BEF's C2 system.[93] John Bourne has summarised Travers's view of it as:

> rigid, hierarchical and inflexible ... reactionary, hostile to technology, preferring a costly 'human solution' to the problems of the battlefield and fatuously determined to overcome the chaos of war by highly detailed and structured planning from above ... The most that can be said in favour of the British system is that it broke down under the impact of the German offensives and the semi-open warfare which followed, to be replaced by 'useful anarchy'.[94]

Bourne takes issue with Travers' views, as do I. The German offensives of March to July 1918 certainly placed the BEF's command and control system under severe strain. The points made about logistics above are also applicable to command and control: the British C2 system proved resilient and flexible enough to absorb and cope with the limited damage inflicted by the German advance. The sudden re-emergence of open warfare left the BEF no choice but to shake off some of their trench-bound habits. Overblown divisional headquarters had to be slimmed down to cope with the new circumstances, the ideal being 'to work as far as possible with a message book only'. Some commanders of divisions 'established advanced H.Q. motor cars', linked by telephone line to the divisional signal office.[95] This is not to underestimate the real C2 problems experienced during the German offensives. Nevertheless, the BEF's C2 system survived, battered but sufficiently intact to allow the BEF to pass onto the offensive. One reason for this was that command at various levels was much less rigid and hidebound than the traditional version would have us believe. The Somme, Arras, Passchendaele and Cambrai battles bred a group of commanders at battalion, brigade and divisional level – perhaps even at corps and army level – able to cope with the changing demands of the battlefield. At even lower levels, subalterns, NCOs and even privates became increasingly accustomed to using initiative and taking responsibility.[96] In Bourne's words, 'The SHLM project on British divisional performance during the war suggests that "useful anarchy" began much before 1918.'[97]

As noted above, the increase in the tempo of offensive operations in the autumn of 1918 placed considerable strain on staff officers. However, in general, operations and logistic staffs coped well with the mobile warfare of the Hundred Days. To take just one example from many, the historian of 5/Leicesters (46th Division) recorded his appreciation of the staff work (and the 'skill and pluck' of the ASC) that enabled the infantry to attack on 29 September carrying only one day's rations.[98] The 1919 Braithwaite Report on Staff Organisation believed that the open warfare phase vindicated 'the soundness of the general principles on which the Staff is organized and was trained before the war'.[99] Although apparently smacking of self-congratulation and even complacency, the historian can accept this conclusion, with reservations, as sound.

The performance of British troops was, then, a vital factor in the Allied victory of 1918. It was not a 'British' victory or even a British Empire victory. British and Dominion forces fought as part of a multi-national coalition, and to think in such terms would be to do a disservice to the considerable French, United States and Belgian contributions. But it was undoubtedly a triumph for the forces of the British Empire. It does not diminish the achievements of the Australian, Canadian, New Zealand and South African forces in any way to recognise that the performance of troops from the British Isles was an indispensable factor in the final victory.

Further Reading

Since this piece was written in 1998 scholars have produced some important work on the BEF in the Hundred Days. Books include Jonathan Boff's

An artist's impression of very early aerial combat. (*Spencer Jones collection*)

-pounder guns camouflaged from enemy aircraft. (*Spencer Jones collection*)

German infantry using flamethrowers against French positions, 1915 – artist's impression. (*Spencer Jones collection*)

Field Marshal Sir John French, Commander-in-Chief of the British Expeditionary Force, 1914–1915. (*Spencer Jones collection*)

ll armies on the Western
ont quickly adjusted to trench
arfare. This German dugout is
n the Aisne. (*Spencer Jones collection*)

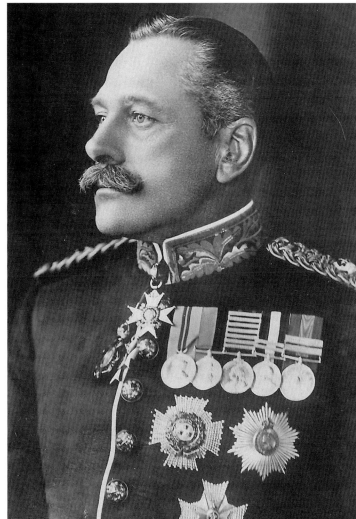

eneral (later Field Marshal)
r Douglas Haig took over
mmand of the BEF from
ench in December 1915 and
ld the position for the rest of
e war. (*Spencer Jones collection*)

Headquarters staff of 1st Canadian Division in 1915. The growth of the experience of staff was to be critical in the improvement of the BEF's performance. (*Spencer Jones collection*)

The Empire made a huge contribution in terms of military manpower. Indian troops were used extensively on the Western Front in 1914–1915 before the bulk were sent to Middle Eastern theatres. (*Spencer Jones collection*)

An artist's impression of a German officer being questioned by his French captors. Interrogation of prisoners was an essential building block of intelligence-gathering. (*Spencer Jones collection*)

A photograph of British infantry, presumably posed, from the earliest days of trench warfare. (*Spencer Jones collection*)

General Sir Henry Rawlinson, commander of Fourth Army on the Somme in 1916 and in the Hundred Days of 1918. (*Spencer Jones collection*)

An imaginative reconstruction of a Royal Field Artillery wireless operator. The combination of wireless, aircraft and guns transformed the conduct of warfare between 1915 and 1918.
(*Spencer Jones collection*)

ritish maritime supremacy was a critical factor in the victory of the Entente in the First World War. ere, an artist depicts aircraft of the Royal Naval Air Service. (*Spencer Jones collection*)

British cavalry regiment, the Royal Scots Greys, in training just before the war. Contrary to myth, orsed cavalry did have a role to play on the Western Front, even under conditions of trench arfare. (*Spencer Jones collection*)

A British tank on the battlefield: the rear wheel dates this photograph to 1916. (*Spencer Jones collection*)

A dramatic cut-away of a German U-boat. The German campaign of unrestricted submarine warfar in 1917 was probably their best chance of forcing Britain out of the war. (*Spencer Jones collection*)

outstanding *Winning and Losing on the Western Front: The British Third Army and the Defeat of Germany in 1918* (Cambridge: Cambridge University Press, 2012). J.P. Harris and Niall Barr produced a good narrative intermingled with analysis, *Amiens to the Armistice* (London: Brassey's, 1999), which is in my view a superior book to Harris's 2008 biography of Haig. Mitchell A. Yockleson brings an interesting perspective on the BEF with his study of US II Corps, *Borrowed Soldiers: Americans under British Command, 1918* (Norman, OK: University of Oklahoma Press, 2008). A key text looking at the Hundred Days from the other side of the hill is David T. Zabecki, *The German 1918 Offensives: A Case Study in the Operational Level of War* (Abingdon: Routledge, 2006). The collection in which this chapter originally appeared, Peter Dennis and Jeffrey Grey (eds), *1918: Defining Victory* (Canberra: Army History Unit, 1999), remains important. Ashley Ekins, *1918: The Year of Victory* (Auckland: Exisle, 2010), is also a key text which contains a number of excellent contributions. In my chapter, I revisited the themes in 'The Indispensable Factor' in the light of more recent research. 'My conclusions of 1998', I wrote, 'remain valid, although the scholarship of the intervening years has produced a more nuanced picture' (p. 54).

Acknowledgements

I would like to thank the usual suspects, especially Chris McCarthy, Peter Simkins, John Lee and Niall Barr, for their advice on this topic.

   I am grateful to Dr Peter H. Liddle for permission to quote from material in the Liddle Collection, University of Leeds; Mrs Pam Bendall for granting me access to material in the library of the Staff College, Camberley; and the Trustees of the Imperial War Museum for granting me access to their collections. Crown Copyright material in the National Archives appears by permission of Her Majesty's Stationery Office.

Notes

1. Robert Blake (ed.), *The Private Papers of Douglas Haig 1914–19* (London: Eyre & Spottis-woode, 1952), p. 340.
2. See Sir Henry Horne to wife, 11 Nov. 1918, Horne Papers, Imperial War Museum [IWM].
3. Jean-Baptiste Duroselle, *La Grande Guerre des Francois 1914–1918* (Paris: Perrin, 1998), pp. 394–5.
4. *The Times*, 17 July 1998, p. 23.
5. In October 1998, in a review of John Keegan's *The First World War*, the influential literary critic Paul Fussell dwelt on the alleged futility of the Somme and Passchendaele while contriving to ignore the Hundred Days – indeed, the Allied victory – altogether: *Guardian Weekly*, 18 October 1998, p. 33.
6. William Moore, *See How They Ran – The British Retreat of 1918* (London: Leo Cooper, 1970).
7. Martin Middlebrook, *The Kaiser's Battle* (London: Allen Lane, 1978).
8. J.E. Edmonds, *Military Operations France and Belgium, 1918* (vols I–III: London: Macmillan, 1935–9; vols IV and V: HMSO, 1947).
9. H. Essame, *The Battle for Europe 1918* (London: Batsford, 1972); Gregory Blaxland, *Amiens 1918* (London: Muller, 1968); John Terraine, *To Win a War: 1918, The Year of Victory* (London: Sidgwick & Jackson, 1978).

10. Tim Travers, *How the War was Won* (London: Routledge, 1992); Robin Prior and Trevor Wilson. *Command on the Western Front: The Military Career of Sir Henry Rawlinson 1914–1918* (Oxford: Blackwell, 1992); Paddy Griffith, *Battle Tactics of the Western Front: The British Army's Art of Attack, 1916–18* (London: Yale University Press, 1994).

11. Hubert C. Johnson, *Breakthrough! Tactics, Technology, and the Search for Victory on the Western Front in World War I* (Novato, CA: Presidio, 1994), p. 247; Denis Winter, *Haig's Command: A Reassessment* (London: Viking, 1991), p. 144.

12. In addition to Prior and Wilson, *Command*, see, among other works, Bill Rawling, *Surviving Trench Warfare: Technology and the Canadian Corps, 1914–1918* (Toronto: University of Toronto Press, 1992); E.M. Andrews, 'Bean and Bullecourt: Weaknesses and Strengths of the Official History of Australia in the First World War', *Revue Internationale d'Histoire Militaire*, 12 (Canberra: Australian Commission of Military History, 1990); Jeffrey Grey, *A Military History of Australia* (Cambridge: Cambridge University Press, 1990), pp. 87–123.

13. Sadly, a projected collaboration between the author, Peter Simkins and John Lee did not come to fruition.

14. For a brilliant pen-portrait of the Regular army of 1914 see Richard Holmes, *Riding the Retreat* (London: Cape, 1995), pp. 26–69.

15. For the character of the mass volunteer army of 1916, see Peter Simkins, *Kitchener's Army* (Manchester: Manchester University Press, 1988), *passim*, and Martin Middlebrook, *The First Day on the Somme* (London: Allen Lane, 1971), pp. 1–28.

16. *Statistics of the Military Effort of the British Empire during the Great War 1914–1920* [SME] (London: HMSO, 1922), p. 364.

17. J.M. Winter, *The Great War and the British People* (London: Macmillan, 1985), pp. 46–8; P.E. Dewey, 'Military recruiting and the British labour force during the First World War', *Historical Journal*, XXXVII (1984), pp. 199–223; J.M. Bourne, *Britain and the Great War 1914–1918* (London: Edward Arnold, 1989), p. 205.

18. Material on 19th Division is drawn from Everard Wyrall, *The History of the 19th Division 1914–1918* (London: Edward Arnold, n.d.); 'Report on Operations undertaken by IX Corps between 27th and 30th May 1918', in WO 95/837, TNA; and Anon, *A Short History of the 19th (Western) Division 1914–1918* (London: John Murray, 1919). Quotations are from the latter source, pp. 61, 78, 30.

19. *Short History of 19th Div.*, p. 100.

20. Shane B. Schrieber, *Shock Army of the British Empire: The Canadian Corps in the last 100 Days of the Great War* (Westport, CT: Praeger, 1997), pp. 20–4; Christopher Pugsley, *On the Fringe of Hell: New Zealanders and Military Discipline in the First World War* (Auckland: Hodder & Stoughton, 1991), p. 259.

21. Schrieber, *Shock Army*, p. 20.

22. Archibald Home (Diana Briscoe, ed.), *Diary of a World War I Cavalry Officer* (Tunbridge Wells: Costello, 1985), p. 105 (29 April 1916).

23. Peter Simkins, 'Co-Stars or Supporting Cast? British Divisions in the "Hundred Days" 1918', in Paddy Griffith (ed.), *British Fighting Methods in the Great War* (London: Cass, 1996), pp. 56–8.

24. Diary, Lieutenant C.R. Benstead, 8 Aug. 1918, Liddle Collection [LC], University of Leeds.

25. Simon Peaple, unpublished paper, 1998.

26. Wyrall, *19th Division*, pp. 211–14.

27. Simkins, 'Co-Stars', p. 66.

28. Peter Simkins, 'The absolute limit: British divisions at Villers-Bretonneux, April 1918', unpublished paper, 1997.

29. 'German Methods in the Attack, and Indications of an Offensive', annex to Tank Corps Summary of Information, 27 February 1918, WO 95/93, TNA.

30. F.C. Grimwade, *The War History of the 4th Battalion The London Regiment (Royal Fusiliers) 1914–19* (London: privately published, 1922), p. 350.
31. 'General Aspects: Officers', item 6, LC.
32. *SME*, p. 163.
33. Edmonds, *Military Operations*, vol. IV, p. 62.
34. James Sambrook, *With the Rank and Pay of a Sapper* (Nuneaton: Paddy Griffith Associates, 1998), p. 204.
35. G.D. Sheffield, *The Morale of the British Army on the Western Front, 1914–1918* (Occasional Paper No. 2, Institute for the Study of War and Society, De Montfort University, Bedford, 1995), reprinted as Chapter 9 of this book.
36. John Keegan, *The Face of Battle* (Harmondsworth: Penguin, 1978), p. 276.
37. Diary, 21–25 Mar. 1918, O.G. Billingham Papers, LC.
38. 'The British Armies in France as gathered from Censorship', Appendix to July 1918, Haig Papers, WO 256/33, TNA; Middlebrook, *Kaiser's Battle*, pp. 105, 300–18, 341.
39. R.B. Marshall to father, 4 June 1918, Marshall Papers, LC.
40. G.D. Sheffield and G.I.S. Inglis (eds), *From Vimy Ridge to the Rhine: The Great War Letters of Christopher Stone DSO MC* (Ramsbury: Crowood, 1989), p. 138 (Stone to wife, 3 October 1918).
41. Ian Malcolm Brown, *British Logistics on the Western Front 1914–1919* (Westport, CT: Praeger, 1998), p. 239.
42. *SME*, p. 181.
43. '[Notes on] Calais Base', November 1917, E436A Joint Services Command and Staff College Library [JSCSCL].
44. 'Notes from a Lecture on Water Supplies in the Field', n.d. (*c.* spring 1917), E435, JSCSCL.
45. 'Forward Tramlines in Trench War', E.inC Field Work notes, No. 22, n.d., E435, JSCSCL.
46. Signaller C.L. Leeson to 'Will', 29 Mar. 1918, Leeson Papers, LC. For details of the soldier's diet in more normal times, see 'Appendix 1, The British Ration in the Field', WO 107/28, TNA.
47. Major General A. Forbes, *A History of the Army Ordnance Services*, vol. III (London: Medici Society, 1929), pp. 153, 164. For an excellent short overview of the work of the Army Ordnance Department, see 'Calais Base', November 1917, E436A, JSCSCL.
48. Forbes, *Army Ordnance Services*, pp. 156–7.
49. Brown, *British Logistics*, devotes only 9 pages (pp. 196–204) to this period out of 261 pages, while A.M. Henniker, *Transportation on the Western Front, 1914–1918* (London: HMSO, 1937), devotes about 50 out of 507 pages of text.
50. Sambrook, *Rank and Pay*, p. 213.
51. Cyril Falls, *The History of the 36th (Ulster) Division* (Belfast: M'Caw, Stevenson & Orr, 1922), pp. 269, 270, 279.
52. 'Operations of the 17th Division from 21st August 1918 to 11 November 1918', 112–13, Conf. 3355, JSCSCL; *Short History of 19th Division*, p. 104.
53. See Griffith, *Battle Tactics*, and Rawling, *Surviving Trench Warfare*.
54. Prior and Wilson, *Command on the Western Front*, p. 311.
55. In *Breakthrough*, p. 224, Hubert C. Johnson misdates this restructuring by twelve months, placing it in 1918.
56. Memorandum, Dawnay to the Armies, 2 November 1918, E434, JSCSCL; Chris McCarthy, 'Nobody's Child: a brief history of the tactical use of Vickers machine guns in the British army 1914–1918', *Imperial War Museum Review* (1993).
57. Travers, *How the War was Won*, pp. 7–9, 175–8.

58. For infantrymen's views on the importance of the 106 fuse, see F.W. Bewsher, *The History of the 51st (Highland) Division 1914–1918* (London/Edinburgh: Blackwood, 1921), p. 141; A.M. McGilchrist, *The Liverpool Scottish 1900–1919* (Liverpool: Young, 1930), p. 223.
59. For the BEF's training regime, see SS152 *Instructions for the Training of the British Armies in France*, January 1918.
60. C.H. Dudley Ward, *History of the Welsh Guards* (London: John Murray, 1920), p. 18.
61 .*Notes on Recent Fighting*, No. 1, 5 April 1918.
62. *Notes on Recent Fighting*, No. 7, 24 April 1918.
63. For example, SS218, *Operations By the Australian Corps Against Hamel, Bois de Hamel and Boise de Vaire*, 4 July 1918.
64. 'First Army no. 1888 (G), lessons of recent fighting …', 30 August 1918, JSCSCL.
65. John Baynes, *Far from a Donkey* (London: Brassey's, 1995), pp. 209–18. For a subaltern's view of Maxse's idiosyncrasies as a trainer, see John Glubb, *Into Battle* (London: Cassell, 1978), pp. 111–12.
66. Training Leaflets issued by the Inspector-General of Training British Armies in France (1919).
67. British tactical pamphlets were also used as source material by the US Army. See *The Attack of the British 9th Corps at Messines Ridge* (Washington: Government Printing Office, 1917) and Jas. A. Moss, *Trench Warfare* (Menasha, WI: Geo. Banta, 1917). The former was effectively a straight reprint of a British pamphlet; the latter was based on the 'latest private and official British publications'.
68. D.V. Kelly, *39 Months with the 'Tigers', 1915–1918* (London: Ernest Benn, 1930), pp. 137–8.
69. Kelly, *39 Months*, p. 138; Edmonds, *Military Operations*, vol. IV, p. 378.
70. Griffith, *Battle Tactics*, p. 22.
71. Home, *Diary*, pp. 163, 166 (1 and 10 April 1918).
72. Diary, 3 Oct. 1916, J.T. Hutton, State Library of New South Wales, ML MSS 1138; Lectures (?) on 'Stopping the German Offensive, 1918' and 'Leadership and Discipline', C.H. Brand Papers, 3 DRL 2750, Australian War Memorial [AWM]; W.D. Joynt, *Saving the Channel Ports 1918* (North Blackburn: Wren Publishing, 1975), pp. 2–5.
73. G.D. Sheffield, *Leadership in the Trenches: Officer–Man Relations. Morale and Discipline in the British Army in the Era of the First World War* (Basingstoke: Macmillan, 2000).
74. McGilchrist, *Liverpool Scottish 1900–1919*, p. 131.
75. Unpublished account (written 1918), p. 45, R.S. Cockburn Papers, P 258, IWM.
76. Author's interview with Roland Whipp.
77. See *Short History of 19th Division*, p. 93.
78. Diary, 22, 23 Oct. 1918, C.R. Benstead Papers, LC.
79. For one such attack in 1917, by the Guards Division on 31 July 1917, see Dudley Ward, *Welsh Guards*, p. 149.
80. Brigadier General A.H. Hussey, *Narrative of the 5th Divisional Artillery* (Woolwich: RA Institution, 1919), p. 36. For examples, see ibid., pp. 34–5.
81. *Notes on Recent Fighting*, No. 21, 25 September 1918, JSCSCL.
82. 'First Army no. 1888 (G), lessons of recent fighting', 30 August 1918, JSCSCL.
83. Prior and Wilson. *Command on the Western Front*; Jonathan Bailey, 'British Artillery in the Great War', in Griffith, *British Fighting Methods*.
84. Appendix G to September 1918, WO 95/1775, TNA.
85. For the BEF's training regime, see S.S 152 *Instructions for the Training of the British Armies in France*, January, 1918.
86. Diary, 5 Nov. 1918, Lieutenant C.R. Benstead, LC. See also Hussey, *Fifth Divisional Artillery*, p. 45.
87. Unpublished account, p. 23, R.S. Cockburn Papers, P 258, IWM.

88. For example, Bernard Brodie, *War and Politics* (London: Cassell, 1973), p. 456.
89. Edmonds, *Military Operations*, vol. V, p. 535.
90. *Short History of 19th Division*, p. 95.
91. Revd J.O. Coop, *The Story of the 55th (West Lancashire) Division* (Liverpool: 'Daily Post' Printers, 1919), pp. 136–8.
92. Martin Samuels, *Command or Control? Command, Training and Tactics in the British and German Armies. 1888–1918* (London: Cass, 1995); Martin van Creveld, *Command in War* (Cambridge, MA: Harvard University Press, 1985), pp. 155–68.
93. Tim Travers, *The Killing Ground* (London: Unwin-Hyman, 1987); Travers, *How the War Was Won*.
94. J.M. Bourne, 'British Generals in the First World War', in G.D. Sheffield (ed.), *Leadership and Command: The Anglo-American Military Experience Since 1861* (London: Brassey's, 1997), p. 110.
95. Notes on Recent Fighting, No. 4, 13 April 1918.
96. See the chapters by Chris McCarthy and John Lee in Gary Sheffield and Dan Todman (eds), *Command and Control on the Western Front: The British Experience 1914–1918* (Staplehurst: Spellmount, 2004).
97. Bourne, 'British Generals', p. 111. For SHLM, see John Lee, 'The SHLM Project – Assessing the Battle Performance of British Divisions', in Griffith, *British Fighting Methods*.
98. J.D. Hills, *The Fifth Leicestershire* (Loughborough: Echo Press, 1919), p. 311.
99. 'Report of the Committee on Staff Organization', 6 March 1919, WO 32/3753, TNA.

PART 3

MORALE

Chapter 9

The Morale of the British Army on the Western Front, 1914–1918

Armed with powerful weapons produced by modern industrialised economies, the armies of 1914–1918 waged a war of unprecedented destructiveness. The Western Front in particular has come to exemplify a form of warfare in which the individual combatant was helpless in the face of high explosives, machine-gun bullets and poison gas. The fearsome weapons created by modern industry and technology seemingly had replaced the sinews and strength of the fighting man. Yet the 'human factor' remained important, even if it has not always received the attention it deserved. The aim of this chapter is to examine one aspect of the human factor: the morale of British Expeditionary Force (BEF) on the Western Front, relating its 'peaks and troughs' to success and failure on the battlefield. Using a broad range of sources, it seeks to build on and amplify the pioneering work of other scholars in the field, particularly two Canadian historians, J.B. Wilson and S.P. MacKenzie.[1]

Between August 1914 and November 1918 the British Army evolved from a small Regular force into a mass army. The original BEF of August 1914 consisted of professional soldiers supplemented by Regular reservists recalled to the colours. By the end of 1914 the BEF's order of battle also included elements of the Territorial Force (TF), a part-time body of amateur soldiers originally intended for home defence. The Territorials were followed by the first New Army (or 'Kitchener's army') units, which arrived in France in the spring of 1915. The New Armies were a mass volunteer force that by 1916 had transformed the nature of the BEF. No longer was it a small, elite, pro-fessional body; it was now a citizen army, the military manifestation of the British 'nation in arms'. The final act in the evolution of the British Army was the introduction of conscription in 1916, conscripts being posted to existing units – Regular, Territorial and Kitchener. The extent of the evolu-tion of the BEF over four years can be gauged by comparing its composition in August 1914 and November 1918. The original BEF consisted of one cavalry and four infantry divisions, all Regular. At the Armistice the BEF had three cavalry and sixty-one infantry divisions, including four Canadian, five Australian and one New Zealand division; and the vast majority of British Empire officers and soldiers on the Western Front in 1918 were essentially civilians in uniform enlisted 'for the duration'.[2]

'Morale', one of the most common terms in the modern military lexicon, is an imprecise term. A number of definitions have been attempted, ranging from the simplistic to the complex. One of the most useful that links the morale of the individual with the morale of the group is that of Irvin L. Child: 'morale pertains to [the individual's] efforts to enhance the effectiveness of the group in accomplishing the task in hand'.[3] The relationship between individual and collective morale can be described as follows: unless the individual soldier is reasonably content, he will not willingly contribute to the unit. He might desert or mutiny but is more likely simply to refuse to work wholeheartedly toward the goals of the group. High group morale, or cohesion, is the product in large part of good morale experienced by the members of that unit; and the state of morale of a larger formation, such as an army, is the product of the cohesion of the units that compose that army. The possession of individual morale sufficiently high that a soldier is willing to engage in combat might be described as 'fighting spirit'.

The work of Carl von Clausewitz gives valuable insights into the nature of collective military morale. He differentiated between professional armies, who possess such attributes as discipline, experience and skill, and nonprofessional armies that have 'bravery, adaptability, stamina and enthusiasm'. Clausewitz divided morale into two components, 'mood' and 'spirit', and warned that one should never confuse the two. The mood of an army is a transient thing, which can change quickly, but an army with 'true military spirit' keeps 'its cohesion under the most murderous fire' and in defeat resists fears, both real and imaginary. Military spirit, Clausewitz argued, is created in two ways: by the waging of victorious wars and by the testing of an army to the very limits of its strength; 'the seed will only grow in the soil of constant activity and exertion, warmed by the sun of victory'.[4] The BEF is a prime example of a largely non-professional force that endured tremendous hardships but continued to fight effectively in a sustained conflict, in part because its morale was boosted at critical moments by a series of minor but significant successes.

Clausewitz's analysis is applicable to individual as well as collective morale. The mood of the soldier might fluctuate from minute to minute, affected by fairly mundane factors such as the state of the weather or the availability of food. An Other Rank of 7/Buffs noted in 1916 that the spirits of the troops were depressed by wet weather but recovered when the rain stopped, while another soldier of 1/5 Londons commented that 'nothing changed one's spirits from buoyancy to utter despondency or vice-versa quicker than a shortage or surfeit of rations'.[5] Thus it was perfectly possible for a soldier's mood to be poor but his military spirit to remain sound.

Interestingly, it seems that local conditions had a greater impact than wider events on the morale of the BEF. The working-class men that provided the BEF with the bulk of its soldiers did not shed their civilian identity on joining the army; their attitudes toward their officers and NCOs were profoundly influenced by their civilian experience, for instance. Leave and letters from home ensured that soldiers in the trenches were aware of developments on the home front, and factors such as food shortages among civilians undoubtedly influenced the mood of individual soldiers. Yet, having examined about 150 collections of unpublished soldiers' writings (letters, diaries and memoirs), I have discovered little evidence that incidents on the home front or wider political affairs such as Lord Lansdowne's 'peace letter' of December 1917 or the Russian Revolution had a significant impact on the 'spirit', that is, the willingness to fight, of the BEF. This is a topic that would undoubtedly repay further research.[6]

Therefore, although this chapter argues that the morale of the BEF remained fundamentally sound throughout the war, it is not suggested that individual soldiers or, indeed, entire units were ecstatically happy all the time. Rather, the combat performance of British soldiers reflected their commitment to winning. It is, of course, possible to find examples of groups or individuals who, at a particular time, lacked the willingness to fight. Some members of 1/Gordon Highlanders were reportedly drunk and undisciplined during the retreat of March 1918.[7] The flight of an Irish battalion on the Somme in September 1916 and the rout of 9/Cheshires on 24 March 1918 provide even more dramatic evidence of the failure of military spirit of specific units at certain times. Cases such as these were, however, exceptional; 9/Cheshires, for example, fought effectively only one month after their rout.[8] The battles of the BEF were far from universally successful, and symptoms of poor morale were discernible on occasion, but the performance of British troops was rarely less than dogged. The British citizen army's mood fluctuated, but its determination to defeat the Germans remained essentially intact. In this respect, the morale of the BEF reflected the morale of the British nation in arms as a whole.[9]

The problems involved in attempting to assess the morale of a formation as large as the BEF are many and obvious. Ideally, an overall picture should be constructed from a series of case studies.[10] Enough evidence exists, however, to draw some tentative general conclusions about the morale of the BEF at certain points during the war. British high command had a strong belief in the importance of moral factors in war, drawn in part from a bastardised version of Clausewitzian theory,[11] and used an attritional strategy that had an explicit aim of destroying enemy morale. Unlike their American and French allies, the British Army did not create a central organisation devoted to the planning, direction, monitoring and sustaining of the morale of their troops.[12] This relatively casual approach is partially explained by the assumption, held by many senior officers, that the morale of their men was fundamentally sound, and likely to remain so;[13] in the jaundiced words of the prime minister, David Lloyd George, generals believed that 'Allied soldiers were infrangible steel, and enemy soldiers ordinary flesh'.[14] This creed was not entirely founded on wishful thinking, for such assumptions were rooted in a belief in the 'character' of the British soldier, and, what is more important, an intimate knowledge of the nature of the British regimental system and the paternalism of the British officer corps. These factors were, indeed, to prove vital in the maintenance of morale.[15]

Moreover, the British regimental system inhibited the establishment of a centralised body concerned with morale; as late as 1940 some senior officers resisted the creation of an Army Welfare Scheme and the use of extra-regimental local welfare officers, on the grounds that the well-being of the soldier was the responsibility of the regimental officer.[16] It is very typical of the British approach to morale that a campaign to mould the opinions of the soldiers of the BEF by a programme of education sprang largely from the initiative of individual staff officers and the Deputy Chaplain-General (although with the encouragement of Field Marshal Sir Douglas Haig, the Commander-in-Chief of the BEF). These schemes were implemented in 1918, the last year of the war, in response to a perceived deterioration in morale. It is arguable that it would have been more sensible to introduce such a scheme earlier, to prevent morale declining in the first place.[17]

This is not to argue that the British high command took no interest in the morale of the troops, rather that the information they received was not always reliable, and some was gathered in a haphazard and unsystematic fashion. Wilson has argued that the high command attempted to ascertain the state of morale and discipline in units by the collection of quantitative data – especially figures for court-martial offences such as drunkenness, looting and desertion – and statistics for trench-foot and shellshock. He concluded, however, that these indices were not, on the whole, very reliable.[18] There was a tendency to confuse morale with discipline. This was misleading, for the two, although related, are not identical. Men serving sentences in military prisons are well disciplined but unlikely to have high morale.[19] Furthermore, not all regimental officers attempted to apply pre-war standards of discipline to their troops, who were mostly civilians in uniform. In some Territorial, Kitchener and Dominion battalions, failure to salute might have betokened neither slack discipline nor low morale. Applying criteria such as propensity to salute to the whole army was an inaccurate way of judging the fighting efficiency of some units.[20]

It is unwise to judge morale by the number of executions within a unit. Men sentenced to death seem to have faced something of a lottery as to whether their sentence would be commuted, for only 10.82 per cent of death sentences were carried out.[21] The composition of the court-martial, whether or not the accused was represented, the attitude of the accuser's hierarchical superiors (from his battalion commander to the C-in-C), whether the accused was Irish or black: all these factors were important in deciding the fate of the individual.[22] The execution of malefactors, who were mostly deserters, was intended to deter others. The commanders of brigades in which condemned men served furnished a report 'as to the state of discipline of the unit and his recommendations as to whether or not an example was necessary'.[23] The decision of the C-in-C, who had the ultimate authority to confirm or commute a death sentence, was influenced by 'the immediate needs of discipline', not necessarily that of the individual's battalion.[24]

The case of Private Skilton (22/Royal Fusiliers), who was executed in December 1916 for deserting during the fighting on the Ancre in November, illustrates the difficulties of generalising about the state of morale of a unit from the execution of an individual. This action was a severe trial for the British infantry, yet his battalion performed well during the battle. The 22/Royal Fusiliers was characterised by an enlightened disciplinary regime, a high level of *esprit de corps* and excellent officer–man relations. The evidence suggests that Skilton was a poor soldier who had been lucky to escape a court-martial after his behaviour in an earlier battle. It was possible that he was shellshocked. In sum, he was an atypical soldier, and it would be unwise to generalise about the state of morale and discipline in 22/Royal Fusiliers from his fate.[25]

Censorship of soldiers' letters represented the most systematic, if far from perfect, method used by the BEF for gauging morale. Reports based on such censorship were submitted at regular intervals to General Headquarters (GHQ) and on occasion to the War Cabinet. Other *ad hoc* methods were also used. The war correspondent Philip Gibbs claimed to have been interviewed in late 1917 by Lord Milner and later by a British liaison officer serving with the French. Both questioned Gibbs as to his opinions of the morale of the BEF in general, and specifically whether he believed the army would accept a compromise peace.[26] Another individual who advised the War Cabinet on British military morale was the South African soldier/statesman J.C. Smuts, who submitted a report on his return from a tour of the front in January 1918.[27]

More junior officers also had quantitative methods of gauging morale. The brigade major of XIV Corps Heavy Artillery 'learned to assess the morale of the infantry' by the number of complaints received from them about British shells dropping short. He believed that many of the reports of 'short-shooting' were 'entirely unreliable', and the better the morale of the infantry, the less likely they were to issue false claims about the inaccuracy of the gunners.[28] In December 1917 the officers of 1/9 King's Liverpool Regiment saw the willingness of troops to subscribe to War Savings Certificates as an indication of *esprit de corps*. The men were initially reluctant to part with their money but became more enthusiastic when the scheme was presented as a way of increasing the prestige of the battalion, and 1/9 King's eventually raised more money than any other unit in their division.[29]

Quite apart from these 'statistical' means of establishing morale, officers used their experience and intuition to keep their finger on the pulse of units. Obvious signs of high morale included spontaneous humour and singing.[30] The junior officer soon learned that when marching men stopped singing and whistling, they were growing weary or approaching danger.[31] R.W.F. Johnston, an officer of 16/Royal Scots, drew a sharp contrast between the demeanour of the battalion before an action on 25–26 August 1917 and one fought two months later. Before the first action, despite a 'sombre and dark' silence on the approach march, the men showed 'keenness' and a degree of *esprit de corps*. By the time of the battle of 22 October, the men were 'tired, dispirited and exhausted ... without thought of victory'. During the latter action logistic arrangements had broken down, leaving the men short of food. It is interesting that Johnston used the absence of 'jokes and singing in the ranks' as a criterion of low morale.[32] Contemporary advice for young officers laid heavy stress on the necessity for the officer to get to know his men.[33] While 'grousing' was not necessarily a sign of low morale, the good officer was able to sense when the morale of his men was low.[34]

Despite the 'scientific' nature of warfare in 1914–1918, the gauging of morale remained an art rather than a science, as it had been throughout history. The use of statistics was fraught with danger, while, conversely, the opinions of regimental and even staff officers (who mostly had recent regimental experience), however subjective, cannot be lightly set aside. Many British officers developed close relationships with their men that made them sensitive to changes in mood and spirit among the rank and file. Likewise, the views of other well-informed individuals are worthy of attention; one such was Philip Gibbs, who built up a close relationship with an infantry battalion, 8/10 Gordon Highlanders. Gibbs claimed that he had 'complete liberty' to visit all parts of the front, spoke to men in the front line and gained much knowledge of 'the spirit and personal experiences of the troops'; one unit did record their satisfaction with his account of a visit to them in July 1915.[35] Finally, combat performance offers valuable evidence of morale, for troops that lack military spirit will not fight effectively. Such evidence, when used alongside the writings of other ranks and the findings of censorship reports, allows us to assess the morale of the BEF.

The first winter of the war was a terrible trial for the soldiers in the trenches, and this experience affected morale; the British official historians referred to the 'depression' experienced by the men in the front lines in the winter of 1914/1915.[36] Wilson argues that this depression was caused by a number of factors, including the harsh climatic conditions, the terrain, the primitive nature of the logistic infrastructure, poor quality of reinforcements for Regular units, and frustration with trench warfare. All these things were important, but most important of all, Wilson suggests, was that the British Army was inadequately prepared to conduct a campaign of static, trench warfare. The paucity of reserves and trench-fighting equipment was symptomatic of the lack of material preparation, but the effort needed to adjust mentally to trench warfare was also of importance. Wilson concludes that this depression, although serious in the short term, was short-lived. The first major British offensive of 1915, launched at Neuve Chapelle in March, demonstrated that the BEF's will to combat had not been undermined.[37]

There is considerable evidence to suggest that the British military leadership regarded the morale and discipline of the BEF with some concern in the winter of 1914/1915. As early as 30 October 1914 a staff officer who had served with 7th Division delivered a lecture to the as-yet-unblooded 8th Division, in which he warned that at Ypres the enemy had attempted to break the morale of the infantry by artillery fire. He also stressed the necessity of maintaining strict discipline, as did General Sir Henry Rawlinson, who spoke after him.[38] In the same month a staff officer treated soldiers arriving at Le Havre to 'a homily upon morale'.[39]

The average regimental officer was well aware of the need to make strenuous efforts to maintain the morale of the ordinary soldier. In 1938 an officer who had served with 2/Rifle Brigade gave a lecture to the Staff College on the upkeep of morale in the winter of 1914/1915. The practical steps that were taken by the officers of this battalion ranged from the enforcement of strict discipline to 'the provision of amusements in the form of organised games, sports, concerts, boxing and horse shows'.[40] Clearly, the depression of the winter of 1914/1915 did not permanently erode the military spirit of the British soldier. Indeed, the fortitude of the Other Ranks impressed contemporary observers.[41] Moreover, this period was not characterised by large-scale desertions or mutinies or by ineffective performances in combat. Morale began to improve in the spring of 1915, when 4/Middlesex, among other units, introduced vigorous training to shake off the sluggish ways of the winter.[42] According to Lieutenant General Sir William Robertson, then Chief of Staff of the BEF, the Battle of Neuve Chapelle, fought that spring, demonstrated that the BEF still possessed a considerable degree of offensive spirit.[43] In Clausewitzian terms, the mood of the BEF may have appeared depressed, but its military spirit remained intact.

A letter written by Private J. Allison in early 1915 perhaps offers a clue to the thinking of the Regular Other Ranks in this period. Allison, a soldier with many years' service, had escaped front-line duty and was working in a base hospital; he may have been wounded. After noting his 'old mob ... getting cut up', Allison opined that 'this War is going to be a very long one so I have settled my mind down for it ... the southafrican (sic) war was not a Patch to this one'. There are a number of interesting points about this letter. Allison had deliberately (and illegally) posted the letter through the French civilian system, thus preventing an officer from censoring it, because, he said, one 'carnt Put anything in it [a letter] to (sic) much' if an officer was going to read it. Even though no one in the military hierarchy would read his letter, Allison concluded with the words 'God save the King'.[44]

Allison's letter is evidence of a Regular private, albeit one who had temporarily escaped front-line duty, coming to terms with the previously unanticipated reality of a long, static war. He accepted the fact with a certain amount of fatalism and even patriotism, tempered by a grumble. His views are consistent with those of other pre-war Regulars in this period. In his memoirs Corporal John Lucy (2/Royal Irish Rifles) wrote of the ebbing of his personal morale and the stultifying effects of trench warfare on soldiers trained for mobile warfare, but his attitude to the war is epitomised by the title of chapter thirty-six: 'Life Goes On'.[45] Likewise, in his memoir Private Frank Richards (2/Royal Welsh Fusiliers) referred in passing to the lowering of morale caused by the harsh conditions of the winter of 1914/1915, but the general tenor of his book is of stoic acceptance of his lot.[46]

Wilson's conclusion that there was an improvement in morale during 1915 and that spirits were generally high by June 1916[47] is broadly correct. There is also evidence, however, of a recurrence of depression among some troops during the winter of 1915/1916. In November 1915, Robertson argued that 'depression at home is beginning to be reflected in the Army in France'.[48] This view was probably influenced by the reports on postal censorship. In November 1916 Captain Martin Hardie (Third Army censor) stated that a year earlier 'Letters containing prolonged grousing' had been 'fairly common'.[49] At the other end of the scale a Territorial private who had served in France for almost a year recorded in October 1915: 'For the first time since the war began, I have heard soldiers say that we are losing.' Although the writer retained his optimism, he believed the modest gains and heavy losses incurred at the Battle of Loos in September had undermined morale: 'It gives one cold shivers to look at a map and see how far the Germans must be driven back.'[50] Philip Gibbs believed that the winter of 1915/1916 was worse even than the winter of 1914/1915 and the one that was to follow the Somme offensive, for the sacrifices of 1915 appeared to have achieved nothing.[51]

This feeling of depression does not appear to have been common to the entire BEF. With the exception of a handful of formations that fought at Loos, few of the New Army units that had arrived in France by the early spring of 1916 had taken part in the battles of 1915. Their morale was generally high. It is also possible to find indications of high morale among troops who had been out in France for some time; a middle-class soldier of 1/21 Londons wrote in October 1915 that 'it is only a matter of time before they [the Germans] give in',[52] while Private Andrews, a professional man serving in a working-class TF unit, 1/4 Black Watch, believed that the men's 'spirit ... was still excellent', although men were more reticent about volunteering for 'dangerous duty' than formerly.[53] The preparation for the Somme appears to have revived spirits in many units. The mood of some of the troops was depressed in the winter of 1915/1916, but the BEF's military spirit remained essentially intact.

The Battle of the Somme was the largest single battle fought by the British Army up to that point. From July to November 1916 the BEF advanced about 7 miles, at the cost of 420,000 British casualties. Some 57,000 casualties were incurred on the first day of the offensive alone, and the German army remained undefeated. Yet in November 1916 a report on the morale of Third Army, based on the censorship of soldiers' letters (the only such records from the period to survive), could report that 'the spirit of the men, their conception of duty, their Moral (sic), has never been higher than at the present moment'. Not surprisingly, General Sir Douglas Haig, the C-in-C, commented on reading the report, 'It is quite excellent.' Although Third Army did not play a major role in the battle after the initial stage, divisions from those armies that bore the brunt of the fighting were sent to Third Army in the course of the offensive. Third Army's censorship reports were complemented by those of other Armies.[54]

The censor's reports offer strong evidence of the reliability of soldiers' letters as indicators of morale and refute a recent suggestion that censors deliberately selected positive statements from soldiers' letters to produce falsely optimistic reports for submission to high command.[55] Captain Hardie, the censor for Third Army, was not a sycophant. His reports in the autumn of 1917 made no attempt to disguise symptoms of poor morale. In view of suggestions that official documents and some private papers were censored or falsified in an attempt to protect the reputations of senior commanders, it is noteworthy that these reports were retained in Hardie's private papers and emerged into the public domain only in the 1980s.[56]

Few consider poor morale a contributory factor in the failure of the British attack on 1 July 1916. Although a staff officer of 32nd Division suggested that a factor in the partial failure of that formation's assault was physical and moral exhaustion caused by excessive digging and a poor system of reliefs,[57] there is general agreement that morale, in the sense of willingness to fight, was high on the eve of the Somme offensive.[58] One artillery officer believed that the change of scenery, from the 'dreary, drab and depressing surroundings of Flanders to the open plains of the Somme' lifted the spirits of the men. Certainly in the first half of 1916 the Somme was a less active sector than the ever-dangerous Ypres salient.[59] The obvious power and apparent effectiveness of the British guns also boosted confidence, leading to a widely held belief, which filtered down from senior officers to the rank and file, that the bombardment of the German positions would ensure the infantry's task would be an easy one, and that the forthcoming offensive would decide the war.[60]

John Keegan has written that the BEF of 1 July 1916 was 'a trusting army'.[61] While there is a great deal of truth in this assertion, it would be wrong to exaggerate the extent to which ordinary soldiers shared their officers' optimism. It is instructive to compare an officer's and a private's recollection of Lieutenant General Sir Aylmer Hunter-Weston's visit to 1/Lancashire Fusiliers on 30 June. The officer recalled that Hunter-Weston's optimism was 'naturally conveyed to my men, it gave us all good heart. In fact we thought that this must be the end of the war!!!' The private recalled 'the ugly mutterings in the ranks' during the general's talk, which told a rather different story.[62] (1/Lancashire Fusiliers was a veteran Regular battalion that was perhaps less impressionable than a green Kitchener unit.)

Rifleman Percy Jones, a soldier of a veteran Territorial battalion, 1/16 Londons, was also unimpressed by a senior officer's assurances that casualties in the assault on 1 July would be low because of the effectiveness of the British artillery. Facing the formidable German defences at Gommecourt, most of Jones's fellow Other Ranks shared his scepticism about 'the carefully drawn up plans'. It is important to note that this cynicism did not undermine the willingness of the men of 1/16 Londons to fight. In two successive diary entries in late June 1916 Jones referred to the men's determination to go on 'until something stops us'.[63] During the week before the assault, only 7 out of 966 men of all ranks of 1/16 Londons reported sick, 'a record', the battalion historian commented, 'rarely beaten in peace time, even under the most favourable conditions', which indicated high morale.[64] Using the most important test of morale of all, both 1/Lancashire Fusiliers and 1/16 Londons fought well on 1 July, even though both their divisions' assaults ended in failure.

Many of the men who attacked on 1 July had never before taken part in a full-scale battle. In a letter of 7 July 1916 a private of 1/13 Londons, newly arrived from England, wryly recorded how his draft's unbridled enthusiasm, which provoked an amazed response from veteran soldiers, was quickly tempered after a few days in the trenches.[65] By July 1916, however, some New Army units had gained as much as nine months' experience of trench warfare, and on active service raw troops experienced a steep learning curve.[66] To choose two regiments at random, of the fourteen battalions of the Northumberland Fusiliers that served with Fourth Army on 1 July 1916, eight had arrived in France in January 1916, two in November 1915, three in September 1915 and one in July 1915, while of the five New Army and Territorial battalions of the Royal Fusiliers serving with Third and Fourth Armies on that date, three had arrived in January, one in March and one in July 1915.[67] There was no repetition of Loos in 1915, where inexperienced New Army troops were pitched into battle without first learning the rudiments of warfare on active service. Thus, in attempting to explain how British morale survived the disappointment and casualties of 1 July, it is necessary to dispense with the idea that the soldiers were 'lambs to the slaughter'.

Writing of the later stages of the Somme campaign, Haig's chaplain suggested that the army's 'old "death or glory" spirit' had largely disappeared. In its place all ranks displayed 'a quiet fortitude and a resolute determination to carry on to the end'.[68] Captain Hardie, Third Army's censor, came to similar conclusions, writing in his report of November 1916 of a 'dogged determination to see the thing through at any cost'.[69] The endurance of the BEF is a theme that echoes through many reports from this period. In this respect, some comments made in September 1916 by B.H. Liddell Hart, then an enthusiastic young company commander of 9/King's Own Yorkshire Light Infantry, were typical. Liddell Hart wrote of the 'wonderful courage and discipline' of the infantry. A few of the men were fearless, a few were too stupid to experience fear, but the majority, he stressed, were just ordinary men.[70]

That is not to suggest that morale was always high during the Somme campaign. Individual actions fought under difficult conditions could place the morale of units under some strain. 35th Division, a 'Bantam' formation recruited from men under the normal height for enlistment, attacked unsuccessfully in August 1916. Some of the division's troops seem to have been little more than children and were found crying during the fighting.[71] In September 49th Division attacked Thiepval. It had already unsuccessfully assaulted this objective, and the evil reputation of Thiepval had adversely affected the division's morale. 12th Division's action at Le Transloy in October, according to one survivor, caused a lowering of morale. Another officer of 12th Division mentioned two factors that indicated the decline of morale: excessive straggling and a tendency for infantry to go to ground under hostile artillery fire. In retrospect, this witness claimed that fighting for 'limited objectives' undermined the morale of the infantry: they were 'murderous affairs to all infantry, with nothing to stir the imagination as to victory'.[72]

This is not the whole picture. One battalion of 12th Division, 7/Suffolks, suffered heavy casualties during July and August, and during the fighting for Le Transloy had the handicap of understrength and untrained companies and the presence of many reinforcements. In addition, the battalion's battle began with an exhausting approach march along 'muddy tracks'. Yet, an officer of the battalion wrote, the morale of the battalion was 'very good' considering all the difficulties.[73] Again, we have evidence that the spirit of the army was essentially sound, although external appearances suggested otherwise.

The ultimate test of morale is willingness to engage in combat, and the BEF's divisions continued to fight, with some degree of success, throughout the campaign. Conditions on the Ancre during the final operations of the campaign were exceptionally bad. The historian of 19th Division declared that it had 'never known greater exhaustion or discomfort than that experienced in November 1916'. J.F.C. Fuller believed that the conditions were responsible for causing 'considerable numbers' of British troops to the desert to the enemy, the only time in the war for which Fuller had evidence of this occurring.[74] In spite of these problems, the operation was a partial success, during which the 51st (Highland) Division seized Beaumont Hamel. In sum, the evidence suggests that the BEF began the Somme campaign with a strong will to fight, and that the subsequent months of fighting, while imposing severe strains on individuals and units, did not erode the military spirit of the army. An artillery officer summed up the change when he wrote that it was not that the 'will to win' disappeared, but that the 'spirit of adventurous participation' that had motivated the New Army in July 1916 'died away' during the Somme offensive.[75]

The year 1917 saw a repetition of the strategy of the previous twelve months. The British Army engaged in two major offensives at Arras (April–May) and at Ypres (July–November). Both battles became attritional affairs, and both resulted in heavy British losses: 150,000 at Arras, 250,000 at Ypres. Yet Captain Hardie's censorship reports and other evidence suggest that in the latter part of 1917 the BEF's morale remained sound, in spite of considerable strains.

The weather in the winter of 1916/1917 was exceptionally cold. In January 1917 one battalion recorded temperatures of '20 to 25 degrees of frost'.[76] The morale of the troops seems to have remained fairly good, however, although at least one unit received a lecture on *esprit de corps* before going into action, which suggests some doubts about their commitment may have existed.[77] Hardie's conclusions on the morale of Third Army in January 1917 are epitomised by the phrase 'Tommy is still in the pink'. Soldiers' letters did contain complaints, but there were 'no indications' of a 'wish for premature peace'; rather, there was a general acceptance that more sacrifices would have to be made before victory could be achieved. Hardie believed that the willingness of the ordinary British soldier to 'submit without a murmur to guidance and authority, and be prepared simply to "carry on" without comment or discussion', indicated confidence in the Allied cause, in the conduct of the war, and in 'the justice and efficiency of our military training and methods'.[78]

Haig, writing at the beginning of May 1917, was, perhaps predictably, at pains to stress the confidence of the BEF and the general belief that German losses were higher than those of the British.[79] Hardie's report of May 1917, the period of the Arras offensive, in which Third Army took a prominent part, confirms this view, registering little change from the generally optimistic tone of previous reports.[80] In the second half of 1917, however, Hardie's reports were indicating a distinct change in the tone of soldiers' letters. In a report based on 900 letters read over the period 8 July to 24 August, he stated that 'it must be frankly admitted that the letters show an increasing amount of war-weariness'. He noted 'a tinge of despondency which has never been apparent before' and considerable 'unsettled feeling about the continuation and conclusion and after-effects of the war', leading to a replacement of 'active enthusiasm' by 'passive acceptance'. Talk of peace, which had been rare earlier in the year, was now 'frequent'. Complaints about matters such as lack of leave outnumbered references to the strain of combat by about five to one, and the average soldier did not seek 'peace at any price', but there was 'an immense and widespread longing for any reasonable and honourable settlement that will bring the war to a close'.[81] A further report of 19 October offered even more alarming conclusions: that the willingness of the soldier to abandon his rights as an individual and obey his military masters without question was beginning to end.[82]

Other evidence supports Hardie's views. Gibbs believed that the Third Battle of Ypres adversely affected morale: 'For the first time the British Army lost its spirit of optimism, and there was a sense of deadly depression among many officers and men. ... They saw no ending of the war ... and nothing except continuous slaughter.'[83]

The French official history also commented on the 'weariness' of the BEF at the beginning of winter,[84] and a recent study demonstrates the extent to which Australian morale had been eroded by the end of the campaign.[85] Yet, as Gibbs himself stated, the discipline of the BEF remained intact.[86] Even Lloyd George, who denounced the 'stupid and squalid strategy' of the last stage of Passchendaele, which, he believed, exhausted the BEF and destroyed its confidence in its leaders, commented on the dogged fighting of the army in this phase.[87] Perhaps the most important piece of evidence for British morale at the end of 1917 is a report to the War Cabinet, dated 18 December 1917. Compiled on the basis of 17,000 front-line soldiers' letters and general impressions formed during the previous three months, this report is 'the nearest thing available to a gallup (sic) poll' for the period. The report stated categorically that 'The Morale of the Army is sound'. Positive and negative letters were about evenly balanced in Second Army, which had taken the lead after the first phase of the offensive at Ypres. Positive letters written by men of other Armies considerably outnumbered negative communications, suggesting that the conditions at Ypres were indeed placing the men of Second Army under considerable stress. Despite much unfavourable news (the 'Russian debacle and the Italian setback') and considerable 'war weariness' and 'an almost universal longing for peace', this report suggested that the BEF remained willing to fight on to achieve victory.[88]

The success of the German counter-attack at Cambrai on 30 November 1917 placed a question-mark against the morale of some British formations. Smuts was sent to France to report on the situation. In two memoranda submitted to the War Cabinet, he concluded that the 'moral (sic) of the army is good'. Smuts proceeded to highlight some major problems that were likely to affect the morale of the BEF. The men, particularly the infantry, were tired, a problem exacerbated by the need to prepare defensive positions. This also reduced the time available for training and 'rest ... a psychological factor of the utmost importance'. Smuts foresaw that, should the British agree to the French request for the British to take over more trenches, 'we shall be running serious risks. We shall be straining the army too far.' In sum, Smuts did not believe that Passchendaele had significantly weakened the resolve of the BEF, although complacency was unwise.[89] The very honesty of censorship reports, and the fact that they included evidence that morale was less than perfect, caused some controversy among the British high command. In October 1917 Robertson, by then Chief of the Imperial General Staff (CIGS), recorded his belief that 'by no means' every British soldier on the Western Front was 'possessed of a good morale', and that this was 'only natural and to a greater or lesser extent common to all armies'.[90] Writing two days later, the ever-optimistic Brigadier General John Charteris, Haig's intelligence chief, complained that Robertson had underestimated 'the extraordinary high morale' revealed by the monthly censorship reports.[91] While a brief report submitted to the cabinet on 13 September certainly supports Charteris's view, the rather more sombre tone of other extant reports tends to support the CIGS.[92]

There are several factors that help to explain why the BEF's morale remained relatively high in early 1917, declined as a result of the offensive at Ypres, but did not collapse. The British won a series of minor but important victories in the first half of 1917. In January the BEF renewed offensive operations on the Somme and gained some success. The German retreat to the Hindenburg Line in March 1917 appeared to be conclusive evidence that the Germans were losing the war and allowed the Somme to be presented as a victory because the Germans had abandoned the field of battle to the Allies.[93] The brief phase of mobile warfare as the British followed up the retreating Germans also seems to have provided a boost to the morale of some units.[94] The initial success in the Arras offensive in April and the seizing of Messines Ridge in June also offered evidence of British victories.

The failure of the initial stages of the Third Battle of Ypres, the heavy casualties sustained and the poor weather help explain the weakening in morale in August. There are several factors that may have helped offset this decline. First was the genuine success of the limited offensives fought by Plumer's Second Army at the battles of the Menin Road, Polygon Wood and Broodseinde (20 and 26 September, 4 October). Second, the fact that the BEF was advancing, albeit slowly and at a high price, was important. On the Somme in October 1916 an officer of 7/East Surreys had written that he was presently back with the battalion transport (i.e., some way behind the forward trenches), but 'even where we are we are some way over where the German front line was before the 1st July which is very satisfactory'.[95] Similarly, thirteen months later the capture of Passchendaele Ridge, although costly in casualties, was proof that the British were advancing steadily: 'Troops were now resting where once they could not have stood up'. The BEF's sacrifices had brought tangible reward.[96] Finally, the offensive at Cambrai in November 1917, although ultimately a failure, was initially brilliantly successful.

The evidence offered in this section could be supplemented by a host of other examples drawn from the lower echelons of the army.[97] The most important testimony to the state of British morale during the Passchendaele offensive is that, with the atypical exception of the Étaples mutiny of September 1917,[98] the men of the BEF continued to obey orders and to fight reasonably effectively. Taken together, the evidence suggests that the morale of the British soldier was severely tested in 1917, but not to destruction.

In 1918 the BEF had to relearn how to conduct mobile operations, first in a major retreat and then advancing to victory. The BEF lost 239,793 men in 40 days in the spring of 1918, compared with the loss of 244,897 in 105 days of the Third Battle of Ypres.[99] As has been pointed out, however, during the period of the Allied offensive (8 August–November 1918), BEF combat fatalities were remarkably low: only about 20,000 for Fourth Army, a spearhead formation.[100] This hitherto little-noticed factor might well have had an effect in maintaining British morale.

The initial success of the German spring offensive that began on 21 March 1918 has been traditionally attributed, in part at least, to 'the poor and cowardly spirit of the officers and men' of Fifth Army.[101] To some extent these accusations were politically inspired, but they have been echoed by some historians.[102] Did British military morale really collapse in the spring of 1918? A censorship report of July 1918, based on the study of 83,621 letters, suggests it did not. This report, covering the period from April, states that 'the high moral quality' shown in March was 'amply confirmed' in the latter part of the period. The comments on the morale of Fourth (formerly Fifth) Army are particularly interesting. The report frankly admits that it would have been 'misleading' to suggest that this formation was 'happy'. Besides a general sense of war weariness, there was a decline in confidence in politicians, and if not in the higher command, at least in the 'higher administration' of the Army. In spite of everything, however, the Fourth Army's 'combative spirit ... remains very high', the letters of the ordinary soldiers containing unambiguous evidence of the men's 'determination to stick it out to the end', to achieve the victory they still longed for. The report also contained comments of a similarly positive nature about the morale of other formations. 'The persistence and determination' of the men of Second Army, who fought a defensive battle on the River Lys in April, was described as 'remarkable'. 'They were *very* tired but unbeaten.'[103]

A soldier of 2/Devons perhaps caught the essence of the morale of the BEF during the spring battles when he wrote of the general belief that, despite all setbacks, they remained confident that everything would be all right in the end.[104] An artillery officer considered Haig's 'Backs to the Wall' message of 11 April 1918 to be damaging to morale because many soldiers 'had not admitted even to themselves' how serious the position was.[105] Furthermore, mere rumours that the British were striking back at the Germans was enough, in good Clausewitzian fashion, to boost morale.[106]

On 21 March 1918 the Germans took 98.5 square miles of ground from the British Third and Fifth Armies (all but 19 square miles from the latter). The British defenders suffered about 38,500 casualties, including 21,000 men taken prisoner. The Germans captured approximately 500 guns, mostly from Fifth Army. Such heavy losses of prisoners and guns are usually the tokens of defeat, and there is also much anecdotal evidence of British soldiers surrendering without putting up much resistance. It would be unwise, however, to deduce from these facts and figures that British morale was low in March 1918. As Martin Middlebrook points out, many factors serve to distort the picture, not least the overall strategic plan and the unfamiliarity of the British forces with the concept of 'defence in depth'. Ignorance of this new doctrine resulted in the advancing Germans cutting off as many as one-third of the defenders, who were crammed into the forward zone. Middlebrook suggests that although Fifth Army's morale was far from 'excellent', the morale of at least some units was 'steady'.[107] The records of stragglers collected by the military police also cast doubt on the traditional belief that Fifth Army routed.[108]

Had the morale of Fifth Army indeed collapsed, the Germans would probably have won the war, for the autumn of 1918 was to demonstrate the serious consequences of a genuine weakening in an army's morale. The German spring offensives were, in Winston Churchill's words, 'judged by the hard test of gains and losses ... decisively defeated'.[109] In short, the British Army's morale was sound enough to allow it to fight the German army to a standstill. Even in a conflict as technologically based as the First World War, sound morale was an indispensable factor in military success.

David Englander has published an interesting analysis of British Army morale and discipline in the last two years of the war. In this article he speculates whether the 1918 German spring offensive forestalled a major mutiny.[110] Moreover, he argues that, although Fifth Army's figures for sick wastage were relatively low, which might be taken as an indicator of sound morale, it would be a mistake to assume 'that the failure of the 5th Army was more of a military defeat due primarily to enemy superiority in manpower and firepower rather than a moral collapse due to fatigue and depression. The evidence from postal surveillance, *should it ever be located*, may well present a different story.'[111]

The evidence presented in this chapter suggests that Englander's arguments are flawed. While the morale of the BEF in early 1918 was not high, it was a very long way from collapse; in March–April 1918 Fifth Army certainly took a battering but it was not defeated, and the postal evidence, which is referred to above and has actually been in the public domain for some years, testifies to the essential soundness of Fifth Army's morale.

The events of the spring of 1918 cannot be divorced from those of the summer and autumn, when the Allies went onto the offensive and won a series of crushing victories. In the absence of a censorship report for the second half of 1918, a book by Major General A.A. Montgomery is probably the nearest we have to an 'official' view of British morale in the final campaigns on the Western Front. Montgomery, the chief of staff of Fourth Army, laid great stress on the increase in British morale and a simultaneous decrease in German morale when the BEF took the offensive in August.[112] More dramatically than during the Somme or Passchendaele offensives, the autumn of 1918 presented the British soldier with tangible evidence of success. The BEF was gaining ground, capturing large numbers of guns and prisoners, and the fighting spirit of many German units was perceptibly deteriorating. In the words of an officer of 46th Division, the BEF 'was at last obtaining a just reward for all its dogged and patient fighting'.[113] It is interesting to compare these comments with those of a German infantry officer, who believed that 'the reason for the slow decline of morale within the German Army over the final months of the war was the feeling of the soldiers that they were being ground to pieces in one useless, pointless, and hopeless offensive action after another'.[114]

It is likely, nevertheless, that the British infantry's morale was somewhat brittle by the time of the Armistice. R.H. Mottram argued that by late 1918 'a new spirit of taking care of one's self' had emerged among the infantry, who would have begun 'not refusing but simply omitting to do duty' if the war had continued beyond 11 November.[115] In the autumn of 1918 there were several mutinies in the Australian Corps, which played a major role in the Allied offensive. Some were protests against the disbandment of units, but two mutinies, those of 59th and 1st Battalions in September, amounted to combat refusals caused by excessive weariness and a sense that the soldiers were being asked to do more than their fair share.[116] One should be wary, however, of drawing firm conclusions about the state of the BEF's morale from such evidence. Mottram was not serving with an infantry battalion at the end of 1918. His views were undoubtedly exaggerated and can profitably be contrasted with a host of other evidence, drawn from the contemporary writings of regimental soldiers and Other Ranks, that suggests morale was high.[117] While the Australian mutinies suggest that these particular troops had reached the end of their tether, it is far from clear that morale in the Australian Corps as a whole was on the point of collapse. Indeed, one can tentatively suggest that much evidence points in the opposite direction.[118] Above all, the ultimate evidence of high morale is willingness to engage in combat. The irrefutable facts are that British Empire troops continued to advance and win battles, taking heavy casualties in the process, until the very end of the war. After the Armistice came into effect, there was a distinct change in the attitude of many soldiers towards their employment – in military terms, there was a collapse of morale and discipline – but this occurred *after*, not before, the end of hostilities.

In conclusion, it would be difficult to improve on Charles Douie's assessment of British morale in 1918. Douie served as a temporary subaltern in 1/Dorsets, and ten years after the war he wrote (in response to the 'disillusioned' school) of the generally 'magnificent' state of morale in the BEF in the last year of the war. He argued that the BEF of 1918 was inferior in quality to its predecessor of 1916, yet it was sufficiently skilled to fight a numerically superior enemy to a standstill in the spring in two great actions, to counter-attack 'and remain continuously on the offensive from August to November. The infantry at least had no doubt that they were winning, and their faith was justified when the greatest military Power of modern times finally collapsed in disordered retreat.'[119]

The BEF of the autumn of 1918 consisted of a blend of veterans of earlier campaigns and young, fresh conscripts who had been spared the rigours of trench warfare and the defensive battles of the spring. This was a winning combination of enthusiasm and experience.

Generally, a rapid and decisive victory can be achieved only if one side is greatly inferior to the other in terms of fighting power. On the Western Front the two sides were roughly equally matched. In the March 1915–March 1918 period British offensive operations frequently began with an attempt to re-open mobile warfare, but when the hoped-for penetration failed to materialise such battles were continued in an attempt to 'wear out' the enemy's strength and morale. Thus, although the opening phases of the Somme in 1916 and the Third Battle of Ypres in 1917 were designed to achieve a breakthrough, they evolved into attritional battles. In early 1915 Haig became convinced that German morale would shortly collapse,[120] and thus continued to fight attritional battles, designed in part to deplete enemy morale. With some justice, in his final dispatch Haig claimed that the battles of the previous four years were 'a single continuous campaign' that had contributed to weakening the German army.[121] Certainly, for a variety of reasons, German military (and civilian) morale began to crumble in the summer and autumn of 1918.[122] In retrospect, the Allied victory of 1918 owed much to the morale of the British soldier remaining intact while that of his German counterpart crumbled. This is not to deny the importance of factors such as improvements in British tactical and operational methods and the arrival of a large United States army on the Western Front, but these would have availed little had the morale of the BEF collapsed. In this respect, the 'human factor' was at least as important as technology in determining the outcome of the First World War.

Acknowledgements
The author is grateful to Peter Simkins, Keith Simpson, Chris McCarthy and Paul MacKenzie for their help and advice.

Thanks are due to the following for allowing me to quote from material for which they hold the copyright: Gertrude Hardie (Martin Hardie Papers); J.B. Gregory (J. Allison Papers); R.G.S. Johnston (R.W.F. Johnston Papers); Paul P.H. Jones (P.H. Jones Papers); the Liddle Collection, University of Leeds (G. Banks-Smith Papers and R.B. Marshall Papers). It has proved impossible to contact the copyright holder of the C.E.L. Lyne Papers, with whom the Imperial War Museum would like to restore contact. Crown Copyright material in the Public Record Office is reproduced by permission of the Controller of Her Majesty's Stationery Office. I would like to thank the trustees of the Imperial War Museum and the trustees of the Royal Military Police for permission to consult material in their possession, and to offer my sincere apologies to anyone whose copyright I have inadvertently infringed.

Notes

1. J.B. Wilson, 'Morale and Discipline in the British Expeditionary Force, 1914–18' (MA, University of New Brunswick, 1978); S.P. MacKenzie, 'Morale and the Cause: The Campaign to Shape the Outlook of Soldiers of the British Expeditionary Force, 1914–18', *Canadian Journal of History*, 25 (1990), pp.215–31; S.P. MacKenzie, *Politics and Military Morale* (Oxford: Clarendon Press, 1992); J.G. Fuller, *Troop Morale and Popular Culture in the British and Dominion Armies 1914–1918* (Oxford, Clarendon Press, 1990).

2. For the expansion of the British Army from 1914 to 1918, see Peter Simkins, *Kitchener's Army* (Manchester: Manchester University Press, 1988); Ian F.W. Beckett and K. Simpson, *A Nation in Arms* (Manchester: Manchester University Press, 1985); Ian F.W. Beckett, 'The Real Unknown Army: British Conscripts 1916–19', *The Great War*, vol, 2, 1 (1989), pp.4–13.

3. See J.H. Sparrow, *The Second World War 1939–45 Army: Morale* (London: HMSO, 1949), pp.1–2; T.T. Paterson, *Morale in War and Work* (London: Max Parrish, 1955), p.99. Child's definition is quoted in Ian McLaine, *Ministry of Morale* (London: Allen & Unwin, 1979), p.8.

4. Carl von Clausewitz, *On War* (Michael Howard and Peter Paret, eds), (Princeton, NJ: Princeton University Press, 1976), pp.187–9.

5. Unpublished account, p.52 (based on a diary entry of 8 Nov. 1916), R. Cude Papers, Imperial War Museum [IWM]; [A. Smith], *Four Years on the Western Front* (London: London Stamp Exchange, 1987 [1922]), p.100.

6. For some indications of possible avenues of research, see David Englander's important article 'Soldiering and Identity: Reflections on the Great War', *War in History*, 1, 3 (1994), pp.300–18.

7. Lieutenant D.D.A. Lockhart's account in War Diary [WD], 1/Gordons, WO 95/1435, TNA.

8. Unpublished account, p.41, H.D. Paviere Papers, 81/19/1, IWM (Paviere erroneously states the division was disbanded a little later); War Diary [WD], 17/Royal Fusiliers, 24 Mar. 1918, WO 95/1363, TNA.

9. For British civilian morale, see note 6, above; Nicholas Reeves, 'The Power of Film Propaganda – Myth or Reality?' *Historical Journal of Film, Radio and Television*, 13, 2 (1993), pp.181–201; J.M. Bourne, *Britain and the Great War* (London: Edward Arnold, 1989), pp.199–214.

10. For an example, see G.D. Sheffield, 'The Effect of War Service on the 22nd Battalion Royal Fusiliers (Kensington) 1914–18, with Special Reference to Morale, Discipline, and the Officer–Man Relationship' (MA thesis, University of Leeds, 1984).

11. K.R. Simpson, 'Capper and the Offensive Spirit', *Journal of the Royal United Services Institution (JRUSI)*, 118, 3 (1973), pp.51–6; G.F.R. Henderson, *The Science of War* (N. Malcolm ed.), (London: Longmans, 1906); *Field Service Regulations, part 1, Operations,*

1909 (reprinted with amendments, 1914), pp. 13, 138, 142; Tim Travers, *The Killing Ground* (London: Unwin Hyman, 1987), pp. 37–82.

12. T.M. Camfield, '"Will to Win" – The U.S. Army Troop Morale Program of World War I', *Military Affairs*, 41, 3 (1977), p. 125; D. Englander, 'The French Soldier, 1914–18', *French History*, 1, 1 (1987), pp. 50–1; E.L. Spears, *Prelude to Victory* (London: Jonathan Cape, 1939), pp. 102–3.

13. See the comments of Haig's Director of Military Operations, John Davidson, in *Haig: Master of the Field* (London: P. Nevill, 1953), pp. 64–5, 125.

14. David Lloyd George, *War Memoirs*, abridged version, vol. I (London: Odhams, 1938), p. 825.

15. See G.D. Sheffield, 'Officer–Man Relations, Morale and Discipline in the British Army 1902–22' (PhD thesis, University of London, 1994), passim.

16. M.C. Morgan, *The Second World War 1939–1945 Army: Army Welfare* (London: HMSO, 1953), p. 1.

17. MacKenzie, 'Morale and the Cause', passim; MacKenzie, *Politics and Military Morale*, pp. 7–31.

18. Wilson, 'Morale and Discipline', p. 311.

19. Sparrow, *Second World War*, p. 2.

20. Sheffield, 'Officer–Man Relations', pp. 37–40; Sheffield, 'Effect of War Service', passim.

21. *Statistics of the Military Effort of the British Empire during the Great War 1914–1920* (London: HMSO, 1922), p. 649.

22. J. Putkowski and J. Sykes, *Shot at Dawn* (Barnsley: Wharncliffe, 1989), p. 9; G. Oram, *Worthless Men: Race, Eugenics and the Death Penalty in the British Army during the First World War* (London: Francis Boutle, 1998), p. 18.

23. Wyndham Childs, *Episodes and Reflections* (London: Cassell, 1930), p. 142.

24. Anthony Babington, *For the Sake of Example* (London: Leo Cooper, 1983), pp. 16–17, 18–19.

25. WD 22/Royal Fusiliers, 26 Dec. 1916, WO 95/1372, TNA; WO 93/49, TNA; H. Berry-cloath, interview with author; H.E. Harvey, *Battleline Narratives* (London: Bretano's, 1928), pp. 135, 157–8.

26. Philip Gibbs, *The Pageant of the Years* (London: William Heinemann, 1946), p. 210.

27. 'Memorandum of a Visit to the Western Front by General Smuts', 27 Jan. 1918, GT 3469, Cabinet Papers (CAB) 24/40, TNA.

28. J.H. Bateson to J.E. Edmonds, 26 May 1934, CAB 45/132, TNA.

29. E.H.G. Roberts, *The Story of the Ninth King's in France* (Liverpool: Northern, 1922), p. 94.

30. William Slim, *Unofficial History* (London: Transworld, 1970 [1959]), p. 12.

31. 'Mark VII' [M. Plowman, pseud.], *A Subaltern on the Somme* (London: J.M. Dent, 1928), p. 66.

32. Unpublished account, pp. 75, 87–8, R.W.F. Johnston Papers, 82/38/1, IWM.

33. E.g., *Notes for Young Officers* (London: HMSO, 1917), p. 3.

34. E.L.M. Burns, *General Mud* (Toronto: Clarke, Irwin, 1970), p. 63.

35. Gibbs, *Pageant*, p. 201; Gibbs to Edmonds, 26 July 1930, CAB 45/134, TNA; Owen Rutter (ed.), *The History of the Seventh Service Battalion of the Royal Sussex Regiment, 1914–19* (London: The Times, 1934), p. 21.

36. J.E. Edmonds and G.C. Wynne, *Military Operations, France and Belgium, 1915*, vol. I (London: Macmillan, 1927), pp. 2–3.

37. Wilson, 'Morale and Discipline', pp. 67–118.

38. 'Lecture delivered by Brigadier General R.A.K. Montgomery, C.B., D.S.O., at the camp of the Eighth Division near Winchester, on 30 October 1914', pp. 5, 9, Department of Printed Books, IWM.

39. 'Around Armentieres and the Ypres Salient', in *Twenty Years After*, supplementary volume (London: Newnes, 1938), p. 503.
40. Colonel M.G.N. Stopford, MC, 'Trench Warfare – General – Winter 1914–15' (lecture to Junior Division, 1938), p. 13, Conf. 3898, Joint Services Command and Staff College Library [JSCSCL]).
41. See B.O. Dewes diary, 17, 21 Nov. 1914, 84/22/1, IWM.
42. T.S. Wollocombe diary, p. 103, 18 Mar. 1915, Royal Military Academy Sandhurst Library.
43. W.R. Robertson, *From Private to Field Marshal* (London: Constable, 1921), pp. 229–30.
44. Letter, 7 Jan. [?] 1915, J. Allison Papers, 85/15/1, IWM.
45. John Lucy, *There's a Devil in the Drum* (London: Faber & Faber, 1938), pp. 255, 267, 311–12.
46. Frank Richards, *Old Soldiers Never Die* (London: Faber & Faber, 1965 [1933]), pp. 60, 97–8.
47. Wilson, 'Morale and Discipline', pp. 139, 157.
48. William Robertson, *Soldiers and Statesmen 1914–1918*, vol. I (London: Cassell, 1926), p. 206.
49. 'Report on Complaints, Moral etc.', pp. 3–4 [Nov. 1916], M. Hardie Papers, 84/46/1, IWM.
50. Letter, 28 Oct. 1915, P.H. Jones Papers, P.246, IWM.
51. Philip Gibbs, *The Battles of the Somme* (London: William Heinemann, 1917), pp. 14–15; Philip Gibbs, *The Realities of War* (London: William Heinemann, 1920), pp. 169–70.
52. Letter, 26 Oct. 1915, G. Banks-Smith Papers, Liddle Collection, University of Leeds.
53. W.L. Andrews, *The Haunting Years* (London: Hutchinson, n.d.), p. 180.
54. 'Report on Complaints, Moral etc.', pp. 6, 12 [Nov. 1916], and 'Summaries of Censorship Reports on General Conditions in British Forces in France', M. Hardie Papers, 84/46/1, IWM.
55. Gerard J. DeGroot, *Douglas Haig 1861–1928* (London: Unwin Hyman, 1988), pp. 1, 235–6.
56. Denis Winter, *Haig's Command* (London: Viking, 1991), pp. 303–15.
57. A.C. Girdwood to J.E. Edmonds, 30 June 1930, CAB 45/143, TNA.
58. See, for example, letter to J.E. Edmonds [signature of writer illegible], 5 Sept. 1930, CAB 45/137, TNA; William Turner, *Pals: 11th (Service) Battalion (Accrington) East Lancashire Regiment* (Barnsley: Wharncliffe, n.d.), pp. 131–2.
59. Letter [signature of writer illegible], n.d., CAB 45/134, TNA.
60. Letter, 6 Nov. 1929, C. Howard, CAB 45/134, TNA; M. Middlebrook, *The First Day on the Somme* (London: Allen Lane, 1971), pp. 96–7, 116.
61. J. Keegan, *The Face of Battle* (Harmondsworth: Penguin, 1978 [1976]), pp. 218–19.
62. J. Collis Browne to J.E. Edmonds, 12 Nov. 1929, CAB 45/132, TNA; George Ashurst, *My Bit: A Lancashire Fusilier at War 1914–18* (Ramsbury: Crowood, 1988), pp. 95–6.
63. Diary, 20–22, 26, 27 June 1916, P.H. Jones Papers, P.246, IWM.
64. J.Q. Henriques, *The War History of the First Battalion Queen's Westminster Rifles 1914–1918* (London: The Medici Society, 1923), p. 84.
65. P.D. Munday to father, 7 July 1916, 80/43/1, IWM.
66. C.E. Carrington, 'Kitchener's Army: The Somme and After', *JRUSI*, 123, 11 (1978), 17. See also Colonel W. Robertson to Edmonds [n.d. but *c*.1936], CAB 45/137, TNA; R.H. Mottram, *Journey to the Western Front* (London: G. Bell & Sons, 1936), p. 144. For an example of 36th (Ulster) Division's learning experience, see Philip Orr, *The Road to the Somme* (Belfast: Blackstaff, 1987), pp. 118–19.
67. E.A. James, *British Regiments, 1914–18* (London: Samson Books, 1978), pp. 46–7, 113; H.C. O'Neill, *The Royal Fusiliers in the Great War* (London: William Heinemann, 1912), p. 6.
68. George S. Duncan, *Douglas Haig as I Knew Him* (London: Allen & Unwin, 1966), p. 45.

69. Censorship Report, Third Army [Nov. 1916], 6, M. Hardie Papers, 84/46/1, IWM.

70. B.H. Liddell Hart, 'Impressions of the Great British Offensive on the Somme', p. 51, CAB 45/135, TNA.

71. Diary, 26 Aug. 1916, Hugh Dalton Papers, Dalton I/I 130, British Library of Political and Economic Science.

72. E. Skinner to Edmonds, 30 Apr. 1936, CAB 45/137, TNA; letter to Edmonds [signature of writer illegible], 13 Apr. 1936, CAB 45/132, TNA.

73. L.A.G. Bowen to Edmonds, 31 Mar. 1930, CAB 45/132, TNA.

74. Anon, *A Short History of the Nineteenth (Western) Division 1914–18* (London, privately published, 1919), p. 29; evidence of J.F.C. Fuller, Parliamentary Papers (PP), 1922, Cmd. 1734, 'Report of the War Office Committee of Enquiry into "Shell-Shock"', p. 22.

75. Unpublished account, p. 176, C.E.L. Lyne Papers, 80/14/1, IWM.

76. C.A.C. Keeson, *The History and Records of Queen Victoria's Rifles* (London: Constable, 1923), p. 212.

77. WD, 1/6 Londons, 17 Feb. 1917, WO 95/2729, TNA.

78. 'Report on Morale etc.' [January 1917], pp. 1, 5, 7, M. Hardie Papers, 84/46/1, IWM. See also Charteris to Macdonogh, 24 Feb. 1917, WO 158/898, TNA, for favourable comments on Second Army's morale.

79. Haig to Robertson, 1 May 1917, WO 158/23, TNA.

80. 'Report on Morale etc.' [May 1917], M. Hardie Papers, 84/46/1, IWM.

81. 'Report on Morale etc.' [Aug. 1917], M. Hardie Papers, 84/46/1, IWM.

82. 'Report on Peace', 19 Oct. 1917, M. Hardie Papers, 84/46/1, IWM.

83. Gibbs, *Realities of War*, p. 396.

84. Quoted in Lloyd George, *War Memoirs*, vol. II, p. 1468.

85. Ashley Ekins, 'The Australians at Passchendaele', in Peter H. Liddle (ed.), *Passchendaele in Perspective: The Third Battle of Ypres* (London: Leo Cooper, 1997), pp. 244–6.

86. Gibbs, *Realities of War*, p. 396.

87. Lloyd George, *War Memoirs*, vol. II, p. 1467.

88. 'The British Armies in France as Gathered from Censorship', 18 Dec. 1917, GT 3044, CAB 24/36, TNA; Gregory Blaxland, *Amiens 1918* (London: W.H. Allen, 1981 [1968]), p. 7. For a useful overview, see Peter Scott, 'Law and Orders: Discipline and Morale in the British Armies in France, 1917', in Liddle, *Passchendaele in Perspective*, pp. 349–70.

89. General Smuts, 'Memorandum', 3 Jan. 1918, GT 3198, CAB 24/37, TNA (see also app. B.1, 'Report by Third Army Commander [Byng]'); 'Memorandum of a Visit to the Western Front by General Smuts', 27 Jan. 1918, GT 3469, CAB 24/40, TNA.

90. Robertson to Haig, 18 Oct. 1917, WO 158/24, TNA.

91. 'Remarks of B.G.G.S., "I",' 20 Oct. 1917, WO 158/24, TNA.

92. 'Note on the Moral of British Troops in France as Disclosed by the Censorship', 13 Sept. 1917, GT 2052, CAB 24/26, TNA.

93. The final frame of a 1917 version of the film *The Battle of the Somme* (IWM video, 1987) makes this point by showing a map of ground abandoned by the Germans in early 1917.

94. *The History of 2/6 Battalion the Royal Warwickshire Regiment 1914–19* (Birmingham, privately published, 1929), p. 47.

95. Captain R.B. Marshall to mother, 3 Oct. 1916, LC.

96. Blaxland, *Amiens 1918*, p. 8.

97. For an example, see A.R. Armfield, letter, Oct. 1963, in correspondence concerning *The Great War* BBC television series, held at IWM.

98. The Étaples mutiny was largely a product of local circumstances. See Sheffield, 'Officer–Man Relations', pp. 295–8; J. Putkowski, 'Toplis, Étaples and "The Monocled Mutineer"', *Stand To!*, 18 (1986), 6–11; Gloden Dallas and Douglas Gill, *The Unknown Army* (London: Verso, 1985), pp. 63–81.

99. John Terraine, *The First World War* (London: Papermac, 1984 [1965]), p. 168.
100. Robin Prior and Trevor Wilson, *Command on the Western Front* (Oxford: Blackwell, 1992), p. 391.
101. Hubert Gough, *Soldiering On* (London: Arthur Barker, 1954), pp. 176–8.
102. e.g., Keegan, *Face of Battle*, p. 276. See also the correspondence on the subject (including from the author and John Keegan) in *Times Literary Supplement*, 13 May; 3, 17 June; 8 July 1994.
103. 'The British Armies in France as Gathered from Censorship, Appx. to July 1918', WO 156/33, TNA. For an example of a soldier's 'grousing' masking a readiness to fight, taken from the 23 Mar. 1918 diary entry of Lieutenant F. Warren (17/King's Royal Rifle Corps), see Anthony Bird (ed.), *Honour Satisfied* (Swindon: Crowood, 1990), p. 87.
104. R.A. Colwill, *Through Hell to Victory* (Torquay: Colwill, 1927), p. 103.
105. 'A Heavy Gunner Looks Back', *Twenty Years After*, vol. I, p. 12.
106. Unpublished account, p. 33, C.J. Lodge Patch Papers, 86/9/1, IWM; Bird (ed.), *Honour Satisfied*, p. 77.
107. Martin Middlebrook, *The Kaiser's Battle* (London: Allen Lane, 1978), pp. 105, 308, 322–39, 341.
108. See Chapter 12.
109. Winston S. Churchill, *The World Crisis 1911–1918*, abridged version, vol. II (London: Odhams, 1938), p. 1289.
110. D. Englander, 'Discipline and Morale in the British Army, 1917–1918', in John Horne (ed.), *State, Society and Mobilization in Europe during the First World War* (Cambridge: Cambridge University Press, 1997), p. 141.
111. Englander, 'Discipline', p. 136; emphasis mine.
112. A.A. Montgomery, *The Story of the Fourth Army in the Battles of the Hundred Days, August 8 to November, 1918* (London: Hodder & Stoughton, 1920), pp. 1, 5, 9, 145–6, 237.
113. R.E. Priestly, *Breaking the Hindenburg Line* (London, T.F. Unwin, 1919), p. 87.
114. G. Ritter, *The Sword and the Sceptre*, vol. IV (London: Allen Lane, 1973), p. 232.
115. R.H. Mottram, J. Easton and E. Partridge, *Three Personal Accounts of the War* (London: Scholartis, 1929), p. 127.
116. C.E.W. Bean, *The Official History of Australia in the War of 1914–1918*, vol. VI: *The A.I.F. in France: May 1918–The Armistice* (St. Lucia, Queensland: University of Queensland Press, 1983 [1942]), pp. 875–6, 933–4, 939–40; Fuller, *Troop Morale*, pp. 24–8.
117. See, for example, the optimistic view of a private of 1/23 Londons: A.E. Abrey, letter, 7 Oct. 1918, 84/4/1, IWM.
118. This comment is based on the examination of primary source material in Australian archives.
119. Charles Douie, *The Weary Road* (London: John Murray, 1931), pp. 15–16.
120. Haig to Lady Haig, 1 Apr. 1915, Haig Papers, National Library of Scotland.
121. J.H. Boraston (ed.), *Sir Douglas Haig's Despatches* (London: Dent, 1979 [1919]), pp. 319–21.
122. 'Why Germany Capitulated on November 11 1918 – A Brief Study Based on Documents in the Possession of the French General Staff', Appx. 2, JSCSCL; R.H. Lutz, *The Causes of the German Collapse in 1918* (Stanford: Stanford University Press, 1934), pp. 176–7.

Chapter 10

Officer–Man Relations, Discipline and Morale in the British Army of the First World War

In 1935 a British wartime Temporary officer wrote that 'An army, like any other human society, is an organism, whose well-being depends on the interplay of human relationships.'[1] This paper examines the relationship of leader and led in the British Army of 1914–1918 and the impact of this relationship upon morale. My remarks are confined largely to infantry and artillery units on the Western Front, and to regimental officers of the rank of lieutenant colonel or below.

It is necessary to examine some of the pre-war foundations of wartime officer–man relations. Modern scholarship has confirmed the essential accuracy of J.F.C. Fuller's view that the pre-war Regular army was 'Recruited from the bottom of Society' but 'led from the top'.[2] An education at a public school, especially a Clarendon school, was an almost essential *rite de passage* for the aspirant officer, while in sharp contrast working-class men filled the ranks. Thus in 1913 unskilled and skilled labourers accounted for over 68 per cent of recruits, while clerks accounted for only 3 per cent.[3] A whole series of influences, including those of the landed interest and the reformed public schools, ensured that by 1914 virtually all Regular officers were thoroughly paternalistic. The core of the officer's creed was *noblesse oblige*, the belief that privilege entailed responsibility for the well-being of their men. A pair of paintings displayed side by side in the Officers' Mess at Sandhurst gives a graphic illustration of this paternal and pragmatic concern. The first depicts a squire and groom standing beside a horse. The squire is saying 'Well, Jim, has he fed all right?' The second shows a group of soldiers sitting round a campfire. An officer is asking 'Dinners all right, men?' Both paintings share a single caption: *Noblesse oblige*.[4]

Somewhat paradoxically, the Regular army combined exemplary paternalism with a rigidly hierarchical approach to discipline and distant, although generally mutually respectful, relations between officers and men.[5] Things were rather different in the pre-war part-time Territorial Force. A whole series of factors, not least the social composition of the ranks and the officer corps, and the practical difficulties involved in enforcing strict discipline on a part-time amateur army, produced a style of officer–man relations and discipline very different from the Regular varieties.[6] An officer of 7/Manchesters wrote of the 'comradeship' which produced an 'easy relationship between officers and men ... [that] was the despair of the more crusted Regular martinet'. A Regular brigadier general described the discipline of another northern Territorial battalion, 6/West Yorkshires, as being that of 'good will'. In this unit, it was claimed, orders were at first obeyed 'because of a mutual confidence and respect' between the ranks, 'similar to that in a workshop or any small society'. Neither battalion set much store by formal discipline. On one pre-war drill in January 1914 the 6/West Yorkshires marched off parade 45 minutes late, only 80 strong, and 'Even this was considered a good attendance!'[7]

Thus there were not one but two distinct strands of officer–man relations and discipline co-existing in the pre-1914 British Army, a 'Regular' and an 'Auxiliary' variety. The paternalism of the Regular officer was passed on to his Temporary wartime successor, and many units raised during the war adopted a 'Regular' style of discipline. However, wartime inter-rank relations tended more towards the 'Territorial' than the 'Regular' end of the spectrum. Most wartime units took elements from both traditions, in varying proportions depending on the battalion, to create a style of officer–man relations and discipline that showed traits inherited from both parents.

It can be misleading to generalise about an organisation as large as the British Army of 1914–1918. It consisted of three, initially distinct, types of unit – Regular, Territorial and New (or 'Kitchener's') Army – and officer–man relations could differ from unit to unit and even from platoon to platoon. Moreover, soldiers had greater opportunities to forge informal relations with their officers on active service than while training at home.[8] Nonetheless, it is possible to make a broad assessment of the subject.

A theme that runs through many wartime officers' letters, diaries and memoirs is that of devotion, even love, for their men. The circumstances of the Western Front were particularly well suited for officers to become fond of their men. While the officer's lot was in many ways better than that of the Other Ranks,[9] all men who served in the trenches suffered from poor living conditions and the fear of sudden death or mutilation. Many officers came to see their men as partners in adversity. In November 1916 Sergeant H.H. Munro (the author 'Saki') was killed. Despite his advanced age and privileged social background, Munro had refused a commission, preferring to stay in the ranks of 22/Royal Fusiliers. One of his officers, Major Christopher Stone, commented that Munro was 'one of the men that I really and honestly admire and revere in this war ... He did very finely for us all.' Two years later Stone expressed similar sentiments about the death of a working-class NCO, describing him as one of 'my friends'.[10]

What might be called the 'bureaucracy of paternalism' ensured that their men were never very far from the thoughts of junior officers. The Regular officers who dominated the wartime army seem to have been concerned that Temporary officers, many of whom lacked the social and educational background of pre-war Regulars, might have neglected their duties towards their men. This concern lay at the root of the much-derided obsession of the staff with apparent trivialities, which were, in fact, manifestations of institutionalised paternalism. Wyn Griffith, a Temporary officer of 15/Royal Welch Fusiliers, described the bureaucracy of paternalism in these words: 'every man above the rank of private is his brother's keeper ... this concern ... can be harassing, and it often is, but it is omnipresent throughout the hierarchy of the command and staff'.[11] Even on the beaches of Gallipoli, one subaltern recorded in 1915, 'endless returns have to be made about one's men – health, clothes, equipment ... etc.'.[12]

Most Temporary officers confounded official fears by displaying an extremely high level of paternal care for their men, which in practice meant ensuring that soldiers were well fed, well clothed and given at least the minimum of comfort. Officers' training emphasised that the well-being of their men should always come before their own comfort. Thus at the end of a march, an officer would routinely ensure that the men were comfortably billeted before even thinking of retiring to his own billet.[13] Many officers provided extra comforts out of their own pockets. Officers' letters home are littered with requests that chocolate, cigarettes and the like be sent out for their men, although the request of one Coldstream Guards officer in December 1915 for 200 large mince pies was perhaps at the upper end of the scale of generosity.[14]

Officers attended to more than just the creature comforts of their men. After breaking down at the graveside of his brother, a private of 1/Coldstream Guards was sent to a convalescent camp by a sympathetic officer.[15] In a revealing casual aside in his memoirs, a Temporary subaltern of 1/North Staffordshires wrote of his disappointment at not being able to keep a 'swanky German' pipe, which would have made his men laugh. Clearly this officer believed that keeping his men amused was an essential part of his duties.[16] What is more important, many officers believed that they had a duty to protect 'their' men against what many perceived as an impersonal and arbitrary coercive military machine. Some officers, such as the CO of 1/Duke of Cornwall's Light Infantry in September 1916, risked their careers by refusing to attack in unfavourable circumstances.[17] Most officers did not take such a personally risky stand. Regimental officers, like the men they commanded, were trapped by the military system, and could only modify that system at an extremely local level.[18]

There were many ways in which officers could make life more bearable for their soldiers. Officers quietly woke exhausted men discovered sleeping on sentry duty and saved them from the full rigour of the disciplinary code.[19] If men were 'crimed', an officer could award minor punishments at company or battalion level to prevent disciplinary cases from going forward to the lottery of a court-martial.[20] More simply, the paternal officer could turn a blind eye to illegal but harmless activities that made the ranker's life worth living. In his great prose/poem, *In Parenthesis*, David Jones (15/Royal Welch Fusiliers) wrote memorably of surreptitious smoking 'under the turnip stack'. Although the 'kind' platoon officer affected not to notice, a look-out watched for signs of authority in the form of 'the Adjutant, or that shit Major Lillywhite'.[21]

By 1917–1918 approximately 40 per cent of British officers were of working-class or at least lower-middle-class origin.[22] The experiences of such officers varied from individual to individual. Henry Williamson, in his semi-autobiographical novel *A Fox Under My Cloak*, wrote of the problems experienced in 1915 by a lower-middle class former ranker in adjusting to commissioned status. In one scene the central character, 'Phillip Maddison', a rather gauche and desperately insecure young man, is subjected to the ordeal of a subaltern's court-martial for infractions of the unwritten social code. By contrast, John Lucy, a former Regular ranker, was treated with kindness when he joined his old battalion as an officer, and had few problems in adapting to his new status.[23] On the whole, it seems that rather more prejudice was experienced by Temporary officers in the earlier years of the war than the latter, and that most were accepted with the same degree of pragmatism that lay behind their commissioning.

There was, however, considerable contemporary criticism of the 'Temporary Gentleman'. This nickname reflects not just social snobbery but also a genuine concern that, lacking a traditional social and educational background, such officers would not be paternalistic. This concern was misplaced. The system of officer training introduced during the war was a pragmatic and highly successful attempt to give potential officers a crash-course in, among other things, paternalistic behaviour.[24] Moreover, the bulk of officers commissioned in the later stages of the war had served in the ranks and knew very well the importance of an officer's care for his men. T.A.H. Nash, for instance, served as a junior NCO in 1/4 Gloucestershires, and the experience served him in good stead when he was commissioned into 16/Manchesters, his divisional commander later paying tribute to Nash's understanding of, and sympathy with, his men.[25] It is true that it is much rarer to find references to officers buying food for their men in 1917–1918 than it is for the earlier period, but this can be explained by purely practical factors, such as food shortages at home and the fact that many ranker-officers did not have enough spare cash to buy gifts in bulk for their men.

The language used by officers when writing about their men indicates that their attitudes were not determined solely by pragmatism or a sense of duty. The bond between the subaltern and his platoon was often described in terms of marriage and parenthood. Both neatly capture the idea of a tender, loving relationship. Sharing as they did, to a greater or lesser degree, the hardships of war, it is perhaps not surprising that boys of similar ages made friends across the rank and class divide, or that older officers had a thoroughly paternal concern for their men, or sympathised with men of their own age enduring life in the ranks. Many officers came to admire the fortitude of their men. 'A private's life out here is a very rotten one' wrote an officer of 9/Duke of Wellington's Regiment in 1916, 'the more one thinks about it, the more one admires the men – they're absolutely wonderful to stick what they do stick.'[26]

The picture was not entirely rosy. Many officers felt that their men seemed incapable of doing anything without their help; the creation of a dependency culture was an almost inevitable consequence of the bureaucracy of paternalism. In 1916 a *Times* journalist commented that the extent to which even intelligent soldiers relied upon their officers was on occasion 'so absolute as to be embarrassing'. This writer believed that this state of affairs was the consequence of the surrender of individual liberty by men when they joined the army.[27] Officers also had to square the circle of demonstrating friendship for their men while retaining their authority as hierarchical leaders by avoiding undue familiarity. Curiously, few officers articulated this dilemma, although it lay at the heart of the question of officer–man relations. One who did succinctly summarised what seems to have been the credo of most officers: 'The men are all topping fellows. But one has to let them know who is master. First an officer has to be an officer, and then he may become a man.'[28] Once this had been established, both officers and men generally observed the principle of 'on parade, on parade; off parade, off parade' – that is, the recognition by both officers and men that 'what was permissible on certain occasions might be a military crime on others'.[29]

What did Other Ranks think of their officers? They tended to judge them by a simple set of criteria. Officers, wrote a private of 2/5 Lancashire Fusiliers, 'fell into two categories. If they passed dirty rifles, handled a spade, or carried a bag of cement they were "aw reet". If not, they were "no bloody *bon*".' A middle-class private of 1/5 Gloucestershires recorded the views of his working-class comrades in similar terms: 'A bad officer, that is, a bully, is a —! A good officer, that is, a considerate (sic), is "a toff." I'd follow him anywhere. The men's friend'; or simply, but in significant tones '*gentleman*!'[30]

As these quotations show, Other Ranks tended to judge officers largely in terms of deference, which can be defined as 'respect for, and obedience to, "leaders" of society'. Deference was one of the principal bonds of Edwardian society. It was both a pragmatic response of working-class men to economic realities, and a 'natural' way of life, inculcated through religion and education. Deference was not, however, the same as subservience. Men in the ranks saw deference as 'the natural exchange' for paternalism. Officers who did not look after their men, who did not show leadership qualities in battle, or who did not behave in a gentlemanly fashion had, in the eyes of the ordinary soldier, forfeited all rights to commissioned status, and the privileges that went with it, including the right to expect rankers to follow them.[31] This point is graphically illustrated by the reaction of some sergeants of 4/5 Black Watch to the unedifying spectacle of a drunken and sexually aroused Temporary officer chasing the hostess around an estaminet. The sergeants, working-class slum dwellers by origin, were 'incensed by such behaviour in an officer of our regiment'.[32]

It is rare indeed to find a blanket condemnation of officers in the writings of Other Ranks. A furious denunciation of one officer is likely to be followed by a complimentary reference to another; thus Private Abraham of 8/Queens attacked the character of one officer, yet went on to say that other officers were natural leaders, who enjoyed the trust and esteem of their soldiers. It is uncommon to discover an officer who was actively hated by his men, as opposed to one who was criticised for neglecting his men or for thoughtlessness. A private described a Northants Yeomanry officer as 'the most detested and hated officer I ever met'. The interesting point is that this officer suffered by comparison with the popular officer he had replaced. Precisely because most officers were paternal and lived up to their side of the unspoken bargain, rankers regarded with especial distaste officers who did not conform to the general pattern of officer–man relations. Private S.B. Abbot (86th Machine Gun Company) was scathing about one officer, who simultaneously risked his men's lives unnecessarily and seemed over-concerned with his own safety. More typical of Abbot's officers was a paternalistic subaltern who was killed at Arras in April 1917, much to Abbot's grief.[33]

The writings of men in the ranks frequently contain favourable references to officers, although not as often as complimentary remarks about soldiers appear in officers' memoirs, letters and writings. In part this is a reflection of differing perceptions of the relationship, but also of the 'unspoken assumption' that officer–man relations were good unless stated otherwise. Only if an officer was exceptionally good, or exceptionally bad, or if he suddenly came to mind through being killed or wounded, was he likely to be mentioned. The first specific death mentioned in the diary of Private Joe Griffiths of 1/King's Royal Rifle Corps was that of Second Lieutenant Bentall. His sense of loss prompted Griffiths to record his appreciation of this officer which otherwise would have gone unknown.[34]

Middle-class rankers were more inclined to complain about the officer–man relationship than their working-class counterparts. The former were perhaps less sympathetic to the concept of deference as a return for paternalism, and tended to resent officers' privileges, particularly if they had been passed over for a commission.[35] For the most part men in the ranks accepted the superior lifestyle of the officer as part of the natural order of things – provided, of course, that the officer did not behave in an 'unofficer-like' way. This obviously placed ranker-officers, that is, officers without a public school education who had previously served in the ranks, in a potentially very difficult situation when faced by a middle-class soldier like John Tucker of

1/13 Londons, who criticised a subaltern for speaking with 'a slight cockney accent', or indeed working-class soldiers who preferred officers to be distinctive in their speech and behaviour.[36] However, if lower-class officers had been widely mistrusted by the men they commanded, the British Army's cohesion would have been placed under severe strain in 1917–1918. In reality, most lower-class ranker officers did meet Other Ranks' expectations of officer-like behaviour, and inter-rank relations remained cordial throughout the war. An officer's leadership skills, competence, paternalism and courage determined his relations with his men, not his social class.

Some soldiers emerged from the khaki mass and formed close relationships with officers. Informal night-time chats between a duty officer and a lonely sentry; the peculiar relationship between officer and soldier servant; the shared experience of battle – all of these circumstances offered opportunities for the barriers of rank to lower, albeit briefly. NCOs, who deserve a major study to themselves, co-operated closely with officers to ensure the smooth running of a unit, although the problems of balancing friendship and discipline could be acute. The officer and NCO had to strike a delicate balance between being part of the platoon or company 'team' and being slightly aloof from it. The successful partnership between the officer and NCO, which was in many ways the lynchpin of the entire disciplinary structure of the army, had to be founded upon mutual goodwill and recognition of the difficulties inherent in the relationship.[37]

In 1915 Donald Hankey, a gentleman-ranker of 7/Rifle Brigade, published 'The Beloved Captain', a short story about an officer who was Christ-like in his concern for his men. 'Beloved Captains' are often to be found in the writings of ordinary soldiers. Some younger soldiers engaged in hero-worship, while other more mature men expressed more measured, but very positive, opinions of some officers. Ernest Shepherd, a pre-war Regular NCO of 1/Dorsets, described Captain Algeo as 'Absolutely fearless ... [his] first and last thought [was] for his men.'[38] A balanced view of the officer corps as a whole appeared in an article published in 1938 in a popular magazine aimed at the ex-servicemen's market. In assessing his officers the author, an anonymous former ranker, certainly did not shrink from pointing out their defects. Nonetheless, like Hankey, he expressed his admiration of brave and paternal officers, and recognised their role in making life bearable for the ordinary soldier: 'We can have nothing but admiration ... tinged with affection ... for almost all of them.'[39]

The generally excellent state of officer–man relations had important consequences for the morale of the army of 1914–1918. As Correlli Barnett has written, British soldiers on the Western Front 'had the moral and material support of an immense organization' devoted to their welfare.[40] Regimental officers had an important role in this organisation, not merely as providers of 'buckshee' cigarettes but as buffers between the soldier and the army; for, as a conscript private noted, while recalling a friendly officer, 'It makes all the difference when one is treated with kindness and consideration by one in authority.'[41] In June 1917 a 'Soldier's and Worker's Council' – a body that would not, one would have thought, have been a natural defender of the officer class – passed resolutions demanding 'more generous treatment' of junior officers and that 'The general treatment of soldiers be brought into line with the spirit of officers and men in daily contact' which alone 'make life endurable'.[42]

British Other Ranks were perfectly capable of conveying their opinions to their superiors by a variety of methods.[43] The most dramatic way was to carry out an act of large-scale mutiny. The only such British mutiny to take place on the Western Front during hostilities occurred at Étaples base camp in September 1917. Here, the army's disciplinary system ran riot and seasoned troops were, much to their disgust, treated as raw recruits. Moreover at Étaples officers were kept well away from the men. The creative tension that existed at unit level between discipline and the protective paternalism of regimental officers was thus absent. Significantly, military police and instructor NCOs, not regimental officers, were the main targets of the mutineers' fury.[44] Without the paternal role of the regimental officers, there might well have been many more such mutinies on the Western Front.

It is important to note the limitations of the paternalistic/deferential relationship. It could not prevent cases of 'rough justice'.[45] It could not prevent the imposition of tough 'Regular' discipline on citizen volunteers and conscripts, although it could help to modify its effects. It helped to sustain a 'dependency culture' in which men relied too heavily on their officers. However, drawing up the balance sheet, the advantages of the inter-rank relationship far outweighed the disadvantages. The excellence of relations between Other Ranks and regimental officers was a factor of absolutely crucial importance in maintaining the morale of the BEF throughout four gruelling years of attrition on the Western Front.[46]

Acknowledgements
Crown Copyright material in The National Archives is reproduced by permission of the Controller of Her Majesty's Stationery Office and material in the Liddle Collection by kind permission of the University of Leeds. It has proved impossible to trace the holders of copyright in the G.S. Chaplin Papers held in the Imperial War Museum.

Notes

1. A.D. Thorburn, *Amateur Gunners* (Liverpool: W. Potter, 1933), p. 5.

2. J.F.C. Fuller, *The Army in My Time* (London: Rich & Cowan, 1935), p. 6. For a study of the social composition of the Victorian and Edwardian army, see Edward M. Spiers, *The Army and Society* (London: Longman, 1980).

3. 'Trades of men offering for enlistment, year ending September 30th 1913', PP, 1921, XX, CMD 1193.

4. The paintings appeared as plates in E.A.H. Alderson, *Pink and Scarlet*, or *Hunting as a School for Soldiering* (London: Hodder & Stoughton, 1913), pp. 198–9.

5. See G.D. Sheffield, 'Officer–Man Relations, Morale and Discipline in the British Army, 1902–22' (PhD, King's College London, 1994), pp. 15–22; unpublished account, p. 2, W.J. Nicholson Papers, Imperial War Museum [IWM]; John F. Lucy, *There's a Devil in the Drum* (London: Faber & Faber, 1938), p. 94.

6. Sheffield, 'Officer–Man Relations', pp. 24–50.

7. G.B. Hurst, *With the Manchesters in the East* (Manchester, Manchester University Press, 1917), p. 2 (see also Hurst's comments in S.J. Wilson, *The Seventh Manchesters* (Manchester, Manchester University Press, 1920, p. xiii); E.V. Tempest, *History of 6th Battalion the West Yorkshire Regiment* (Bradford: Percy Lund, Humphries, 1921), pp. 1–3, 6, 12. For (generally disapproving) views of Regular officers on the discipline of auxiliary units, see the series of 'Reports ... on the progress made by the Territorial Force ...', War Office Library.

8. Unpublished account, p. 4, J. Woollin Papers, PP/MCR/no, IWM; Notebook I, B.D. Parkin Papers, 86/57/1, IWM.

9. I.F.W. Beckett, 'The British Army, 1914–18: The Illusion of Change', in John Turner (ed.), *Britain and the First World War* (London: Unwin-Hyman, 1988), p. 107.

10. G.D. Sheffield and G.I.S. Inglis (eds), *From Vimy Ridge to the Rhine: The Great War Letters of Christopher Stone DSO MC* (Marlborough: Crowood, 1989), pp. 20, 135 (letters of 12 Feb., 16 Nov., 1916, 9 Sept. 1918). For more on Stone, see Chapter 13. For another example, see Lieutenant R.E. Wilson, letter, 9 July 1916, K.R. Simpson Questionnaires [KRS Q]. All quotations from these questionnaires appear by permission of Mr Keith Simpson MP, to whom I am grateful for giving access to this unique archive.

11. Wyn Griffith, *Up to Mametz* (Norwich: Gliddon, 1988 [1931]), pp. 202–3. For an example see memo. from AA&QMG, 66th Division, 28 Feb. 1918, in P. Ingleson Papers, Liddle Collection, University of Leeds [LC].

12. P.M. Campbell, *Letters from Gallipoli* (Edinburgh: privately printed, 1916), p. 26.

13. See Examination paper 1, Dec. 1916, in 'Officers: Officer Cadets' files, LC.

14. Sir W. Baynes Bart, letter, 24 Dec. 1915, LC.

15. H. Venables, diary, 3 June 1915, LC.

16. Bernard Martin, *Poor Bloody Infantry* (London: John Murray, 1987), p. 115.

17. E.W. Flanagan to J.E. Edmonds, 17 Nov. 1935, CAB 45/133, TNA.

18. Robert Graves, *Goodbye to All That* (Harmondsworth: Penguin, 1960 [1929]), p. 192; letter, 7 Oct. 1916, G.S. Taylor Papers, Liddell Hart Centre for Military Archives [LHCMA].

19. [A.M. Burrage] 'Ex-Pte.-X', *War is War* (London: Victor Gollancz, 1930), p. 74; G.H. Cole, KRS Q.

20. P.W. Turner and R.H. Haigh, *Not For Glory* (London: Robert Maxwell, 1969), pp. 86–7; C.E. Carrington, *Soldier From the Wars Returning* (London: Hutchinson, 1965), pp. 169–70.

21. David Jones, *In Parenthesis* (London: Faber & Faber, 1963 [1937]), p. 15.

22. Figures are calculated from *Statistics of the Military Effort of the British Empire during the Great War 1914–1920* (London: HMSO, 1922), p. 707; see also J.M. Winter, *The Great War and the British People* (London: Macmillan, 1987), pp. 83–99.

23. Henry Williamson, *A Fox Under My Cloak* (London: Macdonald, 1985 [1955]), pp. 218–23; Lucy, *Devil*, pp. 352–9.

24. R.T. Rees, *A Schoolmaster at War* (London: Haycock Press, n.d.), p. 79; Sheffield, 'Officer–Man Relations', pp. 138–50; Graves, *Goodbye*, p. 203.

25. T.A.M. Nash (ed.), *The Diary of an Unprofessional Soldier* (Chippenham: Picton, 1991), pp. ix, 27.

26. P. Beaver (ed.), *The Wipers Times* (London: Macmillan, 1988 [1916]), p. 79; G. Macleod Ross, KRS Q; J.W.B. Russell, diary, 15 May 1916, LC.

27. 'A Citizen Army from Within', part III, *The Times*, 5 Dec. 1916; see also E. Taylor, Letters, 12, 13 Dec. 1914, LC. The lack of initiative of the British soldier can be overstressed. For a corrective, see an excellent, and very positive, analysis of British tactics: Paddy Griffith, *Battle Tactics of the Western Front* (New Haven and London: Yale University Press, 1994).

28. R.W. McConnell to father in Laurence Housman, *War Letters of Fallen Englishmen* (London: Victor Gollancz, 1930), p. 186. An excellent description of this dilemma can be found in Rowlands Coldicott, *London Men in Palestine* (London: Edward Arnold, 1919), pp. 66–70.

29. John Brophy and Eric Partridge, *The Long Trail* (London: Andre Deutsch, 1965), p. 225.

30. V.W. Tilsey, *Other Ranks* (London: Cobden-Sanderson, 1931), pp. 126–7; Ivor Gurney (R.K.R. Thornton, ed.) *War Letters* (London: Hogarth Press, 1984), p. 217.

31. For the concept of deference, see Howard Newby, 'The Deferential Dialectic', *Comparative Studies in Society and History*, 17, 2, (1975); Patrick Joyce, *Work, Society and Politics* (London: Methuen, 1980), pp. 91–5.

32. Eric Linklater, *Fanfare for a Tin Hat* (London: Macmillan, 1970), p. 61.

33. Unpublished account, pp. 8a, 54, 84, A.J. Abraham Papers, IWM; unpublished account, (unpaginated), G.S. Chaplin Papers, IWM; unpublished account, S.B. Abbot Papers, 78/36/1, IWM.

34. J. Griffiths, diary, 3 Oct. 1915, IWM.

35. See for instance A. Moffat, diary, 16 Feb. 1916, LC; H. Innes, letter, 5 Sept. 1918, LC; Burrage, *War*, pp. 9, 13, 70–1.

36. John F. Tucker, *Johnny Get Your Gun* (London: William Kimber, 1978), p. 41; G.W. Grossmith, KRS Q.

37. Griffith, *Mametz*, pp. 135–6; R.L. Mackay, diary, 2 Aug. 1917, p. 374, IWM; S.F. Hatton, *The Yarn of a Yeoman* (London: Hutchinson, n.d.), pp. 87–8.

38. Donald Hankey, *A Student in Arms* (London: Andrew Melrose, 1916), pp. 59–7; George Coppard, *With a Machine Gun to Cambrai* (London: Macmillan, 1986 [1978]), p. 5; W.M. Jenner, letter, 24 June 1969, P. Blagrove Papers, LHCMA; Ernest Shepherd (B. Rossor, ed.), *A Sergeant-Major's War* (Marlborough: Crowood, 1987), pp. 82, 97.

39. Anon, 'Memories V', in Sir E. Swinton (ed.), *Twenty Years After*, supplementary vol. (London: George Newnes, n.d. but *c*.1938), pp. 369–72.

40. Correlli Barnett, *The Collapse of British Power* (Gloucester: Alan Sutton, 1984 [1972]), p. 432.

41. Christopher Haworth, *March to Armistice 1918* (London: William Kimber, 1968), p. 28.

42. WO 32/5455, TNA.

43. For a study of 'power relationships' in the French army, which makes some points of relevance to this present study, see Leonard V. Smith, *Between Mutiny and Obedience: The Case of the French Fifth Infantry Division during World War I* (Princeton, NJ: Princeton University Press, 1994).

44. J.H. Dible, diary, 11 Sept. 1917, IWM; War Diary, Commandant, Étaples Base camp, 9–10 Sept. 1917, WO 95/4027, TNA; G.D. Sheffield, *The Redcaps* (London: Brassey's, 1994), p. 80.

45. This is the title of a novel which centres around a military miscarriage of justice that results in an execution. C.E. Montague, *Rough Justice* (London: Chatto & Windus, 1926).

46. The comments on officer–man relations and discipline in J.G. Fuller's otherwise excellent study of an aspect of the BEF's morale merit some adjustment in view of the research presented in this chapter; J.G. Fuller, *Troop Morale and Popular Culture in the British and Dominion Armies 1914–1918* (Oxford, Clarendon Press, 1991), pp. 47–57.

Chapter 11

'A very good type of Londoner and a very good type of colonial': Officer–Man Relations and Discipline in the 22nd Royal Fusiliers, 1914–1918

The importance of the officer–man relationship in the alleviation of battle-field stress and the maintenance of morale has often been noted. Many of the witnesses before the British 'Shellshock Committee' of 1922 stressed the primary importance of officer–man relations in the maintenance of morale, as have many recent writers on the subject. The weight of evidence thus clearly indicates that the relation between the leader and the led is of great importance in holding an army together and making it fight efficiently.[1] This chapter will argue that the leadership of 22nd (Service) Battalion Royal Fusiliers (Kensington) [22/RF], when faced with the challenge of commanding a unit containing a large number of middle-class soldiers, evolved a disciplinary regime that was very different from that of the Regular army, being characterised by an informal inter-rank relationship and a minimum of externally imposed discipline and 'bullshit'. As a result 22/RF came to resemble a pre-war Territorial or even a wartime Dominion unit, rather than a Regular battalion of its parent regiment.

22/RF was one of 557 battalions of the New Armies raised between August 1914 and June 1916. It was formed from the amalgamation of two companies raised by William H. Davison, the Mayor of the London Borough of Kensington, and 600 men recruited to serve in the 'Colonial Light Infantry'. Neither unit was able to recruit up to strength, so the colonials became A and B Companies, the Kensingtons C and D. The resulting unit was described by the historian of the Royal Fusiliers as 'combining a very good type of Londoner and a very good type of colonial, and the two amalgamated very successfully'.[2]

The type of man who made up the bulk of 22/RF was very different from the unskilled workers and unemployed who filled a good proportion of the ranks of the pre-war Army. The colonial companies had their origin in a newspaper advertisement of 12 September 1914 that appealed for men with 'any association with the OVERSEAS DOMINIONS and COLONIES'.

Some of their connections with the Empire were somewhat tenuous, and a steady stream of 'colonials' left the battalion from an early date and were replaced by ordinary British recruits. Much anecdotal evidence suggests that many of the colonials were of relatively high social standing. A resident of Horsham (where 22/RF trained in 1915) contrasted the shabby appearance of some of the London recruits with that of the men from 'Kimberley and Jo'burg' [sic]. Although it is unsafe to assume that all colonials were prosperous, there is no evidence of poverty among the overseas contingent.[3]

C and D companies lacked the initial social homogeneity of the colonial companies. Davison had originally intended to be selective in his recruiting, drawing his men from local business houses, which would have excluded the working classes. The severe competition for recruits put paid to this idea, and Davison was forced to widen his search and accept men of lower social status. From the very beginning Davison decided to work on the 'pals' principle that friends and workmates could serve in the same company.[4] Thus a group of men who belonged to the same rugby football club joined C Company and a small clique of friends from a department store enlisted in 13 Platoon. This policy produced platoons that had the social homogeneity that the battalion as a whole lacked. For example, 12 Platoon consisted almost entirely of working-class men. By contrast, 13 Platoon was recruited from 'solicitors, bank clerks, press men, [and] business men'.[5] There seems to have been some attempt to place men who joined 22/RF as individuals in platoons where they would mix with men of a similar type. In general, it appears that the majority of 22/RF's personnel in 1914–1915 were of middle-class origin, with a strong leavening of workmen. The original 22/RF seems to have contained only a small proportion of men actually resident in Kensington, although it did have a local character of sorts, in that perhaps one-third of its men were drawn from West London and other men may have worked in Kensington but lived outside the area.[6]

To a great extent, military life made social distinctions meaningless. The same process was used to turn both stevedores and solicitors into soldiers, and all men had to take their share of boring and unpleasant duties, regardless of their social position in civilian life. However, the attitudes, lifestyle and even speech of the stevedore were alien to the solicitor. In other battalions some (but by no means all) middle-class men had unhappy experiences while serving in platoons consisting of working-class men. To the inevitable rigours of army life, which came as a shock to some men used to a sedentary existence, was added the loneliness of service amongst men with whom they had little in common, and whose language frequently consisted of a litany of obscenities. In 22/RF social segregation by platoon ensured that the clerk or shop assistant could avoid contact with his social and educational inferiors. A similar result was achieved by elitist 'pals' units and Territorial 'class corps' which charged entrance fees, which effectively excluded the working classes from enlistment.

Paradoxically, such segregation did not produce division within 22/RF. To be allocated companions of a similar background to oneself was a very different matter from being plunged into the company of men with whom one had little in common. The practical application of the 'pals' concept in this way made military life palatable for the middle classes, almost by accident. All platoons were united in loyalty to their officers and to the good name of 22/RF. This had two major consequences. First, it provided ideal conditions for the development of 'primary' or 'buddy' groups within the unit. Second, the solidarity that resulted formed an excellent basis for the development of a disciplinary system based on 'self-', rather than 'imposed' discipline. Such a system would have been impossible to operate in a disunited battalion that lacked morale and cohesion, no matter how educated the soldiers of the battalion might have been.

In September 1914 a Regular officer, Lieutenant Colonel J.A. Innes, was appointed Commanding Officer (CO) of 22/RF. However, Innes's second-in-command, Major Randle Barnett-Barker, seems to have stamped his authority on 22/RF from the very beginning, and 'BB' commanded the battalion on the Western Front from November 1915 until December 1917.[7] Barnett-Barker was also a Regular, who had served with the Royal Welsh Fusiliers before retiring in 1906.[8] In many ways, Barnett-Barker's approach to man-management bore a resemblance to the pre-war ethic of *noblesse oblige* which had characterised pre-war officer–man relations. I have written on this topic elsewhere,[9] and here it will suffice to say that most pre-war officers had recognised that it was their duty, on both philanthropic and pragmatic grounds, to ensure that their men were well cared for. Barnett-Barker clearly recognised that fighting men were more efficient if physical discomfort was minimised. Where Barnett-Barker differed from the majority of his brother Regular officers was in his modification of the basic tenet of the social code of the pre-war army: the rigid separation of the ranks. There are many comments in Barnett-Barker's letters that reveal his genuine affection for his men.[10] As commanding officer of 22/RF, Barnett-Barker was able to make life more bearable for his men, and, as another officer of the battalion commented, the colonel was 'always devising schemes for making this or that man happier'.[11] Barnett-Barker established informal, friendly relationships with his men, anticipating the populist generals of 1939–1945 by moving among his troops, chatting informally and distributing cigarettes.[12] He thus combined the attributes of the typical officer and gentlemen, whose eccentricities and bearing lower-class soldiers are reputed to admire, with those of a Patton or a Montgomery.

Barnett-Barker was shrewd enough to recognise that the better-educated citizen soldier required something more than the odd word of praise or packet of cigarettes to sustain his morale. He sought to bridge the gulf between officer and man, to give a human face to the army, and he largely succeeded. Barnett-Barker was popular with educated and articulate Other Ranks such as the French-Canadian Destrube brothers, and with men such as 'Olly' Berrycloath, a working-class private with a far from unsullied disciplinary record. When he was interviewed in 1984, Berrycloath, unprompted, produced a battered photograph of his old colonel and announced that 'a finer officer and gentleman you could not care to meet'. It was a measure of Barnett-Barker's flexibility and originality of mind that his Kitchener Army subalterns – mere civilians in khaki – felt that this Regular officer was spiritually one of their number, not an officer of the old school.[13]

Most officers of 22/RF followed Barnett-Barker's example, in establishing paternal, but friendly and informal relationships with the Other Ranks. Captain R.E. Banbury, Lieutenant C.J. Fowler and Captain R.L. Roscoe were just three officers who were admired, even loved, by their men; in 1984, for instance, an Other Rank testified to his sense of personal loss at Roscoe's death.[14] Similar evidence could be offered concerning many other officers,[15] but such evidence should not be accepted without qualification. Obituaries, letters written to mourning parents and reminiscences published in OCA magazines might be thought to be prone to exaggerate the positive and minimise or ignore the negative qualities of the individual under discussion. However, even after such qualifications are accepted, it is clear that such men as Fowler were regarded as good officers by the men they commanded, who, in return for paternal care and effective leadership, offered loyalty and obedience.

Soldiers sometimes idealise superior officers as father figures and use them as a focus of loyalty to the group.[16] Many men of 22/RF seem to have extended their trust to officers much more senior than their platoon and company commanders. Not only Barnett-Barker, but Major Christopher Stone and Lieutenant Colonel W.J.P.T. Phythian-Adams (respectively the battalion's last second-in-command and commander) were well regarded, as was Brigadier General R.O. Kellett, the commander of 99 Brigade from 1915 to 1917. Kellett complemented the paternal care for 22/RF demonstrated by almost all the battalion's officers, from Barnett-Barker downwards, and helped to give the upper echelons of the army a human face. The soldiers of 22/RF knew that there was at least one man in the hierarchy who had their best interests at heart and who, in Stone's words, was 'keeping a fatherly eye on "the boys"'. Kellett was a frequent visitor to the trenches, and thus sealed the relationship by showing willingness to share a little of the front-line soldiers' danger and discomfort. At its first general meeting after the war, 22/RF's Old Comrades Association (OCA) voted to send Kellett 'a grateful message to our beloved General' – a remarkable tribute to a senior officer who was bound by informal but very real mutual ties of loyalty and affection to a fighting unit.[17] The commanders of 2nd Division, Major Generals Walker and Pereira, were remoter figures than Kellett but also enjoyed a measure of popularity within 22/RF. Pereira greatly endeared himself to 22/RF OCA after the war by attending children's Christmas parties, at which he introduced himself as 'Uncle General Pereira'.[18]

Clearly many inter-rank relationships in 22/RF moved beyond the usual position of leader and led, and close personal relationships developed. I have argued elsewhere that the conditions on the Western Front were exceptionally favourable for the establishment of good officer–man relations,[19] but there are some specific reasons why this should be so in 22/RF. The ages of the original officers of 22/RF were an important factor in the promotion of good officer–man relations. Many were, by military standards, relatively elderly; about half of all officers and one-third of all subalterns were aged 31 or over. In many cases these men had fifteen years of experience in a civilian profession, and brought to the army their own ideas – experience which did not necessarily accord with traditional army methods of doing business. Some had experience of teaching at public schools, and the age of others encouraged the officer to take a literally paternal attitude towards their men. Second Lieutenant J. 'Pussy' Woods recalled that Major T.H. Boardman acted 'as father and mother to me and the company' when he joined the battalion as a 'grinning boy of 19'.[20] Other officers had only recently left school. Many of the 'men' commanded by these boy subalterns were also very young, and it is perhaps unsurprising that boys of similar ages made friends across the rank and class divide. Of very great importance is the fact that the original officer corps of 22/RF were almost all educated at a public school. The public schools produced ideal officers who were disciplined, dutiful, loyal to the corporate body, resourceful but conformist, paternal, with a keen sense of military virtues.

Relatively few of the original officers of 22/RF had any military experience beyond a little drill in a school Officer Training Corps (OTC), and 65 per cent of those who had seen military service had served in a non-Regular unit.[21] Devoid of the prejudices and preconceptions of the Regular subaltern, the Temporary officers of 22/RF would have been far more amenable to Barnett-Barker's concept of leadership than if they had been products of Sandhurst or Woolwich. In sharp contrast to the state of affairs in the pre-war army, it was relatively easy for Other Ranks to obtain commissions. 22/RF began to receive officers promoted from its own ranks – men such as E.C. Rossell, commissioned from B Company in July 1915, and F.W. Palmer, who was commissioned within the battalion in 1917 after winning the Victoria Cross at Miraumont in February of that year. It appears that these ranker-officers continued to enjoy friendly relations with their erstwhile comrades. Sergeant Roland Whipp, for example, served in the same section as Palmer in

1914 and remained on good terms with him after his elevation to commissioned rank. As the war went on, the officers of 22/RF were increasingly drawn from the lower middle- and even the working classes. In May 1916 Stone commented that 'The old 22nd is being infused with a new element of bourgeoisie', and in September 1917 the battalion's padre lamented the decline in the social standing of the battalion's officers.[22] One veteran suggested that officer–man relations were actually enhanced by this further reduction of the gulf between the ranks. This opinion is in sharp contrast to the widespread dislike of ranker-officers that one often comes across among soldiers of the First World War. Private C. Mizen (23/RF), for example, thought that promoted NCOs, far from having a sympathetic view of the rank and file, found it necessary to assert themselves with officious behaviour.[23]

All the evidence suggests that 22/RF, unlike many other 'pals' battalions, retained its original character, particularly in terms of officer–man relations, discipline and *esprit de corps*, throughout the war. The primary reason for this lies in the continuity of command. Barnett-Barker remained at the helm for all but three months of 22/RF's active service. He was succeeded as commander by Phythian-Adams, who had joined the battalion as a subaltern in 1914 and had, as was described in Barnett-Barker's valedictory address, been 'born and bred a 22nd man'. Christopher Stone, who had joined the battalion in early 1915, was appointed second-in-command. By contrast, the 22nd's sister unit, 17/RF, was commanded by four colonels in the same period, all appointed from outside the battalion. Phythian-Adams and Stone were firmly in the Barnett-Barker mould and enjoyed the latter's full confidence. Indeed, Barnett-Barker had been afraid that one day an officer would be appointed to command who had no respect for 22/RF's idiosyncrasies. In early 1918, shortly after the battalion was disbanded in the reorganisation of the British Expeditionary Force, he wrote: 'On calmly considering things, I am not so sad as I was. If anything had happened to — or — the dear old Regiment would have drifted into strange hands and anything might have happened to them.'[24]

There was also a certain amount of continuity of personnel among the rank and file. If 13 Platoon is typical of the battalion as a whole, approximately 18 per cent or 200 of the original members of 22/RF would still have been serving with the battalion in September 1917.[25] This figure is almost certainly too high, but clearly there was a hard core of survivors who passed on the body of traditions of the unit to new drafts and thus ensured the survival of the spirit and character of the original 22/RF.

Tony Ashworth has suggested that some (although not all) infantry battalions 'evolved into communities and became the core of the soldiers' formal military experience and their socio-emotional lives'. 22/RF was one of these battalions, and it is likely that the state of officer–man relations within the unit was instrumental in helping 22/RF to develop into a community. Many officers and men also testified to the family spirit of the battalion, and 22/RF endured as a community into the post-war period, through the establishment of an OCA, which survived until 1977.[26] The distinctive quality of officer–man relations in 22/RF lay in the destruction of social barriers that had prevented intimacy between diverse social groups in the pre-war Regular army. Some officers and men, particularly in the colonial companies in the early period of the war, were on first-name terms, while others observed the formalities of title but otherwise dispensed with the niceties of military etiquette. Captain C.B. Grant, for example, was always called 'Sir' by his servant, Private Beale, but the two men enjoyed a friendly relationship that even survived the occasion when Grant discovered Beale sleeping in the former's bed, wearing Grant's pyjamas. Many other such friendships could be described.[27]

The importance of the officer–man relationship in the evolution of 22/RF into a community is demonstrated by the reaction of both soldiers and officers to officers who were unwilling to accept the egalitarian nature of 22/RF or who failed to live up to the standard expected of leaders. Major J.B. Scott, who joined 22/RF in 1917, was regarded as an unpredictable and irascible man who was inclined to assert his authority in an officious manner, and both officers and men invented humorous and uncomplimentary songs and verse about him. C.E. Raven, who served as padre in 1917–1918, had somewhat elitist attitudes and failed to adjust to life in 22/RF. As a result Raven was condemned to lead a lonely life and, unlike his predecessor, Padre E.P. St John, he failed to be 'accepted' by the officers and men of 22/RF.[28]

In an altogether different category was another officer found cowering in a trench at the beginning of an attack. His platoon sergeant swore at him and physically bundled him over the parapet. It is possible that this same officer was the one whom Barnett-Barker had transferred with the recommendation that he be court-martialled for cowardice, because of his detrimental effect on battalion morale. A loss of confidence in their officers by soldiers is damaging to any military unit. In 22/RF, where morale was enhanced by the fact that the battalion formed a community in which the ties of friendship and loyalty cut across the formal structure of rank, such a loss of confidence would have been disastrous and Barnett-Barker ruthlessly extirpated inefficient officers. Generally, inter-rank friendships were not allowed to interfere with the operation of discipline, although in 1915, when a colonial sergeant got up a petition that sought to overturn Barnett-Barker's decision (taken on operational grounds) not to allow an officer to go overseas, Barnett-Barker had the sergeant arrested.[29]

The presence of a sizeable number of colonials in 22/RF presented a challenge to traditional notions of military discipline. The original recruits had enlisted in a specifically 'colonial' battalion – on the understanding that they would be paid at the colonial rate, which was higher than that of the British soldier – and some resented amalgamation with a British unit. Some may have feared the imposition of Regular discipline. In October 1914 one newly joined subaltern described the difficult task the battalion's leadership faced in commanding the colonials. They had an egalitarian outlook, and refused automatically to accept the right of a young officer to be their commander. He foresaw problems in teaching them to respect commissioned officers, and believed that the battalion would be unmanageable unless things changed. In the event, the colonial problem was much less traumatic than it appeared in October 1914. The colonials did learn the importance of formal military discipline, but the enlightened regime employed in 22/RF ensured that they were not alienated by an attempt to squeeze them into the Regular mould.[30]

Although many officers conceived an affection for their men, the adoption of a radically different social code in a New Army unit was relatively unusual. Christopher Stone described Barnett-Barker as possessing 'the card player's brain – keen, calculating and decisive, looking far ahead and far behind'. Barnett-Barker therefore 'nursed and trained' the battalion 'on his own lines, with very definite ideas as to the means of extracting the best from the material'. He adapted his methods 'with real liberality of thought to the new conditions of warfare and the new types of soldiers'. Barnett-Barker's approach was possible because the highly motivated and enthusiastic volunteers of 1914 possessed a rather different mentality from that of the average pre-war Regular soldier. While Barnett-Barker grasped this essential fact, Innes did not adapt as easily. He issued Battalion Standing Orders in 1915 which attempted to impose pre-war social relations on 22/RF. One paragraph commands that 'No Sergeant Corporal or Lance Corporal is ever to associate or drink with a Private Soldier'. This instruction was widely, perhaps universally, ignored. When 22/RF was formed, the natural leaders that emerged were often legitimised retrospectively. There was little attempt to enforce the segregation of NCOs from men. Instead, privates and NCOs (and, indeed, officers) fraternised quite happily without any apparent detriment to discipline.[31]

However, informal relations were by no means universal in Kitchener units. Many Regular soldiers believed that spit and polish in the field inculcated pride and enhanced morale. Many temporary soldiers took the opposite view: that it was yet another pointless demand made on them by the army, and Barnett-Barker seems to have leaned towards the latter idea. Although Barnett-Barker himself was invariably impeccably turned out, he tolerated considerable informality and eccentricity in the dress of his officers and men on active service. Before the battalion embarked for active service, he solemnly announced that 'anyone who cleaned his buttons out there would be shot at dawn'. Similarly, Barnett-Barker was quite capable of disregarding the niceties of military discipline. During the Somme fighting in 1916 he dismissed a case brought against a group of men charged with a minor offence because 'The Lewis Gunners did splendidly in Delville Wood'. One man who was involved in this case testified to the positive effect that Barnett-Barker's action had on his morale. Other examples suggest that other officers followed Barnett-Barker's example in applying humanity and common sense to discipline.[32] The soldier of 22/RF was aware that he was not totally impotent and friendless in the face of an impersonal and arbitrary coercive authority. Rather, his officers could usually be relied upon to treat him in a humane and sensible fashion. By contrast, militarily inefficient men did not fare so well, and were transferred out of the unit. One private, described as 'unreliable and useless', was executed for desertion, but it is important to note that he had been under observation for some time, and he was not shot for a momentary lapse.[33] The ultimate test of morale is combat effectiveness, and 22/RF had a good combat record from their first action in May 1916 to their last in December 1917. While good relations between officers and men were the rule rather than the exception in many infantry battalions of the First World War, relatively few units seem to have adopted an enlightened disciplinary approach. 22/RF was indeed fortunate in possessing in Barnett-Barker a commanding officer who encouraged the creation and maintenance of a relatively liberal disciplinary regime.

Acknowledgements

This chapter is based on G.D. Sheffield, 'The Effect of War Service on the 22nd Battalion Royal Fusiliers (Kensington) 1914–18, With Special Reference to Morale, Discipline and the Officer–Man Relationship' (MA thesis, University of Leeds, 1984).

All interviews were conducted by the author in 1983–1985 with veterans of the First World War. Some material was made available and some interviews granted on the understanding that the precise source was not revealed in print. All such material is referred to as 'private source' in the notes.

Notes

1. Parliamentary Papers [PP], *Report of the Committee of Enquiry into Shellshock*, 1922, XII Cmd. 1734, 759, pp. 14, 16, 17, 20; Richard Holmes, *Firing Line* (London: Jonathan Cape, 1985), p. 259.
2. H.C. O'Neill, *The Royal Fusiliers in the Great War* (London: Heinemann, 1922), p. 17. See also Christopher Stone (ed.), *A History of the 22nd (Service) Battalion Royal Fusiliers (Kensington)* (London: privately published, 1923), pp. 7–9.
3. *Evening Standard*, 12 September 1914, p. 4; *W[est] S[ussex] C[ounty] T[imes]*, 12 December 1914, p. 8; *Mufti* [journal of 22/RF Old Comrades Association], Xmas 1937, p. 4.; Roland Whipp, *Interview*; *Mufti*, Summer 1963, pp. 15–16.
4. Stone, *History*, p. 9; Kensington Library, Local History section, Broughshane Cuttings Books, Second Series [BCB], vol. 2, 1914, p. 61.
5. W. Clark, H. Berrycloath, *Interviews*; *22nd Royal Fusiliers Fortnightly Gazette* [22/RF FG], 19 July 1915, p. 131; *Mufti*, Summer 1961, p. 6; *Mufti*, Summer 1945, p. 4.
6. *Mufti*, Xmas 1965, p. 10; Sheffield, 'Effect', p. 28, table 7.
7. For example Davison in Stone, *History*, p. 15; Christopher Stone, *B.B.* (Oxford: Blackwell, 1919), p. 16; B.N.W. William-Powlett, Diary, 6–8 February 1915, I[mperial] W[ar] M[useum].
8. BCB Second Series, vol. II, 1914, p. 74; *Abergavenny Chronicle and Monmouthshire Advertiser*, 5 April 1918, p. 3; Stone, *B.B.*, pp. 26–7.

9. See Chapter 10; G.D. Sheffield, 'The Effect of the Great War on Class Relations in Britain: The Career of Major Christopher Stone DSO MC, *War and Society*, vol. 7, No. 1 (May 1989), pp. 88–9; G.D. Sheffield and G.I.S. Inglis (eds), *From Vimy Ridge to the Rhine: The Great War Letters of Christopher Stone DSO MC* (Ramsbury: Crowood, 1989), pp. 15–16.

10. Barnett-Barker Papers [BB Mss] 6, 13, 17, December 1915, 1 January 1916. All letters in this collection are from Barnett-Barker to his wife. I am indebted to the late J.P.C. Sankey-Barker for giving me access to his father's papers.

11. Stone, *B.B.*, p. 25.

12. BB Mss, 17 December 1915; *Mufti*, June 1954, p. 2; H. Berrycloath, *Interview*.

13. Kensington Mss 8534, P. Destrube letters, 30 January 1917; H. Berrycloath, *Interview*; Stone, *B.B.*, p. 26.

14. *Mufti*, June 1958, p. 9; Christopher Stone Papers, 1 June 1916, IWM [all letters in this collection are from Stone to his wife]; Correspondence relating to the writing of the history of 22nd Royal Fusiliers (71563 Stone, C, 316,322) [IWM Stone Papers], Mrs E. Fowler to Stone, n.d. but *c*.1922, IWM, Department of Printed Books; *Mufti*, Summer 1928, p. 2; George Challis, *Interview*; *Mufti*, January 1920, p. l.

15. See Sheffield, 'Effect', Chapter 4.

16. S.A. Stouffer *et al*, *The American Soldier*, vol. II (Princeton: Princeton University Press, 1949), p. 123.

17. Stone, *History*, p. 56; George Challis, *Interview*; H.E. Harvey, *Battle Line Narratives 1915–1918* (London: Brentano's, 1928), p. 89; C.E. Jacomb, *Torment* (London: Andrew Melrose, 1920), pp. 271–2; *Mufti*, December 1919, p. 3.

18. *Mufti*, Spring 1937, p. 12; see also *Mufti*, June 1954, p. iii and Autumn 1933, p. 4.

19. See Chapter 10 and G.D. Sheffield, *Leadership in the Trenches: Officer–Man Relations, Morale and Discipline in the British Army in the Era of the First World War* (Basingstoke: Macmillan, 2000).

20. See Sheffield, 'Effect', p. 24a, Table 5; Denis Winter, *Death's Men* (Harmondsworth: Penguin, 1979), p. 65; *Mufti*, Xmas 1923, p. 12.

21. Sheffield, 'Effect', p. 27, Table 6.

22. Roland Whipp, *Interview*; Stone, *Vimy*, p. 51; Raven to Burgess, 29 September 1917, C.E. Raven Papers, L[iddle] C[ollection], University of Leeds.

23. Private source; C. Mizen, *Interview*.

24. Everard Wyrall, *The 17th (S) Battalion Royal Fusiliers 1914–19* (London: 1930), pp. 6, 16, 106, 237; Stone, *History*, pp. 55, 61.

25. *Mufti*, Xmas 1945, p. 5.

26. Tony Ashworth, *Trench Warfare* (London: Macmillan, 1980), p. 8; *Mufti*, Xmas 1962, p. 11; C.J. Hancock to Stone, n.d., IWM Stone; *Mufti*, June 1955, p. 5.

27. H. Berrycloath, *Interview*; *Mufti*, June 1948, pp. 3–4; *Mufti*, Autumn 1939, p. 11.

28. George Challis, *Interview*; *Mufti*, December 1951, pp. 3, 12; Raven Mss, 21 May 1917, 29 September 1917, 31 January 1918, LC.

29. Private source; *Mufti*, Xmas 1943, p. 6; *Mufti*, June 1950, p. 3.

30. W.J.T.P. Phythian-Adams, letter of 10 October 1914. I am indebted to Mr Henry Phythian-Adams for allowing me access to his father's papers.

31. Stone, *B.B.*, pp. 25–6; *The Standing Orders of the 22nd Royal Fusiliers* (Horsham: 1915); *West Sussex Gazette*, 4 February 1915, p. 11, 15 April 1915, p. 10; Harvey, *Battleline Narratives*, pp. 129–30, 164–5.

32. Stone, *History*, p. 25; *Mufti*, August–September 1920, p. 6; *Mufti*, Summer 1973, p. 3.

33. WO 93/49, The National Archives.

Chapter 12

The Operational Role of British Military Police on the Western Front[1]

The morale and discipline of the BEF on the Western Front has aroused considerable scholarly and popular interest. However, surprisingly little attention has been paid to a body which had a central role in the enforcement of discipline, namely the Corps of Military Police (CMP, or Redcaps). Furthermore, one of the principal duties of the CMP – traffic control – has been almost entirely ignored. The relationship between an army and its military police is rarely easy, and the First World War perhaps marked the nadir of this relationship as far as the British Army was concerned. Other ranks[2] and officers[3] united in wholehearted condemnation of the CMP. Two former infantry privates claimed that military police were never to be seen 'in the danger area', and that few civil policemen became Redcaps; the latter's job 'was voluntary and few decent men would undertake it if they realised what it implied'.[4] Historians have mostly been content to accept such judgements at face value,[5] and for 'Redcap' have read, it seems, 'martinet', 'sadist' and 'enemy of the ordinary fighting soldier'.[6] This chapter will seek to demonstrate that such views contain a strange mixture of fact, error, opinion and prejudice.

The military police are certainly worthy of study, if for no other reason than that their numbers grew dramatically during the war years. Englander and Osborne have calculated that the growth rate of the CMP 'greatly exceeded that of the army itself'.[7] They link this growth rate to an increase in disciplinary problems in the British Army, but this chapter will argue that other factors should also be considered. Military police were not used solely in their traditional role of enforcing discipline. They also formed traffic control companies, were responsible for the disposal of prisoners of war (POW) and came to have an important role on the battlefield, to mention just three of their duties. The growth of the CMP can be seen as a paradigm of the growth of the BEF as a whole, from a small, relatively unsophisticated organisation into a large and vastly more complex body. The expansion of the numbers of military police should be viewed in the context of the general proliferation of specialist units – such as tank and machine gun units and trench mortar batteries – that became necessary as the BEF adapted and changed to suit the conditions of modern industrialised warfare. In short, the war saw the CMP develop from a small organisation 'concerned solely with the enforcement of discipline at military stations and in the base towns of overseas theatres of war, to a Corps containing thousands of men, which had acquired an essential operational role both in the rear and in the forward areas'.[8] Although tasks such as the enforcement of rear area discipline were important, this chapter will, after a brief survey of organisation and personnel, concentrate on the operational role of the military police in controlling stragglers and traffic, with a particular case study of the 1918 spring retreats.

In 1914 British military policemen fell into three categories: Regimental Police (RP), Garrison Military Police (GMP) and members of the CMP. The first were simply soldiers chosen to perform police duties on a temporary basis in their unit.[9] The GMP were somewhat similar, being seconded from their units to police garrison towns; in 1916 most were incorporated into the CMP.[10] The CMP itself was divided into the Military Mounted Police and Military Foot Police (MMP and MFP).[11] Members of the CMP were volunteers who had served at least four years in the army, were of exemplary character and had transferred to the corps from their parent regiments. They were the only MPs who were entitled to wear the red cap cover.[12]

On 4 August 1914 the strength of the CMP was a mere three officers and 508 NCOs and men. This meagre figure was increased to 776 by the influx of reservists on mobilisation.[13] The demand for military policemen soon outpaced the supply. As early as 2 September 1914 the CMP was opened to direct enlistment for the first time, and (*pace* Brophy and Partridge) a number of civilian policemen did join the corps.[14] In addition, some units were transferred *en bloc* to provost work, without becoming members of the CMP. Paradoxically, considering the strictly limited opportunities for cavalry on the Western Front, the mobility of the mounted military policeman made him an extremely desirable asset for patrolling behind the static front. Three parties from the Bedfordshire Yeomanry, for example, were transferred in the autumn of 1914 to serve as the divisional police of 48th Division.[15] Yeomen were also called upon to serve as dismounted policemen. In January 1917 it was reported that 460 men of the Hampshire Yeomanry, serving in IX Corps, had been trained in traffic control duties – of whom 51 were so employed at any one time. Cyclist units were also much used in this role.[16] While Yeomanry and cyclists had other duties in addition to provost work, some units were transferred permanently to it. From the beginning of 1917 two garrison battalions of infantry regiments served in France under the orders of the Provost-Marshal. In addition, from 1916 onwards substantial numbers of men who had been serving as GMP were temporarily transferred to the CMP, and the CMP received a small number of conscripts.[17] Englander and Osborne calculated that in 1914 the ratio of military policemen to soldiers stood at 1:3,306. In 1918 the ratio was 1:292.[18] Impressive as these figures are, they exclude a large number of men who were used on provost work but did not wear the badge of the CMP. The highest estimate of the number employed on provost duties suggests that some 25,000 were involved world-wide. The Provost-Marshal in France claimed to have 12,000 men under his command on the Western Front, and this figure seems plausible.[19]

Although the CMP expanded to a peak of 151 warrant-officers and 13,325 other ranks in 1918, the Corps could still boast only three officers.[20] Other officers were drafted in as varying grades of Provost-Marshal to command detachments of military police. In October 1918 there were 175 of these officers serving in France. The most common variety of Assistant Provost-Marshal (APM) comprised those graded as staff captains. An analysis of the provenance of the sixty-four officers appointed to this position from August 1914 to May 1915 reveals that about one-third were Regular officers who had retired or were on the reserve. If one adds in Special Reserve, Territorial and other categories of reserve officer, one arrives at a figure of approximately 75 per cent of APMs drawn from reserve sources.[21]

The First World War saw something of a leap in the social quality of the Provost-Marshal. The highest-ranking provost officer in 1914 had been Major R.J.A. Terry, who acted as Provost-Marshal and Commandant of the CMP. By the end of the war there were two brigadier generals who served as provost-marshals in France and Britain respectively.[22] Numerous Guardsmen served as provost officers, including the Honourable Clive Bigham, later Lord Mersey, who was the Provost-Marshal at Gallipoli.[23] The evidence suggests that many provost officers were older men, or men who had been wounded. In short, many officers of the provost branch were not taken from 'teeth-arm' units, but were 'dug-outs' or men who, for one reason or another, were no longer fit for front-line duty. Service as a provost officer allowed them to fulfil a valuable, and increasingly socially acceptable, role.[24]

Did the military police deserve their unsavoury reputation? Some probably did. Much of the fury of the men who mutinied at Étaples Base Camp in September 1917 was directed against military policemen rather than against their own officers,[25] leading one historian to describe the disturbance as 'a case of loyal indiscipline'.[26] As early as May 1916 there seem to have been cases of military policemen abusing their authority at Etaples,[27] and the APM, Captain E. Strachan of the 10th Lancashire Fusiliers, seems to have been an unpopular, although efficient, officer.[28] It was the shooting of an infantryman by a military policeman, Private H. Reeve, that sparked off the mutiny, although, interestingly, Reeve seems to have been a Camp Policeman (a 'species' of GMP) rather than a member of the CMP.[29] However, before damning the entire provost branch on the evidence of Étaples, one must consider certain factors. By the very nature of things, relations between an army and its military police are seldom harmonious. In the case of the First World War, many soldiers felt that they were in the hands of an arbitrary and impersonal military machine,[30] and that the Redcaps were a visible symbol of authority and liable to be hated as such, even if the individual military police-man was not officious. In addition, one cannot ignore the strong probability that the antipathy of the working class towards civilian police was carried over into the army and transferred to the CMP.[31] There was a sharp division between front-line soldiers and those who served in the rear, and a common misperception existed that the CMP carried out their duties very much in the rear, safe from every danger. As will be demonstrated, this was not the case. Broadly speaking, the MFP (many of whom were not fit for front-line duty)[32] performed duties on the lines of communication, while the MMP served just behind the front lines. Controlling traffic within the battle area was a particularly dangerous activity. C.S. Havers, a former Essex policeman, was wounded by shell fire while on traffic duty near Ypres in 1917; while he was recuperating in hospital, his Chief Constable wrote to say that, to date, seven-teen other Essex constables, many of whom apparently served in the CMP, had been killed or died of disease.[33] Over fifty members of the CMP received the DCM and over eighty-five were killed on active service or died of wounds on the Western Front alone, in addition to an unknown number of cyclists, yeomen and the like who became casualties while carrying out provost duties.[34]

What were the attitudes of yeomen, cyclists and other temporary military policemen towards their new employment? Evidence on this point is not easy to find. One historian wrote, somewhat lamely, that 'It has not been recorded that any of these units objected to the transfer',[35] and, in fact, the men of the Bedfordshire Yeomanry, who transferred in autumn 1914, reacted with great enthusiasm to the move, believing that it would mean they would soon see active service – and, indeed, they did cross to France three months before their parent regiment.[36] However, before too rosy a view is taken, it is worth mentioning the evidence of 'Howard', a member of the Royal Wiltshire Yeomanry who was attached to the APM of 4th Division. In a letter of June 1916 he mentioned that, having had several previous posts, he was now serving as a policeman. Two weeks later he wrote that he was now attached to the APM of 7th Division and was not entirely happy in this new role, in part because his peripatetic lifestyle meant that he had difficulty in receiving his mail.[37] Although this is the evidence of just one, possibly unrepresentative, soldier, it acts as a salutary corrective to the traditional infantryman's view that the military police were a collection of danger-shirking martinets who joined this corps in order to give free rein to their sadistic tendencies.

The BEF of 1914 had no clearly defined battlefield role for military police.[38] At the end of the year GHQ found it necessary to issue guidance on provost duties, based on the experience of 5th Division. These instructions amounted to only fourteen paragraphs, of which only one referred to duties on the line of march, and none gave any indication that the CMP might be of use on the battlefield.[39] Nevertheless, by early 1915 they had begun to play a minor but significant role on the battlefield: a role that was to become increasingly important as the war went on.

The CMP had first proved useful in rounding up large numbers of men who straggled from their units during the retreat from Mons, and in shepherding them back to their units – a duty which was reflected in the GHQ instructions mentioned above. Although some limited use was made of military police as a 'battle stop' as early as the Battle of Le Cateau (26 August 1914), the fighting on the Aisne in September was the first occasion on which the CMP were deployed on a large scale to round up battle stragglers.[40] During the First Battle of Ypres in October–November 1914 the problem began to escalate alarmingly.[41] Haig noted in his diary on 4 December 1914 that 'we have to take special precautions during a battle to post police, to prevent more men than necessary from accompanying a wounded man back from the firing line!'[42] The small numbers of military policemen available – twenty-five MMP were allocated to each division, and a further six (or possibly seven) were included in the establishment of a corps – proved to be woefully inadequate and their numbers had to be supplemented by untrained personnel.[43] This seems to have been arranged informally during First Ypres, but by the time of Neuve Chapelle in March 1915 men were detached before the battle from their units for provost work.[44] Neuve Chapelle was the turning point in the history of the CMP: it established beyond a shadow of doubt that the CMP did indeed have a battlefield role.

What was this role? Essentially, the deployment of a line of 'straggler posts' acted as a barrier to men attempting to leave the front line, but it would be wrong to see straggler posts simply as a way of keeping reluctant soldiers in the killing zone. Under the conditions of battle, many men became separated from their units for quite legitimate reasons, and straggler posts served to collect these men, if necessary rearm them, and direct them back to their units. Indeed, a post-war report compiled by the CMP recommended the use of the terms 'battle stop' and 'collecting post' rather than 'straggler post', as the latter term 'is one of often undeserving reproach to a soldier, frequently only anxious to discover his Unit'.[45] A 'battle stop' was defined as the forward straggler post, located just behind the front lines. At Loos, for example, those of one formation of IV Corps, 7th Division, were situated 'at the end of every communication trench'.[46] Those of another corps were situated considerably further back and proved to be far less useful because, in the words of a post-war report, 'the further back stragglers get, the longer is the journey to rejoin their units'.[47] Collecting posts, as the name implies, were the positions where stragglers intercepted by the battle stops were sent, ready for distribution to their units. From First Ypres onwards, the practice was for one CMP NCO to be placed in charge of the battle stop and one or two at each collecting post, with three or four non-CMP personnel under their command.[48] Interestingly, given the CMP's reputation, one of the functions of these posts was to provide food, water and hot tea for stragglers, a policy that foreshadows the modern practice of sympathetic forward treatment of psychiatric casualties.[49] At Neuve Chapelle in March 1915, for example, a number of men who had lost their way were collected by military police, fed at the collecting posts and escorted back to their units the following morning.[50] Straggler posts also proved themselves useful in many other ways: in directing traffic, escorting POW to the rear, and guiding reinforcements.[51] On occasion, straggler posts served the function of a last-ditch fighting reserve. On 11 November 1914 the APM of 1st Division won the DSO leading a mixed party of military police and stragglers in a counterattack near the Menin Road.[52]

Notwithstanding these 'positive' aspects of battlefield provost work, it did of course contain a strong element of coercion: of preventing unauthorised personnel from leaving the battle area. The growth in the importance of this work can be seen by comparing the thin red-capped line of 1914 with the vastly more sophisticated provost arrangements of Third and Fifth Armies in March 1918. By that time Fifth Army had three separate lines of straggler posts, organised by division, corps and army respectively, each comprising forward battle stops and rearward collecting stations. Patrols of MMP visited the posts at regular intervals. VI Corps of Third Army also had military policemen posted at separate collecting stations for walking wounded, ready to remove them to straggler posts if the medical officer believed they were malingering. Behind these three lines were to be found both traffic control units and patrols of MMP, with orders to round up stragglers. Beyond them again were two lines of 'examination posts', which served the same purpose as a fielder placed on the boundary of a cricket field. Unlike the full range of straggler posts which were deployed immediately before action, examination posts were a permanent fixture.[53]

Apart from serving as a general deterrent for would-be absconders, the importance of straggler posts varied with the circumstances of battle and the morale of the army at any given time. Between 1 April 1917 and 11 November 1918 a total of sixty-seven men were arrested as absentees from their units at the examination posts manned by D Company, 2nd (G) Battalion, King's Own Yorkshire Light Infantry (KOYLI). As one might expect, there was a degree of correlation between numbers of arrests and dates of battles. The two months in which most arrests were made coincide with the dates of the battles of Arras and Amiens in April 1917 and August 1918 respectively, although records for the vital March–April 1918 period are incomplete.[54]

The usefulness of straggler posts also varied from battle to battle. At Loos in September 1915 they proved extremely useful in rounding up and re-organising the survivors of the ill-fated attack of 21st and 24th Divisions as they fell back in disorder through the British positions.[55] On the Somme on 1 July 1916, however, there were very few stragglers; despite the disaster to British arms, morale remained relatively high. The APM of 4th Division could remember coming across only one straggler on that day, while 30th Division recorded only seven, and none at all during operations conducted on 23 July.[56] Generally speaking, it would appear that there was a greater need for straggler posts during defensive operations than during offensive ones, and that successful operations produced fewer stragglers than unsuccessful ones. At Bullecourt in 1917 seventy men routed and were stopped by the straggler posts, while during the taking of Messines Ridge several months later IX Corps deployed forty-four men on straggler post duties, but had to deal with only nineteen stragglers in all.[57]

Before they could even reach the lines of straggler posts, stragglers were often confronted with 'battle police'. It is often difficult to disentangle fact from fiction when discussing this subject. According to one historian, before the Somme offensive in July 1916 many units were informed that men who hung back in an attack would be summarily executed by military police. This author goes on to cite an example, based on uncorroborated oral evidence, of the execution of two soldiers by 'Red Caps' (sic) in the trenches.[58] There are a number of difficulties involved in accepting this story, quite apart from the illegality of the executions. First, it is difficult to see what purpose such executions would serve, since it was the policy of GHQ to publicise executions in the belief that they would serve as a deterrent to others.[59] Secondly, MMP were husbanded as a precious resource for use behind the lines and it is unlikely that two Redcaps would have been available to patrol the trenches: the CMP seem to have had responsibility for policing the area behind the trenches but not the trenches themselves.

Although the evidence is not entirely clear, in one corps at least the responsibility for policing the trenches on 1 July rested with the individual brigades, with a troop of yeomanry being provided for patrolling the rearmost communication trenches.[60] Other evidence suggests that 'battle police' were drawn from sources other than the CMP. 2nd West Yorkshires deployed their Provost-Sergeant and the Regimental Police to arrest – but not shoot – men who 'returned improperly' from their attack on Ypres on 31 July 1917. Similarly, in August 1917 3rd Australian Division was posting its RPs in communication trenches to 'form the first line of Battle Stops', among other tasks.[61] Battle police were undoubtedly useful. This is illustrated by the suggestion of one officer that insufficient numbers of them were deployed by 36th (Ulster) Division on 1 July 1916. After their initial attack, the trenches were crowded with stragglers, many of whom were unwounded but lacked arms and any form of organisation, and in some cases were blocking communication trenches.[62] At this point, battle police, if available in sufficient numbers, would have been invaluable in reorganising these stragglers. It would also appear that the deployment or otherwise of battle police depended upon the whim of an individual unit or formation commander. It was not a universal practice, and one historian has concluded that 'most privates were not sure whether battle police existed or not'.[63]

Some extravagant claims have been made about the use of battle police in maintaining the discipline of the BEF,[64] but it is clear that, whatever their composition, on rare occasions they were sometimes used to shoot stragglers. However, most decisions to begin shooting at one's own men seem to have been taken entirely unofficially and at a local level by harassed officers or NCOs faced with routing troops. Rarely was this officially sanctioned. It is instructive to compare the orders given on 25 June 1916 to the straggler posts of the New Zealand Division to fire on men who refused to halt when ordered to do so,[65] or the behaviour of the notorious Brigadier General F.P. Crozier, who had considerable enthusiasm for the practice of shooting his own men, with the reaction of the British high command to the situation on the Aisne in May 1918.[66] During that period of crisis the commander of 19th Division asked GHQ for the power to 'confirm and have carried out' death sentences on stragglers. This request was refused.[67] Although British military justice of the period can be criticised, the fact remains that the processes of military law, which demanded that death sentences be confirmed by the commander-in-chief, were adhered to even at a time of crisis. In sum, the evidence suggests that the image of the brutal Redcap, deployed by a cynical high command to patrol the trenches and force the 'PBI' into action at the point of a revolver, is a misleading caricature of the truth.

The German offensives of March–April 1918 presented the provost branch with its greatest challenge of the war. The experience of XIX Corps may stand as representative of the way in which that challenge was met. This corps, commanded by Sir H.E. Watts, held a frontage of about 12,000 yards on 21 March, and was sandwiched between Congreve's VII Corps to the north and Maxse's XVIII Corps to the south. Two divisions – 66th and 24th – were stationed in the front line.[68] Their divisional straggler posts were established on a line between 3,500 yards and about 6,000 yards from the front line. This was much further back than had been the practice in earlier battles, but is probably a reflection of the fact that defence in depth had been adopted by this stage, and in fact the divisional straggler posts ran down the centre of the Battle Zone, in which the main fighting was expected to take place. Four collecting posts had been established, with the furthest, at Montigny Farm, lying about 6,500 yards behind the front line. The straggler posts were manned at about 6.00am, and by 11.00am the enemy were attacking the Battle Zone, having already cleared the obstacle of the forward zone. This brought chaos to the British line. At about 12.30 Captain Westmacott, APM of 24th Division, arrived at Vermand, where there was both a battle stop and a collecting post. He found a body of wounded and unwounded men from the infantry and artillery, many lacking weapons, streaming back as a mob across the bridge with the military police doing little to prevent them crossing.

Westmacott held up the crowd with his revolver, helped by a sergeant in the North Staffords. He then armed forty men with rifles taken from the wounded, and pressed them into service as temporary military policemen. As soon as his back was turned, these men ran away. Westmacott then took more drastic action, pressing another twenty stragglers into service. Arming his own Redcaps with rifles (normally they only carried revolvers), he ordered them to shoot these men should they attempt to abscond. He and his military policemen then served under the battalion headquarters of 13th Middlesex until he was ordered to retire, having been lightly wounded by shellfire.

This was the pattern for the remainder of the retreat: as the enemy approached, provost personnel fell back to fresh positions and resumed their duties until the approach of the enemy once again forced them to retire. They shared most of the discomforts and many of the experiences of the infantry. On 27 March the situation was so critical that Westmacott was forced to send most of his police to fight in the front line. On other occasions he was able to distribute much-needed rations to the infantry. From his reports it is clear that the military police were not always as efficient as they might have been. A report of 1 April was extremely critical of XIX Corps' straggler posts for being too lenient, and Westmacott used his divisional police to conduct a house-to-house search in rear villages to flush out stragglers, even though this should have been a corps responsibility. Nevertheless, it is clear that the provost staff of XIX Corps on the whole coped well with the enormous responsibilities placed upon them by the retreat.[69]

What were the achievements of military police in the March retreat? A post-war report estimated that at least 25,000 stragglers were collected, fed and put back into the fighting.[70] This figure is almost certainly an under-estimate. A detailed set of figures has survived which reveals that 11,214 stragglers (of whom four were officers) were collected by XIX Corps from 21 March to 5 April.[71] Admittedly this corps was very heavily engaged, but it was only one of four corps in Fifth Army. Third Army also suffered a number of stragglers: for example, IX Corps collected 200 in the first two days of the battle.[72] Where possible, stragglers were directed back to their original units, but sometimes they were formed into composite battalions. Occasionally, at particularly desperate moments, military police led them into action.[73] One account of the fighting by a member of Carey's Force (an *ad hoc* force), who clearly was no admirer of the Redcaps, serves to illustrate the importance of military police during the March retreat. This soldier, A.W. Bradbury, saw men fleeing from their trenches, which were being shelled, only to be rounded up and returned to their positions by armed military police. Although Bradbury expressed incredulity at the notion of military policemen appearing in a place of danger, he admitted that the poor standard of the infantry justified such drastic measures.[74]

The effectiveness of the provost arrangements is indicated by the fact that, according to the report of Fifth Army's Deputy Provost-Marshal (DPM), fewer than a hundred men from the fighting arms got back as far as Army headquarters and he was able to state categorically that 'At no time during the retreat was the straggler position out of hand, and much larger numbers could have been dealt with.'[75] In effect, the CMP maintained a tight cordon behind the Fifth and Third Armies, a cordon that undoubtedly helped maintain cohesion during the retreat. The problem that would have resulted if the BEF had not developed relatively sophisticated provost arrangements by 1918 is demonstrated by the situation which arose when the Guards Division went into action having neglected to deploy straggler posts. This formation, according to one source, claimed that it simply did not need them. As a provost officer of a neighbouring formation commented drily,

> This sounds very well in theory but in practice it broke the continuity of the Straggler Post lines, and allowed the leakage of a number of troops from various divisions. Had these stragglers been directed to their units by posts well up behind the front lines, they would have never have wandered as far back as they ... did.[76]

In fact, relatively few Guardsmen were separated from their units, but those who were wandered a considerable distance before reaching a straggler post that could direct them back – a further reminder that not all 'stragglers' were deliberately running towards safety. Thus not only did the absence of straggler posts behind the Guards Division allow stragglers from neighbouring formations to get much further back than would otherwise have been possible, but valuable time was wasted in getting back into the firing line troops who were fit and ready to fight.

There is much to be learned about the morale and discipline of the army as a whole from a study of straggler control. The impression created in 1918 by Lloyd George and others was that Fifth Army collapsed in rout, a line which has been followed by some historians.[77] It is thus interesting to find that provost sources are unanimous in agreeing that the majority of stragglers in the early stages of the battle were not drawn from front-line units. Fifth Army's DPM wrote in his after-action report that 'During the first two days' fighting Battle stragglers from the firing-lines were few and were chiefly those who were genuinely lost and anxious to rejoin their units.'[78] Who, then, were the stragglers that undoubtedly headed for the rear at the beginning of the German offensive? Many of them appear to have been non-combatants. The Germans attacked when Fifth Army was still constructing its defensive positions on the principles (new to the British Army) of 'elastic' defence in depth. In mid-March 1918 approximately 12,200 Italians, 5,200 Chinese, 10,300 POW, 4,500 Indians and 35,800 British were engaged on labouring duties in Fifth Army's rear.[79] When the blow fell on 21 March, these men were spread out over the length and breadth of the army area. In the words of the army's DPM, although Labour companies may have begun the march out of the fighting area in good order, 'they did not remain so for long without straggling towards the rear along the main routes'. Many of these men were insufficiently fit to march in formation and thus fell out and straggled; many of those who had weapons were unable to carry them, and threw them away. A special collecting post specifically for Labour personnel had to be established at Villers Bretonneux. 'From a spectacular point of view', wrote Fifth Army's DPM, 'anyone might well think these men stragglers from the firing lines but the Deputy Provost-Marshal and other Officers well qualified to speak maintained that stragglers from the fighting troops did not get away.'[80]

As we have seen, there were some 'teeth-arm' men who fled from the battlefield, but it would seem that the real problems of straggling amongst front-line troops did not set in until they had been in retreat for a number of days, and this seems to have been the result of sheer exhaustion. At the beginning of the battle most stragglers were simply directed back to their units, and sometimes went back unescorted: 'they didn't get to the Army back areas, nor did they attempt to after receiving their directions'.[81] Later, stragglers had to be rested and fed at straggler posts and taken (sometimes by bus) to central collecting points, and then distributed to various units.[82] Some statistical material has survived which supports the anecdotal evidence that has been cited. The busiest periods for the straggler posts of 8th, 16th, 24th, 50th and 66th Divisions occurred at least six days after the battle began, on 27–30 March. These figures do not tell the whole story, for of these formations 16th, 24th and 66th Divisions were in action from 21 March, but only 24th Division recorded any figures for the first two days of the battle. Either the other divisions did not collect any stragglers then, which is possible, or their figures are incomplete, but the evidence of 24th Division certainly supports the contention that the worst period for stragglers came only towards the end of March. There were forty stragglers collected on 21 March, fifteen on 22 March, ten on 23 March, six on 24 March, fifty on 27 March and 227 on 30 March.[83] These figures do not necessarily mean that the stragglers belonged to the divisions whose straggler posts collected them, for other corps passed through XIX Corps area.

Naturally, this evidence of the state of British morale in the spring of 1918 should not be treated in isolation. Other factors, such as the numbers of British troops taken prisoner by the Germans and examples of the attackers meeting little resistance from British defenders, should also be taken into account. Nevertheless, an examination of the provost records of the March offensive does not leave the reader with the impression of a beaten army which streamed towards the rear in hopeless rout. In March 1918 the system of straggler posts underwent its first major test in a defensive battle since April

1915, and the military police emerged with considerable credit. Later, the lessons learned from the March retreat were applied with success at the Battle of the Lys, and subsequently during the victorious advance from August to November 1918.

Effective traffic control arrangements were evolved by the provost branch in parallel with those for straggler control. The CMP was involved in traffic control during the early campaigns of the war to a limited extent, but the first major test came during the Battle of Loos, which began on 25 September 1915.[84] The British plan called for two raw formations, 21st and 24th Divisions of XI Corps, to be committed to battle once the crust of the German defences had been broken by Haig's First Army. As these divisions were to be held some miles behind the battle front, the plan called for them to make a long and, in the event, exhausting march before being committed to battle. It was the responsibility of First Army's APM, Major E.R. Fitzpatrick, to ensure that the roads were clear so that XI Corps would be in the right place at the right time.

Fitzpatrick made the best use he could of the limited resources at his disposal, establishing 'control points' at key crossroads and road junctions in the rear area, with divisional and corps APMs stationed at key points and the APMs of I and IV Corps patrolling the main roads in motor cars. In the event the approach march of 21st and 24th Divisions was subject to unnecessary delays, caused in part by poor traffic control, and their attack was an utter failure. The British official historian concluded that traffic control at Loos was reminiscent of an attempt 'to push the Lord Mayor's procession through the streets of London without clearing the route and holding up the traffic'.[85] The affair became entangled in the plots to replace French as Commander-in-Chief by Haig.[86] The failure at Loos had less to do with overzealous and incompetent military policemen than with poor staff work. The problems experienced at Loos led directly to the birth of effective, modern traffic control in the British Army. As a Guards officer was to write after the war, 'I have always understood that the afterwards excellent system of traffic control was evolved as a result of the lessons of that day.'[87]

By the time of the Somme offensive of 1916, it was well understood that the 'Q' (Quartermaster) staff needed to liaise closely with the APM to ensure that traffic on supply routes was properly controlled.[88] While it would be foolish to claim that there were no failures of traffic control,[89] on the whole the system did work well.[90] In July 1916, for example, 18th Division used thirty-seven yeomanry and MMP on traffic control, in addition to some cyclists to man static traffic posts. 18th Division's provost assumed responsibility for 4½ miles of road in the Bray–Carnoy sector on 23 June. The divisional traffic scheme was relatively sophisticated, including diversionary tracks, roadside bays and a breakdown lorry for the clearance of wrecked vehicles. Most traffic was moved under the cover of darkness. On 6–7 July 23 guns, 175 limbers and 300 wagons were counted moving east along the road, with horse-drawn traffic mixed in with motor vehicles and columns of marching infantry.[91]

The battles of 1917 saw traffic control arrangements become increasingly sophisticated. Haig, who clearly recognised the importance of traffic control, fought a bureaucratic battle against the War Office in the autumn of 1917 to retain adequate numbers of traffic control personnel.[92] For the offensive against Messines Ridge in June 1917 IX Corps alone employed 14 officers and 433 other ranks exclusively on traffic duties. Each divisional area was divided into two sections, each under a traffic control officer. Each section head-quarters was linked by telephone to the others, and to the divisional APM. While some problems did arise, the system was fairly successful.[93] An account of a trench raid by 1/6 Londons in February 1917 illustrates traffic management at a much lower level: two-man control posts, apparently manned by RPs, were established in communication trenches for traffic control and to guide wounded and POW.[94]

The British attack at Cambrai on 20 November 1917 demonstrated that surprise could still be achieved on the battlefield. Tanks were brought up to their start lines by night, without lights.[95] Under these conditions, effec-tive traffic control was vital, and the success on this occasion was repeated when the BEF returned to the offensive at Amiens on 8 August 1918, having contained and survived the German spring offensive. The administrative orders issued by Fourth Army on this occasion encapsulated 'the experience of four years of war'. Naturally, traffic control was given careful attention.[96] By 1918 traffic control was taken very seriously indeed by the British Army. The Traffic Control Officer of 31st Division was told on his first morning in the post, 'If you catch Haig breaking traffic regulations, run him in!'[97] Haig himself, a truly 'provost-minded' commander, paid tribute to the importance of traffic control in his final despatch.[98] By 1918 no army could expect to carry out successful operations without having a system of effective traffic control, and the CMP had a vital operational role which was understood and appreciated at the highest level.

In conclusion, it can be seen that the popular view of the Redcaps in the First World War is inaccurate in many ways. The growth of provost was not simply a response to an increase in disciplinary problems. By 1918 the CMP had expanded the scope of its duties and was performing an invaluable operational role in addition to its traditional one. The growth of the provost branch was paralleled by the growth of other specialist formations with highly specialised tasks, and it should be seen in the context of the development of the BEF from a relatively unsophisticated force into what Peter Simkins has described as 'the largest and most complex single organisation created by the British nation up to that time'.[99]

Notes

1. This chapter is an expanded version of the author's earlier article, 'British Military Police and their Battlefield Role, 1914–18', published in the now sadly defunct *Sandhurst Journal of Military Studies*, No. 1 (Camberley: RMA Sandhurst, 1990), pp. 36–46. The present version draws upon material used in his authorised history of the Royal Military Police, *The Redcaps: A History of the Royal Military Police and its Antecedents from the Middle Ages to the Gulf War* (London: Brassey's, 1994), and he is grateful for the support of the Trustees of the RMP and of the Regimental Secretary, Lieutenant Colonel (Retd) P. H.M. Squier. He would also like to thank the following institutions for allowing him to use material in their possession: the Imperial War Museum [IWM], the KOYLI Museum, the National Army Museum [NAM] and The National Archives [TNA].

2. John F. Lucy, *There's Devil in the Drum* (London: Faber & Faber, 1938), p. 50.

3. Hamond Mss, 'Wisdom for Warts. Exuded by an Old Sweat', p. 7. The author is grateful to Dr R. Hamond for permission to use this material.

4. John Brophy and Eric Partridge, *The Long Trail* (London: Andre Deutsch, 1965), pp. 82, 170. For other examples of unfavourable views of the CMP, see Joseph Murray, *Gallipoli 1915* (London: New English Library, 1977), pp. 38–9, 56; H. Warner Mss, p. 462, in IWM.

5. Anthony Babington, *For the Sake of Example* (London: Leo Cooper, 1983), p. xii.

6. See David Englander and James Osborne, 'Jack, Tommy and Henry Dubb: The Armed Forces and the Working Class', *Historical Journal*, vol. 21, No. 3 (1978), p. 599.

7. Englander and Osborne, 'Jack', p. 595.

8. S.F. Crozier, *The History of the Corps of Royal Military Police* (Aldershot: Gale & Polden, 1951), p. 27.

9. For accounts of the work of RPs before and during the war, see J.W. Riddell Mss, IWM 77–73–1; H. Munday, *No Heroes, No Cowards* (Milton Keynes: People's Press, 1981), pp. 28–30.

10. H. Bullock, *A History of the Provost Marshal and the Provost Service* (Aberdeen: Milne & Hutchinson, 1929), p. 68; A.V. Lovell-Knight, *The History of the Office of Provost Marshal and the Corps of Military Police* (Aldershot: Gale & Polden, 1945), pp. 68, 70. For an account of the duties of a garrison policeman in India before the war, see W.H. Davies Mss, in NAM 8201–13.

11. Strictly speaking, the CMP did not come into being until 1926, but the MMP and MFP were often lumped together under the heading 'Corps of Military Police' or 'Military Police Corps' before that date. See *Statistics of the Military Effort of the British Empire during the Great War 1914–1920* [SME] (London: HMSO, 1922), p. 642; Orders 8 May to 9 Oct. 1914, in Royal Military Police Archives (RMPA), Acc. 680.

12. (J.M. Grierson), *The British Army. By a Lieutenant-Colonel in the British Army* (London: Sampson Low, 1899), p. 77; R. Money Barnes, *The British Army of 1914* (London: Seeley Service, 1968), p. 283.

13. Orders 4 and 11 Aug. 1914, in RMPA, Acc. 680; Lovell-Knight, *History*, p. 66.

14. For instance, a party of men from Sheffield City Police enlisted early in 1915: R.C. Brookes, 'The Military Police in the First World War', in *Royal Military Police Journal* (third quarter, 1971), p. 16.

15. Sydney Peel, *O.C. Beds. Yeomanry* (London: Oxford University Press, 1935), pp. 2–3. 17.

16. War Diary (WD), APM IX Corps, 9–10 Jan. 1917, in WO 154/8, TNA; WD, A and Q, 8th Division, appendix, 9 June 1916, in WO 95/1681, TNA.

17. A.V. Lovell-Knight (ed.), *The Corps of Military Police* (Morecambe: Morecambe Bay Printers, 1953), p. 37; WD, 16th (Garrison) Battalion KOYLI, 10 Mar. 1917, in KOYLI Museum; Lovell-Knight, *History*, p. 70; Orders 16 Jan. 1916, in RMPA, Acc. 683, and 24 July, 30 Aug. 1918, in RMPA, Acc. 684.

18. Englander and Osborne, 'Jack', p. 595.

19. Lovell-Knight, *The Corps*, p. 37; H.S. Rogers' application for office of Chief Constable, in RMPA First World War file.
20. *SME*, p. 642.
21. Statistics are drawn from the *Army List* of May 1915.
22. Lovell-Knight, *History*, p. 68.
23. Viscount Mersey, *A Picture of Life 1872–1940* (London: John Murray, 1941), pp. 255–63.
24. Crozier, *History*, p. 18. For an account written by one such APM, see E.A. McKechnie Mss, in RMPA, Acc. 1369.
25. WD, Commandant, Étaples Base Camp, 9–14 Sept. 1917, in WO 95/4027, TNA.
26. J.M. Winter, *The Experience of World War I* (London: Macmillan, 1988), p. 159.
27. WD, APM Lines of Communication, 25 and 29 May 1916, in WO 154/114, TNA.
28. Gloden Dallas and Douglas Gill, *The Unknown Army* (London: Verso, 1985), p. 73; 22 June 1916, in WO 154/114, TNA.
29. 9 Sept. 1917, in WO 95/4027, TNA.
30. This subject is explored further in my 'The Effect of War Service on 22nd Battalion Royal Fusiliers (Kensington) 1914–18 with Special Reference to Morale, Discipline and the Officer–Man Relationship' (MA thesis, University of Leeds, 1984).
31. C. Emsley, *Policing and its Context 1750–1870* (London: Macmillan, 1983), pp. 151–7.
32. 28 Sept. 1915, in WO 54/114, TNA.
33. Questionnaire (CSH DO2), and Letter to C.S. Havers (CSH DO8), in RMPA, Acc. 1667; H.L. Smyth Diary, 25 Sept. 1915, in RMPA First World War file.
34. Lovell-Knight, *History*, p. 171; *Soldiers who Died in the Great War: Part 80, Corps of Military Police* (1921), pp. 87–91.
35. Crozier, *History*, p. 18.
36. Peel, *O.C.*, pp. 2–3.
37. 'Howard' to D. Williams, 1 and 17 June 1916, Miss D. Williams Mss, in IWM 85-4-1.
38. See *Training and Manoeuvre Regulations 1909* (London: HMSO, 1909), pp. 74–5; *Field Service Regulations, Part II* (reprinted London: HMSO, 1911), p. 120.
39. *Notes from the Front. Collated by the General Staff* (1914), pp. 39–41 (copy in NAM).
40. WD, APM 5th Division, 26 Aug. 1914, in WO 154 33, TNA, and 'Straggler Posts', p. 4, in RMPA First World War file. The latter is a short history of the subject which quotes at length from contemporary documents, most of which have now disappeared.
41. RMPA, 'Straggler Posts', p. 4.
42. Robert Blake (ed.), *The Private Papers of Douglas Haig, 1914–19* (London: Eyre & Spottiswode, 1952), p. 79.
43. Lovell-Knight, *History*, p. 77.
44. 'Straggler Posts', p. 4.
45. 'Straggler Posts', p. 5; WD, IV Corps General (GS), 10 Mar. 1915, in WO 95/721, TNA; 'Straggler Posts', p. 2.
46. 'Administrative arrangements during the battle of Loos', lecture given by Lieutenant Colonel the Hon. M.A. Wingfield, 16 Jan. 1916, in IWM Misc 134, item 2072. The author is grateful to Mr Nigel Steel of the IWM for bringing this reference to his attention.
47. 'Straggler Posts', pp. 5–6.
48. 'Straggler Posts', p. 5; Wingfield, 'Administrative arrangements'; 'Provost Arrangements for Defence Scheme', XVII Corps, 7 Mar. 1918, in RMPA, Mss 305.
49. See L. Belensky, S. Noy and Z. Solomon, 'Battle Stress: the Israeli Experience', in *Military Review*, vol. LXV, No. 7, 29–37.
50. 'Straggler Posts', p. 5.
51. WD, First Army GS, Appx D, March 1915, in WO 95 154, TNA; WD, First Army A and Q, Appx B, March 1915, in WO 95/181, TNA; RMPA, Mss 322–425.
52. Lovell-Knight, *History*, p. 87.

53. 'Straggler Posts', p. 25; 'Provost Arrangement VI Corps', 4 April 1918, in RMPA, Mss 300.
54. WD, 2nd (G) Battalion KOYLI, in KOYLI Museum.
55. 'Straggler Posts', p. 5; Wingfield, 'Administrative arrangements', pp. 4–5.
56. 'Straggler Posts', pp. 6–7; WD, 30th Division A and Q, 'Report on Operations', July 1916, and 23 July 1916, in WO 95/2315, TNA.
57. 'Straggler Posts', p. 7; WD, APM IX Corps, Appx III, July 1917, in WO 95/8, TNA.
58. M. Middlebrook, *The First Day on the Somme* (London: Allen Lane, 1971), pp. 94, 221. In fairness to this work, which is in other respects admirable, it should be said that at least one war memoir states that for an attack in August 1916 a battalion appointed battle police and instructed them 'to shoot loiterers': 'Mark VII' (Max Plowman), *A Subaltern on the Somme in 1916* (London: Dent, 1928), pp. 58–9.
59. See Babington, *Example*; Wyndham Childs, *Episodes and Reflections* (London: Cassell, 1930), pp. 143–5.
60. WD, 30th Division GS, Operational Order 18, 16 June 1916, Appx G, June 1916, in WO95/2310, TNA; Appx D in IWM, Sir Ivor Maxse Papers, 69–53–7, file 23.
61. John Terraine (ed.), *General Jack's Diary 1914–18* (London: Eyre & Spottiswode, 1964), p. 237; WD, APM 3rd Australian Division, Appx 3, Aug. 1917, in WO 154 78, TNA.
62. Letter of F.L. Watson. 20 Aug. 1930, in CAB 45/138, TNA. For a detailed discussion of the importance of the straggler post system on the Somme by the Assistant Adjutant and Quarter Master General (AA and QMG) of 2nd Division, see letter of J.P. Villiers-Stuart, 29 Jan. 1937, CAB 45/137, TNA.
63. John Ellis, *Eye Deep in Hell* (London: Fontana, 1977), p. 187.
64. Dave Lamb, *Mutinies: 1917–21* (Oxford and London: Solidarity, n.d.), p. 4.
65. Quoted in Christopher Pugsley, *On the Fringe of Hell: New Zealanders and Military Discipline in the First World War* (Auckland: Hodder & Stoughton, 1991), p. 123.
66. F.P. Crozier, *The Men I Killed* (Bath: Cedric Chivers, 1969 [1937]), pp. 89–90; Lamb, *Mutinies*, pp. 3–4.
67. Gen. Sir George Jeffreys to J.E. Edmonds, n.d. (*c*.1935), CAB 45/114, TNA.
68. J.E. Edmonds, *Military Operations, France and Belgium, 1918*, vol. I (London: Macmillan, 1935), p. 177.
69. This account of XIX Corps' provost branch during the March Retreat is drawn from 'APM XIX Corps Provost Diary ... 21st March to 5th April 1918' and the series of 'APM XIX Corps Report(s) on Operations ... from 21st March to 7th April 1918', in 'Straggler Posts'.
70. 'Straggler Posts', p. 10.
71. 'Straggler Posts', p. 37.
72. 26 March 1918, in WO 154 8, TNA.
73. 'Straggler Posts', p. 33; Lovell-Knight, *History*, pp. 82, 84.
74. A.W. Bradbury Mss. p. 5, in IWM.
75. 'Straggler Posts', pp. 25–6.
76. 'Straggler Posts', p. 22. Earlier in the campaign the Guards Division apparently had made use of straggler posts: see RMPA, Mss. 284.
77. Hubert Gough, *Soldiering On* (London: Arthur Barker, 1954), pp. 176–8; J. Keegan, *The Face of Battle* (Harmondsworth: Penguin, 1978), p. 176.
78. 'Straggler Posts', p. 25.
79. W. Shaw Sparrow, *The Fifth Army in March 1918* (London: Bodley Head, 1921), p. 17.
80. 'Straggler Posts', p. 25.
81. 'Straggler Posts', p. 26.
82. For a divisional commander's testimony to the efficacy of the provost arrangements, see April 1918, Appx F, in WO 95/2315, TNA.
83. 'Straggler Posts', p. 37.

84. Unless otherwise indicated, this account of traffic control at Loos is based on documents in WO 106/390, TNA: 'Handling of the Reserves at Loos on the 25th September 1915'.
85. J.E. Edmonds, *Military Operations, France and Belgium, 1915*, vol. II (London: HMSO, 1928), p. 278.
86. Tim Travers, *The Killing Ground* (London: Unwin Hyman, 1987), pp. 16–19.
87. Letter, Major General Sir G. Jeffreys, n.d., in CAB 45/120, TNA.
88. Letter, H.B. Wilkinson, 6 May 1930, in CAB 45/138, TNA.
89. See letter, L.A.G. Bowen, 31 March 1930, in CAB 45/132, TNA.
90. See diary, 14 July 1916, in H. Dalton Papers, I/I 106, in British Library of Political and Economic Science, London School of Economics.
91. IWM, Sir Ivor Maxse Papers, 69–53–7, file 23.
92. Haig to War Office, 16 Aug. 1917, in WO 32/11355, TNA.
93. WD, APM IX Corps, 'Report on ... action of 7th June 1917', in WO 154/8, TNA. See also *Preliminary Notes on Recent Operations on the Front of the Second Army* (London: HMSO, July 1917), p. 6.
94. WD, 1/6 Londons, Appx III to Feb. 1917, in WO 95/2729, TNA.
95. J.F.C. Fuller, *Memoirs of an Unconventional Soldier* (London: Nicholson & Watson, 1936), p. 204.
96. J.E. Edmonds, *Military Operations, France and Belgium, 1918*, vol. IV (London: HMSO, 1947), p. 18, and Appx VII, 'Fourth Army administrative arrangements of 6th August 1918'.
97. E.L. Roberts, 'Dirty Work at the Crossroads in 1918', in *Great War Adventures* (undated copy in IWM Department of Printed Books), p. 87.
98. J.H. Boraston (ed.), *Sir Douglas Haig's Dispatches* (London: Dent, 1919), p. 341.
99. Peter Simkins, *Kitchener's Army* (Manchester: Manchester University Press, 1988), p. xiv.

Chapter 13

The Effect of the First World War on Class Relations in Britain: The Career of Major Christopher Stone DSO MC

As we saw in Chapter 11, Christopher Stone was one of the key personalities in 22nd (Service) Battalion Royal Fusiliers (Kensington) [22/RF], a New Army unit with exceptionally informal officer–man relations. This chapter examines the impact of service in this battalion on his social philosophy, before making some more general suggestions about the effect of military service on post-war social attitudes in Britain.[1]

Christopher Reynolds Stone (1882–1965) was born in Eton on 19 September 1882.[2] He was the youngest of ten children of a schoolmaster at Eton College, the Revd E.D. Stone. Christopher was educated at Eton and Christ Church College, Oxford. He was to remain devoted to both places, and wrote widely on them.[3] After what was, by his own admission, a fairly undistinguished academic career, he graduated in 1905 with a Second in Greats. After Oxford, Stone lived something of the life of a dilettante. He had a brief spell of schoolmastering at Eton, and was then engaged as a tutor to the daughter of Mrs Alyce (or Alice) Chinnery (1862–1945), a widow nearly twenty years older than himself. They fell in love, and married in 1908. In spite of the age difference, it was a happy marriage; Stone's passionate letters from France to his wife form one of the principal sources for this chapter. His marriage gave Stone a measure of financial security and enabled him to devote the next six years to writing. He published a volume of his poetry and prose, but it was as a novelist that he attempted to make his name.[4] Between 1905 and 1914 Stone wrote a number of novels, which enjoyed some critical, but little commercial success.[5]

In 1912 Stone published what he later called a 'Ruritanian romance', entitled *The Shoe of a Horse*.[6] This was centred around a civil war fought in a mythical East European country and was chiefly notable for some highly romanticized and unrealistic battle scenes. Within five years of writing *The Shoe of a Horse*, Stone was to have some totally unexpected first-hand experience of war. He enlisted as a private in the 16th Battalion, The Middlesex Regiment (Public Schools Battalion) [16/Middlesex] in September 1914, one month after the outbreak of the First World War. This was one of many battalions raised as part of 'Kitchener's Army', and, as its subtitle implied, it was originally recruited from former public schoolboys, although the unit later cast its recruiting net more widely.[7] In March 1915 Stone was commissioned into 22/RF as a second lieutenant. He was then 32 years old. Stone was successively commander of 10 Platoon, C Company; Battalion Signalling Officer; Assistant Adjutant; and Adjutant. At the time when 22/RF was disbanded in February 1918 (a victim of the BEF's chronic manpower shortage), he was a major, the holder of both the Distinguished Service Order (DSO) and the Military Cross (MC) and the second-in-command of the battalion. Stone declined the offer of promotion and the command of another unit, and instead joined the staff of 99 Brigade. After the death of the brigade commander in the March retreat of 1918, he became ADC to Major General Sir Cecil Pereira, commander of 2nd Division.[8]

As we saw in Chapter 11, 22/RF was in many ways an exceptional unit. It was largely the creation of Brigadier General Randle Barnett-Barker, who commanded it in the field from November 1915 until November 1917, having been second-in-command of the battalion from the time it was raised. Under his idiosyncratic leadership an unusually relaxed code of social relations developed. This was in sharp contrast to the pre-war Regular army. Barnett-Barker had served as a regular officer with the Royal Welch Fusiliers before the war, retiring in 1906 with the rank of captain. From this regimental experience he had inherited a full measure of paternalism. However, in 1914 he chose to abandon one of the fundamental tenets of the pre-war system: the separation of the ranks. This was partly from personal preference. In November 1915 he wrote from France: 'I must frankly acknowledge that ... I love [the life] and wouldn't miss it for anything. The comradeship, good feeling and taking everyone's evaluation at their capabilities, regardless of their social position, is delightful.'[9]

Barnett-Barker also had other motives. His primary aim was to produce an efficient fighting unit. To this end, according to Christopher Stone, he 'nursed and trained it on his own lines, with very definite ideas as to the best way of extracting the best from the material'.[10] 22nd RF had originally been raised from a number of 'Colonials', or men with connections with the Empire, and also from men from the west London borough of Kensington. Both groups included large numbers of middle-class volunteers, very different in character from the majority of pre-war recruits to the Regular army, and the colonial element had some rather unorthodox views on discipline. Barnett-Barker responded by adapting 'his methods with real liberality of thought to the new conditions of warfare and the new types of soldiers'.[11] Of course, Barnett-Barker was not the only enlightened battalion commander, but the evidence would appear to suggest that his type was the exception rather than the rule. Thus a paradox appears that, while good officer–man relations were normal in most British battalions, few adopted a 22/RF style of discipline. Most officers were powerless to change the system at any but the most local level. Robert Graves, for instance, deliberately returned to France in 1916 to protect his men from the 'grosser indignities of the military system'.[12]

Trench warfare provided exceptionally favourable circumstances for the development of close inter-rank relationships. All shared (to varying degrees) the same discomforts caused by cold, rain, mud, rats and lice, and the ever-present fear of death or mutilation was common to all ranks. Although the officers had separate dugouts, usually of a higher standard than those of the ordinary soldier, the need to patrol the trenches and the supervision of various activities ensured that contact between the ranks was frequent. Under these conditions, a community of interest developed between the men who, in the words of one Temporary officer, took 'nine-tenths of the risk and ... [did] practically all the hard work in the Army ... the private and the subaltern'.[13] It has been suggested that 'an increase of interaction between persons is accompanied by an increase of sentiments of liking among them'.[14] I would suggest that active service on the Western Front provided the opportunity for 'inter-action' to take place between individuals who would have been unlikely to socialize in peacetime because of the class-bound nature of society. In the national army of 1914–1918 , the 'Two Nations' met each other for the first time.

Christopher Stone was one man from an affluent background whose social philosophy underwent a profound change as a result of war service. Before the war Stone did not appear to have had any great concern for the condition of the working classes. He accepted the conventions of the society in which he lived. In his autobiography Stone described himself as one of many people 'who had never taken the opportunity to emerge from sheltered ignorant lives' until 1914.[15] When working-class characters feature at all in his books, their speech is littered with slang, devoid of aspirates and phoneticised: 'You 'urt me, I tell you ... and if Ah laike Ah c'd 'ave th' law rof you.'[16] In *The Rigour of the Game*, the one proletarian character to be allotted a role of any importance utters lines such as 'Fancy all that pore boy bin through, fighting the Boers and all.'[17] Stone's characterisation is influenced by Kipling's 'Tommy Atkins', although he does not seem to have particularly admired Kipling as an author.[18] In fairness, Stone was not the only plagiarist, for 'Tommy Atkins' had become the primary proletarian archetype replacing 'Sam Weller'.[19] Robert Blatchford commented upon this: 'When Kipling makes all his soldiers speak in this patois: 'We aren't no thin red 'eroes, and we aren't no black-guards too' I think he is fairly open to the charge of offering comic caricature as humorous portrait painting.[20]

Blatchford was well qualified to judge Kipling's portrait, having served in the Victorian army himself and being of working-class origin. Stone's pre-war workers lack the sympathy of Kipling's originals, although Stone was certainly not the worst of Kipling's imitators.[21] Stone's unhesitating adoption of this approach reveals a lack of first-hand experience of his subject matter. Before 1914 he would not have come into contact with the lower classes in anything but a master–servant relationship. He unquestioningly accepted the Edwardian *status quo*: in *Letters to an Eton Boy*, one character writes a letter that contains these sentiments: 'It would be ridiculous if they educated you all at Eton as if you were going to be shopkeepers or the boys in a grammar school as if they were going to be proconsuls or large landowners.'[22]

However, Stone was far from being a reactionary. On the contrary, some of his views revealed a liberal streak. In 1933 he wrote that 'British' and 'Imperial' were words that ever since childhood had 'stuck in my gullet',[23] and at Eton he was a pacifist, deploring 'the whole atmosphere of Kipling that had drenched the country' during the Boer War.[24] He seems to have shared the common prejudice of anti-Semitism, although his writings reveal a curiously ambiguous attitude to this subject.[25] Stone's motives for enlisting as a private in 16/Middlesex (Public Schools Battalion) were complex and perhaps offer the key to understanding his post-war thought. He admitted that he was 'caught up in the general urge' to enlist in August–September 1914, but more importantly he specifically felt that it was his duty to show solidarity with the working classes who were patriotically rallying to the colours.[26] Stone, one senses, felt guilty at the life of self-indulgence he had been leading. All his life Stone had been, although not in the pejorative sense, a parasite: 'It is far too late for me to pretend that I have ever been or shall be anything but an idle spectator ... I would rather be the mistletoe growing in utter uselessness on an apple tree, with the vague prospect of being of service to a youthful lover at a Christmas party, than endure the riotous discipline of the beehive ...'[27]

September 1914 gave men such as he the opportunity of doing something practical, and Stone quickly decided 'that it was "up to" people like myself, softly nurtured and expensively educated for the gentle arts, to assert our essential unanimity with our fellows of sterner breed'.[28] One passage from a pre-war novel perhaps reveals a little of Stone's somewhat paradoxical attitude to the working classes. In *They Also Serve*, the protagonist writes of a meeting with 'about ten men of the labouring class' at a church social: 'I was ashamed of myself for not entering more into the thing, but it was impossible; the men all called me "Sir" when they spoke to me, and the sight of their hands and their greasy cards distressed me continually ... I cursed myself for a stuck-up prig, and came home to read a socialist essay about the equality of man.'[29]

It seems that on the eve of war in 1914 Stone was not unaware of social division, and was indeed vaguely uneasy about it, but he was not stirred sufficiently to do anything about it. Eric J. Leed has argued that 1914 saw a revolt against the alienating effects of industrial society and it seems Stone was one who rejoiced that the trend that inexorably polarised the classes into 'bosses' and 'workers' was suddenly halted.[30] His fictional alter-ego, Peter Currage, is described as hating 'the idea of being at war with his fellow human beings; the idea of the saved and the damned, the aristocrat and the rabble'.[31] Stone's idea of inter-class relations was of a friendly landowner/tenant relationship rather than the divided society produced by the Industrial Revolution. His patronising attitude to the lower classes and laughable caricatures in his novels seem to have been mainly the product of ignorance. The years 1914–1918 were to rectify that ignorance.

The five months Stone spent as a private in 16/Middlesex introduced him to the discomforts of life at the bottom of the military hierarchy, an experience that made a lasting impression on him. The battalion was stationed on Kempton Park racecourse and Stone, and others, was billeted in a horsebox. There were three taps to provide water for 600 men, and while one recruit was heard to say, in an 'Oxford accent', 'we love to rough it',[32] this was not a sentiment that Stone could be expected to share: 'At present it's all pretty beastly . . . and I now understand why soldiers are so accustomed to the use of the word "bloody".'[33]

Unlike his Eton contemporaries who went on to Sandhurst and a commission, Stone carried into the Officers' Mess the knowledge of what life in the ranks was really like: dirty, uncomfortable, unglamorous. The soldier was at the mercy of the arbitrary decisions of officious officers and, above all, life was boring.[34] One middle-class private complained that his platoon commander could not appreciate the suffering of the Other Ranks because he had not experienced them.[35] This could never be said of Christopher Stone. In his autobiography he recorded his admiration for two men who 'stuck it out' in the ranks: R.T. Cooper, an artist who shared a horsebox with Stone in 16/Middlesex and was demobilised with his health much impaired, and L.G. Russell-Davies.[36] The latter was a 'self effacing scholar' who was killed while acting as a sanitary orderly in 22/RF. Russell-Davies was a man of peace who elected to serve as a noncombatant in a front-line unit 'so that he might shirk none of the filth and danger, but might drink the cup to its dregs'. Russell-Davies was, Stone admitted, the only man he had ever envied.[37] Stone recognised the extent of his good fortune. 'When I think of the men who have none of my 1,000 comforts,' he wrote in February 1916, 'I am glad that I didn't stay in the 16th Middlesex.'[38] On the night of an abortive attack on Vimy Ridge, Stone was horrified at the condition of the men. They were exhausted, falling asleep in the trenches where they stood: 'poor dears. It's heartbreaking what they *have* to put up with; there's no getting away from it.'[39]

Perhaps the greatest single influence on the refashioning of Stone's attitudes to the working classes was Randle Barnett-Barker. Stone was personally a kindly man and, like his idol and mentor, came to enjoy living on easy terms with men of all ranks and classes. It was in this relaxed environment, in which a private could tell tall stories to Barnett-Barker, and in which all classes served together both in the ranks and in the Officers' Mess, that Stone experienced 'human loving kindness ... from first to last'.[40]

From his letters home it can be seen that Stone, like many other officers of 22/RF, enjoyed an easy-going relationship with the Other Ranks.[41] From the date of his arrival in France to New Year's Eve 1915 (a mere six weeks), favourable references to the Other Ranks appear seven times in forty-two letters. In these letters he worries about them getting cold, writes of his shopping expeditions to buy them sausages for breakfast, and asks his wife to send cigarettes, chocolate, cake and soup for 'my Signallers' every week.[42] Stone buys them Christmas presents and later, in 1916, rejoices for them when leave for Other Ranks is finally instituted.[43]

Stone's love for his men – particularly the Signal section, or 'Sigs' – grew partly because of his admiration for their fortitude in the face of adversity. In a letter to a local Kensington newspaper he expressed his admiration very clearly:

> This is wonderful, though not unexpected – the amazing spirit of the men. You wouldn't believe it unless you saw it actually under your own eyes. Cool, cheerful, laughing, grousing, covered in mud, drenched to the skin – they are the finest fellows in the world; every day a little more knowing and self-reliant, and able to extract comfort from apparently impossible situations and billets ... They are splendid.[44]

This change of attitude towards the working-classes was not a mere product of admiration; it was also solidly based upon friendship with men with whom he would never have come into contact under normal circumstances. He enjoyed a happy relationship with Private Neale, his orderly, of whom he grew very fond, managing to 'wangle' Neale leave – 'poor boy, he has been out here for over a year'.[45] Above all, Stone became very friendly with A.T. ('Fred') Keeble, his Signals sergeant. Keeble is described as 'a perfect dear' in one of Stone's letters, and their friendship continued long into the post-war era.[46] They worked together for the Old Comrades Association (OCA), Keeble being responsible for fighting for pension rights and the like for disadvantaged members, a field that obviously interested Stone.[47] Their friendship is illuminated by several anecdotes. For instance, Stone passed on complimentary gramophone records for Keeble's young family.[48] Two letters provide an admirable summary of their relationship. In the first, Stone thanks Keeble for a piece of wedding cake he had received. Part of the letter reads: 'I am sending you a little pocket book – not so much as a wedding present, as for a memory of days that we have spent together in a companionship that time cannot efface.'[49] Keeble's reply contains these words: 'At times I think that it is impossible for me to express in words that marked appreciation which I would like to give ... my soldiering under you was one of the greatest pleasures of my life, and I doubt if ever thro [sic] life I shall ever be honoured by serving under a Master such as You.'[50] Seventy years later Christopher Stone remained a family legend among Keeble's (adult) grandchildren.

Stone's 'conversion' should not be over-emphasised. Stone complained bitterly to his wife about the personal habits of his lower-class room-mate, Captain L.C. MacCausland – 'after hearing him "his tubes" in the morning, I can stand anything', and his letters sometimes took a slightly mocking tone when referring to his men.[51] His relations with Keeble, although cordial and clearly marked by mutual respect, were always very correct, not least on Keeble's part. Keeble's letter to Stone quoted above begins, 'Dear Mr. Stone', and concludes 'I remain, Your[s] Faithfully, Alfred T. Keeble'. It would be overstating matters to claim that Keeble and Stone automatically became equals but it is certainly not overstating the case to claim that during the war years Stone's respect for members of the working class greatly increased.

It is reasonable to assume that Stone's war experience demonstrated to him that the type of individual that comprised the other of England's 'Two Nations' was neither a cockney clown nor a dangerous revolutionary: rather he was an ordinary, decent, patriotic man. Thanks to war service, a man from a non-military background was introduced to the paternalism that Regular officers took for granted but was largely missing in civilian society, and was encouraged to convert this paternalism into a more intimate relationship.

One immediate effect on Stone himself was evident in his portrayal of working-class characters in his novels. Drawing on his war experience, Stone created rounded, believable, working-class characters for his post-war novels. One, Philip Grey, a village cobbler, is given an important role to play in the plot of *Flying Buttresses*. His social position could not be gauged from his speech, because he speaks perfectly normal English, instead of the Kipling-esque patois bestowed by Stone on his pre-war proletarian characters.[52] This seems to be a compromise. Because Grey has important advice to give to the main character, his speech cannot be a source of ridicule. With other characters, dialect is hinted at, but Stone is noticeably restrained in comparison to his pre-war works. One figure called Albert has this conversation with the protagonist, 'Peter':

> ''Ere Sir ... let me come with you. I was a batman for over a year with one officer. I can look after you.'
> 'I know you could', said Peter ...
> 'I'll come wi' you, Sir', repeated Albert mulishly ...
> 'But there's no pay. I couldn't pay you.'
> 'Why, you just said money wasn't nothing, Sir.'[53]

Slang is absent, only two words are shortened and, although a double negative is inserted into the last sentence and simple words and sentence structures are employed, this portrait is much less a laboured stereotype than Stone's previous efforts. Albert is depicted sympathetically rather than as a clown or an idiot. Later on in *Flying Buttresses*, Stone neatly circumvents the problem of how to present dialect without descending into caricature: '"You'll excuse me, Sir", he asked in broad Sussex'.[54] Stone indicates the man's origin and social status without resorting to a pastiche of *Barrack Room Ballads* by dropping aspirates or using slang. Stone's post-war characterisation is impor-tant because it is indicative of his new perception of the working classes. Philip Grey is not only represented as both venerable and wise but also as a political radical, a 'socialist and republican'.[55] That Stone should indicate that such a man is to be admired is the measure of the extent to which his prejudices had been modified. Stone did not share these views.[56] He does, however, suggest implicitly that they should be respected.

The most lasting legacy of Stone's military career was that it awoke in him a sense of social responsibility, a realisation of the concept underlying *noblesse oblige*. In the army, Stone expressed this in the familiar terms of the paternal subaltern, common to both the old army and the new, writing, for instance, that while waiting as billeting officer for his exhausted men to arrive 'We have got fires ready for them, and soup and tea, so I hope it won't be too bad'.[57] Immediately after the war, Stone apparently extensively re-evaluated his role in society in the light of his wartime experiences. Two novels written in 1920–1921 give some indication of the state of his mind at this period.[58]

The protagonist of *The Valley of Indecision* and its sequel, *Flying Buttresses*, is Peter Currage, whose portrait is clearly autobiographical. He is profoundly dissatisfied with the civilian upper-class society to which he has returned after being a Signals officer during the war. He rejects the triviality of a hectic social life but is still unsatisfied when he finds the solitude he had craved. The character of the village cobbler, Philip Grey, is used as a device to acquaint Peter forcibly with the realities of poverty. Although Peter explicitly expresses his awakening to the stark facts of social inequality despite his public school and Oxbridge background, the cobbler tells him bluntly: 'You can never know the poor man from the inside: not as I know him.'[59]

Stone was well acquainted with the poverty of many of his former com-rades, both officers and Other Ranks, through his experience as 'father con-fessor' at 22/RF OCA. His books *Valley of Indecision* and *Flying Buttresses* are attempts to find a solution to the problem. He outlines three possibilities: one, expounded by Peter's uncle, contains an element of what would later be called Fascism: a second is a venture into religion to galvanise society into change. The only practical and worthwhile course, Stone suggests, is for the wealthy to recognise their responsibility towards the poor, to be philan-thropic and to work unobtrusively for a better society. This is, of course, simply wartime paternalism translated into a civilian context.

Peter's uncle, General Hayling, hopes that the *Grabenkameradschaft*, the comradeship of the trenches, will continue into civilian life, although his vision is an exclusive one.[60] 'The moment we see the pot-bellied passengers trying to get into the boat again,' threatens Hayling, 'we're going to ... push 'em all back into the water.'[61] Having drilled 'discipline' into the hundreds of thousands of civilians who had passed through the army, Hayling wants to let the young men 'run the show in the way they have learned'.[62] In *Flying Buttresses* he is even more bellicose, wanting to band the ex-soldiers together in order to beat up troublemakers and to bayonet overcharging shopkeepers.[63]

Peter's vision of a religious revival, derived from seeing his father killed on the Somme by a shell which explodes a few feet away from Peter but leaves him unharmed (an incident perhaps inspired by Barnett-Barker's death in action in 1918), leads him to wander from town to town preaching and teaching. Stone gently condemns this because it is ineffectual. Peter's efforts end in failure and are partly responsible for the death of his own mother.

Stone's own view, developed under Barnett-Barker's influence, derives from his own wartime spiritual crisis and reflects military imagery. He makes one character say: 'I believe in sane, straightforward, unobtrusive effort. I believe in working towards a goal, not rushing at it ... What you want to do is as fine and as stupid as if you had rushed across No Man's Land with a bagful of bombs and expected to drive the Boche back to Berlin by the sheer impetus of your self-sacrifice.'[64] Philip Grey's advice to Peter to return to his position as the village squire is in the same vein.

The need to return to a mythical Golden Age when harmony reigned between landlord and tenant shows that Stone's belief in the society he lived in was unshaken and that his ideas for inter-class relationships were far from revolutionary. This Utopian vision, anachronistic even in 1920, reflects his experience in 22/RF and Barnett-Barker's code. Stone has Hayling, say, 'And what have the officer class learned? ... To manage men. How? By example, partly. By setting themselves a higher standard than they expect of their subordinates. And by looking after their men: thinking of their men's comfort, mark you, before their own.' Stone's ideal squire is, in effect, a platoon officer for the village. To look after one's men 'not only pays, but it's *right*'.[65]

In Stone's perfect society, class is not abolished but, rather, institutionalised. Society is reformed, and made more palatable to those at the bottom and more acceptable to the consciences of the elite. Stone's writings at this time are impregnated with the language of class and his political stance is essentially conservative. An aside about industrial relations is revealing: after winning the trust of ex-soldiers at a factory, Peter muses that he believes he could settle any future strikes. It does not occur to him that the workers might be justified in their grievances.[66] Nevertheless, it is clear that by 1919 Stone was aware of social injustice and determined to play his part in rectifying it.

In 1919 several former members of 22/RF met in a public house in Kensington to plan a reunion, but they soon found that Stone had already collected over a thousand names.[67] Stone masterminded the initial founding of the OCA, sending out over 1,300 circulars, convincing Sir William Davison (the raiser of the battalion) and Phythian-Adams of the feasibility of the idea, and then booking a small hall for the reunion, held in July 1919.[68] His motives were a mixture of a wish to recreate wartime solidarity, and a desire to aid the less fortunate of his former comrades. Stone gave small gifts and loans to people in distress. Some men, including L. Hawthorne, received money from Stone, but this was an ineffective means of providing relief. Apart from anything else, Stone was well aware of the working-class tradition of dislike of 'charity', with all its patronising connotations.[69] Money supplied by more prosperous comrades and distributed anonymously through a fund was acceptable to all – it was once compared to sharing parcels in the trenches, an analogy that all could appreciate.[70]

The social work of the OCA was perhaps its most valuable function. In 1920 W.H. Metcalfe invited: 'any member who may be unfortunately out of a job or down on his luck to come ... [to the committee]. All proceedings regarding such cases are strictly private and confidential, and any applicant may feel quite sure that if he comes and lays his case before the committee the very utmost will be done to help him.'[71] Some, like E.J. Rowe, who had been blinded in 1917, were loaned money. Others, like Fred Keeble, battled on behalf of widows for pensions, offered free legal advice, or tried to find work for their comrades. Yet others donated clothing, blankets and toys.[72] The OCA continued in its charitable function as late as 1970.

Stone had apparently foreseen the need for such aid as early as January 1916: 'After the war ... I suppose all of our time will be spent in trying to find work for disreputable old soldiers who will recall these strange days and demand sympathy. And you [Mrs Stone] will hate them all and I shall not be able to resist them.' The following month Stone wrote to his wife that 'I didn't ... [want] those trees cut down ... I said that we could cut down most of them apres la guerre, when men want jobs!'[73]

However, having created the OCA virtually single-handed, he took a back seat. It is clear that the wealthier members of the battalion were expected to provide subscriptions commensurate with their means.[74] Stone appears regularly in the list of contributors to the funds and one suspects that his donation would not have been small. 'If only B.B. had lived ... with what indignation he would have righted our wrongs!'[75] 'B.B.' did not live, but his approach lived on in the form of the OCA. Stone applied Barnett-Barker's methods in civilian life and undoubtedly helped cushion some unfortunates from a harsh, uncaring society. His mentor surely would have approved.

This was not the extent of Stone's philanthropy. He became nationally famous when appointed as the BBC's first 'disc-jockey' in July 1927. Stone quickly became popular with the listening public – *The Era* described him as 'The Man with a Million Friends'.[76] His popularity was based on his relaxed style of presenting gramophone records, which was considered revolutionary in the suffocatingly formal early days of Sir John Reith's BBC. Stone's very human fallibility endeared him to his listeners, who begged him in their letters to 'please go on making mistakes'. After his first broadcast, Stone received 6,000 letters, and from 1927 to about 1940 enjoyed the type of fame and popularity usually reserved for royalty and film stars. His face peered myopically from posters advertising wireless sets, and Radio Luxembourg paid him the then enormous fee of £5,000 per annum simply to play gramophone records. He even had a prize-winning rose named after him. The public's regard for Stone was shared by his fellow broadcasters. Roy Plomley, the doyen of post-war British 'disc-jockeys', described him in 1957 as the 'first gentleman of the gramophone'.[77]

Stone was a little contemptuous of his new-found fame, but he did take his job extremely seriously. He identified his audience as 'the world's workers who switch on the radio for an hour of relaxation'. He perceived his role as one of providing 'the equivalent of a bath and a change for the tired man's ... mind'. Stone had no sympathy for members of his own class who damned him for a lack of 'taste' in playing music-hall songs or novelty records. They were in the position to be able to go out and buy their own records: 'The ten shilling B.B.C. licence means nothing to them. It means a great deal to poor people and to tired people and to bed-ridden people.' Consequently, Stone was delighted when he received letters of appreciation from working people.[78]

Stone's casual and friendly approach to broadcasting may seem diametrically opposed to Reith's conception of the BBC as an instrument 'to raise the cultural and educational standards of listeners'.[79] However, the paternalism implicit in Stone's attitude was not dissimilar to Reith's, although the former did not share Reith's messianic sense of mission. Stone was essentially providing a palliative, relieving some of the pain of an unjust society by providing a little light entertainment, and by helping ex-servicemen in financial trouble. Stone, like Stanley Baldwin, radiated moderation and a belief in 'one nation'. Indeed, it was suggested that a combination of Baldwin and Stone would produce the perfect broadcaster, a notion which embarrassed Stone and delighted Baldwin.[80] The OCA in effect helped to siphon off any anger or hostility against the State that may have existed among former members of 22/RF and thus contributed in a small but significant way to the state of social and political consensus in the inter-war years. Stone was a kindly man, and there is no doubt of his genuine desire to see '[t]he hospitals relieved of their most pressing anxieties [and] the life of the unemployed strengthened and sweetened'.[81] He owed his vision to the war and to Barnett-Barker, who thus helped to provide mid twentieth-century Britain with one of its most familiar voices and characteristic attitudes.

The subalterns of 1916 were the politicians, civil servants and businessmen of twenty years later, and Stone was only one among many who conceived 'an affection and concern for the disadvantaged'. In later years this fuelled 'that transformation of middle class attitudes to the poor which has been the most important social trend in twentieth century Britain'.[82]

Just how common was the transformation in the attitudes of middle-class officers is unclear. Many officers, like Stone, initially served in the ranks: Charles Carrington, Siegfried Sassoon and Donald Hankey, for example. Carrington 'mucked in' with a gasfitter of Communist opinions – an exercise in horizon-broadening that a son of a country vicar was unlikely to have experienced if the war had not broken out.[83]

Others also developed a social conscience. Captain G.D.A. Black of 22/RF indignantly complained of the injustice of a Staff order allowing officers blankets, but denying them to Other Ranks. Thus his men who were 'dead beat and soaking wet after four days in the trenches' had to sleep without any covering on the mud floor of a hut. 'I do wish', continued Black, 'that Tommy had someone in authority to stick up for him.'[84] Ian Hay, whose books on a semi-fictional Highland unit were widely read by other soldiers, had one character state categorically that the army consisted of: '[m]en who had spent three years in getting rid of mutual misapprehensions and assimilating one another's points of view – men who went out to the war ignorant and insular … are coming back wise to all the things that really matter'. Earlier, a character says that: '[w]hen you have experienced a working-man's courage and cheerfulness and reliability in the day of battle, you can't turn round and call him a loafer and an agitator in time of peace – can you?'[85]

While many middle-class men whose attitudes to the masses underwent a transition were officers, others served in the ranks. Sergeant H.H. Munro (the novelist 'Saki'), for instance, had his high Tory attitudes softened somewhat by service in 22/RF. Munro became an extremely paternal NCO carrying the packs of other men and handing out chocolates and acid drops to 'the poorer ones who can't afford much'.[86] One of the most surprising 'conversions' was that of Lance Corporal C.E. Jacomb (23/RF), who had made disparaging remarks about the democratic nature of Australian society in a book published in 1913.[87] Jacomb's dislike of the army exceeded even his dislike of egalitarianism. However, in 1917 we find him writing of the breakdown of barriers between himself and his working-class comrades in these terms: 'If this was the only result of me having been in the army, it would have made all the rest worth while.' In the army Jacomb received some of the treatment that the economically disadvantaged were accustomed to in civilian life. Thereafter he could more readily identify with the working classes, having been 'spoken to and treated like a dog by practically everyone of higher rank than myself'.[88]

Certain officers who were to reach exalted positions in public life were influenced by their wartime experiences, including two Conservative prime ministers noted for their liberal approach to social questions. Anthony Eden served as a subaltern in 21/King's Royal Rifle Corps (the Yeoman Rifles). Writing in the mid-1970s, Eden claimed that he had gained a 'sense of the irrelevance and unreality of class distinction' from a series of conversations with his platoon sergeant in Plugstreet Wood.[89] Eden's successor as prime minister, Harold Macmillan, served in 4/Grenadier Guards. As he admitted, in 1914 he had little knowledge of the masses. Like Stone, military service on the Western Front was to change that.[90] On his death in 1986, the influence of the trenches was singled out in many of the tributes paid to him.[91] In a noticeably conciliatory speech made during the bitterly divisive miners' strike of 1984, he had referred to the miners as the men 'that beat the Kaiser's army'.[92] Clearly, even after seventy years, the memory of his working-class comrades remained a potent force in Macmillan's political thinking, even if he was overly nostalgic, being guilty of harking back to 'an age which may never have existed, in which all coal miners joined the Durham Light Infantry and the Nation was One'.[93] One can, however, tentatively identify a direct correlation between the refashioning of the attitudes of these middle- and upper-class men to the lower classes as a result of military service in the First World War, and perhaps more generally the emergence of consensus attitudes in British society. If this was the case it was a social phenomenon of enormous consequence.

Further Reading for Chapters 9–13

A number of works relevant to the topics covered in Chapters 9 to 13 have been published since my pieces originally appeared. It is gratifying that my work on officer–man relations has entered the mainstream, and works such as Alexander Watson's important book *Enduring the Great War: Combat, Morale and Collapse in the German and British Armies, 1914–1918* (Cambridge: Cambridge University Press, 2008) have drawn upon and built upon it. Turning to morale and discipline, Clive Emsley, *Soldier, Sailor, Beggarman, Thief: Crime and the British Armed Services since 1914* (Oxford: Oxford University Press, 2012) is a ground-breaking study. Peter Stanley, *Bad Characters: Sex, Crime, Mutiny, Murder and the Australian Imperial Force* (Sydney: Pier 9 Books, 2010) is an excellent review of disciplinary problems in one part of the British Empire forces. Michael Snape, *God and the British Soldier: Religion and the British Army in the First and Second World Wars* (London: Routledge, 2005) contains, among other things, much food for thought on how Christianity affected the morale of British soldiers, a topic that I completely neglected in my writings prior to the publication of this book. The ever-controversial question of military executions (the so-called 'Shot at Dawn' debate) continues to generate books and articles: Cathryn Corns and John Hughes-Wilson, *Blindfold and Alone: British Military Executions in the Great War* (London: Cassell, 2001) and Gerard Oram, *Military Executions During World War I* (Basingstoke: Palgrave Macmillan, 2003) are two of the more useful. Two books provide useful context for the motivation of Britain's wartime citizen army: David Silbey, *The British Working Class and Enthusiasm for War,*

1914–1916 (London: Routledge, 2005) and Adrian Gregory, *The Last Great War: British Society and the First World War* (Cambridge: Cambridge University Press, 2008). The 22nd Royal Fusiliers (Kensington) now has an excellent modern history: G.I.S. Inglis, *The Kensington Battalion: 'Never Lost a Yard of Trench'* (Barnsley: Pen & Sword, 2011). Christopher Stone's work is mentioned briefly in David Trotter, 'The British Novel and the War', in Vincent Sherry, *The Cambridge Companion to the Literature of the First World War* (Cambridge: Cambridge University Press, 2005).

Notes

1. This chapter is based on G.D. Sheffield, 'The Effect of War Service on the 22nd Battalion Royal Fusiliers (Kensington), 1914–18, with Special Reference to Morale, Discipline and the Officer–Man Relationship (MA thesis, University of Leeds, 1984). For a selection of Stone's wartime correspondence with an introduction by the author, see G.D. Sheffield and G.I.S. Inglis (eds), *From Vimy Ridge to the Rhine: The War Letters of Christopher Stone 1914–19* (Marlborough: Crowood, 1989).
2. For Stone's early life, see Christopher Stone, *Christopher Stone Speaking* (London: Elkins, Mathews & Marriot, 1933); Faith Compton Mackenzie, *As Much As I Dare* (London: Collins, 1938); Compton Mackenzie, *My Life and Times: Octaves Three to Five* (London: Chatto & Windus, 1964–66).
3. For instance in *Scars* (London: William Heinemann, 1907) and *Letters to an Eton Boy* (London: T. Fisher Unwin, 1913).
4. Christopher Stone, *Lusus* (Oxford: B.H. Blackwell, 1909).
5. Stone, *Speaking*, pp. 34–9.
6. Christopher Stone, *The Shoe of a Horse* (London: Chatto & Windus, 1912).
7. For this unit, see H.W. Wallis Grain, *16th (Public Schools) (S) Battalion, Middlesex Regiment and the Great War* (London: Lewington, 1935).
8. For the details of Stone's military career, see Sheffield and Inglis, *Vimy*.
9. Barnett-Barker Papers, Barnett-Barker to wife, 6 December 1915. The author is grateful to Mr J.P.C. Sankey-Barker for granting permission to use these papers.
10. Christopher Stone, *B.B.* (Oxford: B.H. Blackwell, 1919), p. 26.
11. Stone, *B.B.*, p. 26.
12. Robert Graves, *Goodbye To All That* (Harmondsworth: Penguin, 1960 [1929]), p. 192.
13. Ian Hay, *The First Hundred Thousand* (London: Blackwood, 1916), p. 297.
14. G.C. Homans, *The Human Group* (London: Routledge & Kegan Paul, 1957), p. 113. See Tony Ashworth, *Trench Warfare 1914–18: The Live and Let Live System* (Basingstoke: Macmillan, 1980), p. 248, for qualifications of this statement.
15. Stone, *Speaking*, pp. 54–5. In this article, words such as 'class' and 'working classes' are used purely in their early twentieth-century sense. For use of the language of class, see K.C. Phillips, *Language and Class in Victorian England* (Oxford: Blackwell, 1984); Geoffrey Crossick, 'Classes and the Masses in Victorian England', *History Today*, 37 (March 1987), pp. 29–35.
16. Christopher Stone, *The Noise of Life* (London: Chatto & Windus, 1910), p. 280.
17. Christopher Stone, *The Rigour of the Game* (London: Martin Secker, 1922), p. 157. This book was mostly written in 1914.
18. Stone, *Speaking*, p. 47.
19. Peter Keating, *The Working Classes in Victorian Fiction* (London: Routledge & Kegan Paul, 1971), pp. 141–2.

20. Robert Blatchford, *My Life in the Army* (London: Amalgamated Press, 1910), p. 155, and see also p. 286.
21. See for example D. Ker, 'One Against a Dozen – An Incident of the Peninsular War', *Young England*, XXVII (1906), pp. 222–3.
22. Stone, *Eton Boy*, pp. 245–6. For an excellent analysis of social relations in Britain in this period, see Paul Thompson, *The Edwardians* (London: Paladin, 1977).
23. Stone, *Speaking*, p. 149.
24. Stone, *Speaking*, p. 47.
25. See Stone, *Rigour*, p. 14, and *Eton Boy*, pp. 13–14, 22.
26. Stone, *Speaking*, p. 49.
27. Stone, *Speaking*, pp. 26–7.
28. Stone, *Speaking*, p. 49.
29. Christopher Stone, *They Also Serve* (London: Chatto & Windus, 1910), p. 77.
30. Eric J. Leed, *No Man's Land* (Cambridge 1979), chapter 2.
31. Christopher Stone, *Flying Buttresses* (London: A.M. Philpot, 1927), p. 27.
32. Wallis Grain, *16th Middlesex*, p. 16.
33. Stone Papers, Imperial War Museum, Stone to wife, 18 September 1914. The author would like to thank Mrs Anthea Seeker for permission to use these papers; all letters are from Stone to Mrs Stone unless otherwise stated.
34. Stone Papers, 1, 20 October, 1, 31 December 1914, 11 January 1915.
35. 'Ex Private X' [A.M. Burridge], *War is War* (London: Victor Gollancz, 1930), p. 5.
36. Stone, *Speaking*, p. 49; Christopher Stone (ed.), *A History of the 22nd (Service) Battalion Royal Fusiliers (Kensington)* (London: privately published, 1923), p. 40.
37. Stone Papers, 23 October 1916; Stone, *Speaking*, p. 50.
38. Stone Papers, 12 February 1916.
39. Stone Papers, 23 May 1916.
40. Barnett-Barker Papers, 1 January 1916; Stone, *Speaking*, p. 10.
41. See Chapter 11.
42. Stone Papers, 20, 28 November 1915. Stone was Battalion Signalling Officer from 1915 to 1916.
43. Stone Papers, 19 March 1916.
44. *Kensington News and West London Times*, 14 January 1916.
45. Stone Papers, 23 November 1916.
46. Stone Papers, 3 July 1915.
47. *Mufti* [magazine of 22/RF OCA], Spring 1929, p. 2.
48. Mrs E. Keeble, interview with author.
49. Keeble Papers, Stone to Keeble, 8 October 1919. The author would like to thank Mrs E. Keeble for granting permission to use these papers.
50. Imperial War Museum, Department of Printed Books, 'Correspondence relating to the writing of the history of the 22nd Royal Fusiliers' (Stone, C, 316.322), [Stone IWM Papers], Keeble to Stone, 20 October 1919.
51. Stone Papers, 7 January, 16 May 1916.
52. Stone, *Flying Buttresses*, pp. 33, 102.
53. Stone, *Flying Buttresses*, p. 205.
54. Stone, *Flying Buttresses*, p. 255.
55. Stone, *Flying Buttresses*, p. 31.
56. See Christopher Stone, *The Valley of Indecision* (London: William Collins, 1920), p. 179.
57. Stone Papers, 9 March 1916.
58. For a general overview of the genre, see Hugh Cecil, 'The Literary Legacy of the War: the Post-war British War Novel, a Select Bibliography', in Peter H. Liddle (ed.), *Home Fires and Foreign Fields* (London: Brassey's, 1985), pp. 205–30.

59. Stone, *Flying Buttresses*, p. 33.
60. Stone Papers, 6 December 1915.
61. Stone, *Valley*, p. 189.
62. Stone, *Valley*, pp. 189–90.
63. Stone, *Flying Buttresses*, p. 227.
64. Stone, *Valley*, pp. 174–5.
65. Stone, *Valley*, p. 189.
66. Stone, *Buttresses*, p. 255.
67. Stone IWM Papers, memo by W.H. Metcalfe.
68. Kensington Central Library, Local History Collection, 8961, Stone to Davison, 15 May 1919; 8958, 25 May 1919.
69. Hawthorne to Stone, n.d., and 10 October 1920, Stone IWM Papers; Stone, *Speaking*, p. 150.
70. *Mufti*, June 1948, p. 9.
71. Stone IWM Papers, memo by W.H. Metcalfe.
72. Stone IWM Papers, Davison to Stone, 10 January 1920; Kensington MS, Stone to Davison, 7 May 1919; *Mufti*, passim.
73. Stone Papers, 2 January, 20 February 1916.
74. Stone IWM Papers, circular from OCA, n.d.
75. Stone, *History*, pp. 67–8.
76. *The Era*, 1 July 1931.
77. Stone, *Speaking*, p. 20; obituaries of Stone in *The Times*, 24 May 1965 and *Mufti*, June 1965, p. 2; BBC Sound Archives 24277, *Desert Island Discs*, 9 September 1957.
78. Stone, *Speaking*, pp. 87–8.
79. Mark Pegg, *Broadcasting and Society* (London: Croom Helm, 1983), p. 221.
80. Stone, *Speaking*, p. 9; Stone Papers, Baldwin to Stone, 2 February 1932.
81. Stone, *Speaking*, p. 150.
82. John Keegan, *The Face of Battle* (Harmondsworth: Penguin, 1978 [1976]), p. 225.
83. Charles Edmonds, *A Subaltern's War* (London: Peter Davis, 1929), p. 18.
84. *Mufti*, May 1920, p. 2.
85. Ian Hay, *Carrying On After the First Hundred Thousand* (London: 1917), pp. 312, 313.
86. E.M. Munro, 'Biography of Saki' in Saki, *The Square Egg* (London: John Lane, 1924), pp. 84, 100.
87. C.E. Jacomb, *God's Own Country* (London: Max Goschen, 1913), pp. 43–4.
88. C.E. Jacomb, *Torment* (London: Andrew Melrose, 1917), pp. 227–8, 320. For contrary views on the importance of officer–man relations for post-war society, see I.F.W. Beckett, 'Total War', in G.D. Sheffield and C.J. McInnes (eds), *Warfare in the Twentieth Century: Theory and Practice* (London: Unwin-Hyman, 1988); Richard Bessel and David Englander, 'Up From the Trenches: some recent writing on the Soldiers of the Great War', *European Studies Review*, vol. 11, no. 3 (1981), pp. 387–95.
89. Anthony Eden, *Another World 1897–1917* (London: Allen Lane, 1976), pp. 80–1.
90. Harold Macmillan, *Winds of Change 1914–1939* (London: Macmillan, 1966), pp. 99–101.
91. For example, see *Guardian*, 31 December 1986; *Daily Mail* 30 December 1986.
92. *Guardian*, 14 November 1984.
93. *Daily Mail*, 30 December 1986. (Tribute by Julian Critchley MP.)

Index

Footnotes are shown by a suffix *n*. Suffix *bis* shows two separate entries on a page.

coalition politics 111
decision to continue fight 112
options 112–13
  fall back to Ypres 113
  halt campaign on Ridge 112–13
  secure the Ridge for winter base
  113
strategic objectives 111
Commander First Army 25, 27
  blames Rawlinson for failure 46, 52*n47*
  briefs Gough against Rawlinson 76
  more flexible tactics than Rawlinson 49
  planning for Neuve Chapelle 45–6,
  52*n45*
  prefers collegiate planning 45
commands I Corps, BEF 42, 114
Diary 33*n35, 36*, 52*n41, 42*, 97*n41*,
  97*n43*, 97*n64*, 98*n83*, 99*n112*, 99*n115*,
  99*n122, 123*, 117*n37, 38*, 117*n41*,
  117*n50–52*, 129*n12, 13*, 129*n15*, 200
Haig papers 147*n38*, 174*n79*
Haking, Richard 74
Haldane, Aylmer 40
Hamilton, General Sir Ian 38, 41, 42
Hamilton-Gordon, Alexander 40
Hamond Mss 209*n3*
Hampton, Meleah, historian at the
Australian War Memorial 68
Hancock, C.J. 195*n26*
Hankey, Donald 224
Hankey, Donald, 7/Rifle Brigade 182,
185*n38*
Hardie, Captain M. 160, 161, 163, 164,
  164–5, 173*n49*, 173*n54*, 174*n69*, 174*n78*,
  174*n80–82*
Hardie, Gertrude 171
Harington, General Sir Charles 'Tim', ,
  Second Army Chief of Staff 103, 113,
  116*n9*, 117*n45*
  Life of Lord Plumer 113, 117*n46*
Harper, Glyn 4, 18*n9*
Harris, J.P. 19*n32*
  Douglas Haig and the First World War 115
Harris, J.P. and Niall Barr, *Amiens to the
Armistice* 145
Hart, Brigadier General Herbert
  3 New Zealand (Rifle) Brigade 16, 20*n67*
  4 New Zealand Brigade 16, 20*n64, 65*
Harvey, H.E. 172*n25*, 195*n17*, 195*n31*
Havers, C.S., CMP 199, 210*n33*
Haworth, Christopher 185*n41*

Hawthorne, L., 22/RF 222, 228*n69*
Hay, Ian 224, 226*n13*, 228*n85*
Hayes, Geoffrey, Andrew Iarocci and Mike
  Bechtold, *Vimy Ridge: a Canadian
  Reassessment* 116*n8*, 128
Headlam, Cuthbert 20*n59*
Henderson, G.F.R. 172*n11*
Henniker, A.M. 147*n49*
Henriques, J.Q. 173*n64*
Hermann, David G. 19*n27*
Herwig, Holger H. 19*n29*
Higher Command and Staff Course, Joint
  Services Command and Staff College
  xi–xii
  Staff Ride xii
Hills, J.D. 149*n98*
Hindenburg Line 105, 120, 126, 134, 166
Hindenburg/Ludendorff dictatorship 9
Hobbs, J.J. Talbot, AIF 56
Holland, Robert 20*n48*, 20*n51*
Holmes, Richard x, xii, 43, 52*n35*, 53*n65*,
  146*n14*, 194*n1*
Holt, H.P. 20*n57*
Homans, G.C. 226*n14*
Home, Brigadier General Archibald, Cavalry
  Corps 90, 99*n110*, 146*n22*, 148*n71*
Horne, General Sir Henry 145*n2*
  Commander First Army 122
    clears up potential confusion 123
    consultative command style 123
  Commander XV Corps 63, 123
  commands 2nd Division 47
Horne, John and Alan Kramer 19*n35*
Horspool, David 18*n7*
'Howard' 100, 210*n37*
Howard, C. 173*n60*
Howard, Professor Sir Michael 5, 18*n14*,
  83, 97*n68*, 97*n71*, 131
Howell, Brigadier General Philip, Chief of
  Staff II Corps 62, 65*bis*, 70*n56*, 70*n71*,
  71*n78*, 71*n84*, 74, 84, 85, 98*n87–90*
Howell Papers 98*n83*, 98*n91*, 98*n92*, 98*n94*,
  98*n98*
Hughes, G.B. 68*n7*
Hughes, William Morris, Australian Prime
  Minister 30
Hundred Days offensives 15, 16, 50–1, 66,
  107, 108, 109, 127, 131, 135
  British and Dominion divisions compared
  134
  March retreat 137, 141, 203–7